Archaeology
Essentials

Archae
Essenti

Colin Renfrew & Paul Bahn

ology
als

Fourth Edition

Theories/Methods/Practice

With 303 illustrations

Thames & Hudson

First published in 2007 in paperback in the United States of America by Thames & Hudson Inc., 500 Fifth Avenue, New York, New York 10110

www.thamesandhudsonusa.com

Fourth edition 2018

Library of Congress Control Number 2014944450

Paperback: ISBN 978-0-500-84138-9
Not for Sale: ISBN 978-0-500-29372-0

Printed and bound in China by C & C Offset Printing Co. Ltd

Contents

Preface

Archaeology Essentials is designed for college students taking an introductory course in archaeology. It aims to convey some of the excitement of archaeology in the twenty-first century and to give students a concise and readable account of the ways in which modern archaeologists investigate and understand our remote past. Archaeologists usually make the headlines when they find something spectacular: in 2013, for example, the discovery of the skeleton of King Richard III of England, buried in what remained of the former Greyfriars church in Leicester, now a parking lot, created a sensation. Here were the remains of Richard "Crouchback" (the deformity in the spine clearly visible), the last English monarch to die in battle, at Bosworth Field in 1485. However, most archaeologists spend their time engaged in research that rarely makes the news, but is nevertheless vitally important for our understanding of the past.

Archaeology is still often a matter of the painstaking excavation of an ancient site, but today archaeologists can use new techniques that sometimes avoid the need for excavation altogether. Advances in science and computing, as well as in methods for analyzing and evaluating archaeological finds, mean that archaeologists can reach conclusions that would have been impossible just fifteen or twenty years ago.

This book will introduce students to the methods, new and old, used by archaeologists: from the traditional shovel and trowel to satellite imaging, laser-based mapping using LIDAR (Light Detection and Ranging), and ground-based remote sensing. New technology has affected the work of archaeologists in the laboratory as well as in the field: we cover, for example, the use of genetic evidence.

But the story of modern archaeology is not just about technology. There have been enormous advances in the questions archaeologists ask and in the assumptions and theoretical models they apply to archaeological evidence. Some questions, which an earlier generation of archaeologists might have considered closed, have now been opened up for new examination.

In other words, whatever the focus of an individual college course, it is our intention that students will find in this book an authoritative, concise, and clear explanation of modern archaeological practice.

How to Use This Book

Archaeology Essentials is organized around the most important questions that archaeologists ask. **Chapter 1** looks at the history of archaeology, the kinds of questions asked by archaeologists in the past and the methods they used. In **Chapter 2** we ask the question What Is Left?: the evidence with which archaeologists work. **Chapter 3** examines the question Where?: archaeologists can learn a good deal from the context in which evidence is found, and have developed many techniques for locating and recovering evidence.

In **Chapter 4** the question is When?: how can we know whether something dates from a few hundred years or many thousands of years ago? **Chapter 5** examines the fascinating question of How Were Societies Organized?: the nature, scale, and analysis of past social organization and identity. In **Chapter 6** we look at the world in which ancient people lived: What Was the Environment and What Did They Eat? Technology was an important factor in changing both society and the lives of our ancestors, as were contact and trade with other ancient peoples: the key question for **Chapter 7** is How Were Artifacts Made, Used, and Distributed?

Chapter 8 looks at the archaeology of people: What Were They Like? **Chapter 9** addresses some of the more difficult questions that contemporary archaeologists explore, for instance the ways ancient peoples thought about their world and issues of identity: in other words, What Did They Think? An equally difficult question is the subject of **Chapter 10**: Why Did Things Change? In **Chapter 11** we address the often controversial question Whose Past?: the past may be remote in time but it can be very relevant today if it touches on the beliefs, identity, and wishes of the descendants of those who lived long ago. Finally, in **Chapter 12** we look at both the practice of applied archaeology (a profession that now employs more people than the academic archaeology pursued in universities) and more generally: The Future of the Past. At the end of that chapter we also include a section on building a career in archaeology.

If you follow the questions examined in this book you will understand how archaeologists work, think, analyze, and seek to understand the past. You will also discover that not all questions can be answered, or perhaps that there might be more than one answer.

To help you understand how archaeology works, we have provided some special features in this book. Case studies in boxes, shaded in blue and featured throughout the text, show you archaeology in action and will help you understand the issues that archaeologists deal with in their research and fieldwork. Key Concept boxes summarize and review important concepts, methods, or facts about archaeology. At the end of every chapter there is a summary to recap what you have read and a suggested reading list to guide you to the most important and helpful publications if you want to research any subject further. Archaeological terms in the text that are defined in the glossary are highlighted in bold (e.g. **excavation**) when they first occur in the book.

New to This Edition

This new fourth edition of *Archaeology Essentials* has been updated throughout, to reflect recent advances in methodology, analysis, and understanding, and to highlight the importance of contemporary archaeological issues:

- In Chapter 1, the history of archaeology has been further opened up to new perspectives, with traditionally famous nineteenth-century male figures now balanced with neglected pioneering voices.
- The fast-developing field of digital data capture and 3D modeling is covered in Chapter 3 in a new section, "Excavating the Digital Age," with a particular focus on the potential offered by drone technology.
- The study of isotopes is illustrated with a new case study on the Norse settlement of Greenland in Chapter 6.
- The rapid progress of DNA analysis is reflected throughout this fourth edition, with expanded sections on ancient DNA (aDNA) in Chapters 8 and 10.
- In Chapter 11, the increasing threat posed to the material record by ideological extremism is examined through the destruction of Palmyra by so-called Islamic State (IS), alongside the Taliban's earlier demolition of the sandstone Buddhas at Bamiyan, Afghanistan.

In addition, this new edition of *Archaeology Essentials* includes a range of recent ground-breaking archaeological investigations, for instance the Cultural Resource Management (CRM) work conducted at Hohokam sites in Arizona, along with new and updated case studies on such sites as Mississippian Spiro in Oklahoma, the pyramids of Giza in Egypt, and Must Farm in eastern England.

Student and Instructor Resources

Fully revised student and instructor materials for this fourth edition of *Archaeology Essentials* are found on the website to accompany the book: http://college.thameshudsonusa.com/college/archaeologyessentials4. Readers outside North America should email education@thameshudson.co.uk for further information. *Archaeology Essentials* is also available as an ebook.

Resources for Students

Students benefit from a variety of resources designed to complement the knowledge and skills provided by *Archaeology Essentials*:

- **InQuizitive**, a powerful adaptive learning tool available for the first time in archaeology, and free to use with *Archaeology Essentials* at: http://digital.wwnorton.com/archess4. Developed specifically for introductory archaeology courses, this self-testing tool offers interactive, visually led questions that adapt to students' current knowledge.
- **Active Archaeology Notebook**, available free with purchase of a new copy of *Archaeology Essentials* by prior arrangement with your Norton sales rep. Written by a team of instructors from the SAA Curriculum Committee led by Leah McCurdy, each activity applies a key concept in archaeology and has been tried and tested in archaeology classrooms. Activities are accompanied by online guidance notes for instructors explaining how they can be linked to learning objectives, contribute to students' grades, and build fun and effective in-class activities.
- **Flashcards** of terminological definitions to aid students' learning.
- An online **glossary** that provides easy access to key terms.

Resources for Instructors

Instructors who adopt this fourth edition of *Archaeology Essentials* can get free access to a range of tools to enhance teaching and learning:

- To create visually engaging lectures, the **Archaeology Global Gallery** offers instructors a collection of hundreds of images not included in the book, sourced from museums, Thames & Hudson archives, and from fellow archaeologists, all carefully categorized and captioned. It can be accessed at: http://college.thameshudsonusa.com/college/archaeologyessentials4.
- A range of **videos** exploring ancient sites and featuring interviews with Professor Colin Renfrew and Dr. Kelly Knudson on key topics in archaeology.
- A **test bank** with over 400 multiple choice, true/false, and essay questions.
- **PowerPoint lectures** to help structure and organize teaching.
- **Images** and **diagrams** from *Archaeology Essentials* as JPEGs and PowerPoints.

Acknowledgments

We would like to express our thanks to all those who have provided feedback, reviewed sections of the book, or otherwise helped in the updating of the text and illustrations for this edition: David Aftandilian, Texas Christian University; Lynda Carroll, Binghampton University; Matt Douglass, University of Nebraska-Lincoln; Matthew Johnson, Northwestern University; Timothy Kaiser, Lakehead University; Daniel Kreutzer, Metropolitan State University; Matthew Liebmann, Harvard University; Pamela A. Maack, PhD, San Jacinto College-Central; Heather McKillop, Louisiana State University; C. Jill Minar, Fresno City College; Krysta Ryzewski, Wayne State University; Joshua Samuels, The Catholic University of America; and Michael J. Shott, University of Akron.

1

Searching for the Past
The History of Archaeology

About 5300 years ago, a forty-year-old man made his last journey on a mountain path in the European Alps. He lay undisturbed until his body was discovered in September 1991. Archaeologists were able to determine not only his age, but also the contents of his last meal: meat (probably ibex and venison), plants, wheat, and plums. The Iceman suffered from arthritis, and analysis of a fingernail showed that he had suffered serious illness before he died. At first it was thought that he died from exhaustion in a fog or blizzard. Later analysis, however, revealed what may be an arrowhead in his left shoulder and cuts on his hands, wrists, and ribcage, as well as a blow to the head, so he may well have died a violent death. These observations are just a sample of what archaeologists were able to learn about this long-dead man (see pp. 54–55).

The thrill of discovery and the ability of **archaeology** to reveal at least some of the secrets of our past have been the theme of many famous novels and movies, notably Steven Spielberg's *Indiana Jones* series. But although many discoveries in archaeology are far less spectacular than either the Iceman or those represented in fiction—perhaps a collection of broken pieces of pottery— these kinds of remains too can tell us a lot about the past, through careful collection and analysis of the evidence.

Archaeology is unique in its ability to tell us about the whole history of humankind from its beginnings more than 3 million years ago. Indeed, for more than 99 percent of that huge span of time, archaeology—the study of past **material culture**—is the only source of information. It is the only way that we can answer questions about the **evolution** of our species and the developments in **culture** and society that led to the emergence of the first civilizations and to the more recent societies that are founded upon them.

Archaeology as a Discipline

Many archaeologists consider themselves as part of the broader discipline of **anthropology**. Anthropology in the most general sense is the study of humanity: our physical characteristics as animals, and our unique

The diversity of modern archaeology.

(Right) Urban archaeology: excavation of a Roman site in the heart of London.

(Below left) Working in the on-site archaeobotanical laboratory on finds from Çatalhöyük in Turkey.

(Below right) In the field in Siberia, an ethnoarchaeologist shares and studies the lives of modern Oroqen people, here making blood sausages from the intestines of a recently butchered reindeer.

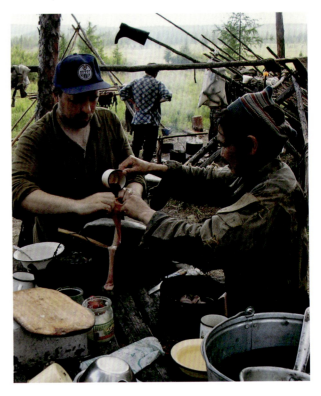

(Right) Underwater archaeology: a huge Egyptian statue found in the now-submerged ruins of an ancient city near Alexandria.

(Below left) An Inca "mummy," now known as the "Ice Maiden," is lifted from her resting place high up on the Ampato volcano in Peru (see p. 56).

(see p. 56).

(Near left) Piecing together fragments of an elaborate mural from the early Maya site of San Bartolo in Guatemala.

(Below right) Archaeologists painstakingly excavate, record, and reconstruct some of the thousands of "terracotta warriors" at the tomb of the first emperor of China, near the city of Xi'an in Shaanxi province.

non-biological characteristics. Anthropology is thus a broad discipline—so broad that it is often broken down into different fields:

- **Physical** or **biological anthropology**: the study of human biological or physical characteristics and how they evolved.
- **Cultural** (or **social**) **anthropology**: the study of human culture and society.
- Linguistic anthropology: the study of how speech varies with social factors and over time.
- Archaeology: the study of former societies through the remains of their material culture and, in the case of such literate cultures as those of Mesopotamia or Mesoamerica, such written records as have survived.

Archaeologists who are interested in the societies of ancient Greece and Rome, their empires and neighboring territories, consider themselves Classical archaeologists. They study the material remains of the Greek and Roman worlds, but can also take into account the extensive written records (literature, history, official records, and so on) that survive.

Similarly, biblical archaeologists work in much the same way as anthropological archaeologists, but with reference to the events set out in the Bible. Like history, archaeology is concerned with documenting and understanding the human past, but archaeologists operate in a time frame much larger than the periods studied by historians. Conventional historical sources begin only with the introduction of written records in around 3000 BCE in Western Asia, and much later in most other parts of the world (not until 1788 CE in Australia, for example). The period before written records and history (meaning the study of the past using written evidence) is known as **prehistory**.

Although archaeologists spend much of their time studying **artifacts** and buildings, it is worth emphasizing that archaeology is about the study of humans and, in that sense, like history, it is a humanity. But although it uses written history, it differs from the study of written history in a fundamental way. Historical records make statements, offer opinions, and pass judgments (even if those statements and judgments themselves need to be interpreted). The objects that archaeologists discover, on the other hand, tell us nothing directly in themselves. It is *we* today who have to make sense of these things. In this respect the practice of archaeology is rather like a science. The scientist collects data, conducts experiments, formulates a hypothesis (a proposition to account for the data), tests the hypothesis against more data, and then devises a model (a description that seems best to summarize the pattern observed in the data). The archaeologist has to develop a picture of the past, just as the scientist has to develop a coherent view of the natural world. It is not found ready made.

Archaeology, in short, is a science as well as a humanity. That is one of its fascinations as a discipline: it reflects the ingenuity of the modern scientist as well as the modern historian. The technical methods of archaeological science are the most obvious, from **radiocarbon dating** to studies of food residues in pots. Equally important are scientific methods of analysis: archaeology is just as much about the analytical concepts of the archaeologist as the instruments in the laboratory. The illustrations on pp. 12–13 give some idea of the diversity of the work that a modern-day archaeologist might be involved in.

The Important Questions

Because the evidence of archaeology cannot speak for itself, it is important that archaeologists ask the right questions of the evidence. If the wrong questions are asked, the wrong conclusions will be drawn. For example, early explanations of the unexplained mounds found east of the Mississippi River assumed that they could not have been built by the indigenous American peoples of the region; it was believed instead that the mounds had been built by a mythical and vanished race of Moundbuilders. As explained in more detail below (p. 18), Thomas Jefferson, later in his career the third President of the United States, decided to test this hypothesis against hard evidence and dug a trench across a mound on his property. He was able to show that the mound had been used as a burial place on many occasions and found no evidence that it could not have been built by the indigenous peoples. In other words, Jefferson asked questions about what the evidence suggested: he did not simply reach a conclusion that fitted his prejudices and assumptions.

Traditional approaches tended to regard the objective of archaeology mainly as reconstruction: piecing together the puzzle. But today it is not enough simply to recreate the material culture of remote periods: how people lived and how they exploited their environment. We also want to know *why* they lived that way, why they had certain patterns of behavior, and how their material culture came to take the form it did. We are interested, in short, in explaining change.

Understanding the History of Archaeology

The history of archaeology is commonly seen as the history of great discoveries: the tomb of Tutankhamun in Egypt, the lost Maya cities of Mexico, the painted caves of the **Paleolithic**, such as Lascaux in France, or the remains of our human ancestors buried deep in the Olduvai Gorge in Tanzania. But even more than that it is the story of how we have come to look with fresh eyes at the material evidence for the human past, and with new methods to aid us in our task.

It is important to remember that just a century and a half ago, most well-read people in the Western world—where archaeology as we know it today was first developed—believed that the world had been created only a few thousand years earlier (in the year 4004 BCE, according to the then-standard interpretation of the Bible), and that all that could be known of the remote past had to be gleaned from the earliest historians, notably those of the ancient Near East, Egypt, and Greece. There was no awareness that any kind of coherent history of the periods before the development of writing was possible at all.

But today we can indeed penetrate the depths of the remote past. This is not simply because new discoveries are being made. It is because we have learned to ask some of the right questions, and have developed some of the right methods for answering them. The material evidence of the archaeological record has been lying around for a long time. What is new is our awareness that the methods of archaeology can give us information about the past, even the prehistoric past (before the invention of writing). The history of archaeology is therefore in the first instance a history of ideas, of theory, of ways of looking at the past. Next it is a history of developing research methods, employing those ideas, and investigating those questions. And only thirdly is it a history of actual discoveries.

In this book it is the development of the questions and ideas that we shall emphasize, and the application of new research methods. The main thing to remember is that every view of the past is a product of its own time: ideas and theories are constantly evolving, and so are methods. When we describe the archaeological research methods of today we are simply speaking of one point on the trajectory of the subject's evolution. In a few decades' or even a few years' time these methods will certainly look old-fashioned and out of date. That is the dynamic nature of archaeology as a discipline.

The First Searchers: The Speculative Phase

Humans have always speculated about their past, and most cultures have their own foundation myths to explain why society is how it is. Most cultures, too, have been fascinated by the societies that preceded them. The Aztecs exaggerated their Toltec ancestry, and were so interested in Teotihuacan—the huge Mexican city abandoned hundreds of years earlier, which they mistakenly linked with the Toltecs—that they incorporated ceremonial stone masks from that **site** in the foundation deposits of their own Great Temple. A rather more detached curiosity about the relics of bygone ages developed in several other early civilizations, where scholars and even rulers collected and studied objects from the past.

During the revival of learning in Europe known as the Renaissance (fourteenth to seventeenth centuries), princes and people of refinement began to form "cabinets of curiosities," in which curios and ancient artifacts were displayed rather haphazardly with exotic minerals and all manner of specimens illustrative of what was called "natural history." During the

Renaissance also, scholars began to study and collect the relics of ancient Greece and Rome. And they began too in more northern lands to study the local relics of their own remote past. At this time these were mainly the field monuments—those conspicuous sites, often made of stone, which immediately attracted attention, such as Stonehenge. Careful scholars, such as the Englishman William Stukeley, made systematic studies of some of these monuments, with accurate plans that are still useful today. Stukeley and his colleagues successfully demonstrated that these monuments had not been constructed by giants or devils, as suggested by such local names as the Devil's Arrows, but by people in antiquity. Stukeley was also successful in phasing field monuments, demonstrating that, since Roman roads intersected barrows, the former must have been built after the latter.

The First Excavations

In the eighteenth century more adventurous researchers initiated **excavation** of some of the most prominent sites. The Roman city of Pompeii in Italy was one of the first of these. Buried under meters of volcanic ash after the cataclysmic eruption of nearby Mount Vesuvius, Pompeii was only

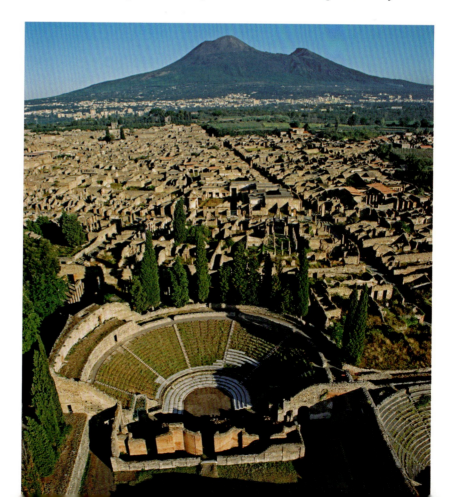

The Roman city of Pompeii lies in the shadow of Mount Vesuvius in Italy. When the volcano erupted in 79 CE, the entire city was buried, all but forgotten until excavations began in the mid-eighteenth century. Such spectacular discoveries generated huge interest in the past, and greatly influenced the arts.

Thomas Jefferson, later to become President of the United States, conducted the "first scientific excavation" in Virginia in 1784

By carefully digging a trench across a Native American burial mound, Jefferson was able to observe different layers and to draw reasoned conclusions from the data

rediscovered in 1748. Although to begin with the motivation of the excavators was to find valuable ancient masterpieces, it was not long before published finds from Pompeii were attracting enormous international attention, influencing **styles** of furniture and interior decoration, and even inspiring several pieces of romantic fiction. Not until 1860, however, did well-recorded excavations begin.

The credit for conducting what has been called "the first scientific excavation in the history of archaeology" traditionally goes to Thomas Jefferson, who in 1784 dug a trench or section across a burial mound on his property in Virginia. Jefferson's work marks the beginning of the end of the Speculative Phase.

In Jefferson's time people were speculating that the hundreds of unexplained mounds known east of the Mississippi River had been built not by the indigenous Americans, but by a mythical and vanished race of "Moundbuilders." Jefferson adopted what today we would call a scientific approach, that is, he tested ideas about the mounds against hard evidence—by excavating one of them. His methods were careful enough to allow him to recognize different layers (or **stratigraphy**) in his trench, and to see that the many human bones present were less well preserved in the lower layers. From this he deduced that the mound had been reused as a place of burial on many separate occasions. Although Jefferson admitted, rightly, that more evidence was needed to resolve the Moundbuilder question, he saw no reason why ancestors of the present-day Native Americans themselves could not have raised the mounds.

Jefferson was ahead of his time. His sound approach—logical **deduction** from carefully excavated evidence, in many ways the basis of modern archaeology—was not taken up by any of his immediate successors in North America. In Europe, meanwhile, extensive excavations were being conducted, for instance by the Englishman Sir Richard Colt Hoare, who dug into hundreds of burial mounds in southern Britain during the first decade of the nineteenth century. None of these excavations, however, did much to advance the cause of knowledge about the distant past, since their interpretation was still within the biblical framework, which insisted on a short span for human existence.

The Beginnings of Modern Archaeology

It was not until the middle of the nineteenth century that the discipline of archaeology became truly established. Already in the background there were the significant achievements of the newly developed science of geology. The study of the **stratification** of rocks (their arrangement in superimposed layers or strata) established principles that were to be the basis of archaeological excavation, as foreshadowed by Jefferson. It was demonstrated that the stratification of rocks was due to processes that were still going on in

(Above) Early excavations: Sir Richard Colt Hoare and William Cunnington direct a dig north of Stonehenge in 1805.

(Below) Charles Darwin caricatured as an ape, published in 1874. The drawing was captioned with a line from William Shakespeare's *Love's Labour's Lost*: "This is the ape of form."

seas, rivers, and lakes. This was the principle of **uniformitarianism**: that geologically ancient conditions were in essence similar to, or "uniform with," those of our own time, introduced by the great geologist Sir Charles Lyell. This idea could be applied to the human past also, and it marks one of the fundamental notions of modern archaeology: that in many ways the past was much like the present.

The Antiquity of Humankind and the Concept of Evolution

These advances in geology did much to lay the groundwork for what was one of the most significant events in the intellectual history of the nineteenth century (and an indispensable one for the discipline of archaeology): the establishment of the antiquity of humankind. It had become widely agreed that Earth's origins extended far back into a remote past, so that the biblical notion of the creation of the world and all its contents just a few thousand years before our own time could no longer be accepted. The possibility of a prehistory of humankind, indeed the need for one, was established.

This harmonized well with the findings of Charles Darwin, whose fundamental work, *On the Origin of Species*, published in 1859, established the concept of evolution to explain the origin and development of all plants and animals. The idea of evolution itself was not new—earlier scholars had suggested that living things must have changed or evolved through the ages. What Darwin demonstrated was how this change occurred. The key mechanism was, in Darwin's words, "natural selection," or the survival of the fittest. In the struggle for existence, environmentally better-adapted individuals of a particular species would survive (or be "naturally selected"),

Key Early Advances

The rejection of a literal interpretation of the biblical account of early human history and the establishment of the antiquity of humankind

Charles Darwin's theories of evolution and natural selection

The establishment of the Three Age System that divided prehistory into a Stone Age followed by a Bronze Age and an Iron Age

The development of archaeological field techniques

whereas less well-adapted ones would die. The surviving individuals would pass on their advantageous traits to their offspring and gradually the characteristics of a species would change to such an extent that a new species emerged. This was the process of evolution. The implications were clear: that the human species had emerged as part of this same process. The search for human origins in the material record, using the techniques of archaeology, could begin.

Darwin's work on evolution also had an immediate impact on archaeologists who were laying the foundations for the study of artifacts and how they develop over time. But his influence on social thinkers and anthropologists has been even more significant. The principles of evolution can also be applied to social organization, for culture can be seen as learned and passed on between generations, albeit in a more general way than in biological evolution.

The Three Age System

As we have noted, some archaeological techniques, notably those in the field of excavation, were already being developed. So too was another conceptual device that proved very useful for the progress of European prehistory: the **Three Age System**. As early as 1808, Colt Hoare had recognized a sequence of stone, "brass," and iron artifacts within the barrows he excavated, but this was first systematically studied in the 1830s by the Danish scholar C.J. Thomsen. He proposed that prehistoric artifacts could be divided into those coming from a Stone Age, a Bronze Age, and an Iron Age, and this **classification** was soon found useful by scholars throughout Europe. Later a division in the Stone Age was established—between the Paleolithic or Old Stone Age and the **Neolithic** or New Stone Age.

These terms were less applicable to Africa, where bronze was not used south of the Sahara, or to the Americas, where bronze was less important and iron was not in use before the European conquest. But it was conceptually significant. The Three Age System established the principle that by studying and classifying prehistoric artifacts, they could be ordered chronologically. Archaeology was moving beyond mere speculation about the past, and becoming instead a discipline involving careful excavation and the systematic study of the artifacts unearthed. Although superseded by modern dating methods, the Three Age System remains one of the fundamental divisions of archaeological materials today.

Ethnography and Archaeology

Another important strand in the thought of the time was the realization that the study by ethnographers of living communities in different parts of the world could be a useful starting point for archaeologists seeking to understand something of the lifestyles of their own early native inhabitants, who clearly had comparably simple tools and crafts. For example, as early as the sixteenth century, contact with native communities in North America provided antiquarians and historians with models for tattooed images of Celts and Britons.

Soon ethnographers and anthropologists were themselves producing schemes of human progress. Strongly influenced by Darwin's ideas about evolution, the British anthropologist Edward Tylor and his American counterpart Lewis Henry Morgan both published important works in the 1870s arguing that human societies had evolved from a state of savagery (primitive hunting) through barbarism (simple farming) to civilization (the highest form of society). Morgan's work was partly based on his great knowledge of living Native Americans.

Discovering the Early Civilizations

By the 1880s, then, many of the ideas underlying modern archaeology had been developed. But these ideas themselves took shape against a background of major nineteenth-century discoveries of ancient civilizations in the Old World and the New.

The splendors of ancient Egyptian civilization had already been brought to the attention of an avid public after Napoleon's military expedition there of 1798–1800. It was the discovery by one of his soldiers of the Rosetta Stone that eventually provided the key to understanding Egyptian hieroglyphic writing. Inscribed on the stone were parallel texts written in both Egyptian and Greek scripts. The Frenchman Jean-François Champollion used this bilingual inscription finally to decipher the hieroglyphs in 1822, after fourteen years' work. A similar piece of brilliant scholarly detection helped unlock the secrets of cuneiform writing, the script used for many languages in ancient Mesopotamia.

Egypt and the Near East also held a fascination for the American lawyer and diplomat John Lloyd Stephens, but it was in the New World that he was to make his name. His travels in Yucatan, Mexico, with the English artist Frederick Catherwood, and the superbly illustrated books they produced together in the early 1840s, revealed for the first time to an enthusiastic public the ruined cities of the ancient Maya. Unlike contemporary researchers in North America, who continued to argue for a vanished white race of Moundbuilders as the architects of the earthworks there, Stephens rightly believed that the Maya monuments were, in his own words, "the creation of the same races who inhabited the country at the time of the Spanish conquest." Stephens also noted that there were similar hieroglyphic inscriptions at the different sites, which led him to argue for Maya cultural unity—but no Champollion was to emerge to decipher the glyphs until the 1960s.

Frederick Catherwood's accurate, if somewhat romantic, drawing of a stela at Copan; at the time of his visit to the site, in 1840, Maya glyphs had not been deciphered.

(Right) General Pitt-Rivers, excavator of Cranborne Chase, and pioneer in recording techniques.

(Far right) Pitt-Rivers's meticulous plan of a barrow on Cranborne Chase.

Dorothy Garrod, one of the first to study the prehistoric Near East systematically.

The Development of Field Techniques

It was only in the late nineteenth century that a sound methodology of scientific excavation began to be generally adopted. From that time some major figures stand out, who in their various ways have helped create the modern field methods we use today.

General Augustus Lane-Fox Pitt-Rivers, for much of his life a professional soldier, brought long experience of military methods, survey, and precision to impeccably organized excavations on his estates in southern England. Plans, sections, and even models were made, and the exact position of every object was recorded. He was not concerned with retrieving beautiful treasures, but with recovering all objects, no matter how mundane. He was a pioneer in his insistence on total recording, and his four privately printed volumes, describing his excavations on Cranborne Chase from 1887 to 1898, represent the highest standards of archaeological publication.

A younger contemporary of Pitt-Rivers, Sir William Flinders Petrie was likewise noted for his meticulous excavations and his insistence on the collection and description of everything found, not just the fine objects, as well as on full publication. He employed these methods in his exemplary excavations in Egypt, and later in Palestine, from the 1880s until his death.

In 1937 Dorothy Garrod became the first woman professor in any subject at Cambridge, and probably the first woman prehistorian to achieve professorial status anywhere in the world. Her ground-breaking excavations at Zarzi in Iraq and Mount Carmel in Palestine provided the key to a large section of the Near East, from the Middle Paleolithic to the **Mesolithic**, and her find of the fossil skull of a Neanderthal child in 1925 became crucial to the understanding of the relationship between Neanderthals and *Homo sapiens*. And with her discovery of the Natufian culture, the predecessor of the world's first farming societies, she posed a series of new problems still not fully resolved today.

Flinders Petrie outside the tomb in which he lived in Giza, Egypt, in the early 1880s.

Sir Mortimer Wheeler fought in the British army in both world wars and, like Pitt-Rivers, brought military precision to his excavations, notably through such techniques as the grid-square method of dividing and digging a site. He is particularly well known for his work at British hillforts, notably Maiden Castle. Equally outstanding, however, was his achievement as Director-General of the Archaeological Survey of India, where he held training schools in modern field methods, and excavated at many important sites.

Sir Mortimer Wheeler (below), and his excavation at Arikamedu, India, in 1945 (right).

(Right) Kathleen Kenyon was a great excavator who worked at two of the most important and complex sites in the Near East, Jericho and Jerusalem.

(Below) Julio Tello, arguably the greatest Native American social scientist of the twentieth century—he was a Quechua Indian—and the father of Peruvian archaeology.

Alfred Kidder (below left) and his cross-sectional drawing of the stratigraphy at the Pecos pueblo site (below right).

Kathleen Kenyon trained on Roman sites in Britain under Sir Mortimer Wheeler, and adopted and developed his method, with its close control over stratigraphy. She subsequently applied this approach in the Near East at two of the most complex and most excavated sites in Palestine: Jericho and Jerusalem. At Jericho, in 1952–58, she found evidence that pushed back the date of occupation to the end of the Ice Age, and uncovered the walled village of the Neolithic farming community commonly referred to as "the earliest town in the world."

Julio Tello, "America's first indigenous archaeologist," was born and worked in Peru, began his career with studies in Peruvian linguistics, and qualified as a medical doctor before taking up anthropology. He did much to awaken an awareness of the archaeological heritage of Peru, and was the first to recognize the importance of the key site of Chavín de Huantar and indeed of such other major sites as Sechín Alto, Cerro Sechín, and Wari. He was one of the first to stress the autonomous rise of civilization in Peru, and he also founded the Peruvian National Museum of Archaeology.

Alfred Kidder was the leading Americanist of his time. As well as being a major figure in Maya archaeology, he was largely responsible for putting the Southwest on the archaeological map with his excavations at Pecos Ruin, a large pueblo in northern New Mexico, from 1915 to 1929. His survey of the region, *An Introduction to the Study of Southwestern Archaeology* (1924), has become a classic. Kidder was one of the first archaeologists to use a team of specialists to help analyze artifacts and human remains. He is also important for his "blueprint" for a regional strategy: (1) **reconnaissance**; (2) selection of criteria for ranking the remains of sites chronologically; (3) organizing them into a probable sequence; (4) stratigraphic excavation to elucidate specific problems; followed by (5) more detailed regional survey and dating.

Classification and Consolidation

As we have seen, well before the end of the nineteenth century many of the principal features of modern archaeology had been established and many of the early civilizations had been discovered. There now ensued a period, lasting until about 1960, that has been described as the "classificatory-historical period." Its central concern was chronology. Much effort went into the establishment of regional chronologies, and the description of the development of culture in each area.

It was scholars studying the prehistoric societies of Europe and North America who made some of the most significant contributions to the subject. In the United States there was a close link between anthropologists and archaeologists studying the Native Americans. The anthropologist Franz Boas reacted against the broad evolutionary schemes of his predecessors and demanded much greater attention to the collection and classification of information in the field. Huge inventories of cultural traits, such as pot and basket designs or types of moccasins, were built up. This tied in with the so-called "direct historical approach" of the archaeologists, who attempted to trace modern Native American pottery and other styles "directly" back into the distant past. By the 1930s the number of separate regional sequences was so great that a group of scholars led by W.C. McKern devised what became known as the **Midwestern Taxonomic System**, which correlated sequences in the Midwest by identifying similarities between artifact collections.

Meanwhile, Gordon Childe, a brilliant Australian based in Britain and a leading thinker and writer about European prehistory, had almost single-handedly been making comparisons of this sort between prehistoric sequences in Europe. Both his methods and the Midwestern Taxonomic System were designed to order the material, to answer: To what period do these artifacts date? And also: With which other materials do they belong? This latter question usually carried with it an assumption that Childe made explicit: that a constantly recurring collection or **assemblage** of artifacts (a "culture" in his terminology) could be attributed to a particular group of people. This approach thus offered the hope of answering, in a very general sense, the question: To whom did these artifacts belong?

But Childe went beyond merely describing and correlating the culture sequences, and attempted to account for their origin. In the late nineteenth

Professor Gordon Childe at the site of the Neolithic settlement at Skara Brae, Orkney, Scotland, in 1930.

century scholars had argued that all the attributes of civilization, from stone architecture to metal weapons, had spread or "diffused" to Europe from the Near East by trade or migration of people. With the much greater range of evidence available to him, Childe modified this approach and argued that Europe had undergone some indigenous development—but he nevertheless attributed the major cultural changes to Near Eastern influences.

Later Childe went on to try and answer the much more difficult question: Why had civilization arisen in the Near East? Himself influenced by Marxist ideas and the relatively recent Marxist revolution in Russia, he proposed that there had been a **Neolithic Revolution** that gave rise to the development of farming, and later an Urban Revolution, which led to the first towns and cities. Childe was one of the few archaeologists of his generation bold enough to address this whole broad issue of why things happened or changed in the past. Most of his contemporaries were more concerned with establishing chronologies and cultural sequences. But after World War II scholars with new ideas began to challenge conventional approaches.

The Ecological Approach

One of the most influential new thinkers in North America was the anthropologist Julian Steward. Like Childe he was interested in explaining cultural change, but he brought to the question an anthropologist's understanding of how living cultures work. Moreover he highlighted the fact that cultures do not interact simply with each other, but with the environment as well. Steward christened the study of ways in which adaptation to the environment could cause cultural change "**cultural ecology**." Perhaps the most direct archaeological impact of these ideas can be seen in the work of Gordon Willey, one of Steward's graduate associates, who carried out a pioneering investigation in the Virú Valley, Peru, in the late 1940s. This study of some 1500 years of pre-Columbian occupation involved a combination of observations from detailed maps and aerial photographs, survey at ground level, and excavation and surface potsherd collection to establish dates for the hundreds of prehistoric sites identified. Willey then plotted the geographical distribution of these many sites in the valley at different periods and set the results against the changing local environment.

Quite independently of Steward, however, the British archaeologist Grahame Clark developed an ecological approach with even more direct relevance for archaeological fieldwork. Breaking away from the artifact-dominated **culture-historical approach** of his contemporaries, he argued that by studying how human populations adapted to their environments we can understand many aspects of ancient society. Collaboration with new kinds of specialists was essential: for example, specialists who could identify animal

Key Developments

The early twentieth-century establishment of regional chronologies and sequences of artifacts

The development of scientific aids for archaeology, notably radiocarbon dating

The post-World War II development of an environmental or ecological explanation for past change

Increasing collaboration with specialists in other disciplines, such as animal or plant studies

Gordon Childe's bold questioning of why things happened or changed in the past bones or plant remains in the archaeological record could help build up a picture not only of what prehistoric environments were like, but also what foods prehistoric peoples ate.

The Rise of Archaeological Science

The other striking development of the period immediately after World War II was the rapid development of scientific aids for archaeology. We have already seen how pioneers of the ecological approach forged an alliance with specialists from the environmental sciences. Even more important, however, was the application to archaeology of the physical and chemical sciences.

The greatest breakthrough came in the field of dating. In 1949 the American chemist Willard Libby announced his invention of radiocarbon dating. It was not until well over a decade later that the full impact of this momentous technical achievement began to be felt, but the implications were clear: here at last archaeologists might have a means of directly determining the age of undated sites and finds anywhere in the world without complicated cross-cultural comparisons. Traditionally, prehistoric Europe had been dated by supposed contacts with early Greece and hence (indirectly) with ancient Egypt, which could itself be dated historically. The radiocarbon method now promised a completely independent chronology for ancient Europe. It also meant that to establish a date was no longer one of the main end products of research. It was still important, but it could now be done much more efficiently, allowing the archaeologist to go on to ask more challenging questions than merely chronological ones.

Archaeological applications for scientific techniques now include plant and animal studies, and methods for analyzing human remains and artifacts. Over the past decade developments in biochemistry and molecular genetics have led to the emergence of the new disciplines of molecular archaeology and archaeogenetics. Sensitive techniques in the field of chemistry are beginning to allow the precise identification of organic residues and are giving fresh insights into both diet and nutrition. The study of **DNA (deoxyribonucleic acid)**, both modern and ancient, has offered novel approaches to the study of human evolution, and is now beginning to give the study of plant and animal domestication a systematic, molecular basis.

A Turning Point in Archaeology

The 1960s mark a turning point in the development of archaeology. By this time some archaeologists were dissatisfied with the way research in the subject was being conducted. These dissatisfactions were not so much with excavation techniques, or with the newly developed scientific aids in archaeology, but with the way conclusions were drawn from them—how archaeologists explain things.

The fundamental cause for dissatisfaction with the traditional archaeology was that it never seemed to explain anything, other than in terms of migrations of peoples and supposed "influences." Already in 1948 the American archaeologist Walter W. Taylor had argued for an approach that would take into consideration the full range of a culture system. And in 1958 Gordon Willey and Philip Phillips argued for a greater emphasis on the social aspect, for a broader study of the general processes at work in culture history (a "processual interpretation").

That was all very well, but what would it mean in practice?

The Birth of the New Archaeology

In the United States the answer was provided, at least in part, by a group of younger archaeologists, led by Lewis Binford, who set out to offer a new approach to the problems of archaeological interpretation, which was soon dubbed the **New Archaeology**. Binford and his colleagues argued against trying to use archaeological data to write a kind of "counterfeit history." They maintained that the potential of the archaeological evidence was much greater than had been realized for the investigation of social and economic aspects of past societies. It was a more optimistic view than that of many of their predecessors.

They also argued that archaeological reasoning should be made explicit. Conclusions should be based not simply on the authority of the scholar making the interpretation, but on an explicit framework of logical argument. Thus conclusions, if they are to be considered valid, must be open to testing.

These advocates of **processual archaeology** sought to explain rather than simply to describe, and to do so, as in all sciences, by seeking to make valid generalizations (**induction**). They tried to avoid the rather vague talk of the "influences" of one culture upon another, but rather to analyze a culture as a system that could be broken down into subsystems (such as technology, trade, or ideology), which could be studied in their own right. They placed much less emphasis on artifact **typology** (a sequence of design styles) and classification.

In order to fulfill these aims, the New Archaeologists to a large extent turned away from the approaches of history toward those of the sciences. There was a great willingness to employ more sophisticated quantitative techniques and to draw on ideas from other disciplines, notably geography.

In their enthusiasm to use a battery of new techniques and analytical tools, the New Archaeologists drew also on a range of previously unfamiliar vocabularies, which their critics tended to dismiss as jargon. Indeed in recent years, several critics have reacted against some of those aspirations to be scientific. But there can be no doubt that archaeology will never be the same again. Most researchers today, even the critics of the early New Archaeology, implicitly recognize its influence when they agree that it is indeed the goal

Lewis Binford, the founder of the "New Archaeology," lecturing on his work among the Nunamiut hunters of Alaska.

Key Concepts
Processual Archaeology

In the early days of the New Archaeology, its principal exponents were very conscious of the limitations of the older, traditional archaeology. The following contrasts were among those that they often emphasized:

The Nature of Archaeology:
Explanatory vs Descriptive
Archaeology's role was now to explain past change, not simply to reconstruct the past and how people had lived. This involved the use of explicit theory

Explanation:
Culture Process vs Culture History
Traditional archaeology was seen to rely on historical explanation: the New Archaeology, drawing on the philosophy of science, would think in terms of culture process, of how changes in economic and social systems take place. This implies generalization

Reasoning:
Deductive vs Inductive
Instead of the traditional task of "piecing together the past," like a jigsaw puzzle, the appropriate procedure was now to formulate hypotheses, constructing models, and deducing their consequences

Validation:
Testing vs Authority
Hypotheses were to be tested, and conclusions should not be accepted on the basis of the authority or standing of the research worker

Research Focus:
Project Design vs Data Accumulation
Research should be designed to answer specific questions economically, not simply to generate more information, which might not be relevant

Choice of Approach:
Quantitative vs Simply Qualitative
Quantitative data allowed computerized statistical treatment, with the possibility of sampling and significance testing. This was often preferred to the purely verbal traditional approach

Scope:
Optimism vs Pessimism
Traditional archaeologists often stressed that archaeological data were not well suited to the reconstruction of social organization or cognitive systems. The New Archaeologists were more positive, and argued that it would never be known how hard these problems were until archaeologists had tried to solve them

of archaeology to explain what happened in the past as well as simply to describe it. Most of them agree too that in order to practice good archaeology it is necessary to make explicit, and then to examine, our underlying assumptions.

Increasingly also there has been a readiness to apply the techniques of archaeological investigation to more recent times. In the United States James Deetz made significant contributions, and, more widely, medieval archaeology and industrial archaeology are now recognized fields.

The Postprocessual Debate of the 1980s and 1990s

Postmodernist currents of thought in the 1980s and 1990s encouraged a great diversity of approaches to the past. While many field archaeologists were relatively untouched by theoretical debates, and the processual tradition established by the New Archaeology rolled on, there were several new approaches, sometimes collectively termed **postprocessual archaeology**, which dealt with interesting and difficult questions.

Influential arguments, some of them first advanced by the archaeologist Ian Hodder and his students, have stressed that there is no single, correct way to undertake archaeological inference, and that the goal of objectivity is unattainable. They argued that archaeological interpretation can be underpinned by social and political bias, which the ideal of objectivism only works to obscure. This well-justified critique of the scientism of the early New Archaeology sometimes overlooks more recent developments in scientific methodology. It can also lead to charges of relativism, where one person's view has to be taken to be as good as another's, and where, in interpretive matters, "anything goes."

For its early proponents, postprocessual archaeology represented so radical a critique of processual archaeology as to establish a new beginning in archaeological theory. Others, however, saw postprocessualism as simply a development of some of the ideas and theoretical problems introduced by the New Archaeology. The term interpretive archaeologies (plural) has been suggested as a more positive label than postprocessual.

The majority of postprocessual approaches used in more recent times are less aggressively anti-scientific, and the emphasis has instead been upon the use of a variety of personal and often humanistic insights to develop a range of different fields and interests, recognizing the varied perspectives of different social groups. Ian Hodder's work at the early farming site of Çatalhöyük in Turkey provides a good example of this approach in action. It is now recognized that there is no single or coherent postprocessual archaeology, but rather a whole series of interpretive approaches and interests.

One of the strengths of the interpretive approach is to bring into central focus the actions and thoughts of individuals in the past. It argues that in order to understand and interpret the past, it is necessary to "get inside the minds" and think the thoughts of the people in question. This might seem a logical goal when examining symbolic systems (for example figurative

Key Concepts
Interpretive or Postprocessual Archaeologies

Postprocessualism is a collective term for a number of approaches to the past, all of which have roots in the post-modernist current of thought that developed in the 1980s and 1990s

The **neo-Marxist** element has a strong commitment to social awareness: that it is the duty of the archaeologist not only to describe the past, but also to use such insights to change the present world. This contrasts quite strikingly with the aspirations towards objectivity of many processual archaeologists

The **post-positivist** approach rejects the emphasis on the systematic procedures of scientific method that are such a feature of processual archaeology, sometimes seeing modern science as hostile to the individual, as forming an integral part of the "systems of domination" by which the forces of capitalism exert their "hegemony"

The **phenomenological** approach lays stress on the personal experiences of the individual and on the way in which encounters with the material world and with the objects in it shape our understanding of the world. In landscape archaeology, for example, the archaeologist sets out to experience the humanly shaped landscape as it has been modified and formed by human activities

The **praxis** (or *practice*) approach lays stress upon the central role of the human "agent" and upon the primary significance of human actions (praxis) in shaping social structure. Many social norms and social structures are established and shaped by habitual experience (and the notion of **habitus** similarly refers to the unspoken strategy-generating principles employed by the individual, which mediate between social structure and practice). The role of the individual as a significant agent is thus emphasized

The **hermeneutic** (or interpretive) view rejects generalization, another feature of processual archaeology. Emphasis is laid, rather, upon the uniqueness of each society and culture and on the need to study the full context of each in all its rich diversity. A related view stresses that there can be no single correct interpretation: each observer or analyst is entitled to his or her own opinion about the past. There will therefore be a diversity of opinions, and a wide range of perspectives—which is why the emphasis is on interpretive archaeologies (plural)

artworks employing a complex **iconography**) but there is in reality no easy way to get into other people's minds, especially past minds. Nevertheless, in Chapter 9 we examine some of the ways in which we *can* start to answer the question: What did they think?

Whatever the methodological problems, the consequence of the various debates has been to broaden the range of archaeological theory in a positive manner and to emphasize the symbolic and cognitive aspects of human endeavor in a way that the early New Archaeology failed to do.

Pluralizing Pasts

The postprocessual archaeologists are certainly right in arguing that our own interpretation and presentation of the past involve choices that depend less on an objective assessment of the data than on the feelings and opinions of the researchers and of the clients whom they aim to please. The great national museum of the United States, the Smithsonian Institution in Washington, D.C., found it almost impossible to mount an exhibition in 1995 dealing with the destruction of Hiroshima fifty years earlier, without exciting the anger both of ex-servicemen and of those respectful of Japanese sensibilities.

It is evident that archaeology cannot avoid being caught up in and influenced by the issues of the day, social and political as well as intellectual. An example is the influence of feminist thinking and the growth of feminist archaeology, which overlaps with the field of gender studies. A pioneer in the emphasis of the importance of women in prehistory was Marija Gimbutas. Her research in the Balkans led her to create a vision of an "Old Europe" associated with the first farmers whose central focus was (or so she argued) a belief in a great Mother Goddess figure. Although many feminist archaeologists today would take issue with certain aspects of Gimbutas's approach, she has certainly helped foster the current debate on gender roles.

In an article of 1984, Margaret Conkey and Janet Spector drew attention to the androcentrism (male bias) of the discipline of archaeology. As Margaret Conkey pointed out, there existed a need "to reclaim women's experience as valid, to theorize this experience, and to use this to build a program of political action."

The deeply pervasive nature of androcentric thinking in most interpretations of the past should not be underestimated: the gender-specific terminology of "Man the Toolmaker," even when swept away with every reference to "mankind" corrected to "humankind," does in fact conceal further, widely held assumptions or prejudices—for instance that Paleolithic stone tools were mainly made by men rather than women, for which there is little or no evidence.

The box overleaf profiles a number of eminent female archaeologists (in addition to Dorothy Garrod and Kathleen Kenyon, whose pioneering fieldwork is described above, pp. 22–24) who have made important contributions to the discipline, but feminist archaeologists can with justice point to the persistent imbalances between female and male professionals among archaeologists today; the goal of "political action" may be seen as justified by current social realities. In the 1990s feminist concern over androcentrism became one voice among many questioning the supposed objectivity and political neutrality of archaeology. Today, it is common practice to acknowledge the voices and interests of multiple stakeholders in the past, including postcolonial perspectives, local communities, and indigenous archaeology (see below, pp. 35–36).

The Development of Public Archaeology

A further turning point came during the later twentieth century with the development of public archaeology—that is to say, archaeology supported through resources made available as a public obligation. This came with the growing realization that the potential knowledge about the historic (or prehistoric) past embedded in the archaeological record—the material remains of that past—is a resource of public importance, both nationally and internationally, and that the destruction of that past without adequate record should be prevented.

From these realizations came the widespread acceptance that these material remains of the past should be protected and conserved. Moreover, if commercial development sometimes required damage or destruction to that resource, steps should be taken to mitigate that damage through conservation and through recording. There are three key principles here:

- The material record of the past is a public resource that should be managed for the public good.
- When practical circumstances make inevitable some damage to the material record, steps should be taken to mitigate the impact through appropriate survey, excavation, and research.
- The developer pays: the persons or organizations initiating the eventual impact (usually through building works undertaken for economic reasons) should fund the necessary actions in mitigation.

The nations of the world have in practice developed different legal frameworks to deal with these problems. They vary from country to country. In France the approach is termed preventive archaeology, in Britain **rescue archaeology**, and in the United States **Cultural Resource Management** (**CRM**).

These issues are worth emphasizing. In those countries with legislation protecting the material record of the past, a large proportion of the resources devoted toward archaeology come through these practices of conservation and mitigation, as governed by national legislation. The protective system in place is influential for the way archaeology is conducted and for the way students are trained. We return to these important issues in Chapter 12.

Further Women Pioneers of Archaeology

In the history of archaeology we have met Dorothy Garrod and Kathleen Kenyon, who are only two of many early female archaeologists who achieved success against a backdrop of exclusion, discrimination, and lack of recognition and promotion. Through the early history of archaeology many brilliant academic women accepted that, after marriage, professional careers were no longer possible, and they were left to support the academic work of their husbands with little public recognition. This has remained so until the present time, so the achievements of the following pioneers, spanning the nineteenth and twentieth centuries, are all the more impressive and noteworthy.

(Below) Harriet Boyd Hawes (in 1892), discoverer of the Minoan town site of Gournia, Crete.

Harriet Boyd Hawes

This well-educated American majored in Classics and was fluent in Greek. Just after graduating, in her early twenties, she spent several seasons riding around Crete on muleback, in dangerous territory, alone or in the company of a woman friend, looking for prehistoric sites. In 1901 she discovered the Bronze Age site of Gournia—the first Minoan town site ever unearthed—which she excavated for the next three years, supervising a hundred local workmen. She published her findings in exemplary fashion in a lavishly illustrated report that is still consulted today.

Beatrice de Cardi

Initially an assistant of Sir Mortimer Wheeler, Beatrice de Cardi (1914–2016) undertook field surveys in the Persian Gulf and Baluchistan and then in Qatar and the United Arab Emirates. At the age of ninety-three she ceased active fieldwork and concentrated on writing. At the time of her death she was "the world's oldest practicing archaeologist."

(Above) Gertrude Caton-Thompson: her work at Great Zimbabwe confirmed that the site was the work of a major African culture.

Gertrude Caton-Thompson

A wealthy British researcher who followed courses in prehistory and anthropology at Cambridge, Caton-Thompson subsequently became well known for her pioneering inter-disciplinary project of survey and excavation in the Faiyum of Egypt; and later, perhaps most famously, at Great Zimbabwe, where her excavations in 1929 unearthed datable artifacts from a stratified context, and confirmed that the site represented a major culture of African origin.

(Near left) Beatrice de Cardi stated of her fieldwork that "I have never had any difficulties.... I am not a woman or a man when I am working in the Gulf or anywhere else. I am a professional and [my colleagues] have always accepted that."

(Above left) Anna O. Shepard was an acknowledged expert in the ceramics of the American Southwest and Mesoamerica.

(Above center) Tatiana Proskouriakoff: her work on Maya glyphs contributed greatly to their final decipherment.

(Above right) Mary Leakey working on the fossilized hominin footprints at Laetoli, Tanzania.

Anna O. Shepard

An American who studied archaeology as well as a wide range of hard sciences, Shepard subsequently became a specialist in ceramics, as well as Mesoamerican and Southwestern archaeology. She was one of the pioneers of petrographic analysis of archaeological pottery, focusing on sherd paste, paint, and temper. She published extensively on the technology of New World pottery, and wrote a standard work, *Ceramics for the Archaeologist*.

Tatiana Proskouriakoff

Born in Siberia, Proskouriakoff moved with her family to Pennsylvania in 1916. Unemployed after graduating as an architect in 1930 during the Great Depression, she ended up working as a museum artist in the University of Pennsylvania. A visit to the Maya site of Piedras Negras led her to devote the rest of her life to Maya architecture, art, and hieroglyphs.

Mary Leakey

A cigar-smoking, whiskey-drinking, British archaeologist who, together with her husband Louis, transformed their chosen field. They worked for almost half a century at many sites in East Africa, most notably at Olduvai Gorge, Tanzania, and at Laetoli, where she excavated the famous trails of fossilized hominin footprints, made 3.7 million years ago.

Indigenous Archaeologies

Comparable questions have continued to emerge in the developing indigenous archaeologies in former colonies, now freed from imperial power. The appropriate policy for cultural heritage management, and indeed the very nature of the cultural heritage itself, are often contested, sometimes along ethnic lines. Marginalized groups, such as the Australian Aborigines, have sought to attain greater influence in the heritage sphere, and have often found their interests overlooked and misunderstood.

Deeper questions arise, however, about the nature of the globalization process, itself the outcome of technological advances developed in the West, and whether the very notion of cultural heritage, as commonly understood, may not be a product of Western thought. The Western-conceived notion of Cultural Heritage Management has been seen by postcolonial thinkers as an imposition of Western values, with officially endorsed notions of heritage perhaps leading to homogenization and the undervaluation of cultural diversity. Even the UNESCO-sponsored listing of World Heritage Sites, from the standpoint of this critique, is dominated by Western-formulated notions of heritage.

While some aspects of archaeology at the beginning of the new millennium were inevitably controversial, they were also in some ways very positive. They emphasized the value and importance of the past for the contemporary world, and they led to the realization that the cultural heritage is an important part of the human environment, and can be as fragile as the natural environment. They imply, then, that the archaeologist has an important role to play in achieving a balanced view also of our present world, which is inescapably the product of the worlds that have preceded it. The task of interpretation is now seen as very much more complex than it once seemed.

Today, archaeology—once largely the preserve (and the product) of white, upper class, European or North American males—has changed. Many active archaeologists are women. All nationalities are represented. Indigenous archaeologists play an increasing role. Yet the nineteenth- and twentieth-century origins of the discipline are still all too evident today.

Study Questions

1   Why is the study of stratification important to archaeology?
2   Why was the invention of radiocarbon dating so momentous?
3   How did the New Archaeology differ from classificatory-historical archaeology?
4   What are some postprocessual approaches to archaeology?
5   What is feminist archaeology?
6   Why has "public archaeology" become important in recent decades?

Summary

THE HISTORY OF ARCHAEOLOGY is a history of new ideas, methods, and discoveries. Modern archaeology took root in the nineteenth century with the acceptance of three key concepts: the great antiquity of humanity, Darwin's principle of evolution, and the Three Age System for ordering material culture. By the 1880s, many of the early civilizations, especially in the Old World, had been discovered, and some of their ancient scripts deciphered. This was followed by a long phase of consolidation—of improvements in fieldwork and the establishment of regional chronologies.

AFTER WORLD WAR II the pace of change in the discipline quickened. New ecological approaches sought to help us understand human adaptation to the environment. New scientific techniques introduced among other things reliable means of dating the prehistoric past. The New Archaeology of the 1960s and 1970s turned to questions not just of what happened when, but also why, in an attempt to explain processes of change. Meanwhile, pioneer fieldworkers studying whole regions opened up a truly world archaeology in time and space—in time, back from the present to the earliest toolmakers, and in space, across all the world's continents.

MORE RECENTLY a diversity of theoretical approaches, often grouped under the label postprocessual, highlighted the variety of possible interpretations and the sensitivity of their political implications. Today archaeology plays a significant role in the establishment of national and ethnic identities.

PRECISELY HOW ARCHAEOLOGISTS are continuing to push back the frontiers of knowledge about our planet's human past forms the subject of the rest of this book.

Further Reading

Good introductions to the history of archaeology include:

Bahn, P. G. (ed.). 1999. *The Cambridge Illustrated History of Archaeology*. Cambridge University Press: Cambridge & New York.

Bahn, P. G. (ed.). 2014. *The History of Archaeology: An Introduction*. Routledge: London.

Cohen, G. M. & Joukowsky, M. S. (eds). 2007. *Pioneering Women Archaeologists*. Michigan University Press: Ann Arbor.

Deetz, J. 1996. *In Small Things Forgotten: An Archaeology of Early American Life* (2nd ed.). Anchor Books: New York.

Fagan, B. M. 2004. *A Brief History of Archaeology: Classical Times to the Twenty-First Century*. Prentice Hall: Upper Saddle River, NJ.

Johnson, M. 2010. *Archaeological Theory: An Introduction* (2nd ed.). Wiley-Blackwell: Oxford.

Lowenthal, D. 1999. *The Past is a Foreign Country*. Cambridge University Press: Cambridge & New York.

Renfrew, C. & Bahn, P. (eds). 2004. *Key Concepts in Archaeology*. Routledge: London & New York.

Trigger, B. G. 2006. *A History of Archaeological Thought* (2nd ed.). Cambridge University Press: Cambridge & New York.

Willey, G. R. & Sabloff, J. A. 1993. *A History of American Archaeology* (3rd ed.). Freeman: New York.

[See p. 345 for a list of useful websites]

2

What Is Left?
The Variety of the Evidence

The relics of past human activity are all around us. Some of them were deliberate constructions, built to last, for example the pyramids of Egypt, the Great Wall of China, or the temples of Mesoamerica and India. Others, such as the remains of the Maya irrigation systems of Mexico and Belize, are the visible relics of activities, the aim of which was not primarily to impress the observer, but that still command respect today for the scale of the enterprise they document.

Most of the remains of archaeology are far more modest, however. They are the discarded garbage from the daily activities of human existence: the food remains, the bits of broken pottery, the fractured stone tools, the debris that is formed everywhere as people go about their daily lives.

In this chapter we define the basic archaeological terms, briefly survey the scope of the surviving evidence, and look at the great variety of ways in which it has been preserved for us. From the frozen soil of the Russian steppes, for instance, have come the wonderful finds of Pazyryk, those great chieftains' burials where wood and textiles and skins are splendidly preserved. From the dry caves of Peru and other arid environments have come remarkable textiles, baskets, and other remains that often perish completely. And by contrast, from wetlands, whether the swamps of Florida or the lake villages of Switzerland, further organic remains are being recovered, this time preserved not by the absence of moisture, but by its abundant presence to the exclusion of air.

Extremes of temperature and of humidity have preserved much. So too have natural disasters. The volcanic eruption that destroyed Pompeii in Italy is the most famous of them, but there have been others, such as the eruption of the Ilopango volcano in El Salvador in the second century CE, which buried land surfaces and settlement remains in a large part of the southern Maya area.

Unfortunately most archaeological sites are not in areas subjected to extremes of climate or volcanic activity, and levels of preservation can vary enormously. Our knowledge of the early human past is dependent in this way on the human activities and natural processes that have formed the archaeological record, and on those further processes that determine, over long periods of time, what is left and what is gone for ever. Today we can hope to recover much of what remains, and to learn from it by asking the right questions in the right way.

Basic Categories of Archaeological Evidence

The evidence studied by archaeologists very often includes artifacts—objects used, modified, or made by people. But equally important is the study of organic and environmental remains—known as **ecofacts**—that, although not made by humans, can still be very revealing about many aspects of past human activity. Much archaeological research concentrates on the analysis of these artifacts and ecofacts that are found together on sites, which in turn are most productively studied together with their surrounding landscapes and grouped together into regions. Some of these different scales at which archaeologists operate, as well as the terminology they use, are illustrated above and opposite.

Artifacts are humanly made or modified portable objects, such as stone tools, pottery, and metal weapons. But artifacts provide evidence to help us answer all the key questions—not just technological ones—addressed in this book. A single clay vessel or pot can be analyzed in a number of different ways. The clay may be tested to produce a date for the vessel and thus perhaps a date for the location where it was found. It could also be tested to find the source of the clay and thus give evidence for the range and contacts of the group that made the vessel. Pictorial decoration on the pot's surface could help to form or be related to a sequence of design styles (a typology), and it could tell us something about ancient beliefs, particularly if it shows gods or other figures. And analysis of the vessel's shape and any food or other residues found in it can yield information about the pot's use, perhaps in cooking, as well as about ancient diet.

SMALL REGION

Areas with soils suitable for first farmers (loess soils)

Rhine River

Sites

1 : 400,000

GROUP OF SITES in association with river

Merzbach River

1 : 40,000

INDIVIDUAL SITE (SMALL VILLAGE)

Early phase house (*structure*)

Garbage pit (*feature*) containing organic remains (*ecofacts*)

Path (*feature*)

Silo (*small structure*)

Later phase house (*structure*)

1 : 4000

INDIVIDUAL STRUCTURE (HOUSE)

Scatter of *artifacts*

Posthole (*feature*)

1 : 400

Artifacts and features are found *in association with* the structure

Different scales and terminology used in archaeology, from the continental region (opposite page, top left) to the individual structure (this page, bottom right). In this representation of the pattern of settlement of Europe's first farmers (fifth millennium BCE), the archaeologist might study—at the broader scale—the interesting association between sites and light, easily worked soils near rivers. At the smaller scale, the association—established by excavation—of houses with other houses and with such structures as silos for grain storage raises questions, for example about social organization and permanence of occupation during this period.

Key Concepts
Types of Evidence

Artifacts: portable objects used, modified, or made by humans

Ecofacts: organic and environmental remains not made by humans

Features: non-portable artifacts

Sites: places where artifacts, ecofacts, and features are found together

Key Concepts
Context

Matrix: the material surrounding a find (an artifact, ecofact, or feature)

Provenience: the exact position of a find within the matrix

Association: a find's relationship with other finds

Without context, an artifact loses much of its archaeological value

Some researchers broaden the meaning of the term artifact to include all humanly modified components of a site or landscape, such as hearths, postholes, and storage pits—but these non-portable artifacts are more usefully described as **features**. Such simple features as postholes may themselves, or in combination with remains of hearths, floors, ditches, etc., give evidence for complex features or structures, defined as buildings of all kinds, from houses and granaries to palaces and temples.

Non-artifactual organic and environmental remains, or ecofacts, include human skeletons, animal bones, and plant remains, but also soils and sediments—all of which may shed light on past human activities. They are important because they can indicate, for example, what people ate or the environmental conditions in which they lived.

Archaeological sites may be thought of as the huge variety of places where artifacts, features, structures, and organic and environmental remains are found together. For working purposes we can simplify this still further and define sites as places where significant traces of human activity are identified. Thus a village or town is a site, and so too is an isolated monument, such as Serpent Mound in Ohio. Equally, a surface scatter of stone tools or potsherds may represent a site occupied for no more than a few hours, whereas a Near Eastern **tell** or mound is a site indicating human occupation over perhaps thousands of years.

The Importance of Context

In order to reconstruct past human activity at a site it is crucially important to understand the **context** of a find, whether artifact, ecofact, or feature. A find's context consists of its immediate **matrix** (the material surrounding it, usually some sort of sediment, such as gravel, sand, or clay), its **provenience** (horizontal and vertical position within the matrix), and its **association** with other finds (occurrence together with other archaeological remains, usually in the same matrix). In the nineteenth century the demonstration that stone tools were often associated with the bones of extinct animals in a sealed matrix helped establish the idea of the great antiquity of humankind.

Increasingly since then archaeologists have recognized the importance of identifying and accurately recording associations between remains on sites. This is why it is such a tragedy when looters dig up a site indiscriminately, looking for rich finds, without recording its matrix, provenience, or associations. All the contextual information is lost. A looted vase may be attractive for a collector, but far more could have been learnt about the society that produced it had archaeologists been able to record where it was found (in a tomb, ditch, or house?) and in association with what other artifacts or organic remains (weapons, tools, or animal bones?). Much information about the Mimbres people of the American Southwest has been lost for ever because looters bulldozed their sites, hunting for the superbly painted—and highly sought after—bowls made by the Mimbres 1000 years ago (see box, p. 310).

When modern (or ancient) looters disturb a site, perhaps shifting aside material they are not interested in, they destroy that material's primary context. If archaeologists subsequently excavate that shifted material, they need to be able to recognize that it is in a secondary context. This may be straightforward for, say, a Mimbres site, looted quite recently, but it is much more difficult for a site disturbed in antiquity. Nor is disturbance confined to human activity: archaeologists dealing with the tens of thousands of years of the Paleolithic or Old Stone Age period know well that the forces of nature—encroaching seas or ice sheets, wind and water action—invariably destroy primary context. A great many of the Stone Age tools found in European river gravels are in a secondary context, transported by water action far from their original, primary context.

Formation Processes

In recent years archaeologists have become increasingly aware that a whole series of **formation processes** may have affected both the way in which finds came to be buried and what happened to them after they were buried. The study of these processes is called **taphonomy**.

A useful distinction has been made between cultural formation processes and non-cultural or natural formation processes. Cultural formation processes involve the deliberate or accidental activities of human beings as they make or use artifacts, build or abandon buildings, plow their fields, and so on. Natural formation processes are natural events that govern both the burial and the survival of the archaeological record. The sudden fall of volcanic ash that covered Pompeii is an exceptional example; a more common one would be the gradual burial of artifacts or features by wind-borne sand or soil. Likewise the transporting of stone tools by river action, referred to above, or the activities of animals—burrowing into a site or chewing bones and pieces of wood—are also examples of natural formation processes.

At first sight these distinctions may seem of little interest to the archaeologist. In fact they are vital to the accurate reconstruction of past human activities. It can be important to know whether certain archaeological evidence is the product of human or non-human (cultural or natural) activity. If, for example, you are trying to reconstruct human woodworking activities by studying cutmarks on timber, then you should learn to recognize certain kinds of marks made by beavers using their teeth and to distinguish these from cutmarks made by humans using stone or metal tools.

Let us take an even more significant example. For the earliest phases of human existence in Africa, at the beginning of the Paleolithic or Old Stone Age period, theories about our primitive hunting ability have been based on the

Early humans as mere scavengers (above) or mighty hunters (right)? Our understanding of formation processes governs the way in which we interpret associations of human tools with animal bones from the fossil record in Africa.

association between stone tools and animal bones found at archaeological sites. The bones were assumed to be those of animals hunted and slaughtered by the early humans who made the tools. But studies of animal behavior and cutmarks on animal bones suggest that in many cases the excavated bones are the remains of animals hunted and largely eaten by other predatory animals. The humans with their stone tools would have come upon the

Experimental Archaeology

One effective way to study formation processes is through long-term experimental archaeology. An excellent example is the experimental earthwork constructed on Overton Down, southern England, in 1960.

The earthwork consists of a substantial chalk and turf bank, 21 m (69 ft.) long, 7 m (25 ft.) wide, and 2 m (6 ft. 7 in.) high, with a ditch cut parallel to it. The aim of the experiment has been to assess not only how the bank and ditch alter through time, but also what happens to buried materials, such as pottery, leather, and textiles. Sections (trenches) have been—or will be—cut across the bank and ditch at intervals of 2, 4, 8, 16, 32, 64, and 128 years (in real time, 1962, 1964, 1968, 1976, 1992, 2024, and 2088): a considerable commitment for all concerned.

The project is nearing the halfway point, and preliminary results have been interesting. In the 1960s the bank dropped some 25 cm (10 in.) in height and the ditch silted up quite rapidly;

since the mid-1970s, the structure has stabilized. As for the buried materials, tests after four years showed that pottery was unchanged and leather little affected, but textiles were already becoming weakened and discolored.

The excavations in 1992 revealed that preservation was better in the chalk bank, which is less biologically active, than in the turf core, where textiles and some wood had completely disappeared. The structure itself had changed little since 1976, though there

The bank and ditch as cut in 1960, together with the changes revealed by sections cut across the earthwork in 1962 and 1976.

was considerable reworking and transporting of fine sediment by earthworms.

The experiment has already shown that many of the changes that interest archaeologists occur within decades of burial, and that the extent of these changes can be far greater than had hitherto been suspected.

---

scene as mere scavengers, at the end of a pecking order of different animal species. By no means everyone agrees with this scavenging hypothesis. The point to emphasize here is that the issue can best be resolved by improving our techniques for distinguishing between cultural and natural formation processes—between human and non-human activity. Many studies are now focusing on the need to clarify how to differentiate cutmarks on bones made by stone tools from those made by the teeth of animal predators. Modern experiments using replica stone tools to cut meat off bones are one helpful approach. Other kinds of **experimental archaeology** can be most instructive about some of the formation processes that affect the physical preservation of archaeological material (see box above).

The remainder of this chapter is devoted to a more detailed discussion of the different cultural and natural formation processes.

Cultural Formation Processes—How People Have Affected What Survives in the Archaeological Record

We may separate these processes rather crudely into two kinds: those that reflect the original human behavior and activity before a find or site became buried; and those (such as plowing or looting) that came after burial. Now of course most major archaeological sites are formed as the result of a complex sequence of use, burial, and reuse repeated many times over, so that a simple two-fold division of cultural formation processes may not be so simple to apply in practice. Nevertheless, since one of our main aims is to reconstruct original human behavior and activity, we must make the attempt.

Original human behavior is often reflected archaeologically in at least four major activities: in the case of a tool (see diagram below) there may be:

1 acquisition of the raw material;
2 manufacture;
3 use (and distribution); and finally
4 disposal or discard when the tool is worn out or broken.

(The tool may of course be reworked and recycled, i.e. repeating stages 2 and 3.) Similarly, a food crop, such as wheat, will be acquired (harvested), manufactured (processed), used (eaten), and discarded (digested and the

An artifact, a stone tool in this case, may have entered the archaeological record at any one of these four stages in its life cycle. The archaeologist's task is to determine which stage is represented by the find in question.

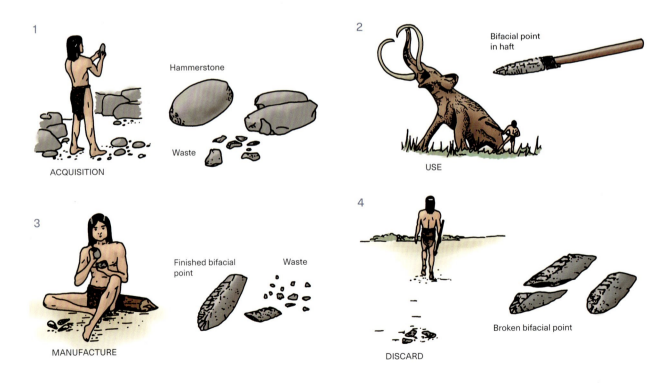

1 ACQUISITION

Hammerstone

Waste

2 USE

Bifacial point in haft

3 MANUFACTURE

Finished bifacial point

Waste

4 DISCARD

Broken bifacial point

waste products excreted)—here we might add a common intermediate stage of storage before use. From the archaeologist's point of view the critical factor is that remains can enter the archaeological record at any one of these stages—a tool may be lost or thrown out as inferior quality during manufacture, or a crop may be accidentally burnt and thus preserved during processing. In order to reconstruct accurately the original activity it is therefore crucial to try to understand which one of the stages we are examining. It may be quite easy to identify, say, the first stage for stone tools, because stone quarries can often be recognized by deep holes in the ground, with piles of associated waste flakes and blanks, which survive well. But it is much more difficult to know beyond reasonable doubt whether a sample of charred plant remains comes from, say, a threshing area or an occupation area—and this may also make it difficult to reconstruct the true plant diet, since certain activities may favor the preservation of certain species of plant.

Deliberate burial of valuables is another major aspect of original human behavior that has left its mark on the archaeological record. In times of conflict or war people often deposit prized possessions in the ground, intending to reclaim them at a later date but sometimes for one reason or another failing to do so. These **hoards** are a prime source of evidence for certain periods, such as the European Bronze Age, for which hoards of metal goods are common, or later Roman Britain, which has yielded buried treasures of silver and other precious metals. The archaeologist, however, may not find it easy to distinguish between hoards originally intended to be recovered and valuables buried with no reclamation intended, perhaps to placate supernatural powers (placed for example at a particularly dangerous part of a crossing over a bog).

How archaeologists set about trying to demonstrate belief in supernatural powers and an afterlife will be seen in Chapter 9. Here we may note that, in addition to hoards, the major source of evidence comes from burial of the dead, whether in simple graves, elaborate burial mounds, or giant pyramids, usually with such grave-goods as ceramic vessels or weapons, and sometimes with painted tomb-chamber walls, as in ancient Mexico or Egypt. The Egyptians indeed went so far as to mummify their dead—to preserve them, they hoped, for eternity—as did the Incas of Peru, whose kings were kept in the Temple of the Sun at Cuzco and brought outside for special ceremonies.

Human destruction of the archaeological record might be caused by burials of the kind just described being dug into earlier deposits. But people in the past deliberately or accidentally obliterated traces of their predecessors in innumerable other ways. Rulers, for instance, often destroyed monuments or erased inscriptions belonging to previous chiefs or monarchs. Some human destruction meant to obliterate has inadvertently preserved material for the archaeologist to find. Burning, for example, may not always destroy.

It can often improve the chances of survival of a variety of remains, such as of plants: the conversion into carbon greatly increases the powers of resistance to the ravages of time. Clay daubing and adobe usually decay, but if a structure has been fired, the mud is baked to the consistency of a brick. In the same way thousands of clay writing tablets from the Near East have been baked accidentally or deliberately in fires and thus preserved. Timbers too may char and survive in structures, or at least leave a clear impression in the hardened mud.

Today human destruction of the archaeological record continues at a frightening pace, through land drainage, plowing, building work, looting, etc. In Chapter 12 we discuss how this affects archaeology generally and what the potential implications are for the future.

Natural Formation Processes—How Nature Affects What Survives in the Archaeological Record

We saw above how natural formation processes, such as river action, can disturb or destroy the primary context of archaeological material. Here we will focus on that material itself, and the natural processes that cause decay or lead to preservation.

Practically any archaeological material can survive in exceptional circumstances. Usually, however, inorganic materials survive far better than organic ones.

Inorganic Materials

The most common inorganic materials to survive archaeologically are stone, clay, and metals.

Stone tools survive extraordinarily well—some are more than 2 million years old. Not surprisingly they have always been our main source of evidence for human activities during the Paleolithic period, even though wooden and bone tools (which are less likely to be preserved) may originally have equaled stone ones in importance. Stone tools sometimes come down to us so little damaged or altered from their primary state that archaeologists can examine microscopic patterns of wear on their cutting edges and learn, for example, whether the tools were used to cut wood or animal hides. This is now a major branch of archaeological inquiry.

Fired clay, such as pottery and baked mud brick or adobe, is virtually indestructible if well fired. It is therefore again not surprising that for the periods after the introduction of pottery-making (some 16,000 years ago in Japan, and 9000 years ago in the Near East and parts of South America) ceramics have traditionally been the archaeologist's main source of evidence. As we saw earlier in this chapter, pots can be studied for their shape, surface decoration, mineral content, and even the food or other residues left inside

This bronze head from a statue of a Greek male athlete was found off the coast of Croatia in 2001. Bronze survives well in seawater, but some 2000 years of encrustation had to be painstakingly removed by restorers.

them. Acid soils can damage the surface of fired clay, and porous or badly fired clay vessels or mud brick can become fragile in humid conditions. Even disintegrated mud brick, however, can help to assess rebuilding phases in, for instance, Peruvian villages or Near Eastern tells.

Such metals as gold, silver, and lead survive well. Copper, and bronze with a low-quality alloy, are attacked by acid soils, and can become so oxidized that only a green deposit or stain is left. Oxidation is also a rapid and powerful agent of the destruction of iron, which rusts and may similarly leave only a discoloration in the soil.

The sea is potentially very destructive. Underwater remains can be broken and scattered by currents, waves, or tidal action. On the other hand, the sea can cause metals to be coated with a thick, hard casing of metallic salts from the objects themselves; this helps to preserve the artifacts. If the remains are simply taken out of the water and not treated, the salts react with air, and give off acid that destroys the remaining metal. But the use of **electrolysis**— placing the object in a chemical solution and passing a weak current through it—leaves the metal artifact clean and safe. This is a standard procedure in underwater archaeology and is used on all types of objects from cannons to the finds recovered from the *Titanic*.

Organic Materials

Survival of organic materials is determined largely by the matrix (the surrounding material) and by climate (local and regional)—with the occasional influence of such natural disasters as volcanic eruptions, which are often far from disastrous for archaeologists.

The matrix, as we saw earlier, is usually some kind of sediment or soil. These vary in their effects on organic material; chalk, for example, preserves human and animal bone well (in addition to inorganic metals). Acid soils destroy bones and wood within a few years, but will leave telltale discolorations where postholes or hut foundations once stood. Similar brown or black marks survive in sandy soils, as do dark silhouettes that used to be skeletons.

But the immediate matrix may in exceptional circumstances have an additional component, such as metal ore, salt, or oil. Copper can favor the preservation of organic remains, perhaps by preventing the activity of destructive micro-organisms. The prehistoric copper (and salt) mines of central and southeastern Europe, for example, contain many remains of wood, leather, and textiles.

A combination of salt and oil ensured the preservation of a woolly rhinoceros at Starunia, Ukraine, with skin intact, and the leaves and fruits of tundra vegetation around it. The animal had been carried by a strong current into a pool saturated with crude oil and salt from a natural oil

Matrix: the conditions and makeup
of the soil or sediment surrounding
organic material dictate whether the
latter survives

Climate: the local and regional
weather conditions in turn affect
soils, erosion, flora, and fauna

Natural disasters, such as volcanic
eruptions, and extremes of dry,
cold, and wet conditions, can
lead to exceptional preservation
of organic materials

seep, which prevented decomposition: bacteria could not operate in these conditions, while salt had permeated the skin and preserved it. Similarly, the asphalt pits of La Brea, Los Angeles, are world famous for the large quantities and fine condition of the skeletons of a wide range of prehistoric animals and birds recovered from them.

Climate plays an important role too in the preservation of organic remains. Occasionally the "local climate" of an environment, such as a cave, preserves finds. Caves are natural "conservatories" because their interiors are protected from outside climatic effects, and (in the case of limestone caves) their alkaline conditions permit excellent preservation. If undisturbed by floods or the trampling feet of animals and people, they can preserve bones and even such fragile remains as footprints.

More usually, however, it is the regional climate that is important. Tropical climates are the most destructive, with their combination of heavy rains, acid soils, warm temperatures, high humidity, erosion, and wealth of vegetation and insect life. Tropical rainforests can overwhelm a site remarkably quickly, with roots that dislodge masonry and tear buildings apart, while torrential downpours gradually destroy paint and plasterwork, and woodwork rots away completely. Archaeologists in southern Mexico, for example, constantly have to battle to keep back the jungle. On the other hand, jungle conditions can be positive, in that they hinder looters from easily reaching even more sites than they do already.

Temperate climates, as in much of Europe and North America, are not good, as a rule, for the preservation of organic materials; their relatively warm but variable temperatures and fluctuating rainfall usually combine to accelerate the processes of decay. In some circumstances, however, local conditions can counteract these processes. At the Roman fort of Vindolanda, near Hadrian's Wall in northern England, more than 1300 letters and documents, written in ink on wafer-thin sheets of birch and alderwood, have been found. Offering a remarkable insight into both military and personal matters on the frontier, the fragments, dating to about 100 CE, have survived because of the soil's unusual chemical condition: clay compacted between layers in the site created oxygen-free pockets (the exclusion of oxygen is vital to the preservation of organic materials), while chemicals produced by bracken, bone, and other remains effectively made the land sterile in that locality, thus preventing disturbance by vegetation and other forms of life.

Natural disasters sometimes preserve sites, including organic remains, for the archaeologist. The most common are violent storms, such as the one that covered the coastal Neolithic village of Skara Brae, in the Orkney Islands, off the north coast of Scotland, with sand; the mudslide that engulfed the prehistoric village of Ozette on America's Northwest Coast (see box, p. 58); or volcanic eruptions, such as that of Vesuvius, which buried and preserved

Roman Pompeii under a blanket of ash. Another volcanic eruption, this time in El Salvador in about 595 CE, deposited a thick and widespread layer of ash over a densely populated area of Maya settlement. Work here has uncovered a variety of organic remains at the site of Cerén, including palm and grass roofing, mats, baskets, stored grain, and even preserved agricultural furrows.

Apart from these special circumstances, the survival of organic materials is limited to cases involving extremes of moisture: that is, very dry, frozen, or waterlogged conditions.

Preservation of Organic Materials: Extreme Conditions

DRY ENVIRONMENTS.   Great aridity or dryness prevents decay through the shortage of water, which ensures that many destructive micro-organisms are unable to flourish. Archaeologists first became aware of the phenomenon in Egypt (see Tutankhamun box overleaf), where much of the Nile Valley has such a dry atmosphere that bodies of the Predynastic period (before 3000 BCE) have survived intact, with skin, hair, and nails, without any artificial mummification or coffins—the corpses were simply placed in shallow graves in the sand. Rapid drying out, plus the draining qualities of the sand, produced such spectacular preservative effects that they probably suggested the practice of mummification to the later Egyptians of the Dynastic period.

The pueblo dwellers of the American Southwest (c. 700–1400 CE) buried their dead in dry caves and rockshelters where, as in Egypt, natural desiccation took place: these are not therefore true, humanly created mummies, although they are often referred to as such. The bodies survive, sometimes wrapped in fur blankets or tanned skins, and in such good condition that it has been possible to study hair styles. Clothing (from fiber sandals to string aprons) also remains, together with a wide range of goods, such as basketry, feathered ornaments, and leather. Some far earlier sites in the same region also contain organic remains: Danger Cave, Utah (occupied from 9000 BCE onward), yielded wooden arrows, trap springs, knife handles, and other wooden tools, while caves near Durango, Colorado, had preserved maize cobs, squashes, and sunflower and mustard seeds. Plant finds of this type have been crucial in helping to reconstruct ancient diet.

The coastal dwellers of central and southern Peru lived—and died—in a similarly dry environment, so that it is possible today to see the tattoos on their desiccated bodies, and admire the huge and dazzlingly colorful textiles from cemeteries at Ica and Nazca, as well as basketry and featherwork, and also maize cobs and other items of food. In Chile, the oldest deliberately made mummies have been found at Chinchorro, preserved again by the aridity of the desert environment.

Dry Preservation: The Tomb of Tutankhamun

EGYPT

Thebes

The arid conditions that prevail in Egypt have helped preserve a wide range of ancient materials, ranging from numerous written documents on papyrus (made of the pith of a Nile water plant) to two full-size wooden boats buried beside the Great Pyramid at Giza. But the best-known and most spectacular array of objects was that discovered in 1922 by Howard Carter and Lord Carnarvon in the tomb at Thebes of the pharaoh Tutankhamun, dating to the fourteenth century BCE.

Tutankhamun had a short reign and was relatively insignificant in Egyptian history, a fact reflected in his burial, a poor one by pharaonic standards. But within the small tomb, originally built for someone else, was a wealth of treasure. For Tutankhamun was buried with everything he might need in the next life. The entrance corridor and the four chambers were crammed with thousands of individual grave-goods. They included objects of precious metal, such as jewelry and the famous gold mask, and food and clothing. But wooden objects, such as statues, chests, shrines, and two of the three coffins, made up a large part of the tomb's contents.

The grave furniture was not all originally intended for Tutankhamun. Some of it had been made for other members of his family, and then hastily

(Above) The outermost of Tutankhamun's three coffins was made of cypress wood, overlaid with gold foil.

(Left) A gilded ritual couch found remarkably well preserved among the contents of the tomb of Tutankhamun.

adopted when the young king died unexpectedly. There were also touching items, such as a chair the king had used as a child, and a simple reed stick mounted in gold labeled as "A reed which His Majesty cut with his own hand." Even wreaths and funerary bouquets had survived in the dry conditions, left on the second and third coffins by mourners.

(Below) A cutaway view of the tomb and its treasures, as found in 1922.

A slightly different phenomenon occurred in the Aleutian Islands, off the west coast of Alaska, where the dead were kept and naturally preserved in volcanically warmed caves that were extremely dry. Here the islanders seem to have enhanced the natural desiccation by periodically drying the bodies by wiping or suspension over a fire; in some cases they removed the internal organs and placed dry grass in the cavity.

COLD ENVIRONMENTS. Natural refrigeration can hold the processes of decay in check for thousands of years. Perhaps the first frozen finds to be discovered were the numerous remains of mammoths encountered in the permafrost (permanently frozen soil) of Siberia, a few with their flesh, hair, and stomach contents intact. The unlucky creatures probably fell into crevices in snow, and were buried by silt in what became a giant deep-freeze. The best-known are Beresovka, recovered in 1901, and baby Dima, found in 1977. Preservation can be still so good that dogs will eat the meat and they have to be kept well away from the carcasses.

The most famous frozen archaeological remains are those from the burial mounds of steppe nomads at Pazyryk in the Altai Mountains, southern Siberia, dating to the Iron Age, about 400 BCE. They comprise pits dug deep into the ground, lined with logs, and covered with a low cairn of stones. They could only have been dug in the warm season, before the ground froze solid. Any warm air in the graves rose and deposited its moisture on the stones of the cairn; moisture also gradually infiltrated down into the burial chambers, and froze so hard there during the harsh winter that it never thawed during subsequent summers, since the cairns were poor conductors of heat and shielded the pits from the warming and drying effects of wind and sun. Consequently, even the most fragile materials have survived intact—despite the boiling water that had to be used by excavators to recover them.

The Pazyryk bodies had been placed inside log coffins, with wooden pillows, and survived so well that their spectacular tattoos can still be seen. Clothing included linen shirts, decorated caftans, aprons, stockings, and headdresses of felt and leather. There were also rugs, wall-coverings, tables laden with food, and horse carcasses complete with elaborate bridles, saddles, and other trappings. A further well-preserved burial has been found in the region, containing a female accompanied by six horses, and grave-goods including a silver mirror and various wooden objects.

Similar standards of preservation have also been encountered in other regions, such as Greenland and Alaska. More southerly regions can produce the same effect at high altitude, for instance the Inca-period "mummies" found at a number of high-altitude sites in the Andes; or the 5300-year-old Iceman found preserved in the ice in the Alps near the border between Italy and Austria (see boxes, overleaf and p. 56).

Frozen conditions in southern Siberia helped to preserve many remarkable finds from the burial mounds of steppe nomads at Pazyryk, dating from about 400 BCE, including this tattoo pattern on the torso and arms of a chieftain.

Cold Preservation 1: The Iceman

The world's oldest fully preserved human body was found in September 1991 by German hikers near the Similaun glacier, in the Ötztal Alps of South Tyrol. They spotted a human body, its skin yellowish-brown and desiccated, at an altitude of 3200 m (10,500 ft.). The Iceman is the first prehistoric human ever found with his everyday clothing and equipment; other similarly intact bodies from prehistory have been either carefully buried or sacrificed.

The body was placed in a freezer in Austria, but subsequent investigation determined that the corpse—called Similaun Man, Ötzi, or simply the Iceman—had lain *c.* 90 m (300 ft.) inside Italy, and he has been housed there, in a museum in Bolzano, since 1998. Fifteen radiocarbon dates have been obtained from the body, the artifacts, and the grass in the boots: they are all in rough agreement, averaging at 3300 BCE.

It was initially thought the Iceman was overcome by exhaustion—perhaps caught in a fog or a blizzard. After death, he was dried out by a warm autumn wind, before becoming encased in ice. Since the body lay in a depression, it was protected from the movement of the glacier above it for 5300 years, until a storm from the Sahara laid a layer of dust on the ice that absorbed sunlight and finally thawed it out.

(Above right) The body of the Iceman after preservation.

(Right) The Iceman, the oldest fully preserved human, as found in 1991, emerging from the melting ice that had preserved him for more than 5000 years.

Calf leather belt and pouch, with three flint tools, a bone awl, and organic material (for tinder)

Dagger: flint blade with ashwood haft in woven grass sheath

Leather loincloth

Leather leggings

Coat of tanned domestic goat hide

Copper axe with yew haft and leather binding

Shoes: bearskin soles with deerskin uppers; filled with grass

Yew longbow (unfinished)

Hazel and larchwood frame for a fur backpack

Bearskin cap

Deerskin quiver with fourteen arrows (only two finished) of viburnum and dogwood, an antler point and two fragments, coiled string, and two bundles of animal sinews

Cape of woven grass or reeds

Sewn birch-bark containers (one with evidence of fire)

He was a dark-skinned male, aged in his mid- to late forties. Only about 1.56–1.6 m (5 ft. 2 in.) tall, his size and stature fit well within the measurement ranges of late Neolithic populations in Italy and Switzerland. Preliminary analysis of his DNA confirms his links to northern Europe.

The corpse currently weighs only about 54 kg (120 lb). His teeth are very worn, especially the front incisors, suggesting that he ate coarse ground grain, or that he regularly used them as a tool. When found he was bald, but hundreds of curly brownish-black human hairs, about 9 cm (3.5 in.) long, were recovered from the vicinity of the body. These had fallen out after death, and it is possible he had a beard.

A body scan has shown that the brain, muscle tissues, lungs, heart, liver, and digestive organs are in excellent condition, though the lungs are blackened by smoke, probably from open fires, and he has hardening of the arteries and blood vessels. Traces

of meat have been found in his colon (probably ibex and venison), along with wheat, plants, and plums.

Traces of chronic frostbite were noted in one little toe, and eight of his ribs were fractured, though these had healed or were healing when he died.

Groups of tattoos, mostly short parallel vertical blue lines, were discovered on both sides of his lower spine, on his left calf and right ankle, his wrists, and he had a blue cross on his inner right knee. These marks, probably made with soot, may be therapeutic, aimed at relieving the arthritis that he had in his neck, lower back, and right hip.

His nails had dropped off, but one fingernail was recovered. Its analysis revealed not only that he undertook manual labor, but also that he experienced periods of reduced nail growth corresponding to episodes of serious illness—four, three, and two months before he died. The fact that he was prone to periodic crippling disease

The equipment and clothing of the Iceman are a virtual time-capsule of everyday life—more than seventy objects were found associated with him.

supported the view that he fell prey to adverse weather and froze to death. Recent work, however, has revealed what appears to be an arrowhead lodged in the Iceman's left shoulder, cuts on his hands, wrists, and ribcage, and a blow to the head—either from being struck or from falling—which is probably what killed him.

The items found with him constitute a unique time-capsule of everyday life. A great variety of woods and a range of sophisticated techniques of working with leather and grasses were used to create the collection of seventy objects, which add a new dimension to our knowledge of the period.

Cold Preservation 2: Mountain "Mummies"

Since the 1950s, sporadic discoveries have been made of frozen bodies high in the Andes mountains of South America—these finds have become

The older, better-preserved Llullaillaco girl had neatly braided hair and wore a selection of ornaments.

known as mummies, even though they were preserved only by the cold, not by any process of artificial mummification. The Incas of the fifteenth to sixteenth centuries CE built more than 100 ceremonial centers on many of the highest peaks in their empire, since they worshiped the snowcapped mountains, believing that they provided the water for irrigating fields, and hence controlled the fertility of crops and animals.

Among the offerings left for the mountain gods were food, alcoholic drinks, textiles, pottery, and figurines—but also human sacrifices, often young children. In the 1990s, American archaeologist Johan Reinhard carried

out a series of expeditions to high peaks in the Andes, and discovered some of the best-preserved ancient bodies ever found, thanks to this "extreme archaeology."

On the Ampato volcano, at 6312 m (20,708 ft.), he found a bundle lying on the ice that contained an Inca girl—dubbed the "Ice Maiden" or "Juanita"—who had been ritually sacrificed (by a blow to the head) at the age of about fourteen, and buried with figurines, food, textiles, and pottery. The buried bodies of a boy and girl were later excavated at 5850 m (19,193 ft.).

In 1999, on the peak of Llullaillaco—at 6739 m (22,109 ft.)—he encountered a seven-year-old boy, and two girls of fifteen and six, all with figurines and textiles. So perfect is the preservation of all these bodies that detailed analyses can be carried out on their internal organs, their DNA, and their hair. For example, isotopes in the hair suggest that they chewed coca leaves, a common practice in the region even today.

WATERLOGGED ENVIRONMENTS. A useful distinction in land archaeology (as opposed to archaeology beneath the sea) can be drawn between dryland and wetland sites. The great majority of sites are "dry" in the sense that moisture content is low and preservation of organic remains is poor. Wetland sites include all those found in lakes, swamps, marshes, fens, and peat bogs. In these situations organic materials are effectively sealed in a wet and airless environment that favors their preservation, as long as the waterlogging is more or less permanent up to the time of excavation. (If a wet site dries out, even only seasonally, decomposition of the organic materials can occur.)

It has been estimated that on a wet site often 75–90 percent, sometimes 100 percent, of the finds are organic. Little or none of this material, such as wood, leather, textiles, basketry, and plant remains of all kinds, would survive on most dryland sites. It is for this reason that archaeologists are turning their attention more and more to the rich sources of evidence about past human activities to be found on wet sites. Growing threats from drainage and peatcutting in the wetlands, which form only about 6 percent of the world's total land area, give this work an added urgency.

Wetlands vary a great deal in their preservative qualities. Acidic peat bogs preserve wood and plant remains, but may destroy bone, iron, and even pottery. The lake sites of the Alpine regions of Switzerland, Italy, France, and southern Germany, on the other hand, preserve most materials well. Sometimes other forces can help to preserve waterlogged remains, such as the mudslide that buried the Ozette site in Washington State (see box overleaf).

An important recent example of wet preservation is the Must Farm settlement in Cambridgeshire, in the east of England, where some of the best-preserved Bronze Age dwellings in the world have been excavated. The remains include two circular wooden houses dating from 1000–800 BCE, which appear to have been damaged by fire before then sliding into the river, where the fire was extinguished. The buildings and objects within them were then buried and preserved in silt. Many remarkable objects have now been recovered from the site, including pots still containing food, textiles woven from lime tree bark and other plant fibers, and sections of wattle walls. In 2016, a large wooden wheel about 1 m (3 ft.) in diameter was found, the most complete and earliest of its type in Britain. Through its waterlogged preservation, Must Farm offers a rare insight into the everyday life of a Bronze Age village.

Peat bogs, nearly all of which occur in northern latitudes, are some of the most important environments for wetland archaeology. The Somerset Levels in southern England, for example, have been the scene not only of excavations in the early twentieth century to recover the well-preserved Iron Age lake villages of Glastonbury and Meare, but also of a much wider campaign in the last few decades that has unearthed numerous wooden trackways (including

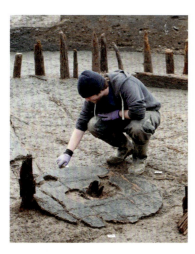

Excavations at Must Farm in Cambridgeshire, in the east of England, uncovered extensive Bronze Age remains including structures and many objects, among them a well-preserved wheel.

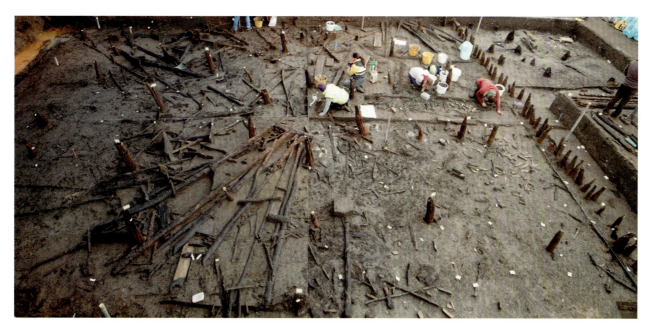

Wet Preservation: The Ozette Site

A special kind of waterlogging occurred at the Ozette site, Washington, on the US Northwest Coast. In about 1700 CE, a huge mudslide buried part of a Makah Indian whale-hunting village. Ruins of huge cedar-plank houses lay protected by the mud for three centuries—but not forgotten, for the descendants kept the memory of their ancestors' home alive. Then the sea began to strip away the mud, and it seemed that the site might fall prey to looters. The Makah tribal chairman asked Washington State University archaeologist Richard Daugherty to excavate the site and salvage its remains. Clearing the mud with water pumped from the ocean and sprayed through hoses revealed a wealth of wood and fiber objects.

The houses, where several related families would have lived, were up to 21 m (68 ft. 3 in.) in length and 14 m (45 ft. 6 in.) wide. They had adzed and carved panels (with designs including wolves and thunderbirds), roof-support posts, and low partition walls. There were also hearths, sleeping platforms, storage boxes, mats, and baskets.

More than 55,000 artifacts—mostly wooden—were recovered. They had been preserved by the wet mud, which excluded oxygen. The most spectacular was a block of red cedar, a meter high, carved in the form of a whale's dorsal fin. Even leaves—still green—survived, together with many whale bones.

Field excavation and laboratory preservation continued non-stop for eleven years, an outstanding example

Cleaning a basket holding a comb and a spindle whorl.

of cooperation between archaeologists and indigenous people. Makah elders helped to identify artifacts; young Makah helped to excavate; and a museum now displays the results.

(Below left) A Makah Indian crew member measures a find in one of the Ozette houses.

(Below right) A red cedar carving in the shape of a whale's dorsal fin, inlaid with 700 sea-otter teeth (some forming the shape of a thunderbird holding a serpent, which would stun the whale so that the thunderbird could pick it up in its claws).

The surviving parts of Oldcroghan Man's body are superbly preserved, particularly his hands: the well-kept fingernails and absence of calluses suggest that he may have been an individual of relatively high status. Analysis of his stomach contents revealed a final meal of cereals and buttermilk.

the world's "oldest road," a 6000-year-old 1.6-km (1-mile) stretch of track), and many details about early woodworking skills, and the ancient environment. On the continent of Europe, and in Ireland, peat bogs have likewise preserved many trackways—sometimes with evidence for the wooden carts that ran along them—and other fragile remains. Other types of European wetlands, such as coastal marshes, have yielded dugout logboats, paddles, even fish-nets and fish-weirs.

Bog bodies, however, are undoubtedly the best-known finds from the peat bogs of northwestern Europe. Most of them date from the Iron Age. The degree of preservation varies widely, and depends on the particular conditions in which the corpses were deposited. Most individuals met a violent death and were probably either executed as criminals or killed as a sacrifice before being thrown into the bog. For example, in 2003 the huge (1.91 m (6 ft. 3½ in.) tall) Oldcroghan Man was recovered from a peat bog in Ireland: he had been stabbed, decapitated, and tied down to the bottom of a bog pool.

The best-preserved specimens, such as Denmark's Tollund Man, were in a truly remarkable state, with only the staining caused by bog water and tannic acid as an indication that they were ancient rather than modern. Within the skin, the bones have often disappeared, as have most of the internal organs, although the stomach and its contents may survive. In Florida, prehistoric human brains have even been recovered.

Occasionally, waterlogged conditions can occur inside burial mounds. The oak-coffin burials of Bronze Age northern Europe, and most notably those of Denmark dating to about 1000 BCE, had an inner core of stones packed round the tree-trunk coffin, with a round barrow built above. Water infiltrated the inside of the mound, and, by combining with tannin from the tree trunks, created acidic conditions that destroyed the skeleton but preserved the skin (discolored like the bog bodies), hair, and ligaments of the bodies inside the coffins, as well as their clothing and such objects as birch-bark pails.

A somewhat similar phenomenon occurred with the ships that the Vikings used as coffins. The Oseberg ship in Norway, for example, held the body of a Viking queen of about 800 CE, and was buried in clay, covered by a packing of stones and a layer of peat that sealed it in and ensured its preservation.

Lake-dwellings have rivaled bog bodies in popular interest ever since the discovery of wooden piles or house supports in Swiss lakes more than a century ago. The range of preserved material is astonishing, not simply wooden structures, artifacts, and textiles but, at Neolithic Charavines in France for example, even nuts, berries, and other fruits.

Perhaps the greatest contribution to archaeology that lake-dwellings and other European wetland sites have made in recent years, however, is to provide abundant well-preserved timber for the study of tree-rings, the annual growth rings in trees, for dating purposes. In Chapter 4 we explore the breakthrough this has brought about in the establishment of an accurate tree-ring chronology for parts of northern Europe stretching back thousands of years.

Another rich source of waterlogged and preserved timbers can be found in the old waterfronts of towns and cities. Archaeologists have been particularly successful in uncovering parts of London's Roman and medieval waterfront, but such discoveries are not restricted to Europe. In the early 1980s archaeologists in New York excavated a well-preserved eighteenth-century ship that had been sunk to support the East River waterfront. Underwater archaeology itself is, not surprisingly, the richest source of all for waterlogged finds (see pp. 100–102).

The major problem with waterlogged finds, and particularly wood, is that they deteriorate rapidly when they are uncovered, beginning to dry and crack almost at once. They therefore need to be kept wet until they can be treated or freeze-dried at a laboratory. Conservation measures of this kind help to explain the enormous cost of both wetland and underwater archaeology. It has been estimated that "wet archaeology" costs four times as much as "dry archaeology." But the rewards, as we have seen above, are enormous.

The rewards in the future, too, will be very great. Florida, for example, has about 1.2 million ha (3 million acres) of peat deposits, and on present evidence these probably contain more organic artifacts than anywhere else in the world. So far the wetlands here have yielded the largest number of prehistoric watercraft from any one region, together with totems, masks, and figurines dating as far back as 5000 BCE. In the Okeechobee Basin, for instance, a first-millennium BCE burial platform has been found, decorated with a series of large carved wooden totem posts, representing an array of animals and birds. After a fire, the platform had collapsed into its pond. Yet it is only recently that wet finds in Florida have come to us from careful excavation rather than through the drainage that is destroying large areas of peat deposits and, with them, untold quantities of the richest kinds of archaeological evidence.

Study Questions

1 What is the difference between an artifact and an ecofact?
2 Why is it important for archaeologists to distinguish between cultural and natural formation processes?
3 Why is the context of an artifact so very important to archaeologists?
4 Why do inorganic materials survive better than organic materials?
5 Why are archaeologists particularly interested in wet or waterlogged sites?
6 What is experimental archaeology?

Summary

THE ARCHAEOLOGICAL EVIDENCE available to us depends on a number of important factors:

WHAT PEOPLE, PAST AND PRESENT, have done to it (cultural formation processes).

WHAT NATURAL CONDITIONS, such as soil and climate, have preserved or destroyed (natural formation processes). Inorganic materials usually survive far better than organics, but the latter can be well preserved in a range of special environments— the dry, the cold, and the waterlogged.

OUR ABILITY to find, recognize, recover, and conserve it.

WE CAN DO NOTHING about the first two factors, being at the mercy of the elements and previous human behavior. But the third factor, which is the subject of this book, is constantly improving, as we understand better the processes of decay and destruction, and design research strategies and technical aids to make the most of what archaeological evidence actually survives.

Further Reading

Good introductions to the problems of differential preservation of archaeological materials can be found in:

Aldhouse-Green, M. 2015. *Bog Bodies Uncovered: Solving Europe's Ancient Mystery*. Thames & Hudson: London & New York.

Binford, L. R. 2002. *In Pursuit of the Past: Decoding the Archaeological Record*. University of California Press: Berkeley & London.

Lillie, M. C. & Ellis, S. (eds). 2007. *Wetland Archaeology and Environments: Regional Issues, Global Perspectives*. Oxbow Books: Oxford.

Menotti, F. & O'Sullivan, M. 2012. *Oxford Handbook of Wetland Archaeology*. Oxford University Press: Oxford.

Schiffer, M. B. 2002. *Formation Processes of the Archaeological Record*. University of Utah Press: Salt Lake City.

Sheets, P. D. 2006. *The Ceren Site: An Ancient Village Buried by Volcanic Ash in Central America* (2nd ed.). Wadsworth: Stamford, CT.

[See p. 345 for a list of useful websites]

3

Where?
Survey and Excavation of Sites and Features

Traditionally, archaeologists are known for finding and excavating sites, but today, while sites and their excavation do remain of paramount importance, the focus has broadened. Archaeologists have become aware that there is a great range of **off-site** or **non-site evidence**, from scatters of artifacts to such features as plowmarks and field boundaries, that provides important information about the past. The study of entire landscapes by regional survey, for example, is now a major part of archaeological fieldwork.

It should also not be forgotten that suitable evidence for study often comes from new work at sites already the subject of fieldwork. Much potentially rich and rewarding material also lies locked away in museum and institution vaults, waiting to be analyzed by imaginative modern techniques. It is only recently, for example, that the plant remains discovered in Tutankhamun's tomb in the 1920s have received thorough analysis. Yet it remains true that the great majority of archaeological research is still dependent on the collection of new material by fresh fieldwork. The main way that archaeologists find this new material—in other words new sites and features—is by survey, either on the ground or from the air.

In the early days of archaeology the next step would have been to excavate. But when archaeologists excavate a site, digging through the layers of evidence, uncovering features and removing artifacts that may have been lying undisturbed for thousands of years, it is important to remember that this is essentially a destructive act—there is just one chance to record exactly what is found and the "experiment" can never be repeated. Excavation is also very expensive, but after the digging the excavators must be prepared to put considerable time, effort, and money into the conservation and storage of their finds, and into the interpretation and publication of their results. Non-destructive means of assessing the layout of sites and features, using, for example, site **surface survey** or **remote sensing** devices, have therefore taken on a new importance, often providing enough information for archaeologists to interpret features at a site, and making large-scale excavation unnecessary.

The Great Wall of China, more than 2000 km (1250 miles) long, was begun in the third century BCE. Like the pyramids of Egypt, it has never been lost to posterity.

Although excavation does remain a very important aspect of archaeology, archaeologists are becoming increasingly aware that it should not be undertaken lightly, and that it is only absolutely vital where sites would otherwise be destroyed by modern development or natural erosion.

Before any archaeological fieldwork begins, archaeologists try to make explicit what their objectives are and what their plan of campaign will be. This procedure is commonly called devising a **research design**, which broadly has four stages (listed in the box at left). There is seldom if ever a straightforward progression through these stages. In real life the research strategy will constantly be refined as evidence is collected and analyzed. All too often, and inexcusably, publication may be neglected. But in the best-planned research the overall objective—the broad question or questions to be answered—will stand, even if the strategy for achieving it alters.

In this chapter we are focusing on stage 2 of the research process—on the methods and techniques archaeologists use to obtain evidence against which to test their ideas. We will distinguish between methods used in the discovery of archaeological sites and non-site features or artifact scatters, which include a variety of ground-based and aerial survey techniques, and those employed once those sites and features have been identified, which include detailed survey and selective excavation at individual sites.

Locating Archaeological Sites and Features

One major task of the archaeologist is to locate and record the whereabouts of sites and features. In this section we will be reviewing some of the principal techniques used to locate sites. But we should not forget that many monuments have never been lost: the massive pyramids of Egypt have always been known to succeeding generations, as has the Great Wall of China. Their exact function or purpose may indeed have aroused controversy down the centuries, but their presence, the fact of their existence, was never in doubt.

And not all those sites that were once lost were discovered by archaeologists. No one has ever made a precise count, but a significant number of sites known today were found by accident, from the decorated French cave of Lascaux, and more recently Cosquer, the underwater entrance to which was discovered by a deep-sea diver in 1985, to the amazing terracotta army of China's first emperor, unearthed in 1974 by farmers digging for a well, as well as the countless underwater wrecks first spotted by fishermen, sponge-gatherers, and sport-divers. Construction workers building new roads, subways, dams, and office blocks have made their fair share of discoveries too.

Nevertheless, it is archaeologists who have systematically attempted to record these sites, and it is archaeologists who seek out the full range of sites and features, large or small, that make up the great diversity of past landscapes. How do they achieve this?

A practical distinction can be drawn between site identification conducted at ground level (**ground survey**) and identification from the air or from space (**aerial survey**), although any one field project will usually employ both types of survey.

Ground Survey

Methods for identifying individual sites include the consultation of documentary sources and place-name evidence, but primarily actual fieldwork, whether the monitoring of building developers' progress in "applied archaeology" (see pp. 324–27), or survey in circumstances where the archaeologist is more of a free agent.

DOCUMENTARY SOURCES. In the nineteenth century, Homer's account of the Trojan Wars in his narrative poem the *Iliad* fired the imagination of German banker Heinrich Schliemann, sending him on a quest for the city of Troy; with remarkable luck and good judgment he successfully identified it in western Turkey. A more recent success story of the same kind was the location and excavation by Helge and Anne Stine Ingstad of the Viking settlement of L'Anse aux Meadows in Newfoundland, thanks in large part to clues contained in the medieval Viking sagas. Much of modern biblical archaeology concerns itself with the search in the Near East for evidence of the places—as well as the people and events—described in the Old and New Testaments. Treated objectively as one possible source of information about Near Eastern sites, the Bible can be a rich source of documentary material, but there is certainly the danger that belief in the absolute religious truth of the texts can cloud an impartial assessment of their archaeological validity.

Much research in biblical archaeology involves attempting to link named biblical sites with archaeologically known ones. Place-name evidence, however, can also lead to actual discoveries of new archaeological sites. In southwestern Europe, for example, many prehistoric stone tombs have been found thanks to old names printed on maps that incorporate local words for "stone" or "tomb."

The low mounds at L'Anse aux Meadows turned out to be the remains of huts with walls of piled turf and roofs of turf supported by a wood frame—those seen here have been reconstructed for visitors. Lack of evidence for rebuilding indicates that this was a short-lived settlement.

CULTURAL RESOURCE MANAGEMENT AND APPLIED ARCHAEOLOGY. In this specialized work—discussed more fully in Chapter 12—the archaeologist's role is to locate and record sites, in some cases before they are destroyed by new roads, buildings, or dams, or by peatcutting and drainage in wetlands.

In the USA a large number of sites are located and recorded in inventories every year under Cultural Resource Management (CRM) laws, which were considerably broadened and strengthened in the 1970s. Proper liaison with a developer should allow archaeological survey to take place in advance along the projected line of road or in the path of development. Important sites thus discovered may require excavation, and in some cases can even cause construction plans to be altered. Certain archaeological remains unearthed during the digging of subways in Rome and Mexico City, for instance, were incorporated into the final station architecture.

SURVEY. How does the archaeologist set about locating sites, other than through documentary sources and salvage work? A conventional and still valid method is to look for the most prominent remains in a landscape, particularly surviving remnants of walled buildings, and burial mounds, such as those in eastern North America or Wessex in southern Britain. But many sites are visible on the surface only as a scatter of artifacts and thus require more thorough survey—what we may call survey—to be detected.

Furthermore, in recent years, as archaeologists have become more interested in reconstructing the full human use of the landscape, they have begun to realize that there are very faint scatters of artifacts that might not qualify as sites, but that nevertheless represent significant human activity. Some scholars have suggested that these off-site or non-site areas (that is, areas with a low density of artifacts) should be located and recorded, which can only be done by **systematic survey** work involving careful sampling procedures (see p. 69). This approach is particularly useful in areas where people leading a mobile way of life have left only a sparse archaeological record, as in much of Africa.

Survey has become important for another major reason: the growth of regional studies. Thanks to the pioneering researches of such scholars as Gordon Willey in the Virú Valley, Peru, and William T. Sanders in the Basin of Mexico, archaeologists increasingly seek to study settlement patterns—the distribution of sites across the landscape within a given region. The significance of such work for the understanding of past societies is discussed further in Chapter 5. Here we may note its impact on archaeological fieldwork: it is rarely enough now simply to locate an individual site and then to survey it and/or excavate it in isolation from other sites. Whole regions need to be explored, involving a program of surveys.

In the last few decades, survey has developed from being simply a preliminary stage in fieldwork (looking for appropriate sites to excavate) to a more or less independent kind of inquiry, an area of research in its own right that can produce information quite different from that achieved by digging. In some cases excavation may not take place at all, perhaps because permission to dig was not forthcoming, or because of a lack of time or funds—modern excavation is slow and costly, whereas survey is cheap, quick, relatively non-destructive, and requires only maps, compasses, and tapes. Usually, however, archaeologists deliberately choose a surface approach as a source of regional data in order to investigate specific questions that interest them and that excavation could not answer.

Survey encompasses a broad range of techniques: no longer just the identification of sites and the recording or collection of surface artifacts, but sometimes also the sampling of natural and mineral resources, such as stone and clay. Much survey today is aimed at studying the spatial distribution of human activities, variations between regions, changes in population through time, and relationships between people, land, and resources.

SURVEY IN PRACTICE.   For questions formulated in regional terms, it is necessary to collect data on a regional scale, but in a way that provides a maximum of information for a minimum of cost and effort. First, the region to be surveyed needs to be defined: its boundaries may be either natural (such as a valley or island), cultural (such as the extent of an artifact style), or purely arbitrary, though natural boundaries are the easiest to establish.

The area's history of development needs to be examined, not only to familiarize oneself with previous archaeological work and with the local materials but also to assess the extent to which surface material may have been covered or removed by natural processes. There is little point, for example, in searching for prehistoric material in sediments only recently laid down by river action. Other factors may have affected surface evidence as well. In much of Africa, for example, great animal herds or burrowing animals will often have disturbed surface material, so that the archaeologist may be able to examine only very broad distribution patterns. Geologists and environmental specialists can generally provide useful advice.

This background information will help determine the intensity of the surface coverage of the survey. Other factors to take into consideration are the time and resources available, and how easy it is actually to reach and record an area. Arid (dry) and semi-arid environments with little vegetation are among the best for this type of work, whereas in equatorial rainforest, survey may be limited to soil exposures along river banks, unless time and labor permit the cutting of trails. Many regions, of course, contain a variety of landscapes, and more than one strategy for survey is often needed. Moreover, it must be remembered that some archaeological phases (with easily distinguishable artifacts or pottery styles, for example) are more visible than others, and that mobile **hunter-gatherer** or pastoral communities leave a very different—and generally sparser—imprint on the landscape than do agricultural or urban communities. All these factors must be taken into account when planning search patterns and recovery techniques.

There are two basic kinds of survey: the unsystematic and the systematic. The former is the simpler, involving walking across each part of the area (for example, each plowed field), scanning a strip of ground, collecting or examining artifacts on the surface, and recording their location together with that of any surface features. It is generally felt, however, that the results may be biased: walkers have an inherent desire to find material, and will therefore tend to concentrate on those areas that seem richer, rather than obtaining a sample representative of the whole area that would enable the archaeologist to assess the varying distribution of material of different periods or **types**. On the other hand, the method is flexible, enabling the team to focus greater efforts on the areas that have proved most likely to contain sites or finds.

Much modern survey is done in a systematic way, employing either a grid system or a series of equally spaced transects (straight paths) across the area. The area to be searched is divided into sectors, and these are walked systematically. Because of the constraints of time and money, it is often not possible to survey the entirety of an area in this way, so archaeologists have to employ a sampling strategy (see box opposite) where only certain sectors or transects are picked to be searched. Systematic survey also makes it easier to plot the location of finds since an exact position is always known.

For example, from 1992 to 1998 the Sydney Cyprus Survey Project, led by Bernard Knapp and Michael Given of the University of Glasgow in Scotland, undertook an intensive archaeological survey in a 75-sq. km (29-sq. mile) area in the northern Troodos Mountains of Cyprus. This is an area famed for its copper sulphide ore deposits, exploited as early as the Bronze Age. The project examined the human transformation of the landscape over a period of 5000 years and placed it in its regional context. A first requirement for the systematic intensive survey strategy was good maps. Enlarged aerial photographs were used to create a base map of the entire survey region. The main survey approach was a transect survey with the aim of obtaining a broad systematic sample of the area; areas with extensive evidence of early industrial, agricultural, or settlement activities, and locales with high densities of artifacts, were investigated more closely. It took the team around 6 years to survey just 10 percent of the area. The survey identified 11 Special Interest Areas and 142 Places of Special Interest for investigation. The count in the field totalled 87,600 sherds of pottery, 8111 tile fragments, and 3092 lithics. About one third of these were collected and analyzed and entered into the project's database.

Results tend to be more reliable from long-term projects that cover a region repeatedly, since the visibility of sites and artifacts can vary widely from year

Key Concepts
Locating Sites Using Ground Survey

Documentary Sources: mainly of use in locating Classical, biblical, and relatively recent sites

Cultural Resource Management: sites in areas that may be under threat from development are located, recorded, and sometimes excavated prior to their destruction

Survey: surveys can be either **unsystematic** (where archaeologists randomly search an area on foot for artifacts or evidence of features) or, more commonly, **systematic** (where archaeologists walk an area using carefully laid out grid systems or transects). A **sampling strategy**, where only a representative part of an area is actually searched, is often used to save time and money. Small-scale excavations can be undertaken to check survey results

Sampling Strategies

Archaeologists cannot usually afford the time and money necessary to investigate the whole of a large site or all sites in a given region, so they need to sample the area being researched. In a ground survey this will involve using one of the methods described below to choose a number of smaller areas to be searched, with the objective being to draw reliable conclusions about the whole area.

The way archaeologists use sampling is similar to the way it is employed in public opinion polls, which make generalizations about the opinions of millions of people using samples of just a few thousand. Surprisingly often the polls are more or less right. This is because the structure of sampled populations is well known—for example, we know their ages and occupations. We have much less background information to work with in archaeology, so must be more careful when we extrapolate generalizations from a sample. But as with opinion polls, in archaeological work the larger and better designed the sample, the more likely the results are to be valid.

Some sites in a given region, however, may be more accessible than others, or more prominent in the landscape, which may prompt a more informal sampling strategy. Long years of experience in the field will also give some archaeologists an intuitive "feel" for the right places to undertake work.

Types of Sampling

The simplest form is a simple random sample, where the areas to be sampled are chosen using a table of random numbers. The nature of random numbers, however, results in some areas being allotted clusters of squares, while others remain untouched—the sample is, therefore, inherently biased.

One answer is the stratified random sample, where the region or site is divided into its natural zones (strata, hence the technique's name), such as cultivated land and forest, and squares are then chosen by the same random-number procedure, except that each zone has the number of squares proportional to its area. Thus, if forest comprises 85 percent of the area, it must be allotted 85 percent of the squares.

Another solution, systematic sampling, entails the selection of a grid of equally spaced locations—e.g. choosing every other square. By adopting such a regular spacing one runs the risk of missing (or hitting) every single example in an equally regular pattern of distribution—this is another source of potential bias.

A more satisfactory method is to use a stratified unaligned systematic sample, which combines the main elements from the other techniques. In collecting artifacts from the surface of a large tell or mound site at Girik-i-Haciyan in Turkey, Charles Redman and Patty Jo Watson used a grid of 5-m squares, but orientated the grid along the site's main N-S/E-W axes. The squares were selected with reference to these axes. The strata chosen were blocks of nine squares (3 x 3), and one square in each block was picked for excavation by selecting its N-S/E-W coordinates randomly.

Transects vs Squares

In large-scale surveys, transects (straight paths) are sometimes preferable to squares, particularly in areas of dense vegetation, such as tropical rainforest. It is far easier to walk along a path than to locate accurately and investigate a square. In addition, transects can easily be segmented into units, whereas it may be difficult to locate or describe a specific part of a square; transects are equally useful not merely for finding sites but also for recording artifact densities across the landscape. On the other hand, squares have the advantage of exposing more area to the survey, thus increasing the probability of intersecting sites. A combination of the two methods is often best: using transects to cover long distances, but squares when larger concentrations of material are encountered.

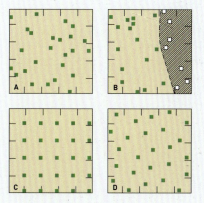

Types of sampling: (A) simple random; (B) stratified random; (C) systematic; (D) stratified unaligned systematic.

Systematic surface survey in the Egyptian desert: using GPS, archaeologists sample small areas spaced 100 m (330 ft.) apart, looking for Middle Paleolithic stone tools (top). Finds are then processed in the field using electronic calipers and handheld computers (above).

to year or even with the seasons, thanks to vegetation and changing land-use. In addition, members of field crews inevitably differ in the accuracy of their observations, and in their ability to recognize and describe sites (the more carefully we look, and the more experience we have, the more we see); this factor can never be totally eliminated, but repeated coverage can help to counter its effects. The use of standardized recording forms makes it easy to put the data into a computer at a later stage; alternatively, handheld computers can be used in the field.

Finally, it may be necessary or desirable to carry out small excavations to supplement or check the surface data (particularly for questions of chronology, contemporaneity, or site function), or to test hypotheses that have arisen from the survey. The two types of investigation are complementary, not mutually exclusive. Their major difference can be summarized as follows: excavation tells us a lot about a little of a site, and can only be done once, whereas survey tells us a little about a lot of sites, and can be repeated.

EXTENSIVE AND INTENSIVE SURVEY. Surveys can be made more extensive by combining results from a series of individual projects in neighboring regions to produce very large-scale views of change in landscape, land-use, and settlement through time—though, as with individual members of a field crew, the accuracy and quality of different survey projects may vary widely. Alternatively survey can be made more intensive by aiming at total coverage of a single large site or site-cluster. It is a paradox that some of the world's greatest and most famous archaeological sites have never, or only recently, been studied in this way, since attention has traditionally focused on the grander monuments rather than on any attempt to place them within even a local context. At Teotihuacan, near Mexico City, a major mapping project initiated in the 1960s has added hugely to our knowledge of the area around the great pyramid-temples (see pp. 82–84).

Ground survey has a vital place in archaeological work, and one that continues to grow in importance. In modern projects, however, it is usually supplemented (and often preceded) by survey from the air, one of the most important advances made by archaeology in the twentieth century. In fact, the availability of air photographs can be an important factor in selecting and delineating an area for ground survey.

Aerial Survey

Archaeological survey using airborne or spaceborne remote sensing can be divided into two component parts: data collection, which comprises taking photographs or images from aircraft or satellites; and data analysis, in which such images are analyzed, interpreted, and (often) integrated with other evidence from field survey, ground-based remote sensing, or documentary evidence. From the viewpoint of the photo interpreter or image analyst there is little difference between satellite images, multispectral/hyperspectral data, and traditional air photographs other than that of scale and resolution. The source itself is irrelevant and these data will collectively be referred to as "aerial images."

Millions of aerial images have already been taken: some of these are available for consultation in specialist libraries, and a lesser quantity is freely available online. Most result from "area survey" in which aerial images are taken in overlapping series to cover predefined areas, and a small number are taken each year by archaeologists who undertake prospective surveys using a light aircraft. It must be stressed that aerial images, even those resulting from prospective survey, are used for a wide range of archaeological purposes, from the discovery and recording of sites, to monitoring changes in them through time, photographing buildings, urban (and other) development—and, in fact, recording almost anything that "may not be there tomorrow." Nevertheless, the taking and analysis of aerial images from aircraft or satellite have led to a large number of archaeological discoveries, and the tally grows every year.

HOW ARE AERIAL IMAGES USED? Images taken from the air are merely tools; they are means to an end. Images do not themselves reveal sites—it is the image taker and the interpreter who do so, by examination of the terrain and the pictures. These are specialized skills. Long experience and a keen eye are needed to differentiate archaeological traces from other features, such as vehicle tracks, old river beds, and canals. Indeed, most military intelligence units during the final years of World War II had archaeologists on their staff as interpreters of air photographs.

Aerial images are of two types: oblique and vertical. Each has its advantages and drawbacks, but oblique images have usually been taken of sites observed from the air by an archaeologist and thought to be of archaeological significance, whereas most vertical images result from non-archaeological surveys (for instance, cartographic). Both types can be used to provide overlapping stereoscopic pairs of prints that enable a scene to be examined in three dimensions and so add confidence to any interpretation. Stereoscopic pictures taken of the ancient city of Mohenjodaro in Pakistan

Aerial photographs are of two types: oblique and vertical. Obliques are easier to view and understand than verticals but may present more difficulty to the interpreter, who must transform the information to plan views. The photo (bottom) is an oblique aerial photograph of Newark earthworks, Ohio. An octagon and circle joined by a small strip of land are clearly visible, as are the small mounds just inside the octagon's corners.

from a tethered balloon, for example, have enabled photogrammetric—accurately contoured—plans to be made of its surviving structures. Similarly, large areas can be surveyed with overlapping images, which are then processed into a very accurate photogrammetric base map of all the archaeological evidence identified from the air. Analytical ground survey can then proceed on a much surer basis.

Oblique images are often targeted on archaeological features that may show clearly, while vertical images may need to be more thoroughly examined by an interpreter seeking such information. Both types of image can be rectified or georeferenced using computer programs. This removes the scale and perspective distortions of oblique images and can correct for tilt and distortion in vertical views. After computer transformation the resulting image may be layered in graphics software or a **GIS** (**Geographic Information System**—see pp. 79–82) and interpreted by overdrawing the archaeological features that have been identified.

The clearest way to indicate what a person has identified on aerial images is to produce a map that shows their interpretation. Such maps have many uses: to provide a guide for conservation and management; to show the relations between sites and their environment; to give context for field-walking; and to show accurate locations of archaeological features for ground surveys. For example, although it was known that prehistoric roadways existed within Chaco Canyon in the American Southwest, it was only when a major aerial survey project was undertaken by the National Park Service in the 1970s that the full extent of the road system was appreciated. Using the extensive coverage provided by the aerial images, a whole network of prehistoric roadways was identified and mapped. This was followed by selective ground surveys and some archaeological investigation. From the aerial coverage it has been estimated that the network, thought to date to the eleventh and twelfth centuries CE, extends to some 2400 km (1500 miles), though of this only 208 km (130 miles) have been verified by examination at ground level.

IDENTIFYING ARCHAEOLOGICAL SITES FROM ABOVE. Successful identification of archaeological sites on aerial images requires knowledge of the types of feature that might be expected and of the post-depositional (formation) processes that may have affected them since their abandonment. In general, for a site to be detected by any remote sensing method, it needs to have altered the soil or subsoil. These alterations can vary between holes cut into the ground (such as ditches and pits) and features placed upon it (such as banks, mounds, and walls), and these may now survive in relief—i.e. as lumps and bumps on the surface—or be completely buried under leveled cultivated land.

It is important to remember that similar holes and bumps may have been caused by natural disturbances or from recent human activity (leveling field

(Right) How crop-marks are formed: crops grow taller and more thickly over sunken features, such as ditches (1), and show stunted growth over buried walls (2). Such variations may not be obvious at ground level, but are often visible from the air, as different-colored bands of vegetation.

(Below) Features in relief on the left of this photograph show the remains of a Romano-British farm at Holbeach in the East Anglian fens of eastern England. Ditches were cut to form field and other property boundaries, flank tracks, and drain the land. These features continue into the field on the right, where they have been filled and are now under a level field growing cereal. The track that runs across the upper part of the left field can be seen to the right, marked by a darker band where crop growth has been boosted by the deeper soil that fills the former ditch. Silted channels of former watercourses show as broad light-toned bands where the crop is growing sparsely in poorer soil. These differences illustrate how changes in crop growth can mark subsurface features.

boundaries or digging small quarries, for example), and an experienced image analyst should be able to identify these, and distinguish them from archaeological features, in an area with which they are familiar.

Aerial images record relief sites through a combination of highlight and shadow, so the time of day and season of the year are important factors in creating the most informative image of such sites. It may be necessary to obtain images taken at different times to maximize the information visible through light and shade, although such new techniques as **LIDAR** (**Light Detection and Ranging**)—also known as **ALS** (**Airborne Laser Scanning**)— allow a viewer to move the position of the sun at will (see overleaf).

In some parts of the world, archaeological sites have been leveled and now lie in arable land. Although these sites have suffered a degree of destruction (and many continue to be destroyed by annual cultivation), these landscapes can be rewarding when examined on aerial images. In summer months, crops may grow differently above different soils and above different depths of soil and can thus indicate the presence of archaeological and natural features. These crop differences, sometimes called crop-marks, have been the main way in which aerial survey has recorded the presence of archaeological features; indeed, more features have been discovered via crop-marks than with any other form of prospection.

RECENT DEVELOPMENTS.   New technology is having an impact on aerial survey in different ways. Although the majority of existing images have been taken on film—black and white, color, or false color infrared—primarily digital sensors are now used in precision vertical cameras and the handheld cameras used by airborne archaeologists. Modern flying, be this to capture a series of parallel overlapping strips of vertical photographs or to examine a chosen area by an archaeologist, is usually planned and recorded to take advantage of GPS (Global Positioning System) navigation.

The application of digital image analysis is now a basic element in the survey archaeologist's toolkit. Just as in excavation and aerial survey, remote sensing research must be well planned and well executed, using a comprehensive methodology. Automated and semi-automated image analysis is commonplace in disciplines such as environmental remote sensing, where work is undertaken on extensive datasets. Field observations, archaeological interpretation, and human expertise, however, remain indispensable.

The use of drones (or Unmanned Aerial Vehicles—UAVs) has become increasingly popular. Small battery-powered drones carry a range of instruments and cameras and can take scores of pictures that produce an overlapping set, recording a site, excavation, or feature from all possible angles. Structure from Motion (SfM) software can combine these images to produce a 3D model that can be georeferenced and used for making accurate drawings.

LIDAR AND SLAR.   Use of LIDAR has proved extremely valuable in the past few years. This technique uses an aircraft (or drone), whose exact position is known through GPS, carrying a laser scanner that rapidly pulses a series of beams to the ground. By measuring the time taken for these to return to the aircraft an accurate picture of the ground in the form of a digital elevation model (or digital surface model) is created. Software used with LIDAR provides archaeologists with two great advantages over conventional aerial photography: tree canopies can be eliminated by switching off the "first return," so the sensor can see into woodland; and the angle and azimuth of the sun can be moved to enable ground features to be viewed under optimal

---

Key Concepts
Locating Sites Using Aerial Survey

Aerial Photography: aerial photographs can be either oblique (better for pictorial effect and perspective) or vertical (better for maps and plans). Features visible from the air are classed as either earthworks, soil-marks, or crop-marks

Drones: Unmanned Aerial Vehicles (UAVs) are now commonly used to produce overlapping sets of pictures and 3D models of sites

LIDAR: a new laser-scanning technique that can accurately map whole landscapes, even beneath tree cover. Resulting digital plans can be manipulated to reveal such subtle features as the remains of ancient field systems

Satellite Photography: useful primarily at the largest scales, for example mapping very large sites or tracing ancient irrigation systems

LIDAR in operation: the Iron Age hillfort of Welshbury in the Forest of Dean, England, is almost invisible in conventional aerial photographs (left). The initial LIDAR image shows little improvement (center) but once reflections from leaves and trees (the "first return") have been filtered out using a software algorithm the earthworks are clearly visible (right).

(and sometimes naturally impossible) lighting. Both facilities have been used to advantage in England where new sites—mostly enlargements to field systems—have been found, and locational corrections made to the existing record of the landscape around Stonehenge.

An excellent example of the practical application of LIDAR to an archaeological site comes from Caracol, a Maya city in Belize that flourished between 550 and 900 CE. Arlen and Diane Chase of the University of Nevada have been excavating at this site for more than twenty-five years, and during that time, despite the dense tropical forest, had managed to map 23 sq. km (9 sq. miles) of settlement. Survey from the air, however, enabled them within a few weeks to surpass the results of those twenty-five years, by covering a far larger area and discovering that the city actually extended over 177 sq. km (68 sq. miles). Images taken at the end of the dry season in 2009 took about four days (twenty-four hours of flight time) to capture, the small aircraft passing back and forth over the city, and making more than 4 billion measurements of the landscape below. This was then followed by three weeks of analysis by remote sensing experts.

Caracol's entire landscape can now be viewed in 3D, which has led to the discovery of new ruins, agricultural terraces, and stone causeways leading to more distant settlements (see illustration overleaf). This was the first application of LIDAR to such a large archaeological site, and it is clear that the technique will radically transform research on sites in challenging environments of this kind. However, just as only excavation can verify the findings of ground-based remote sensing, so the data produced from the air at Caracol will need to be confirmed on the ground.

Only a tiny proportion of the city of Caracol's total area has been cleared of jungle—the photo (top) shows Plaza A at the site, closely surrounded by thick vegetation. A 3D LIDAR projection of the site (above), however, reveals the features beneath the jungle canopy; agricultural terraces show up as ripples in valleys and hillsides.

Another remote sensing technique, Side-Looking Airborne Radar (SLAR), has yielded evidence suggesting that Maya agriculture was more intensive than previously imagined. The technique involves recording in radar images the return of pulses of electromagnetic radiation sent out from a flying aircraft. Since radar will penetrate cloud cover and to some extent dense rainforest, Richard Adams and his colleagues were able to use SLAR from a high-flying NASA aircraft to scan 80,000 sq. km (31,200 sq. miles) of the Maya lowlands. The SLAR images revealed not only ancient cities and field systems, but also an enormous lattice of gray lines, some of which may have been canals, to judge by subsequent inspections by canoe. If field testing reveals that the canals are ancient, it will show that the Maya had an elaborate irrigation and water transport system.

SATELLITE IMAGERY AND GOOGLE EARTH. It is now routine to access Google Earth and use the high-resolution air photos and satellite cover there, or to buy copies of them. The high-resolution images available from the IKONOS (about 1 m resolution), QuickBird (60 cm), and GeoEye (40 cm) satellites offer data comparable with aerial photographs, while Google Earth has basic world cover from NASA's LANDSAT series (28.5 m) but includes blocks of IKONOS, QuickBird, and GeoEye images, some other satellite imagery, and some conventional aerial photographs. The imagery can be imported into remote sensing image-processing software, as well as into GIS packages for analysis.

The introduction of Google Earth has been a true aerial revolution, since it offers every archaeologist the opportunity to examine the ground and look for archaeological sites—for example, it is being used by paleontologists in Africa to hunt for fossils, and in 2008 it revealed 500 new caves in South Africa, including the one that yielded the bones of **Australopithecus** *sediba* (see p. 135); and hundreds of new archaeological sites in Afghanistan are also being discovered by this method. But the same rules of visibility apply to those images as they do to conventional aerial photos, and absence of evidence on one particular date is not evidence of absence. Most users have never been trained to interpret such images and many expect sites to be visible at all times.

QuickBird and IKONOS/GeoEye images can be taken to order, although the minimum cost may be high for some archaeological projects. Libraries of older images are lower in price. In parts of the world where maps are still regarded as secret or do not exist, an up-to-date satellite image may be the only way to provide a base map for archaeological investigations.

Much use has been made of the Cold War CORONA satellite photographs (at best about 2 m resolution), and these too provide a useful base map and allow provisional interpretation of sites that can later be checked by

Two satellite images of the Urartian citadel of Erebuni, near Yerevan, Armenia, founded in 782 BCE: on the left, with resolution of about 2 m (10 ft.), is an image from the American CORONA series taken in 1971; on the right is a higher resolution screen shot from Google Earth of a QuickBird image taken in 2006. Both images are displayed with south to the top so that shadows assist photo-reading of topography and structures.

CORONA photograph (above, with false color added) of radial trackways around Tell Brak, northeastern Syria, dating from around 2600 to 2000 BCE. Thousands of miles of trackways in the region have been mapped by Jason Ur using a GIS database. The area shown at top is about 80 km (50 miles) wide. Tell Brak is at center right, north of the Khabur River.

fieldwork—for example, CORONA images have led to the detection and detailed mapping of numerous kinds of archaeological remains, such as ancient roads, ruins, irrigation networks, and so forth.

Jason Ur of Harvard University has used CORONA imagery to examine linear trackways ("hollow ways") across northern Mesopotamia (Syria, Turkey, and Iraq). These broad and shallow features were formed over time as people walked between settlements, and from settlements to fields and pasture. Because depressed features collect moisture and vegetation, they are easily visible on CORONA images. Some 6025 km (3750 miles) of premodern features have been identified, primarily dating to a phase of Bronze Age urban expansion from around 2600 to 2000 BCE. Most commonly, trackways radiated out 2–5 km (1–3 miles) from sites, in a spoke-like pattern. Although there were several major centers, all movement was done by moving from place to place; no direct tracks existed between the major centers. From that we can deduce that political centralization and authority was probably weak.

OTHER SATELLITE TECHNIQUES.   Another recent addition to the archaeologist's arsenal is SAR (Synthetic Aperture Radar), in which multiple radar images (usually taken from space, but also from aircraft) are processed to yield extremely detailed high-resolution results that can provide data for maps, databases, land-use studies, and so forth. SAR records height information and can provide terrain models of territory being surveyed. One of its many advantages is that, unlike conventional aerial photography, it provides results day or night and regardless of weather conditions. It can be used with multispectral data from satellites to make inventories of archaeological sites in a survey area—a rapid, non-destructive alternative to surface survey that does not involve the collection of artifacts and can thus save a great deal of time and effort in some circumstances.

A satellite image of the huge ancient site of Angkor in Cambodia.

The international Greater Angkor Project has found that the vast ruins of the 1000-year-old temple complex of Angkor in northern Cambodia may cover an area of up to 3000 sq. km (11,500 sq. miles). The ruins, shrouded in dense jungle and surrounded by landmines, have been the subject of studies using high-resolution SAR imagery obtained from NASA satellites. The resulting dark squares and rectangles on the images are stone moats and reflecting pools around the temples. The most important discovery for archaeologists so far has been the network of ancient canals surrounding the city (visible as light lines) that irrigated rice fields and fed the pools and moats. They were probably also used to transport the massive stones needed for constructing the complex.

ASTER (Advanced Spaceborne Thermal Emission and Reflection Radiometer) is an imaging instrument that flies on Terra, a satellite launched in 1999 as part of NASA's Earth Observing System (EOS), and is used to obtain detailed maps of land surface temperature, reflectance, and elevation.

Satellite remote sensing projects carried out by those with backgrounds in both remote sensing and archaeology have much to offer, but satellite archaeology should not be regarded as a substitute for archaeological excavation or survey work. It is just one among a number of tools that archaeologists may want to employ in their research. Besides revealing the presence of (sub)surface archaeological features (even in areas previously surveyed), satellite remote sensing can place archaeological sites in a much larger context, showing past social landscapes in all their complexity and helping greatly with quality assessment. Analysis of satellite imagery may further aid in determining where to excavate and may precede archaeological survey. Archaeologists will therefore need to rethink their surveying and excavation strategies in light of this new information, especially as image resolution continues to increase.

Geographic Information Systems

The standard approach to archaeological mapping is now the use of Geographic Information Systems (GIS), described in one official report as "the biggest step forward in the handling of geographic information since the invention of the map." A GIS is a collection of computer hardware and software and of geographic data, designed to obtain, store, manage, manipulate, analyze, and display a wide range of spatial information. A GIS combines a database with powerful digital mapping tools. GIS developed out of computer-aided design and computer-aided mapping (CAD/CAM) programs during the 1970s. Some CAD programs, such as AutoCAD, can be linked to commercial databases and have proved valuable in allowing the automatic mapping of archaeological sites held in a computer database. A true GIS, however, also incorporates the ability to carry out a statistical analysis of site distribution, and to generate new information.

DATA LAYERS

Actual
landscape

Diagram showing possible GIS data layers:
from top to bottom, drainage, human activity,
and relief.

A GIS may include an enormous amount of topographic and environmental data on relief, communications, hydrology, etc. To make the information easier to handle, it can be divided into different layers, each representing a single variable (see illustration at left). Archaeological data may themselves be split into several layers, often so that each layer represents a discrete time-slice. As long as they can be spatially located, many different types of data can be integrated, including site plans, satellite images, aerial photographs, geophysical survey, as well as maps. A good example of many different types of data being incorporated into a GIS is the Giza Plateau Mapping Project in Egypt (see box opposite).

The ability to incorporate aerial imagery can be particularly valuable for site survey, as it can provide detailed and current land-use information. Many topographic data already exist in the form of digital maps that can be taken directly into a GIS. Knowing exact ground coordinates is essential in archaeological practice for mapping purposes and learning about distribution patterns. This is done by means of a handheld GPS, which allows archaeologists to map their ground position (in some cases to within as little as 3 cm) by connecting to a global satellite system. A minimum of four satellites has to be communicating with the GPS to provide close X and Y data, which can display the received information in longitude/latitude (degrees, minutes, seconds), or to a UTM (Universal Transverse Mercator) coordinate system that provides data in eastings and northings. These data are extremely useful where a region is unmapped, or where the maps are old or inaccurate.

Once the basic outlines of a site have been mapped with reasonable accuracy by means of the GPS, and control points placed around the site, standard practice is to use a **total station** to record its more detailed features to a greater degree of accuracy. This instrument is an electronic theodolite integrated with an electronic distance meter, used to read distances to a particular point. Angles and distances are measured from the total station to points under survey and the coordinates (X, Y, Z, or northing, easting, and elevation) of the surveyed points relative to the total station position are calculated. These data can then be downloaded from the total station to a computer to generate a map of the surveyed area. All the information is recorded and then submitted as GIS data to the client or sponsoring organization of the work as a matter of course.

Once data are stored within a GIS it is relatively straightforward to generate maps on demand, and to query the database to select particular categories of site to be displayed. Individual map layers, or combinations of layers, can be selected according to the subject under investigation.

One of the earliest, and most widespread, uses of GIS within archaeology has been the construction of predictive models of site locations. Most

Survey and Excavation on the Giza Plateau

For nearly thirty years American Egyptologist Mark Lehner has been systematically exploring Egypt's Giza Plateau in an effort to find the settlements that housed the workforce that built the pyramids. To the south of the Great Sphinx, 4500-year-old paved streets have been uncovered, as well as various buildings, from barracks to bakeries. The Giza Plateau Mapping Project (GPMP) has so far exposed a vast urban center attached to the pyramids, sometimes known as the "Lost City of the Pyramid Builders."

Directed by Camilla Mazzucato and Rebekah Miracle, GIS is being used to integrate all the project's drawings, forms, survey data, and artifact databases into a single organized digital archive. This enables the team to map patterns of architecture, burials, artifacts, and other materials, such as foodstuffs: for example, it has been found that the people who resided in the bigger houses ate the best meat (beef) and fish (perch), while the others ate more pig and goat. Color-coded graphs and charts can be produced, representing the densities and distributions of various artifact types in different areas, buildings, rooms, or even features.

Data collected over almost 30 years, incorporated in the GIS:

- over 6000 field drawings
- over 19,000 archaeological features
- survey and remote sensing data
- aerial and satellite imagery
- historical maps
- artifact/ecofact distribution information

(Above left) The Giza Plateau Mapping Project began with an extremely accurate survey of the cultural and natural features of the entire area. The survey grid is centered on the Great Pyramid.

(Left) Using digitized 1-meter contours of the plateau and CAD data depicting the architectural components of the pyramid complex, the GPMP GIS team created a nearly three-dimensional surface called a TIN, or triangulated irregular network, over which they can lay other data layers, such as maps. Here (left), the GPMP survey grid is draped over the surface of the plateau. The "Lost City of the Pyramid Builders," Heit el-Ghurab, is clearly visible in the foreground.

Menkaure Valley Temple

Khentkawes Town

Heit el-Ghurab

of the development of these techniques has taken place within North American archaeology, where the enormous spatial extent of some archaeological landscapes means that it is not always possible to survey them comprehensively. The underlying premise of all predictive models is that particular kinds of sites tend to occur in the same kinds of place. For example, certain settlement sites tend to occur close to sources of fresh water and on southerly aspects, because these provide ideal conditions in which humans can live (not too cold, and within easy walking distance of a water source). Using this information it is possible to model how likely a given location is to contain an archaeological site from the known environmental characteristics of that location. In a GIS environment this operation can be undertaken for an entire landscape, producing a predictive model map for the whole area.

An example was developed by the Illinois State Museum for the Shawnee National Forest in southern Illinois. It predicts the likelihood of finding a prehistoric site anywhere within the 91 sq. km (35 sq. miles) of the forest by using the observed characteristics of the 68 sites that are known from the 12 sq. km (4.6 sq. miles) that have been surveyed. A GIS database was constructed for the entire area and the characteristics of the known sites were compared with the characteristics of the locations known not to contain sites. This resulted in a model that can be used to predict the likelihood that any location with known characteristics will contain a prehistoric site.

Assessing the Layout of Sites and Features

Finding and recording sites and features is the first stage in fieldwork, but the next stage is to make some assessment of site size, type, and layout. These are crucial factors for archaeologists, not only for those who are trying to decide whether, where, and how to excavate, but also for those whose main focus may be site management, the study of settlement patterns, site systems, and **landscape archaeology**, and who are not planning to carry out any excavation.

We have already seen how aerial images may be used to plot the layout of sites as well as helping to locate them in the first place. What are the other main methods for investigating sites without excavating them?

Site Surface Survey

The simplest way to gain some idea of a site's extent and layout is through a site surface survey—by studying the distribution of surviving features, and recording and possibly collecting artifacts from the surface.

The Teotihuacan Mapping Project, for instance, used site surface survey to investigate the layout and orientation of the city, which had been the largest and most powerful urban center in Mesoamerica in its heyday from 200 to 650 CE. The layout and orientation of the city had intrigued scholars for decades; however, they considered the grandiose pyramid-temples, plazas,

MEXICO
Teotihuacan

(Above) Archaeological and topographic map of Teotihuacan produced by the Teotihuacan Mapping Project. The survey grid system of 500-m squares is oriented to the north–south axis of the city, in particular the central "Street of the Dead" (dividing W1 and E1 on the map).

(Right) View south along the Street of the Dead, with the Pyramid of the Sun prominent on the left, echoing the shape of the mountain behind.

and the major avenue—an area now known as the ceremonial center—to be the entire extent of the metropolis. It was not until the survey conducted by the Teotihuacan Mapping Project that the outer limits, the great east–west axis, and the grid plan of the city were discovered and defined.

Fortunately, structural remains lay just beneath the surface, so that the team were able to undertake the mapping from a combination of aerial and surface survey, with only small-scale excavation to test the survey results. Millions of potsherds were collected, and more than 5000 structures and activity areas recorded. Teotihuacan had been laid out on a regular plan, with four quadrants orientated on the great north–south "Street of the Dead" and another major avenue running east–west across it. Construction had occurred over several centuries, but always following the master plan.

For artifacts and other objects collected or observed during site surface survey, it may not be worth mapping their individual locations if they appear to come from badly disturbed secondary contexts. Or there may simply be too many artifacts to record all their individual proveniences. In this latter instance the archaeologist will probably use sampling procedures for the selective recording of finds. Where time and funds are sufficient and the site is small enough, however, the collection and recording of artifacts from the total site area may prove possible.

For example, a site surface survey was conducted at the Bronze Age city of Mohenjodaro in Pakistan. Here, a team of archaeologists from Pakistan, Germany, and Italy investigated the distribution of craft-working debris and found, to their surprise, that craft activities were not confined to a specific manufacturing zone within the city, but were scattered throughout the site, representing assorted small-scale workshops.

RELIABILITY OF SURFACE FINDS. Archaeologists have always used limited surface collection of artifacts as one way of trying to assess the date and layout of a site prior to excavation. However, now that surface survey has become not merely a preliminary to excavation, but also in some instances a substitute for it—for cost and time reasons—a vigorous debate is taking place in archaeology about how far surface traces do in fact reflect distributions below ground.

We would logically expect single-period or shallow sites to show the most reliable surface evidence of what lies beneath. Equally one might predict that multi-period, deep sites, such as Near Eastern village mounds, would show few if any traces on the surface of the earliest and deepest levels. This is by no means always true, however—for example, at Tell Halula in northern Syria, a survey was carried out by an Australian team in 1986, involving the collection of such artifacts as potsherds and stone tools from the surface, using **stratified random sampling** procedures based on a grid system. 46 squares in this grid were sampled, amounting to 4 percent of the 12.5-ha (31-acre) site

(Left) The survey and collection team at Tell Halula using a theodolite.

Tell Halula

SYRIA

Tigris R.

Euphrates R.

Topography and Collection Areas

200m

N

Pre-Pottery Neolithic B

8.0 ha

Halaf

6.9 ha

Ubaid–Late Chalcolithic

2.3 ha

Uruk–Early Bronze Age

1.9 ha

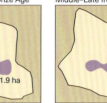

Middle–Late Iron Age

1.2 ha

(Above) Plan of Tell Halula showing the layout of collection squares, plus outline plans showing the changing location and size of settlement during five of the ten occupation phases.

satellite image © USGS

(Left) CORONA satellite image of the Halula district, showing the location of the tell and the boundary of the sampling area.

area. Typological analysis of the artifacts made it possible to identify ten major occupation phases, representing fifteen different cultural periods.

Those who support the validity of surface survey, while agreeing that there is bound to be a quantitative bias in favor of the most recent periods on the surface, nevertheless point out that one of the surprises for most survey archaeologists is how many of their sites, if collected with care, are truly multi-period, reflecting many phases of a site's use, not just the latest one. The reasons for this are not yet entirely clear, but they certainly have something to do with the kind of formation processes discussed in Chapter 2—from erosion and animal disturbance to such human activity as plowing.

The relationship between surface and subsurface evidence is undoubtedly complex and varies from site to site. It is therefore wise wherever possible to try to determine what really does lie beneath the ground, perhaps by digging test pits (usually meter squares) to assess a site's horizontal extent, or by more thorough excavation (see below, pp. 91–105). There is, however, a whole battery of **subsurface detection** devices that can be used before—or indeed sometimes instead of—excavation, which of course is destructive as well as expensive.

Subsurface Detection

PROBES.   The most traditional technique is that of probing the soil with rods or augers, and noting the positions where they strike solids or hollows. Metal rods with a T-shaped handle are the most common, but augers—large corkscrews with a similar handle—are also used, and have the advantage of bringing samples of soil to the surface, clinging to the screw. Many archaeologists use hand-held probes that yield small, solid cores. Probing of this type was used, for example, by Chinese archaeologists to plot the 300 pits remaining to be investigated near the first emperor's famous buried terracotta army. There is always, however, a risk of damaging fragile artifacts or features.

One notable advance in this technique was developed by Carlo Lerici in Italy in the 1950s as part of the search for Etruscan tombs of the sixth century BCE. Having detected the precise location of a tomb through aerial photography and **soil resistivity** (see pp. 88–89), he would bore down into it a hole 8 cm (3 in.) in diameter, and insert a long tube with a periscope head and a light, and also a tiny camera attached if needed. Lerici examined some 3500 Etruscan tombs in this way, and found that almost all were completely empty, thus saving future excavators a great deal of wasted effort. He also discovered more than twenty with painted walls, thus doubling the known heritage of Etruscan painted tombs at a stroke.

SHOVEL-TEST PITS (STPS).   To gain a preliminary idea of what lies beneath the surface, small pits may often be dug into the ground at consistent distances from each other; in Europe these are usually in the form of meter-squares, but in some parts of North America small round holes are dug, about the diameter of a dinner-plate and less than a meter deep. These pits help show what an area has to offer, and help identify the extent of a possible site, while analysis and plotting of the material retrieved from them by sieving of the soil can produce maps showing areas with high concentrations of different kinds of artifacts. This method is commonly employed as part of site surveys for CRM projects in areas of the USA with poor surface visibility, such as forested areas of the east coast.

PROBING THE PYRAMIDS.   Modern technology has taken such work even further, with the development of the endoscope and miniature TV cameras. In a project reminiscent of Lerici's, a probe was carried out in 1987 of a boat pit beside the Great Pyramid of Cheops (Khufu), in Egypt. This lies adjacent to another pit, excavated in 1954, that contained the perfectly preserved and disassembled parts of a 43-m- (141-ft.-) long royal cedarwood boat of the third millennium BCE. The 1987 probe revealed that the unopened pit contained all the dismantled timbers of a second boat. In 2008 a team from Waseda University in Tokyo, Japan, inserted a second miniature camera to reexamine the boat's condition and ascertain whether it could be safely lifted.The covering stone blocks and boat's timbers were duly removed in 2011. Robot probes with miniature cameras have been sent up two of the so-called "airshafts" of the Great Pyramid to discover whether or not they link up to hidden chambers— tantalizingly, stone blocking part-way up hinders further investigation.

Projects of this kind are beyond the resources of most archaeologists. But in future, funds permitting, probes of this type could equally well be applied to other Egyptian sites, to cavities in Maya structures, or to the many unexcavated tombs in China. The Great Pyramid itself has been the subject of further probes by French and Japanese teams, who believe it may contain as yet undiscovered chambers or corridors. Using ultrasensitive microgravimetric equipment—which is normally employed to search for deficiencies in dam walls, and can tell if a stone has a hollow behind it—they detected what they think is a cavity some 3 m (10 ft.) beyond one of the passage walls. Test drilling to support this claim has not been completed, however, and all tests are carefully monitored by the Egyptian authorities until their potential contribution to Egyptology has been established.

Ground-based Remote Sensing

Probing techniques are useful, but inevitably involve some disturbance of the site. There are, however, a wide range of non-destructive techniques ideal for the archaeologist seeking to learn more about a site before— or increasingly often without—excavation. These are geophysical sensing devices, which can be either active (i.e. they pass energy of various kinds through the soil and measure the response in order to "read" what lies below the surface); or passive (i.e. they measure such physical properties as magnetism and gravity without the need to use energy to obtain a response).

ELECTROMAGNETIC METHODS.   The ground-penetrating (or probing) radar (GPR) method employs radio pulses. An emitter sends short pulses through the soil, and the echoes not only reflect back any changes in the soil and sediment conditions encountered, such as filled ditches, graves, walls, etc., but also measure the depth at which the changes occur on the basis of the travel time of the pulses. Three-dimensional maps of buried archaeological remains can then be produced from data processing and image-generation programs.

In archaeological exploration and mapping, the radar antenna is generally dragged along the ground with the aid of a low trolley at walking speed in transects, sending out and receiving many pulses per second. The reflection data are stored digitally, which enables sophisticated data processing and analysis to be carried out, producing records that are relatively easy to interpret. Powerful computers and software programs make it possible to store and process very large three-dimensional sets of GPR data, and computer advances now permit automated data and image processing that can help to interpret complicated reflection profiles.

One such advance is the use of time-slices or slice-maps. Thousands of individual reflections are combined into a single three-dimensional dataset that can then be "sliced" horizontally, each slice corresponding to a specific estimated depth in the ground, and revealing the general shape and location of buried features at successive depths. A variety of colors (or shades of gray) are used to make a visual image that the brain can interpret more easily—e.g. areas with little or no subsurface reflection may be colored blue, those with high reflection may be red. Each slice therefore becomes like a horizontal surface, and can illustrate the buried components of the site.

Amplitude slice-maps from the Forum Novum site, Italy. The top slice, at 0–10 ns (nanosecond, equivalent to 0–50 cm) reveals a Y-shaped anomaly, reflecting two gravel roads. As the slices go deeper, the Roman walls begin to emerge very clearly, showing a well-organized plan of rooms, doors, and corridors. The deepest slice shows the actual floor levels of the rooms and the objects preserved on them.

For example, at Forum Novum, an ancient Roman marketplace about 100 km (60 miles) north of Rome, archaeologists from the University of Birmingham in England and the British School of Archaeology in Rome needed a fuller picture of an unexcavated area than they had been able to obtain from aerial photographs and other techniques, such as resistivity (see below). GPR slices of the area revealed a whole series of walls, rooms, doorways, and courtyards—in short, they produced an architectural layout of the site that means that future excavation can be concentrated on a representative sample of the structures, thus avoiding a costly and time-consuming uncovering of the whole area.

EARTH RESISTANCE SURVEY.   A commonly used method that has been employed on archaeological sites for several decades, particularly in Europe, is **earth resistance survey**. The technique derives from the principle that the damper the soil the more easily it will conduct electricity, i.e. the less resistance it will show to an electric current. A **resistivity meter** attached to electrodes in the ground can thus measure varying degrees of subsurface resistance to a current passed between the electrodes. Silted-up ditches or filled-in pits retain more moisture than stone walls or roads, and will therefore display lower resistivity than stone structures.

The technique works particularly well for ditches and pits in chalk and gravel, and masonry in clay. It usually involves first placing two remote probes, which remain stationary, in the ground. Two mobile probes, fixed to a frame that also supports the meter, are then inserted into the earth for each reading. A variation of the method is resistivity profiling, which involves the measurement of earth resistance at increasing depths by widening the probe spacings and thus building up a vertical "pseudosection" across a site.

MAGNETIC SURVEY METHODS.   These are particularly helpful in locating such fired-clay structures as hearths and pottery kilns; iron objects; and pits and ditches. Such buried features all produce slight but measurable distortions in the Earth's magnetic field. The reasons for this vary according to the type of feature, but are based on the presence of minute amounts of iron. For example, grains of iron oxide in clay, their magnetism randomly orientated if the clay is unbaked, will line up and become permanently fixed in the direction of the Earth's magnetic field when heated to about 700°C (1292°F) or more. The baked clay thus becomes a weak permanent magnet, creating an anomaly in the surrounding magnetic field. Anomalies caused by pits and ditches, on the other hand, occur because the so-called magnetic susceptibility of their contents is greater than that of the surrounding subsoil.

Magnetic instruments, such as **fluxgate magnetometers** (see box overleaf), can produce informative site plans that help to delimit archaeological potential. Today, multiple types of sensors—both electromagnetic and magnetic—are often integrated on moving platforms or mobile arrays, which allow for simultaneous measurements. Color and grayscale maps are produced that, along with contour maps, are used to display earth resistance survey results. In the case of magnetic survey, the contour map has lines that join all points of the same value of the magnetic field intensity—this can reveal separate anomalies, such as tombs in a cemetery.

METAL DETECTORS.   These electromagnetic devices are also helpful in detecting buried remains. An alternating magnetic field is generated by passing an electrical current through a transmitter coil. Buried metal objects distort this field and are detected as a result of an electrical signal picked up by a receiver coil. Metal detectors can be of great value to archaeologists, particularly as they can provide general results and are able to locate modern metal objects that may lie near the surface. They are also very widely used by non-archaeologists, most of whom are responsible enthusiasts. Some, however, vandalize sites mindlessly and often illegally dig holes without recording or reporting the finds they make, which are therefore without context.

So far, we have discovered sites and mapped as many of their surface and subsurface features as possible. But, despite the growing importance of survey, the only way to check the reliability of surface data, confirm the accuracy of the remote sensing techniques, and actually see what remains of these sites is to excavate them. Furthermore, survey can tell us a little about a large area, but only excavation can tell us a great deal about a relatively small area.

Measuring Magnetism

Most terrestrial magnetometer surveys are undertaken either with fluxgate or with alkali-metal vapor magnetometers.

Fluxgate instruments usually comprise two sensors fixed rigidly at either end of a vertically held tube, and measure only the vertical component of the local magnetic field strength. The magnetometer is carried along a succession of traverses, usually 0.5–1.0 m apart, tied in to an overall pre-surveyed grid, until the entire site is covered. The signal is logged automatically and stored in the instrument's memory, to be downloaded and processed later. To speed up the coverage of large areas, two or more fluxgate instruments can be moved across the site at once—either on a frame carried by the operator, or sometimes on a wheeled cart. In this way, many hectares of ground can be covered quite quickly, revealing such features as pits, ditches, hearths, kilns, or entire settlement complexes and

their associated roads, trackways, and cemeteries.

An alternative and sometimes more effective magnetometer is the alkali-metal vapor type, typically a cesium magnetometer. Although more expensive and quite difficult to operate, an advantage these magnetometers have over fluxgate types is that they are more sensitive and can therefore detect features that are only very weakly magnetic, or more deeply buried than usual. Such instruments have been used for many years with great success in continental Europe and are finding favor elsewhere. Unlike a fluxgate gradiometer they measure the total magnetic field (but can be operated as a total-field gradiometer if configured with two vertically mounted sensors). It is also usual for two or more of these sensors to be used at once—often

The Bartington Grad601-2 single-axis, vertical-component, high-stability fluxgate gradiometer system.

mounted on a non-magnetic wheeled cart. Surveys with such systems can cover up to about 5 ha (12 acres) each day at a high resolution sampling interval (0.5 m × 0.25 m). Arrays of fluxgate sensors are now also being introduced, but many surveys are conducted with a dual sensor system (as in the photograph above) with a sample interval of *c.* 0.1 m × 0.25 m. Fluxgates are often favored for their lower cost, versatility, and ability to detect a similar range of features to cesium systems.

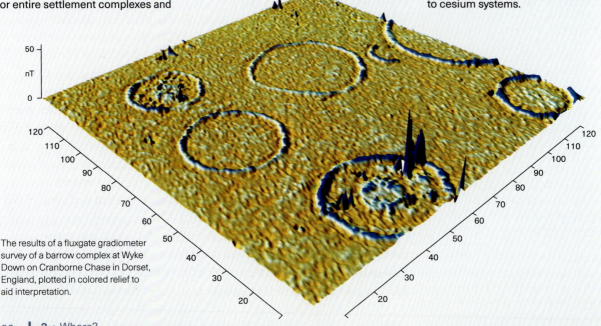

The results of a fluxgate gradiometer survey of a barrow complex at Wyke Down on Cranborne Chase in Dorset, England, plotted in colored relief to aid interpretation.

Excavation

Excavation retains its central role in fieldwork because it yields the most reliable evidence for the two main kinds of information archaeologists are interested in: (1) human activities at a particular period in the past; and (2) changes in those activities from period to period. Very broadly we can say that contemporary activities take place horizontally in space, whereas changes in those activities occur vertically through time. It is this distinction between horizontal slices of time and vertical sequences through time that forms the basis of most excavation methodology.

In the horizontal dimension, archaeologists demonstrate that activities occurred at the same time by proving through excavation that artifacts and features are found in association in an undisturbed context. Of course, as we saw in Chapter 2, there are many formation processes that may disturb this primary context. One of the main purposes of the survey and remote sensing procedures outlined in earlier sections is to select for excavation sites, or areas within sites, that are reasonably undisturbed. On a single-period site, such as an East African early human camp site, this is vital if human behavior at the camp is to be reconstructed at all accurately. But on a multi-period site, such as a long-lived European town or Near Eastern village mound, finding large areas of undisturbed deposits will be almost impossible. Here archaeologists have to try to reconstruct during and after excavation just what disturbance there has been, and then decide how to interpret it. Clearly, adequate records must be made as excavation progresses if the task of interpretation is to be undertaken with any chance of success. In the vertical dimension archaeologists analyze changes through time by the study of stratigraphy.

Stratigraphy

As we saw in Chapter 1, one of the first steps in understanding the great antiquity of humankind was the recognition by geologists of the process of stratification—that layers or strata are laid down, one on top of the other, according to processes that still continue. Archaeological strata (the layers of cultural or natural debris visible in the side of any excavation) accumulate over much shorter periods of time than geological ones, but nevertheless conform to the same law of superposition. Put simply, this states that where one layer overlies another, the lower was deposited first. Hence, an excavated vertical profile showing a series of layers constitutes a sequence that has accumulated through time.

Chapter 4 explores the significance of this for dating purposes. Here we should note that the law of superposition refers only to the sequence of deposition, not to the age of the material in the different strata. The contents of lower layers are indeed usually older than those of upper layers, but the archaeologist must not simply assume this. Pits dug down from a higher layer or burrowing animals (even earthworms) may introduce later materials into lower levels. Moreover, occasionally strata can become inverted, as when they are eroded all the way from the top of a bank to the bottom of a ditch.

Archaeologists have developed an ingenious and effective method of checking that artifacts—so far mostly of stone or bone—discovered in a particular deposit are contemporaneous and not intrusive. They have found that in a surprising number of cases flakes of stone or bone can be fitted back together again: reassembled in the shape of the original stone block or pieces of bone from which they came. At the Mesolithic (Middle Stone Age) site of Hengistbury Head in southern England, for example, reanalysis of an old excavation showed that two groups of flint flakes, found in two different layers, could be **refitted**. This cast doubt on the stratigraphic separation of the two layers, and demolished the original excavator's argument that the flints had been made by two different groups of people. As well as clarifying questions of stratification, these refitting or **conjoining** exercises are transforming archaeological studies of early technology (see Chapter 7).

The complexity of stratification varies with the type of site. This hypothetical section through an urban deposit indicates the kind of complicated stratigraphy, in both vertical and horizontal dimensions, that the archaeologist can encounter. There may be few undisturbed stratified layers. The chances of finding preserved organic material increase as one approaches the water table, near which deposits may be waterlogged.

modern disturbance

present ground surface

natural soil level

drain

intact stratification

preserved organic material

wall foundations

water table

Excavation yields evidence of contemporary activities (which are found horizontally through space) and changes through time (which are found vertically in sequences)

Stratigraphy is the study of archaeological layers found during excavations. The law of superposition states that where one layer overlies another, the lower was deposited first. This forms the basis of the way archaeologists investigate changes through time

Excavation methods should be adapted to the site and the particular questions that need to be answered. The two main strategies are the Wheeler box-grid and open-area excavation; a combination of both is often used. A sampling strategy of some kind can be required to save time and money

Stratigraphy, then, is the study and validating of stratification—the analysis in the vertical, time dimension of a series of layers in the horizontal, space dimension (although in practice few layers are precisely horizontal).

What are the best excavation methods for retrieving this information?

Methods of Excavation

Excavation is both costly and destructive, and therefore never to be undertaken lightly. Wherever possible, non-destructive approaches (outlined earlier) should be used to meet research objectives in preference to excavation. But assuming excavation is to proceed, and the necessary funding and permission to dig have been obtained, what are the best methods to adopt?

This book is not an excavation or field manual, but although such things do exist, a few days or weeks spent on a well-run dig are worth far more than reading any book on the subject. Nevertheless, some brief guidance as to the main methods is given here. In addition, we look at the excavation of one site, the Jamestown settlement in Virginia, in a little more detail (see box overleaf).

It goes without saying that all excavation methods need to be adapted to the research question in hand and the nature of the site. It is no good digging a deeply stratified urban site, with hundreds of complex structures, thousands of intercutting pits, and tens of thousands of artifacts, as if it were the same as a shallow Paleolithic open site, where only one or two structures and a few hundred artifacts may survive. On the Paleolithic site, for example, it may be possible to uncover all the structures and record the exact position or provenience, vertically and horizontally, of each and every artifact. On the urban site there is no chance of doing this, given time and funding constraints. Instead, we have to adopt a sampling strategy, and only key artifacts, such as coins (important for dating purposes: see Chapter 4), will have their provenience recorded with three-dimensional precision, the remainder being allocated simply to the layer and perhaps the grid-square in which they were found (sites are usually divided up into grid-squares, just like maps are, in order to aid in accurate recording; naturally, the size and number of the grid squares will depend on the type, size, and likely depth of the site).

It should be noted, however, that we have already reintroduced the idea of the vertical and horizontal dimensions. These are as crucial to the methods of excavation as they are to the principles behind excavation. Broadly speaking we can divide excavation techniques into:

1 those that emphasize the vertical dimension, by cutting into deep deposits to reveal stratification; and
2 those that emphasize the horizontal dimension, by opening up large areas of a particular layer to reveal the spatial relationships between artifacts and features in that layer.

Jamestown Rediscovery: The Excavation Process

On May 13, 1607, a hundred Englishmen established a settlement on Jamestown Island in Virginia. Soon under attack from Native Americans, they quickly built a wooden fort. Periodic resupply of settlers and stores, investment by the sponsoring Virginia Company of London, and the discovery of a cash crop, tobacco, kept the venture alive. Ultimately, Jamestown proved to be the first permanent English colony in North America. For centuries the site of the fort was thought to have been eroded away by the adjacent James River, but archaeological excavations from 1994 onward by the Jamestown Rediscovery project have proved that the "lost" site has actually escaped erosion. Most of the archaeological footprint of the fort and more than one million artifacts have been recovered, at least half of these dating to the first three struggling years of settlement.

The Jamestown Rediscovery research design is straightforward: uncover, record, and interpret the remnants of the James Fort; determine the original and evolving fort plan; learn as much as possible about the daily lives of the settlers and the Native Americans; and record prehistoric and post-James Fort occupations. From the outset, it was clear that the best way to record and recover all this required a hybridized excavation process combining the traditional grid-based control system with open-area excavation. A thorough documentary search was also essential, both to pinpoint areas to investigate, and to reassess the records continually in light of new and more complex questions raised by the digging.

The Ongoing Field Process

Initially, a grid of 3-m (10-ft.) squares is employed in each area to be excavated, facilitating the recording of artifacts deposited in post-fort layers. Once the seventeenth-century level is exposed, the grid is replaced with a feature-based open-area recording method. At this stage, both physical remains and variations in soil color and texture

Delicate field recovery of arms and armor in a backfilled metalworking shop/bakery cellar after full feature definition by open-area excavation.

together delineate features: building foundations, fireplaces, postholes, cellars, wells, pits, ditches, and graves. These defined contexts are assigned ascending "JR" numbers, which are then entered into a GIS site map.

The decision to excavate partially or fully (or leave unexcavated) features or related components of features is dependent upon whether or not they can be associated with other known James Fort/Jamestown period (1607–24) remains, such as wall lines. More recent features are usually mapped but left unexcavated. Once it is decided that a given feature is likely to be a remnant of the fort occupation, excavation determines the cultural deposition sequence, indicated by changes in the soil color, texture, or inclusions of strata. Each layer is then sequentially assigned a letter of the alphabet. In this manner, the JR number and letter permanently label each individual feature, and layers within them, as distinct contexts. Most contexts are then drawn, photographed, systematically archived, and eventually linked to the GIS site map.

The artifacts are recovered in two stages: as the feature layers are excavated and then as the loose spoil is wet- or dry-screened (the latter either by hand or mechanically). The specific

The grid-based (foreground) and open-area (background) excavations at James Fort.

GIS site map of the James Fort open-area excavations, 1994–2010.

0   30 m
0   100 ft.

N

☐ Grid areas excavated between 1994 and 2011

* Features shown in red are circa James Fort period

screening process employed depends on the age and integrity of the context. The resulting artifact collections are washed, conserved, and cataloged in a laboratory on site, permanently carrying their JR number and letter.

Soil samples of individual layers are collected and archived for future flotation and/or chemical analysis. Once selected features in an area have been excavated and/or recorded, that area is covered with a geotextile fabric and backfilled, usually with 50 cm (20 in.) of soil. As of 2011, about 15 percent of features in the fort have been partially or fully excavated, with the remainder preserved for future investigation.

Collections Management

After initial cleaning, artifacts are sorted according to conservation requirements, balancing the need for rescue and long-term preservation with interpretive potential. A number of techniques, including X-ray recording and mechanical/chemical treatments, are applied to metallic objects and organic materials.

The computer cataloging program is straightforward and searchable, utilizing minimal attribute fields (number, material, form, and design), but with the ability to enter other useful data in a separate field. To facilitate analysis and publication, the digital catalog is linked to the GIS site map so that plans, photos, and artifacts can be interpreted at a single computer station. Descriptive reports are generated for each year of the excavation, but interpretation is limited because of the ongoing nature of the project.

Reconstruction of James Fort based on excavated evidence and historical records.

Most excavators employ a combination of both strategies, but there are different ways of achieving this. All presuppose that the site has first been surveyed and a grid of squares laid down over it. A site grid is laid out from a datum, which is simply a selected location that serves as a reference point for all horizontal and vertical measurements taken, so that the site can be accurately mapped and the exact location of any artifact or feature can be recorded in three dimensions if that is necessary or feasible.

The **Wheeler box-grid**—developed from the work of Pitt-Rivers, as noted in Chapter 1—seeks to satisfy both vertical and horizontal requirements by retaining intact balks of earth between the squares of the grid, as can be clearly seen in the picture to the right, so that different layers can be traced and correlated across the site in vertical profiles. Once the general extent and layout of the site have been ascertained, some of the balks can be removed and the squares joined into an open excavation to expose any features (such as a mosaic floor) that are of special interest.

Advocates of **open-area excavation** criticize this method, arguing that the balks are invariably in the wrong place or wrongly orientated to illustrate the relationships required from sections, and that they prevent the distinguishing of spatial patterning over large areas. It is far better, these critics say, not to have such permanent or semi-permanent balks, but to open up large areas and only to cut vertical sections (at whatever angle is necessary to the main site grid) where they are needed to elucidate particularly complex stratigraphic relationships. Apart from these "running sections," the vertical dimension is recorded by accurate three-dimensional measurements as the dig proceeds and reconstructed on paper after the end of the excavation. The introduction since Wheeler's day of more advanced recording methods, including field computers, makes this more demanding open-area method feasible, and it has become the norm, for instance, in much of British archaeology. The open-area method is particularly effective where single-period deposits lie near the surface, as for instance with remains of Native American or European Neolithic long houses. Here the time dimension may be represented by lateral movement (a settlement rebuilt adjacent to, not on top of, an earlier one) and it is essential to expose large horizontal areas in order to understand the complex pattern of rebuilding. Large open-area excavations are often undertaken in applied archaeology when land is going to be destroyed—otherwise farmers are naturally opposed to stripping large areas of plow-disturbed soil. The box-grid method is still widely used in parts of South Asia, where it was introduced by Wheeler in the 1940s. It remains popular as it enables large numbers of untrained workers in individual boxes to be easily supervised by small numbers of staff.

No single method, however, is ever going to be universally applicable. The rigid box-grid, for instance, has rarely been employed to excavate very

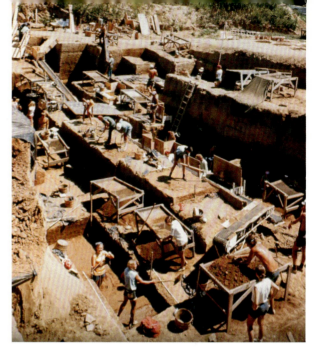

(Above left) Box-grid excavation trenches at Anuradhapura's Abhayagiri Buddhist monastery, Sri Lanka.

(Above right) The Native American site of Koster, in the Illinois River Valley: large horizontal areas were uncovered to locate living floors and activity zones. However, in order for the vertical dimension to be analyzed at this deep site, vertical sections were cut as steps as the excavation descended. At this complex site fourteen occupation levels were identified, dating from c. 7500 BCE to 1200 CE.

deep sites, such as Near Eastern tells, because the trench squares rapidly become uncomfortable and dangerous as the dig proceeds downward. One solution commonly adopted is **step-trenching**, with a large area opened at the top that gradually narrows as the dig descends in a series of large steps. This technique was used effectively at the Koster site, Illinois.

Each site is different and one needs to adapt to its conditions—for example, in some cases by following the natural geological strata or the cultural layers instead of using arbitrary spits or imposing a false regularity where it does not exist. Whatever the method of excavation, a dig is only as good as its methods of recovery and recording. Since excavation involves destruction of much of the evidence, it is an unrepeatable exercise. Well-thought-out recovery methods are essential, and careful records must be kept of every stage of the dig.

Excavating in the Digital Age

The development of new digital technologies has revolutionized archaeological survey in recent years, and the same is true of excavation and site recording. Image-based 3D modeling is proving of special importance.

A 3D computer-generated model of a site is created before work starts, and then every stage of the excavation is documented in the same way as with paper recording. Anyone can visit the virtual dig, as if they were standing on the site itself as the work took place. They can thus examine the evidence as it appears, and pool their expertise to interpret it. In contrast to 3D laser scanning, which requires expensive and specialized equipment

Excavating an Urban Site

Archaeological sites in continuously occupied towns and cities present two special challenges. The first is how to identify, record, and interpret the features left by centuries of building and rebuilding, which may result in meters of complex archaeology. The second concerns the economic pressures of modern development. In the case of the modern City of London, which lies on top of Roman Londinium, these are particularly acute. Archaeological work has to be planned rigorously and integrated with demolition and construction programs to avoid expensive delays.

A phase plan of part of the site, illustrating Roman masonry walls, timbers and floor surfaces, generated from digitized records. The numbers indicate ground levels in meters.

The Bloomberg Excavation
The 3-acre site lies over a buried river, known today as the Walbrook. In the 1950s limited excavations revealed remains of a third-century Roman temple. In 2010 the global financial information company Bloomberg decided to redevelop the site for its European headquarters. A Museum of London Archaeology (MOLA) project manager was integrated into the Bloomberg design team.

Planning and Strategy
Desk-based research and site work by MOLA showed that up to 7 m (23 ft.) of waterlogged deposits might have survived in certain areas. An area of 650 sq. m (2130 sq. ft.) needed to be excavated. Some of the key research objectives were to understand local landscape formation processes and how these influenced the siting of the earliest settlement, the management and use of the Walbrook, and the landscape contemporary with the Roman temple.

Field Techniques
Urban sites, with their hundreds of interrelated and intercutting deposits, require the use of a single-context recording system, where evidence of each archaeological "event" is

A team of fifty archaeologists from MOLA excavated the Bloomberg London site for over six months. It is the most extensive excavation to take place in the City of London for twenty years.

allocated a context number, planned on an individual sheet, and recorded on a context sheet. Every find or environmental sample is attributed to its context, linking each aspect of the project to its origin on the site, allowing the archaeology to be reconstructed after the excavation. Use of the Harris matrix (a diagram representing the stratigraphic relationship of the contexts) is vital.

Post-excavation Analysis and Public Engagement
The excavation produced a huge archaeological assemblage: 3 tons of Roman pottery, nearly 400 fragments of wooden writing tablets, and the best assemblage of Roman textiles from Roman Britain. In addition to publishing the excavations, the project also employed a public engagement strategy, including the Walbrook Discovery Program blog, professionally video-recording the excavation and interviews with site staff.

to produce high-quality results, the new method needs nothing more than a simple camera and some software—in other words, it is cheap and accessible to all.

For example, if archaeologists are digging a burial, they no longer need to draw the skeleton and grave in plan view (an acquired skill); instead they merely take a series of digital photos (fifteen to eighty) from as many angles as possible, at every stage of the excavation as the burial is uncovered. A software program called PhotoScan can then generate the 3D contours of the burial from the photos, as well as digitized plans of the skeleton.

The method need not only be applied to small-scale digs or individual features. It is now being extended to entire excavations—for example at the Boudelo-2 site in Belgium, a twelfth- to thirteenth-century Cistercian abbey on reclaimed medieval wetland. During an excavation campaign in 2012, a 60-m- (195-ft.-) long soil profile and all unearthed brick structures were recorded both by image-based 3D modeling and by traditional manual techniques, plus oblique photography. The work then proceeded to a complete 3D recording of the excavation—everything that would normally have been recorded on paper was logged digitally. Manual recording was thus relegated to a backup system.

Labels, notes, descriptions, and interpretations are still necessary in the course of any excavation, and these more subjective aspects cannot be added immediately to the recording; hence they need to be stored elsewhere and linked to the excavation record later. Such data are therefore first logged in database form on tablet PCs. These are now sufficiently robust and cheap for use in the field, and have already proved invaluable at many sites—for example at Pompeii, where Apple iPads replaced field notebooks some years ago.

The recording of a single brick structure from Boudelo-2 in Belgium: the excavation process is visualized in a series of orthophotos and corresponding digital surface models (below left), and vertical ortho-images show the structure in profile from all four sides (below right).

North profile

South profile

East profile

West profile

Reconstruction of the Arch of Triumph from Palmyra, Syria, on display in Trafalgar Square, London, in 2016. The original arch, built by the Romans some 1800 years ago, was destroyed by militants of the so-called Islamic State (IS) in 2015. Using 3D and 2D photographs taken before the destruction, the replica was modeled and effectively "printed" in real stone (albeit at two-thirds scale) using a computer-controlled milling machine. The arch has also been displayed in New York and other cities.

In short, new technology is encouraging a significant improvement in the quality of recording in comparison with traditional methods, especially as the latter are often subject to error. The accurate documentation of 3D shape and texture is of great importance in archaeology: the combination of accurate metrics, 3D shape and detailed texture produces a far more objective and reliable record of an excavation.

Computer technology is advancing so rapidly that new software developments, together with decreasing costs and increasing computing power, will undoubtedly further streamline and improve many aspects of excavation in the next few decades. Digital data capture, however, is not a panacea for all situations; computers may introduce their own bias to matters of observation and interpretation, introducing their own issues of subjectivity. Archaeologists need always to carefully consider what a digital output is actually telling them.

3D printing is also increasing the possibilities of collaboration in an archaeological project. Excavated objects can now be scanned and the data sent to other locations to be replicated by 3D printing. These replicas can be examined off-site by specialists, or used for teaching purposes, and can extend the visibility of artifacts and architecture across the world.

Underwater Archaeology

One special category of both survey and excavation is constituted by underwater archaeology, which is generally considered to have been given its first major impetus during the winter of 1853–54, when a particularly low water level in the Swiss lakes laid bare enormous quantities of wooden posts, pottery, and other artifacts. From the earliest investigations, using crude diving-bells, it has developed into a valuable complement to work on land. It encompasses a wide variety of sites, including wells, sink holes, and springs (e.g. the great sacrificial well at Chichen Itza, Mexico); submerged lakeside settlements; and marine sites ranging from shipwrecks to sunken harbors and drowned cities.

The invention in recent times of miniature submarines, other submersible craft, and above all of scuba diving gear has been of enormous value, enabling divers to stay underwater for much longer, and to reach sites at previously impossible depths. As a result, the pace and scale of discovery have greatly increased. More than 1000 shipwrecks are known in shallow Mediterranean waters, but recent explorations using deep-sea submersibles, such as

(Above) Three methods of geophysical underwater survey. (1) The proton magnetometer is towed well behind the survey boat, detecting iron and steel objects (e.g. cannons, steel hulls) that distort the Earth's magnetic field. (2) Side-scan sonar transmits sound waves in a fan-shaped beam to produce a graphic image of surface (but not subsurface) features on the seafloor. (3) The sub-bottom profiler emits sound pulses that bounce back from features and objects buried beneath the seafloor.

(Below) Underwater excavation techniques: left, the lift bag for raising objects; center, measuring and recording finds in situ; right, the air lift for removing sediment.

miniature unmanned submarines (remotely operated vehicles—ROVs) with sonar, high-powered lighting, and video cameras, have begun to find Roman wrecks at depths of up to 850 m (2790 ft.). And two Phoenician wrecks packed with amphorae (storage jars) discovered off the coast of Israel are the oldest vessels ever found in the deep sea.

UNDERWATER SURVEY. Geophysical methods are as useful in **underwater survey** as they are for locating land sites. For example, in 1979 it was magnetometry combined with **side-scan sonar** that discovered the *Hamilton* and the *Scourge*, two armed schooners sunk during the War of 1812 at a depth of 90 m (295 ft.) in Lake Ontario, Canada. The latest multibeam side-scan sonar gives brilliantly clear images and allows accurate measurements to be taken of shipwrecks on the seabed. Nevertheless, in such regions as the Mediterranean the majority of finds have resulted from methods as simple as talking to local sponge-divers, who collectively have spent thousands of hours scouring the seabed.

UNDERWATER EXCAVATION. Excavation underwater is complex and expensive (not to mention the highly demanding post-excavation conservation and analytical work that is also required). Once under way, the excavation may involve shifting vast quantities of sediment, and recording and removing bulky objects as diverse as amphorae, metal ingots, and cannons. George Bass, founder of the Institute of Nautical Archaeology in Texas, and others have developed many helpful devices, such as baskets attached to balloons to raise objects, and air lifts (suction hoses) to remove sediment. If the vessel's hull survives at all, a 3D plan must be made so that specialists can later reconstruct the overall form and lines, either on paper or in three dimensions as a model or full-size replica. In some rare cases, for example that of England's *Mary Rose* (a sixteenth-century CE warship that sank off Portsmouth), preservation is sufficiently good for the remains of the hull to be raised—funds permitting.

Nautical archaeologists have now excavated more than 100 sunken vessels, revealing not only how they were constructed but also many insights into shipboard life, cargoes, trade routes, early metallurgy, and glassmaking. For example, a Basque whaling ship, the *San Juan*, which had sunk in Red Bay, Labrador, in 1565, was excavated in the 1980s from a specially equipped barge, anchored above the site, that contained a workshop, storage baths for artifacts, a crane for lifting timbers, and a compressor able to run 12 air lifts for removing silt. Salt water was heated on board and pumped down through hoses direct to the divers' suits to maintain body warmth in the near-freezing conditions. An important technique devised during the project was the use of latex rubber to mold large sections of the ship's timbers in position

(Above left) Model, at a scale of 1:10, to show how the *San Juan*'s surviving timbers may have fitted together.

(Above right) Structural plan of the wreck on the harbor bottom (2-m grid squares).

underwater, thereby reproducing accurately the hull shape and such details as toolmarks and wood grain. The remains of the vessel were also raised in pieces to the surface for precise recording, but the latex molds eliminated the need for costly conservation of the original timbers, which were reburied on-site.

Recovery and Recording of the Evidence

As we saw above, different sites have different requirements. We should aim to recover and plot the three-dimensional provenience of every artifact from a shallow single-period Paleolithic or Neolithic site, an objective that is simply not feasible for the urban archaeologist. On both types of site, a decision may be made to save time by using mechanical diggers to remove topsoil, but thereafter the Paleolithic or Neolithic specialist will usually want to screen or sieve as much excavated soil as possible in order to recover tiny artifacts, animal bones, and plant remains. The urban archaeologist on the other hand will only be able to adopt sieving much more selectively, as part of a sampling strategy, for instance where plant remains can be expected to survive, as in a latrine or garbage pit. Decisions need to be made about the type of sieving to be undertaken, the size of the screen and its mesh, and whether dry or wet sieving will yield the best results. Naturally all these factors will depend on the resources of the excavation project, the period and scale of the site, whether it is dry or waterlogged, and what kind of material can be expected to have survived and to be retrievable.

Once an artifact has been recovered, and its provenience recorded, it must be given a number that is entered in a catalog book or field computer and on the bag in which it is to be stored. Day-to-day progress of the dig is recorded in site notebooks, or on data sheets preprinted with specific questions to be answered (which helps produce uniform data suitable for later analysis by computer).

Unlike artifacts, which can be removed for later analysis, features and structures usually have to be left where they were found (or in situ), or destroyed as the excavation proceeds to another layer. It is thus imperative to record them, not simply by written description in site notebooks, but by accurately scaled drawings and photography. The same applies to vertical profiles (sections), and for each horizontally exposed layer, good overhead photographs taken from a stand or tethered balloon are also essential.

It is the site notebooks, scaled drawings, photographs and digital media—in addition to recovered artifacts, animal bones, and plant remains—that form the total record of the excavation, on the basis of which all interpretations of the site will be made. This post-excavation analysis will take many months, perhaps years, often much longer than the excavation itself. Some preliminary analysis, however, particularly sorting and classification of the artifacts, will be made in the field during the course of the excavation.

Processing and Classification

Like excavation itself, the processing of excavated materials in the field laboratory is a specialized activity that demands careful planning and organization. For example, an archaeologist excavating a wet site will need experts in the conservation of waterlogged wood, and facilities for coping with such material.

Two important aspects of field laboratory procedure are cleaning artifacts, and sorting and classifying them. In both cases the archaeologist always needs to consider in advance what kinds of questions the newly excavated material might be able to answer. Thorough cleaning of artifacts, for example, is a traditional part of excavations worldwide. But many of the new scientific techniques discussed later in this book make it quite evident that artifacts should not necessarily be cleaned thoroughly before a specialist has had a chance to study them. For instance, we now know that food residues are often preserved in pots, and possible blood residues on stone tools. The chances of such preservation need to be assessed before evidence is destroyed.

Nevertheless most artifacts eventually have to be cleaned to some degree if they are to be sorted and classified. Initial sorting is into such broad categories as stone tools, pottery, and metal objects. These categories are then subdivided or classified, so as to create more manageable groups that can later be analyzed. Classification is commonly done on the basis of three kinds of characteristics or **attributes**: surface attributes (including decoration and color); shape attributes (dimensions as well as shape itself); and technological attributes (primarily raw material). Artifacts with similar attributes are grouped together into artifact types—hence the term typology, which simply refers to the creation of such types.

Typology dominated archaeological thinking until the 1950s, and still plays an important role. The reason for this is straightforward. Artifacts make up a large part of the archaeological record, and typology helps archaeologists create order in this mass of evidence. As we saw in Chapter 1, C.J. Thomsen demonstrated early on that artifacts could be ordered in a Three Age System or sequence of stone, bronze, and iron. This discovery underlies the continuing use of typology as a method of dating (see Chapter 4). Typology has also been used as a means of defining archaeological entities at a particular moment in time: groups of artifact (and building) types at a particular time and place are termed assemblages, and groups of assemblages have been taken to define **archaeological cultures**. These definitions are also long established, but, as we shall see later, the difficulty comes when one tries to translate this

Terms used in archaeological classification, from attributes (shape, decoration) of a pot to the complete archaeological culture: a diagram developed by the American archaeologist James Deetz. The columns at left and right give the inferred human meaning of the terms.

INDIVIDUALS   ATTRIBUTES   ARTIFACTS   Attribute patterning reflects individual behavior patterns

GROUPS   ARTIFACTS   SUBASSEMBLAGES   Artifact patterning reflects group behavior patterns

COMMUNITIES   SUBASSEMBLAGES   ASSEMBLAGES   Subassemblage patterning reflects community behavior patterns

SOCIETIES   ASSEMBLAGES   ARCHAEOLOGICAL CULTURES   Assemblage patterning reflects societal behavior patterns terminology into human terms and to relate an archaeological "culture" with an actual group of people in the past.

This brings us back to the purpose of classification. Types, assemblages, and cultures are all concepts designed to put order into disordered evidence—they are artificial. The trap that former generations of scholars fell into was to allow these concepts to determine the way they thought about the past, rather than using them merely as one means of giving shape to the evidence. We now recognize more clearly that different classifications are needed for the different kinds of questions we want to ask. A student of ceramic technology would base a classification on variations in raw material and methods of manufacture, whereas a scholar studying the various functions of pottery for storage, cooking, and so forth might classify the vessels according to shape and size. Our ability to construct and make good use of new classifications has been immeasurably enhanced by computers, which allow archaeologists to compare the association of different attributes of thousands of objects at once.

Post-excavation work in the laboratory or store does not cease with cleaning, labeling, and classification. Curation is also of immense importance, and the conservation of objects and materials plays a major role, not only for the arrangement of long-term storage but also for collections management in general. The material needs to be preserved and readily available for future research, reinterpretation and, in some cases, display to the public, whether permanently or in temporary exhibitions.

In conclusion, it cannot be stressed too strongly that all the effort put into survey, excavation, and post-excavation analysis will have been largely wasted unless the results are published.

Study Questions

1   What are the pros and cons of the unsystematic and systematic survey methods?
2   What types of archaeological sites can be identified through aerial photography?
3   What is a GIS and how can archaeologists use it?
4   How is archaeological excavation different from archaeological survey?
5   What are the benefits and drawbacks of the Wheeler box-grid method of excavation?
6   What are some of the ways in which artifacts can be classified?

Summary

THE ARCHAEOLOGIST has a barrage of ground and aerial survey techniques available with which to find new sites.

INDIVIDUAL SITES have traditionally been the main focus of archaeological attention, but today archaeologists study whole regions, often employing sampling techniques. Having located sites within those regions, and mapped them (usually using GIS), archaeologists can then turn to remote sensing site survey devices able to detect buried features without excavation.

REMOTE SENSING METHODS almost all involve measuring either energy that has been passed into the ground or the intensity of the Earth's magnetic field. In both cases, they depend on contrast between the buried features and their surroundings. The various techniques allow archaeologists to be more selective in deciding which parts of a site, if any, should be fully excavated.

EXCAVATION elucidates the horizontal extent of a site in space, as well as its vertical stratification, representing changes through time. Good recording methods are essential, together with a well-equipped field laboratory for processing and classifying finds. Classification based on selected attributes (decoration, shape, material) of each artifact is the fundamental means of organizing excavated material, usually into types—hence typology. But classification is only a means to an end, and different schemes are needed for the different questions archaeologists want to address.

MATERIAL RETRIEVED during survey and excavation will only be of use if it can be dated in some way. In the next chapter we turn to this crucial aspect of archaeology.

Further Reading

Useful introductions to methods of survey and excavation can be found in:

Collis, J. 2004. *Digging up the Past: An Introduction to Archaeological Excavation*. Sutton: Stroud.

Conyers, L. B. 2012. *Interpreting Ground-Penetrating Radar for Archaeology*. Left Coast Press: Walnut Creek, CA.

English Heritage 2008. *Geophysical Survey in Archaeological Field Evaluation* (2nd ed.). English Heritage: London.

Gaffney, V. & Gater, J. 2003. *Revealing the Buried Past: Geophysics for Archaeologists*. Tempus: Stroud.

Hester, T. N., Shafer, H. J., & Feder, K. L. 2008. *Field Methods in Archaeology* (7th ed.). Left Coast Press: Walnut Creek, CA.

Oswin, J. 2009. *A Field Guide to Geophysics in Archaeology*. Springer: Berlin.

Wheatley, D. & Gillings, M. 2002. *Spatial Technology and Archaeology: The Archaeological Applications of GIS*. Routledge: London.

Wiseman, J. R. & El-Baz, F. (eds). 2007. *Remote Sensing in Archaeology*. Springer: Berlin.

[See p. 345 for a list of useful websites]

4

When?
Dating Methods and Chronology

All human beings experience time. An individual experiences a lifetime of perhaps seventy years or so. That person, through the memories of his or her parents and grandparents, may also indirectly experience earlier periods of time, back over more than 100 years. The study of history gives us access to hundreds more years of recorded time. But it is only archaeology that opens up the almost unimaginable vistas of thousands and even a few millions of years of past human existence. This chapter will examine the various ways in which we, as archaeologists, date past events within this great expanse of time.

RELATIVE AND ABSOLUTE DATING. It might seem surprising that in order to study the past it is not always essential to know precisely how long ago (in years) a particular period or event occurred. It is often very helpful simply to know whether one event happened before or after another. By ordering artifacts, deposits, societies, and events into sequences, earlier before later, we can study developments in the past without knowing how long each stage lasted or how many years ago the changes took place. This idea that something is older (or younger) relative to something else is the basis of **relative dating**.

Ultimately, however, we want to know the full or absolute age in years before the present of different events or parts of a sequence—we need methods of **absolute dating**. Absolute dates help us find out how quickly such changes as the introduction of agriculture occurred, and whether they occurred simultaneously or at different times in different regions of the world. Only in the last sixty-five years or so have independent means of absolute dating become available, transforming archaeology in the process. Before then, virtually the only reliable absolute dates were historical ones, such as the date of the reign of the ancient Egyptian pharaoh Tutankhamun.

MEASURING TIME. How do we detect the passage of time? We can all observe its passing through the alternating darkness and light of nights and days, and then through the annual cycle of the seasons. In fact, for most of human history these were the only ways of measuring time, other than by the human lifespan. As we shall see, some dating methods still rely on the annual passage of the seasons. Increasingly, however, dating methods in archaeology have come to rely on other physical processes, many of them not observable to the human eye. The most significant of these is the use of radioactive clocks.

Some degree of error, usually expressed as an age bracket that can stretch over several centuries or even millennia, is inevitable when using any dating technique. But while the science behind dating methods is being ever more refined, the main source of errors remains the archaeologist— by poor choice of samples to be dated, by contaminating those samples, or by misinterpreting results.

DATING CONVENTIONS.   To be meaningful, our timescale in years must relate to a fixed point in time. In the Christian world, this is by convention taken as the birth of Christ, supposedly in the year AD 1 (there is no year 0), with years counted back before Christ (BC) and forward after Christ (AD or *Anno Domini*, which is Latin for "In the Year of Our Lord"). However, this is by no means the only system. In the Muslim world, for example, the basic fixed point is the date of the Prophet's departure from Mecca (AD 622 in the Christian calendar). As a result of these differences some scholars prefer to use the terms "Before the Common Era" (BCE) and "in the Common Era" (CE) instead of BC and AD, and that is the convention we follow in this book.

Scientists who derive dates from radioactive methods want a neutral international system, and have chosen to count years back from the present (BP). But since scientists too require a firm fixed point to count from, they take BP to mean "before 1950" (the approximate year of the establishment of the first radioactive method, radiocarbon). This may be convenient for scientists, but can be confusing for everyone else (a date of 400 BP is not 400 years ago but 1550 CE, currently more than 465 years ago). It is therefore clearest to convert any BP date for the last few thousand years into the BCE/CE system.

For the Paleolithic period, however (stretching back two or three million years before 10,000 BCE), archaeologists use the terms "BP" and "years ago" interchangeably, since a difference of fifty years or so between them is irrelevant. For this remote epoch we are dating sites or events at best only to within several thousand years of their true date. If even the most precise dates for the Paleolithic give us glimpses of that epoch only at intervals of several thousand years, clearly archaeologists can never hope to reconstruct a conventional history of Paleolithic events. On the other hand, Paleolithic archaeologists can gain insights into some of the broad long-term changes that shaped the way modern humans evolved—insights that are denied archaeologists working with shorter periods of time, where in any case there may be too much detail for the broader pattern to be apparent.

The way in which archaeologists carry out their research therefore depends very much on the precision of dating obtainable for the period of time in question. In what follows we deal first with relative dating, whereby principles of sequence—what comes before, what comes after—are established. That is what stratigraphy is all about. Then we deal with absolute dating, establishing dates in years. There radiocarbon dating and its calibration are crucial. Other methods of absolute dating are then briefly discussed.

RELATIVE DATING

The first, and in some ways the most important, step in much archaeological research involves ordering things into sequences. The things to be put into sequence can be archaeological deposits in a stratigraphic excavation, or they can be artifacts, as in a typological sequence. Changes in the Earth's climate also give rise to local, regional, and global environmental sequences—the most notable being the sequence of global fluctuations during the Ice Age. All these sequences can be used for relative dating.

Stratigraphy: Ordering Archaeological Layers

Stratigraphy, as we saw in Chapter 3, is the study of stratification—the laying down or depositing of strata or layers (also called deposits) one above the other. From the point of view of relative dating, the important principle is that the underlying layer was deposited first and therefore earlier than the overlying layer. A succession of layers provides a relative chronological sequence, from earliest (bottom) to latest (top).

Good stratigraphic excavation at an archaeological site is designed to obtain such a sequence. Part of this work involves detecting whether there has been any human or natural disturbance of the layers since they were originally deposited (such as garbage pits dug down by later occupants of a site into earlier layers, or animals burrowing holes). Armed with carefully observed stratigraphic information, the archaeologist can hope to construct a reliable relative chronological sequence for the deposition of the different layers.

But of course what we mostly want to date are not so much the layers or deposits themselves as the materials that humans have left within them—artifacts, structures, organic remains—that ultimately reveal past human activities at the site. Here the idea of association is important. When we say that two objects were found in association within the same archaeological deposit, we generally mean that they became buried at the same time. Provided that the deposit is a sealed one, without stratigraphic intrusions from another deposit, the associated objects can be said to be no more recent than the deposit itself. A sequence of sealed deposits thus gives a

Key Concepts
Relative Dating Methods

Stratigraphy: in a succession of layers the bottom layer is the earliest and the top layer the latest

Association: objects found in the same stratigraphic layer were buried at the same time

Typological Sequences: artifacts with similar characteristics were produced at the same time— "like goes with like"

Seriation: assemblages of objects can be arranged in serial order to create a relative chronology

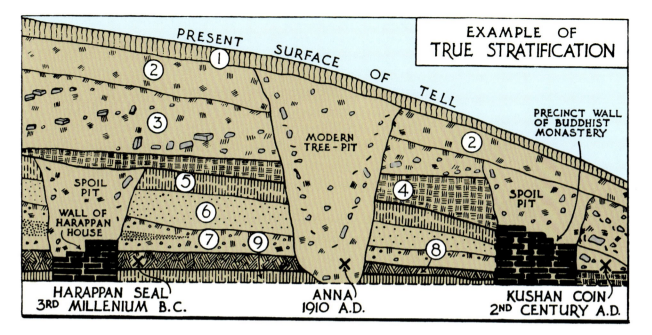

EXAMPLE OF
TRUE STRATIFICATION

PRESENT SURFACE OF TELL

① ② ③ ⑤ ⑥ ⑦ ⑨

SPOIL PIT

WALL OF HARAPPAN HOUSE

MODERN TREE-PIT

④ ⑧ ②

PRECINCT WALL OF BUDDHIST MONASTERY

SPOIL PIT

HARAPPAN SEAL
3RD MILLENIUM B.C.

ANNA
1910 A.D.

KUSHAN COIN
2ND CENTURY A.D.

Stratigraphy in action: a section across a mound or tell in the Indus Valley. Attention to stratigraphy is crucial because, as with the coins and the seal here, not everything found at the same level is always equally old.

sequence—and relative chronology—for the time of burial of the objects found associated in those deposits.

This is a crucial concept to grasp, because if one of those objects can later be given an absolute date—say a datable coin or a piece of charcoal that can be dated by radiocarbon in the laboratory—then it is possible to assign that absolute date not only to the charcoal but to the sealed deposit and the other objects associated with it as well. A series of such dates from different deposits will give an absolute chronology for the whole sequence. It is this interconnecting of stratigraphic sequences with absolute dating methods that provides the most reliable basis for dating archaeological sites and their contents. The example shown above is Sir Mortimer Wheeler's drawing of a section across an ancient mound in the Indus Valley (modern Pakistan). The site has been disturbed by more recent pits, but the sequence of layers is still visible, and the Harappan seal, of known age and found in an undisturbed context in layer 8, helps to date that layer and the wall next to it.

But there is another important point to consider. So far we have dated, relatively and, with luck, absolutely, the time of burial of the deposits and their associated material. As we have observed, however, what we want ultimately to reconstruct and date are the past human activities and behavior that those deposits and materials represent. If a deposit is a garbage pit with pottery in it, the deposit itself is of interest as an example of human activity, and the date for it is the date of human use of the pit. This will also be the date of final burial of the pottery—but it will *not* be the date of human use of that pottery, which could have been in circulation tens or hundreds of years

Gradual changes in design are evident in the history of the automobile and of the prehistoric European axe—(1) stone; (2–5) bronze.

earlier, before being discarded with other garbage in the pit. It is necessary therefore always to be clear about which activity we are trying to date, or can reliably date in the circumstances.

Typological Sequences: Comparing Objects

When we look at the artifacts, buildings, or any of the human creations around us, most of us can mentally arrange them into a rough chronological sequence. One kind of aircraft looks older than another, one set of clothes looks more old-fashioned than the next. How do archaeologists exploit this ability for relative dating?

Archaeologists define the form of such an artifact as a pot by its specific attributes of material, shape, and decoration. Several pots with the same attributes constitute a pot type, and typology groups artifacts into such types. Underlying the notion of relative dating through typology are two other ideas.

The first is that the products of a given period and place have a recognizable style: through their distinctive shape and decoration they are in some sense characteristic of the society that produced them. The archaeologist or anthropologist can often recognize and classify individual artifacts by their style, and hence assign them to a particular place in a typological sequence.

The second idea is that the change in style (shape and decoration) of artifacts is often quite gradual, or evolutionary. This idea came from the Darwinian theory of the evolution of species, and was used by nineteenth-century archaeologists who applied a very convenient rule, that "like goes with like." In other words, particular artifacts (e.g. bronze daggers) produced at about the same time are often alike, but those produced several centuries apart will be different as a result of centuries of change. It follows, then, that when studying a series of daggers of unknown date, it is logical first to arrange them in a sequence in such a way that the most closely similar are located beside each other. This is then likely to be the true chronological sequence, because it best reflects the principle that "like goes with like." In the diagram to the left, designs of automobiles and prehistoric European axes have been arranged in a relative chronological sequence; however, the rate of change (a century for the automobile, millennia for the axe) has to be deduced from absolute dating methods.

For many purposes, the best way to assign a relative date to an artifact is to match it with an artifact already recognized within a well-established typological system. Pottery typologies usually form the backbone of the chronological system, and nearly every area has its own well-established ceramic sequence. One example is the very extensive ceramic sequence for the ancient societies of the American Southwest, a part of which is shown in the diagram opposite. If such a typology is tied into a stratigraphic sequence of deposits that can be dated by radiocarbon or other absolute means, then

PHASE	DECORATION	SHAPE
SACATON 1000–1175 CE		
SANTA CRUZ 875–1000 CE		
GILA BUTTE 800–875 CE		
SNAKETOWN 750–800 CE		
SWEETWATER 700–750 CE		
ESTRELLA 650–700 CE		

Pottery typology, as exemplified by this 500-year sequence of Hohokam bowl styles from the American Southwest.

the artifacts in the typological sequence can themselves be assigned absolute dates in years.

Different types of artifact change in style (decoration and shape) at different rates, and therefore vary in the chronological distinctions that they indicate. Usually, with pottery, surface decoration changes most rapidly (often over periods of just a few decades) and is therefore the best attribute to use for a typological sequence. On the other hand, the shape of a vessel or container may be most strongly influenced by a practical requirement, such as water storage, which need not alter for hundreds of years.

Other artifacts, such as metal weapons or tools, can change in style quite rapidly, and so may be useful chronological indicators. By contrast, stone tools, such as **hand-axes**, are often very slow to change in form and therefore rarely make useful indicators of the passage of time (and are more useful in making general distinctions between much longer periods).

Seriation: Comparing Assemblages of Objects

The insights of the principle that "like goes with like" have been developed further to deal with associations of finds (assemblages) rather than with the forms of single objects taken in isolation. The technique of **seriation** allows assemblages of artifacts to be arranged in a succession or serial order, which is then taken to indicate their ordering in time, or their relative chronology.

The great pioneer of Egyptian archaeology, Sir William Flinders Petrie, was one of the first to develop a technique for arranging the graves of a cemetery in relative order by considering carefully and systematically the associations of the various pottery forms found within them. His lead in the late nineteenth century was taken up half a century later by American scholars who realized that the frequency of a particular ceramic style, as documented in the successive layers of a settlement, is usually small to start with, rises to a peak as the style gains popularity, and then declines again (which diagrammatically produces a shape like a battleship viewed from above, known as a battleship curve). Using this insight they were able to compare the pottery assemblages from different sites in the same area, each with a limited stratigraphic sequence,

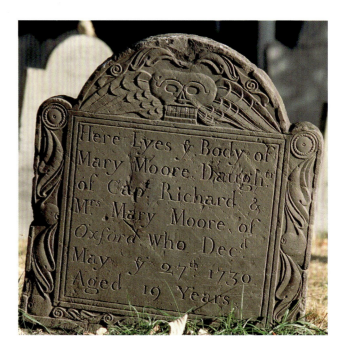

	Death's Head	Cherub	Urn and Willow

1860–69			
1850–59			■■■■■
1840–49			■■■■■
1830–39		■	■■■■
1820–29		■	■■■■
1810–19	■	■	■■■
1800–09		■	■■■
1790–99	■■	■■	■■
1780–89	■■	■■■	■
1770–79	■■■	■■■	
1760–69	■■	■■■■	
1750–59	■■■	■■■	
1740–49	■■■■	■■	
1730–39	■■■■■		
1720–29	■■■■■		
1710–19	■■■■■		
1700–09	■■■	■	

■ = 10 percent of the stones in a 10-year period

(Above left) Seriation: changes in the popularity of central Connecticut tombstone designs.

(Above right) The death's head design.

and arrange these sites into chronological order so that the ceramic frequencies would conform to the pattern of rising to a maximum and then declining.

The diagram above shows how this technique has been applied to changes in the popularity of three tombstone designs found in central Connecticut cemeteries dating from 1700 to 1860. The fluctuating fortunes of each design produce characteristic and successive battleship curves—as elsewhere in New England, the death's head design (peak popularity 1710–1739) was gradually replaced by the cherub (peak 1760–1789), which in turn was replaced by the urn and willow tree (peak 1840–1859).

Seriation has been used in an archaeological context by the American archaeologist Frank Hole in his excavations on the Deh Luran Plain in Iran. The Neolithic ceramic assemblages he was studying were derived from stratigraphic excavations, so it was possible to compare the sequences obtained through **frequency seriation** with the true stratigraphic sequences discovered in their excavations. There were no serious contradictions, again proving the validity of the method.

Environmental Sequences

So far in this chapter we have been discussing sequences that can be established either stratigraphically for individual sites, or typologically for artifacts. In addition, there is a major class of sequences, based on changes in the Earth's climate, that has proved useful for relative dating on a local, regional, and even global scale. Some of these environmental sequences can also be dated by various absolute methods.

The Ice Age (or Pleistocene epoch, dating from 2.6 million years ago to 11,700 years ago), when world temperatures were usually much lower and ice covered large parts of the Earth's surface, was not one long unbroken spell of cold. A complex sequence of cold periods (called glacials) were separated by warmer interludes (called interglacials). The interglacial period we now live in, known as the Holocene, covers the last 11,700 years. These climatic fluctuations are recorded in **deep-sea cores**, **ice cores**, and sediments containing pollen.

DEEP-SEA CORES AND ICE CORES.   The most coherent record of climatic changes on a worldwide scale is provided by deep-sea cores. These contain shells of microscopic marine organisms known as foraminifera, laid down on the ocean floor through the slow continuous process of sedimentation. Variations in the chemical structure of these shells are a good indicator of the sea temperature at the time the organisms were alive. Cold episodes in the deep-sea cores relate to glacial periods of ice advance, and the warm episodes to interglacial periods of ice retreat. Radiocarbon and **uranium-series dating** (see pp. 123–30) can also be applied to the foraminiferan shells to provide absolute dates for the sequence, which now stretches back 2.3 million years.

As with deep-sea cores, cores extracted from the polar ice of the Arctic and Antarctic have yielded impressive sequences revealing past climatic changes. The layers of compacted ice represent annual deposits for the last 2000–3000 years that can be counted—thus giving an absolute chronology for this part of the sequence. For earlier time periods—at greater depths—the annual stratification is no longer visible, and dating of the ice cores is much less certain. Good correlations have been made with climatic variations deduced from the study of the deep-sea cores.

Evidence of major volcanic eruptions can also be preserved in the ice cores, theoretically meaning that particular eruptions, such as the huge Thera eruption in the Aegean roughly 3500 years ago (associated by some scholars with the destruction of Minoan palaces on Crete), can be given a precise absolute date. In practice, though, it is hard to be certain that a volcanic event preserved in the ice actually relates to a particular historically documented eruption—it could relate to an unknown eruption that happened somewhere else in the world.

POLLEN DATING.   All flowering plants produce grains called pollen, and these are almost indestructible, surviving for many thousands (and even millions) of years in all types of conditions. The preservation of pollen in bogs and lake

Foraminifera. These tiny (up to 1 mm-long) shells form the deep-sea sediments of the ocean floor. Analysis of shells in successive sediment layers gives a record of world sea temperature change.

sediments has allowed pollen experts (palynologists) to construct detailed sequences of past vegetation and climate. These sequences are an immense help in understanding ancient environments, but they have also been—and to some extent still are—important as a method of relative dating.

The best-known pollen sequences are those developed for the Holocene of northern Europe, where an elaborate succession of so-called pollen zones covers the last 10,000 years. By studying pollen samples from a particular site, that site can often be fitted into a broader pollen zone sequence and thus assigned a relative date. Isolated artifacts and such finds as bog bodies discovered in contexts where pollen is preserved can also be dated in the same way. It is important to remember, however, that the pollen zones are not uniform across large areas. Regional pollen zone sequences must first be established, and then the sites and finds in the area can be linked to them. If tree-ring or radiocarbon dates are available for all or part of the sequence, we can work out an absolute chronology for the region.

Thanks to the durability of pollen grains, they can yield environmental evidence even as far back as 3 million years ago for sites in East Africa. Different interglacial periods in such areas as northern Europe have also been shown to have characteristic pollen sequences, which means that the pollen evidence at an individual site in the area can sometimes be matched to a particular interglacial—a useful dating mechanism since radiocarbon cannot be used for these early time periods.

ABSOLUTE DATING

Although relative dating methods can be extremely useful, archaeologists ultimately want to know how old sequences, sites, and artifacts are in calendar years. To achieve this they need to use the methods of absolute dating described in the following sections. The three most commonly used and most important to the archaeologist are calendars and historical chronologies, **tree-ring dating**, and radiocarbon dating. For the Paleolithic period, **potassium-argon dating** and uranium-series dating are vital. Genetic dating is also now beginning to be used to date population events.

Calendars and Historical Chronologies

Until the development of the first scientific dating techniques around the beginning of the twentieth century, dating in archaeology depended almost entirely on historical methods. That is to say, it relied on archaeological connections with chronologies and calendars that people in ancient times had themselves established. Such dating methods are still of immense value today. In the ancient world, literate societies recorded their own history in written documents. In Egypt, the Near East, and ancient China, for example, history was recorded in terms of the successive kings, who were organized in groups of dynasties. As we shall see, there were also very precise calendrical systems in Mesoamerica.

Archaeologists have to bear in mind three main points when working with early historical chronologies. First, the chronological system requires careful reconstruction, and any list of rulers or kings needs to be reasonably complete. Second, the list, although it may reliably record the number of years in each reign, has still to be linked with our own calendar. Third, the artifacts, features, or structures to be dated at a particular site have somehow to be related to the historical chronology, for example by their association with an inscription referring to the ruler of the time.

These points can be well illustrated by the Egyptian and Maya chronologies. Egyptian history is arranged in terms of thirty-one dynasties, themselves organized into the Old, Middle, and New Kingdoms. The modern view is a synthesis based on several documents including the so-called Turin Royal Canon. This synthesis gives an estimate of the number of years in each reign, right down to the conquest of Egypt by Alexander the Great in the year 332 BCE

Chronological table summarizing the spans of time for which different absolute dating methods are applicable.

A Maya Long Count date in a tomb at the city of Río Azul, Guatemala. In modern terms the date given equates to September 27, 417 CE.

(a date recorded by Greek historians). So the Egyptian dynasties can be dated by working backward from there, although the exact length of every reign is not known. This system can be confirmed and refined using astronomy: Egyptian historical records describe observations of certain astronomical events that can be independently dated using current astronomical knowledge and knowledge of where in Egypt the ancient observations were carried out. Egyptian dates are generally considered to be quite reliable after about 1500 BCE, with a margin of error of perhaps one or two decades at most, but by the time we go back to the beginning of the dynastic period, around 3100 BCE, the accumulated errors might amount to some 200 years or so.

Of the calendrical systems of Mesoamerica, the Maya calendar was the most elaborate and precise. It was used for recording exact dates of historical (and mythical) events in inscriptions on stone columns or **stelae** erected at Maya sites during the so-called Classic period (300–900 CE). The Maya had glyphs or signs for the days and the months, and a straightforward system of numerals, with a stylized shell representing zero, a dot "one," and a bar "five." The Maya actually had two concurrent calendrical systems, the first of which, the Calendar Round, was used for everyday purposes. Any day in the Calendar Round was identified by the conjunction of two different cycles: a Sacred Round of 260 named days, and a solar year of 365 named days. A specific day would only recur once every fifty-two years.

The second system, the Long Count, recorded days past since a mythical zero or starting point—August 13 3113 BCE in terms of our own calendar—and was used to refer to historical (or future) dates. The understanding of the Maya calendar, and the more recent decipherment of the Maya glyphs, mean that a well-dated Maya history is now emerging in a way that seemed impossible a few decades ago.

Using a Historical Chronology

It is relatively easy for the archaeologist to use a historical chronology when abundant artifacts are found that can be related closely to it. Thus, at major Maya sites, such as Tikal or Copan, there are numerous stelae with calendrical inscriptions that can often be used to date the buildings with which they are associated. The artifacts associated with the buildings can in turn be dated: for instance, if a pottery typology has been worked out, the finding of known types of pottery in such historically dated contexts allows the pottery typology itself to be dated. Contexts and buildings on other sites lacking inscriptions can be dated approximately through the occurrence of similar pot types.

Sometimes artifacts themselves carry dates, or the names of rulers that can be dated. This is the case with many Maya ceramics that bear hieroglyphic inscriptions. For the Roman and medieval periods of Europe, coins normally carry the name of the issuing ruler, and inscriptions or records elsewhere usually allow the ruler to be dated. But it is crucial to remember that to date a coin or an artifact is not the same thing as to date the context in which it is found. The date of the coin indicates the year in which it was made. Its inclusion within a sealed archaeological deposit establishes simply a *terminus post quem* (Latin for "date after which"): in other words, the deposit can be no earlier than the date on the coin—but it could be later (perhaps much later) than that date.

A well-established historical chronology in one country may be used to date events in neighboring and more far-flung lands that lack their own historical records but are mentioned in the histories of the literate society. Similarly, archaeologists can use exports and imports of objects to extend chronological linkages by means of cross-dating with other regions. For instance, the presence of foreign pottery in well-dated ancient Egyptian contexts establishes a *terminus ante quem* ("date before which") for the manufacture of that pottery: it cannot be more recent than the Egyptian context. In addition, Egyptian objects, some with inscriptions allowing them to be accurately dated in Egyptian terms, occur at various sites outside Egypt, thereby helping to date the contexts in which they are found.

Dating by historical methods remains the most important procedure for the archaeologist in countries with a reliable calendar supported by a significant degree of literacy. Where there are serious uncertainties over the calendar, or over its correlation with the modern calendrical system, the correlations can often be checked using other absolute dating methods, to be described below.

Outside the historic and literate lands, however, cross-dating and broad typological comparisons have been almost entirely superseded by the various scientifically based dating methods described below. Now, all the world's cultures can be assigned absolute dates.

Annual Cycles

Any absolute dating method depends on the existence of a regular, time-dependent process. The most obvious of these is the system by which we order our modern calendar: the rotation of the Earth around the sun once each year. Because this yearly cycle produces regular annual fluctuations in climate, it has an impact on features of the environment that can in certain cases be measured to create a chronology. For absolute dating purposes the sequence needs to be a long one (with no gaps), linked somehow to the present day, and capable of being related to the structures or artifacts we actually want to date.

Evidence of these annual fluctuations in climate is widespread. For example, the changes in temperature in polar regions result in annual variations in the thickness of polar ice, which scientists can study from cores drilled through the ice (see p. 115). Similarly, in lands bordering the polar regions, the melting of the ice sheets each year when temperatures rise leads to the formation of annual deposits of sediment in lake beds, called **varves**, which can be counted. Considerable deposits of varves were found in Scandinavia, representing thousands of years, stretching (when linked together) from the present back to the beginning of the retreat of the glacial ice sheets in that region some 13,000 years ago. The method allowed, for the first time, a fairly reliable estimate for the date of the end of the last Ice Age, and hence made a contribution to archaeological chronology not only in Scandinavia but also in many other parts of the world.

But today, while varves remain of restricted use, another annual cycle, that of tree-rings, has come to rival radiocarbon as the main method of dating for the last few thousand years in many parts of Europe, North America, and Japan.

Tree-ring Dating

The modern technique of tree-ring dating (**dendrochronology**) was developed by an American astronomer, A.E. Douglass, in the early decades of the last century—although many of the principles had been understood long before that. Working on well-preserved timbers in the arid American Southwest, by 1930 Douglass could assign absolute dates to many of the major sites there, such as Mesa Verde and Pueblo Bonito. But it was not until the end of the 1930s that the technique was introduced to Europe, and only in the 1960s that the use of statistical procedures and computers laid the foundations for the establishment of the long tree-ring chronologies now so fundamental to modern archaeology. Today dendrochronology has two distinct archaeological uses: (1) as a successful means of calibrating or correcting radiocarbon dates (see below, pp. 125–28); and (2) as an independent method of absolute dating in its own right.

BASIS OF METHOD.   Most trees produce a ring of new wood each year, and these circles of growth can easily be seen in a cross-section of the trunk of a felled tree. These rings are not of uniform thickness. In an individual tree, they will vary for two reasons. First, the rings become narrower with the increasing age of the tree. Second, the amount a tree grows each year is affected by fluctuations in climate. In arid regions, rainfall above the average one year will produce a particularly thick annual ring. In more temperate regions, sunlight and temperature may be more critical than rainfall in affecting a tree's growth. Here, a sharp cold spell in spring may produce a narrow growth ring.

Dendrochronologists measure and plot these rings and produce a diagram indicating the thickness of successive rings in an individual tree. Trees of the same species growing in the same area will generally show the same pattern of rings so that the growth sequence can be matched between successively older

Section of an oak beam from the wall of a log cabin in Hanover, Pennsylvania: the annual growth rings are clearly visible, and since this sample contains complete sapwood (top of image), a precise felling date of 1850/1 can be established.

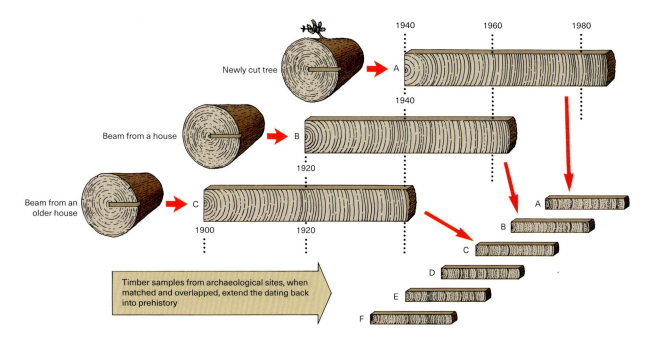

Tree-ring dating: annual growth rings can be counted, matched, and overlapped, to build up a master sequence for a particular region.

timbers to build up a chronology for an area. (It is not necessary to fell trees in order to study the ring sequence: a usable sample can be extracted by boring without harming the tree.) By matching sequences of rings from living trees of different ages as well as from old timber, dendrochronologists can produce a long, continuous sequence, such as that in the diagram above, extending back hundreds, even thousands, of years from the present. Thus, when an ancient timber of the same species (e.g. Douglas fir in the American Southwest or oak in Europe) is found, it should be possible to match its tree-ring sequence of, say, 100 years with the appropriate 100-year length of the master sequence or chronology. In this way, the felling date for that piece of timber can usually be dated to within a year.

APPLICATIONS.   One of the most important uses of tree-ring dating has been the development of long tree-ring sequences, against which it is possible to check radiocarbon dates. The pioneering research was done in Arizona on a remarkable species, the Californian bristlecone pine, which can live up to 4900 years. By matching samples from dead trees also, an unbroken sequence was built up back from the present as far as 6700 BCE. The importance of this for the calibration of radiocarbon dates is discussed below. The research in the American Southwest has been complemented by studies in Europe of tree-rings of oak, often well preserved in waterlogged deposits. The oak sequence in Northern Ireland stretches back unbroken to c. 5300 BCE, and the master sequence in western Germany to c. 8500 BCE.

Direct tree-ring dating of preserved timber found in archaeological contexts has itself been important in several areas, but results are particularly impressive in the American Southwest, where the technique is longest established and wood is well preserved in the arid conditions. For instance, Betatakin, a cliff dwelling in Arizona, has been precision dated using dendrochronology so that not only do we know that the settlement was founded in 1267 CE, but we also can track the expansion of the site room by room, year by year, until it reached a peak in the mid-1280s, before being abandoned shortly thereafter.

LIMITING FACTORS.   Unlike radiocarbon, dendrochronology is not a worldwide dating method because of two basic limitations:

1 it applies only to trees in regions outside the tropics where pronounced differences between the seasons produce clearly defined annual rings; and
2 a direct tree-ring date is restricted to wood from those species that (a) have yielded a master sequence back from the present; (b) people actually used in the past; and where (c) the sample affords a sufficiently long record to give a unique match.

In addition, there are important questions of interpretation to consider. A tree-ring date refers to the date of felling of the tree. This is determined by matching the tree-ring sample ending with the outermost rings (the sapwood) to a regional sequence. Where most or all of the sapwood is missing, the felling date cannot be identified. But even with an accurate felling date, the archaeologist has to make a judgment—based on context as well as formation processes—about how soon after felling the timber entered the archaeological deposit. Timbers may be older or younger than the structures into which they were finally incorporated, depending on whether they were reused from somewhere else, or used to make a repair in a long-established structure. The best solution is to take multiple samples, and to check the evidence carefully on-site. Despite these qualifications, dendrochronology looks set to become the major dating technique, alongside radiocarbon, for the last 8000 years in temperate and arid lands.

Radioactive Clocks

Many of the most important developments in absolute dating have come from the use of what might be called radioactive clocks, based on a widespread and regular feature in the natural world, **radioactive decay**. The best known of these methods is radiocarbon, today the main dating tool for the last 50,000 years or so.

Radiocarbon Dating

Radiocarbon is the single most useful method of dating for the archaeologist. As we shall see, it has its limitations, both in terms of accuracy, and for the time range where it is useful. Archaeologists themselves are also the cause of major errors, thanks to poor sampling procedures and careless interpretation. Nevertheless, radiocarbon has transformed our understanding of the past, helping archaeologists to establish for the first time a reliable chronology of world cultures.

HISTORY AND BASIS OF METHOD. In 1949, the American chemist Willard Libby published the first radiocarbon dates. During World War II he had been studying cosmic radiation, the sub-atomic particles that constantly bombard the Earth. These produce high-energy neutrons, which in turn react with nitrogen atoms in the atmosphere to produce atoms of carbon-14 (^{14}C), or radiocarbon, which are unstable because they have eight neutrons in the nucleus instead of the usual six as for ordinary carbon (see box overleaf). This instability leads to radioactive decay of ^{14}C at a regular rate. Libby estimated that it took 5568 years for half the ^{14}C in any sample to decay—its **half-life** (see diagram below)—although modern research indicates that the more accurate figure is 5730 years.

Libby realized that the decay of radiocarbon at a constant rate should be balanced by its constant production through cosmic radiation, and that therefore the proportion of ^{14}C in the atmosphere should remain the same

(Below left) Radiocarbon is produced in the atmosphere and absorbed by plants through carbon dioxide, and by animals through feeding off plants or other animals. Uptake of ^{14}C ceases when the plant or animal dies.

(Below right) After death, the amount of ^{14}C decays at a known rate (50 percent after 5730 years, etc.). Measurement of the amount left in a sample gives the date.

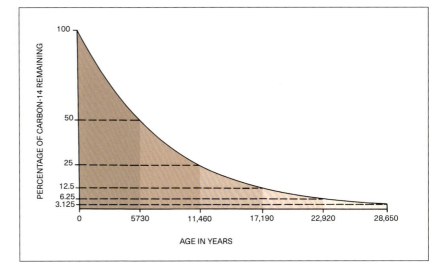

The Principles of
Radioactive Decay

Like most elements occurring in nature, carbon exists in more than one isotopic form. It has three isotopes: ^{12}C, ^{13}C, and ^{14}C—the numbers correspond to the atomic masses of these isotopes. In any sample of carbon, 98.9 percent of atoms are of ^{12}C type and have six protons and six neutrons in the nucleus, and 1.1 percent are of the ^{13}C type with six protons and seven neutrons. Only one atom in a million millions of atoms of carbon will be that of the isotope ^{14}C, with eight neutrons in the nucleus. This isotope of carbon is produced in the upper atmosphere by cosmic rays bombarding nitrogen (^{14}N) and it contains an excess of neutrons, making it unstable. It decays by the emission of weak beta radiation back to its precursor isotope of nitrogen—^{14}N—with seven protons and seven neutrons in a nucleus. Like all types of radioactive decay the process takes place at a constant rate, independent of all environmental conditions.

The time taken for half of the atoms of a radioactive isotope to decay is called its half-life. In other words, after one half-life, there will be half of the atoms left; after two half-lives, one-quarter of the original quantity of the isotope remains, and so on. In the case of ^{14}C, the half-life is now agreed to be 5730 years.

Half-lives of radioactive isotopes of other elements can range from thousands of millions of years to a minute fraction of a second. But in every case, there is a regular pattern to the decay.

Carbon-12 atom   Carbon-14 atom

● Neutron

● Proton

throughout time. Furthermore, this steady atmospheric concentration of radiocarbon is passed on uniformly to all living things through carbon dioxide, as part of what is known as the carbon cycle. Plants take up carbon dioxide during photosynthesis, they are eaten by herbivorous animals, which in turn are eaten by carnivores. When a plant or animal dies the uptake of ^{14}C ceases, and the steady concentration of ^{14}C begins to decline through radioactive decay. Thus, knowing the decay rate or half-life of ^{14}C, Libby recognized that the age of dead plant or animal tissue could be calculated by measuring the amount of radiocarbon left in a sample. Samples usually consist of organic materials found on archaeological sites, such as charcoal, wood, seeds, and other plant remains, and human or animal bone. Inorganic materials, for example stone, are not part of the carbon cycle and so cannot be radiocarbon dated.

Libby's great practical achievement was to devise an accurate means of measurement. He discovered that each atom of ^{14}C decays by releasing a beta particle, and he succeeded in counting these emissions using a Geiger counter, still the basis of the conventional method employed by many radiocarbon laboratories today. Advances were made in the late 1970s and early 1980s with the introduction of special gas counters capable of taking measurements from very small samples.

In the conventional method some 5 g of pure carbon after purification was needed, which means an original sample of some 10–20 g of wood or charcoal, or 100–200 g of bone. The special gas-counting equipment required only a few hundred milligrams (mg) of charcoal.

Increasingly, the accelerator mass spectrometry (AMS) method is becoming the dominant technique used in radiocarbon dating. This requires smaller samples still. Disregarding their radioactivity, AMS counts the atoms of ^{14}C directly. The minimum sample size is reduced to as little as 5–10 mg—thus enabling precious organic materials, such as the Turin Shroud (see p. 129), to be sampled and directly dated, and making feasible the direct dating of pollen. Initially it was hoped that the datable timespan for radiocarbon using AMS could be pushed back from 50,000 to 80,000 years, although this is proving difficult to achieve, in part because of sample contamination.

Radiocarbon dates are usually quoted in years BP (before the present, currently taken to be 1950 CE), but because the accurate measurement of the ^{14}C activity of a sample is affected by counting errors, background cosmic radiation, and other intrinsic factors, there is always an element of uncertainty to the measurements. Thus there is always a statistical error or standard deviation attached to a radiocarbon date, expressed as a plus/minus term. Radiocarbon dates are quoted with an error of one standard deviation. For a date of 3700 ±100 BP, for example, this means that there is a 68.2 percent probability, or roughly two chances in three, that the correct estimate in radiocarbon years lies between 3800 and 3600 BP (of course this also means that there is a one in three chance that it doesn't). Double to two standard deviations, and there is a 95.4 percent chance (nineteen chances in twenty) that the radiocarbon age of the sample lies between 3900 and 3500 BP, or in other words 3700 ±200 BP.

But there is a complication: these dates still do not, unfortunately, equate with true calendar years. To convert radiocarbon years into calendar years requires calibration.

CALIBRATION OF RADIOCARBON DATES. One of the basic assumptions of the radiocarbon method has turned out to be not quite correct. Libby assumed that the concentration of ^{14}C in the atmosphere has been constant through time, but we now know that it has varied. The method that demonstrated the inaccuracy—tree-ring dating—has also provided the means of correcting or calibrating radiocarbon dates.

Radiocarbon dates obtained from tree-rings show that before about 1000 BCE dates expressed in radiocarbon years are increasingly too young in relation to true calendar years. In other words, before 1000 BCE trees (and all other living things) were exposed to greater concentrations of atmospheric ^{14}C than they are today. By obtaining radiocarbon dates systematically from the long

Key Concepts
Radiocarbon Dating

Method: based on the regular decay of a radioactive isotope of carbon

Range: 400–50,000 years ago (AMS)

Precision: many complicating factors, but often to within *c.* 50–100 years

Applications: dating of any organic matter (containing carbon); new techniques allow very small sample sizes, meaning grain, seeds, and precious objects can be dated

Calibration: radiocarbon dates must be calibrated to arrive at a calendar date

Limitations: samples must be carefully chosen; samples can easily be contaminated; results can be difficult to interpret correctly and require statistical treatment

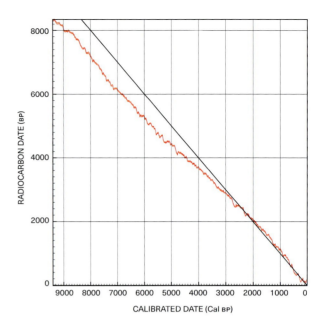

The wiggles of the INTCAL09 calibration curve over the last 9000 years. The straight line indicates the ideal 1:1 timescale.

tree-ring master sequences of bristlecone pine and oak (see above, p. 121), scientists have been able to plot radiocarbon ages against tree-ring ages (in calendar years) to produce calibration curves, such as that illustrated above. Broadly, these curves show that radiocarbon ages diverge increasingly from true ages before 1000 BCE, so that by 5000 BCE in calendar years the radiocarbon age is 900 years too young. Thus an age estimate in radiocarbon years of 6050 BP might well in fact when calibrated be somewhere near 5000 BCE. For dates beyond 12,600 years ago, the current scope of tree-ring dating, scientists have been able to use data from uranium-thorium dated corals and varve-counted marine sediments to produce a calibration curve going back some 50,000 years. The box opposite gives a more detailed explanation of the calibration process.

CONTAMINATION AND INTERPRETATION OF RADIOCARBON SAMPLES.
Although radiocarbon dates have certain inescapable levels of error associated with them, inaccurate results are as likely to derive from poor sampling and incorrect interpretation by the archaeologist as from inadequate laboratory procedures. The major sources of error in the field are summed up below:

- *Contamination before sampling.* Problems of contamination of the sample within the ground can be serious. For instance, groundwater on waterlogged sites can dissolve organic materials and also deposit them, thus changing the amount of ^{14}C in a sample. These matters can usually be tackled in the laboratory.

How to Calibrate Radiocarbon Dates

Radiocarbon laboratories will generally supply calibrated dates of their samples, but archaeologists may need to calibrate raw radiocarbon dates themselves.

The calibration curve, part of which is illustrated opposite, shows the relationship between radiocarbon years (BP) and samples dated in actual calendar years (Calibrated or "Cal" BP or BCE/CE). In order to find the calibrated age range of a radiocarbon sample, a computer program is most often used. There are several that are freely available on the Internet (OxCal, BCal, CALIB, etc.). With OxCal (http://c14.arch.ox.ac.uk/oxcal) a simple plot is generated of a single calibrated result, such as in the diagram below. In this example one can see the radiocarbon date of 470 ±35 BP is represented in the form of a probability distribution on the y-axis. This distribution is transformed, using the calibration curve, into a probability distribution on the x-axis, representing calendar years. The calibrated date at one standard deviation is thus 530–503 Cal BP, or 1420–1447 Cal CE. The parts of the radiocarbon distribution that have higher levels of probability also have a higher probability on the calendar scale.

The calibration curve is full of steep and sometimes wiggly sections, including sections with plateaux where the amount of radiocarbon in the atmosphere remains the same over long periods of time. Here the calibration precision is always wide (the problem is particularly irksome for dating in the period 800–400 BCE). Even dating single samples at high levels of precision (some laboratories are able to produce dates with a ± of 15–20 years), or dating multiple samples (which can then be averaged), cannot substantially improve the situation.

This diagram shows the calibration of a single radiocarbon date using OxCal. The y-axis shows the probability distribution of the radiocarbon age 470 ±35 BP (in pink). The measured age is calibrated using the INTCAL09 calibration curve (in blue), forming the new probability distribution (in gray), which is the calibrated age. Age ranges at 68.2 and 95.4 percent probability are given.

OxCal v4.1.7 Bronk Ramsey (2010); r:5; Atmospheric data from Reimer et al. (2009)

OxA-124512 (470 ± 35 BP)

68.2% probability
  (68.2%) 530–503 Cal BP
95.4% probability
  (95.4%) 546–478 Cal BP

- *Contamination during or after sampling.* Any modern organic material coming into contact with a sample can contaminate it, but some, such as roots and earth, cannot always be prevented. Such sources of contamination, however, can be eliminated in the laboratory.
- *Context of deposition.* Many errors arise because the excavator has not fully understood the formation processes of the context in question. Unless it is appreciated how the dated material found its way to its find spot, and how and when it came to be buried, then precise interpretation is impossible.
- *Date of context.* Too often, it is assumed that a radiocarbon determination, e.g. on charcoal, will simply date the charcoal's burial. If that charcoal derives from roof timbers that might themselves have been several centuries old when destroyed by fire, however, then some early construction is being dated, not the fire. For this reason, samples with a short life are often preferred, such as twigs or charred cereal grains, which are not likely to be old at the time of burial.

A strategy for sampling should be based on the wise saying that "one date is no date": several are needed. The best procedure is to work toward an internal relative sequence of dates—for instance, in the stratigraphic succession on a well-stratified site, such as Gatecliff Shelter, Monitor Valley, Nevada, shown left. If the samples can be arranged in relative sequence in this way, with the lowest unit having the earliest date and so on, then there is an internal check on the coherence of the laboratory determinations and on the quality of field sampling. Some of the dates from such a sequence may come out older than expected. This is quite reasonable as some of the material may have been old at the time of burial. But if they come out younger (i.e. more recent) than expected, then there is something wrong. Either some contamination has affected the samples, or the laboratory has made a serious error, or the stratigraphic interpretation is wrong.

Master profile for Gatecliff Shelter, Nevada, showing how dates derived from radiocarbon determinations are consistent with the stratigraphic succession.

Natural Strata

1300 CE

700 CE

1250 BCE

1300 BCE

1400 BCE

2100–1450 BCE
2300–2150 BCE
3050–2300 BCE
3150–3050 BCE

3300–3150 BCE

3400–3300 BCE
3550–3400 BCE

THE IMPACT OF RADIOCARBON DATING. Radiocarbon has undoubtedly offered the most generally useful way of answering the question "When?" in archaeology. The greatest advantage is that the method can be used anywhere, whatever the climate, as long as there is material of organic (i.e. living) origin. Thus the method works as well in South America or Polynesia as it does in Egypt or Mesopotamia. And it can take us back 50,000 years—although at the other end of the timescale it is too imprecise to be of much use for the 400 years of the most recent past. Radiocarbon has been incredibly important in establishing for the first time broad chronologies for the world's cultures that previously lacked timescales (such as calendars) of their own. Calibration of radiocarbon has increased, not diminished, this success.

Radiocarbon dating by the AMS technique is opening up new possibilities. Precious objects and works of art can now be dated because minute samples are all that is required. In 1988 AMS dating was used on the Turin Shroud, a piece of cloth with the image of a man's body on it that many genuinely believed to be the actual imprint of the body of Christ. Laboratories at Tucson, Oxford, and Zurich all placed it in the range of the late thirteenth to fourteenth centuries CE, not from the time of Christ at all, although this remains a matter of controversy.

Part of the Turin Shroud. Radiocarbon AMS dating has given a calibrated age range for the cloth of 1260–1390 CE.

Other Radiometric Methods

Radiocarbon is likely to maintain its position as the main dating tool back to 50,000 years ago for organic materials, but the half-life of radiocarbon is such that, for particularly old samples, there is hardly any radioactivity left to measure. So, for inorganic or very ancient materials, other methods have to be used.

The most important of them are also radiometric—they depend upon the measurement of natural radioactivity. But they use elements the radioactive isotopes of which have very much longer half-lives than the 5730 years of carbon-14. They have two drawbacks. In the first place, they depend upon elements less frequently found in archaeological contexts than is carbon. And secondly, the long half-lives generally mean datings are less precise.

POTASSIUM-ARGON DATING. The potassium-argon (K-Ar) method is used by geologists to date volcanic rocks hundreds or even thousands of millions of years old, but no more recent than around 80,000 years old.

K-Ar dating is based on the steady but very slow decay of the radioactive isotope potassium-40 (^{40}K) to the inert gas argon-40 (^{40}Ar) in volcanic rock. Knowing the decay rate of ^{40}K—its half-life is around 1.3 billion years—a measure of the quantity of ^{40}Ar trapped within a 10 g rock sample gives an estimate of the date of the rock's formation. The principal limitation of the technique is that it can only be used to date sites buried by volcanic rock.

The results are effectively geological dates for the eruption leading to the formation of volcanic strata. Fortunately, some of the most important areas for the study of the Lower Paleolithic, notably the Rift Valley in East Africa, are volcanic areas. The chronology of Olduvai Gorge, for example, which has

Key Concepts
Potassium-argon Dating

Method: based on the decay of radioactive potassium-40 into argon-40

Range: older than 80,000 years ago

Precision: ± 10 percent

Applications: dates volcanic rocks, and the archaeological remains associated with them provided important fossil remains of *Australopithecus*, *Homo habilis*, and *Homo erectus*, has been well established by K-Ar dating. At this and other similar sites, archaeological remains frequently lie on volcanic strata, and moreover they are often overlain by comparable volcanic rock, so that K-Ar dates for the two strata provide a time range for the material we are trying to date. The K-Ar method, in conjunction with a variety of other techniques, has also been used to date the important early human site at Atapuerca in Spain (see box opposite).

URANIUM-SERIES DATING. This dating method is based on the radioactive decay of isotopes of uranium. It has proved particularly useful for the period 500,000 to 50,000 years ago, which again lies outside the time range of radiocarbon dating. In Europe, where there are relatively few volcanic rocks suitable for dating by the potassium-argon technique, uranium-series (U-series) dating may be the method of first choice for early human sites— it has been used effectively, for example, on the skulls and other skeletal remains of very early *Homo sapiens* found at Qafzeh and Skhul caves in Israel. It has also been used successfully at Atapuerca in Spain (also see box opposite).

The method dates the time of formation of travertine (calcium carbonate), which is often deposited on cave walls and floors, and hence can be used to date any material, such as an artifact or bone, embedded in a layer of travertine or in another type of sediment between two layers of it. The method is also applicable to teeth, since these absorb water-soluble uranium when buried. High-precision measurement can give an error margin of fewer than 1000 years for a 100,000-year-old sample, and the method can also be cross-checked with **electron spin resonance** dates using the same materials (see p. 133).

FISSION-TRACK DATING. **Fission-track dating** depends upon the spontaneous fission (or division) of radioactive uranium atoms (^{238}U), present in a wide range of rocks and minerals, which causes damage to the structures of the minerals involved. In materials where ^{238}U is present, including volcanic and manufactured glasses, and such minerals as zircon and apatite, found within rock formations, the damage is recorded in pathways called fission tracks. The tracks can be counted in the laboratory under an optical microscope. Since we know the rate of fission of ^{238}U, this allows the date of formation of the rock or glass to be determined.

In this case, the radioactive clock is set at zero by the formation of the mineral or glass, either in nature (as with **obsidian**) or at the time of manufacture (as with manufactured glass). The method produces useful dates from suitable rocks that contain or are adjacent to those containing archaeological evidence, and has been used with success at early Paleolithic sites, such as Olduvai Gorge, Tanzania, providing independent confirmation of potassium-argon and other results.

Examples of fission tracks, after etching.

Dating Early Europeans at Atapuerca, Spain

The Sierra de Atapuerca, near Burgos in northern Spain, is a veritable treasure house of sites—mostly infilled caves—that are rewriting the early prehistory of western Europe, where human occupation before 500,000 years ago had been doubtful. Excavations there have been continuing for decades, but still only a tiny fraction of the Sierra's contents have been investigated. Atapuerca ranks as one the world's most important archaeological areas.

A variety of dating techniques has been used, from faunal analysis (making comparisons between animal remains found at the site and others of known date) to radiocarbon, potassium-argon, and uranium-series. They have combined to present evidence of human occupation stretching back more than 1 million years. Of particular importance are levels at the Gran Dolina site, dating from c. 800,000 to 1 million years ago. In 1994 human remains and stone tools found in them provided the first undeniable evidence for hominins in Europe during the Lower Pleistocene—the hominins were given a new species name, *Homo antecessor*. Electron spin resonance and uranium-series dating of teeth confirmed the Lower Pleistocene dates.

At the Galeria site, the lowest layers have been dated to more than 780,000 years ago by means of archaeomagnetism (which indicated a period of reversed polarity known as the Matuyama epoch), while younger layers have been dated by electron spin resonance and uranium-series to 350,000–300,000 and 200,000 years ago.

The Sima del Elefante has a deep stratigraphy; faunal, microfaunal, and archaeomagnetic analyses here

(Above) Some of the 5500 human fossils from the Sima de los Huesos, dating to more than 430,000 years ago.

have shown that the lowest section—which has yielded stone flakes made by humans—dates to the Lower Pleistocene, more than 1 million years ago. In 1998 it was announced that a human jaw together with stone tools had been recovered from a layer that a number of methods has combined to place at 1.1–1.2 million years ago, making it the oldest and most securely dated record of human occupation in Europe.

Microfaunal analysis, electron spin resonance, and uranium-series methods in the Sima de los Huesos have established that a speleothem (mineral deposit) that covers the layer containing human bones dates to at least 430,000 years ago, while high-resolution uranium-series dates have shown that the bodies were placed here about 600,000 years ago.

(Center) The skull of *Homo antecessor*, found at Gran Dolina.

(Left) Excavation at Gran Dolina.

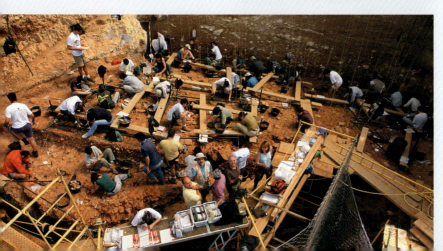

Other Absolute Dating Methods

There are several more dating methods that can be used in special circumstances, but none is as important in practice to archaeologists as those already described. Some are of relevance to the solution of specific problems, such as the dating of Paleolithic rock art. Several of the most significant are mentioned below, so that the overview given in this chapter is reasonably complete. But the discussion here is deliberately kept brief, to give a flavour of a field that can easily become rather complicated, and that is not directly relevant to much mainstream archaeology. The rather special case of DNA dating is of particular interest.

THERMOLUMINESCENCE DATING. **Thermoluminescence (TL) dating** can be used to date crystalline materials (minerals) buried in the ground that have been fired—usually pottery, but also baked clay, burnt stone, and in some circumstances burnt soil. But unfortunately it is a method that is difficult to make precise, and so it is generally used when other methods, such as radiocarbon dating, are not available.

Like many other methods it depends upon radioactive decay, but in this case it is the amount of radioactivity received by the specimen since the start date that is of interest, not the radiation emitted by the specimen itself. When atoms located within the structure of a mineral are exposed to radiation from the decay of radioactive elements in the nearby environment, some of that energy is "trapped." If the amount of radiation remains constant over time, then this energy will accumulate at a uniform rate and the total amount of energy will depend upon the total time of exposure. When a sample is heated to 500°C or more, the trapped energy is released as thermoluminescence, and the radioactive clock is set back to zero.

This means that archaeological artifacts, such as pottery, will have had their clocks reset when they were originally fired, and that by reheating samples from these objects, we can measure the thermoluminescence released and hence date the material. The main complication of the method is that the level of background radiation that a sample might have been exposed to is not uniform—it must be measured for every sample by burying a small capsule containing a radiation-sensitive material, or by using a radiation counter at the exact spot the sample was found. In general, the difficulties of making these measurements mean that TL dates rarely have a precision of better than ±10 percent of the age of the sample.

A good example of the archaeological application of TL is the dating of the terracotta head known as the Jemaa head, from the alluvium of a tin mine near the Jos Plateau of Nigeria. The head and similar examples belong to the Nok culture, but such sculptures could not be dated reliably at the site of Nok itself because of the lack of any plausible radiocarbon dates.

Key Concepts
Thermoluminescence Dating

Range: up to 100,000 years ago

Precision: ± 5–10 percent on site; 25 percent otherwise

Applications: dates minerals that have been sufficiently heated and then buried. Can be applied to pottery, other baked clay, and burnt stone

A TL reading on the head gave an age of 1520 ±260 BCE, allowing this and similar heads from the Nok region to be given a firm chronological position for the first time.

OPTICAL DATING.   This method is similar in principle to TL, but it is used to date minerals that have been exposed to light, rather than heat. Most minerals contain some trapped energy that will be released by several minutes' exposure to sunlight. Such exposure is in effect the start point. Once buried they begin to accumulate electrons once more, as a result of radioactive radiation experienced in the soil. In the laboratory, optically stimulated luminescence (OSL) is produced by directing light of a visible wavelength onto the sample, and the resultant luminescence is measured. And once again the background radiation at the place of burial has to be measured, so optical dating suffers from many of the same complications as TL.

ELECTRON SPIN RESONANCE DATING.   Electron spin resonance (ESR) is a technique similar to but less sensitive than TL, but it can be used for materials that decompose when heated and thus where TL is not applicable. Its most successful application so far has been for the dating of tooth enamel. Newly formed tooth enamel contains no trapped energy, but it begins to accumulate once the tooth is buried and exposed to natural background radiation. The precision of the method when used to date tooth enamel is in the order of 10–20 percent, but it is still very useful for the study of early humans and the cross-checking of other dating methods.

ARCHAEOMAGNETIC DATING AND GEOMAGNETIC REVERSALS.
Archaeomagnetic (or **paleomagnetic**) **dating** has so far been of limited use in archaeology. It is based on the constant change, both in direction and intensity, of the Earth's magnetic field. The direction of that magnetic field at a particular time is recorded in any baked-clay structure (oven, kiln, hearth, etc.) that has been heated to a temperature of 650 to 700°C. At that temperature the iron particles in the clay permanently take up the Earth's magnetic direction and intensity at the time of firing. This principle is called thermoremanent magnetism (TRM). Charts can be built up of the variation through time that can be used to date baked-clay structures of unknown age, the TRM of which is measured and then matched to a particular point on the master sequence.

Another aspect of archaeomagnetism, relevant for the dating of the Lower Paleolithic, is the phenomenon of complete reversals (**geomagnetic reversals**) in the Earth's magnetic field—magnetic north becomes magnetic south, and vice versa. The most recent major reversal occurred about 780,000 years ago, and a sequence of such reversals stretching back several millions of years has been built up with the aid of potassium-argon and other dating techniques.

GENETIC DATING. The methods now being used by molecular geneticists present rather a special case. They use DNA samples from living human populations to date population events, notably migrations. Genetic dating is now well established as one of the principal dating methods available in human population studies. Using assumptions about genetic mutation rates, they can date approximately the appearance of new genetic categories and thus give a date to such important processes as the "Out of Africa" dispersal of our species (around 60,000–50,000 years ago; see below). It is the information within living humans that provides the data, not ancient excavated samples: our past within us! Recently, however, techniques of analysis have improved, so that it is now sometimes also possible to analyze the DNA from human bones found in secure archaeological contexts. But in such cases the date of the bones derives from the context, not from the DNA.

World Chronology

As a result of the application of the various dating techniques discussed above, it is possible to summarize the world archaeological chronology, from the evolution of human ancestors millions of years ago in Africa, to the spread of our own species around the world, and the eventual development of agriculture and complex societies.

Paleoanthropologists hold strongly differing views on how the fossil remains for human evolution should be interpreted. This diagram presents the evidence as four adaptive radiations: the australopithecines (blue), paranthropines (green), early *Homo* (purple), and later *Homo* (including modern humans; also purple).

The human story as understood at present begins in East Africa, with the emergence there of the earliest **hominins** of the genus *Australopithecus*, such as *Australopithecus afarensis*, around 4 million years ago, and the possibly earlier *Ardipithecus*. By around 2 million years ago, there is clear fossil evidence for the first known representative of our own genus, *Homo habilis*, from such sites as Koobi Fora (Kenya) and Olduvai Gorge (Tanzania). The earliest stone tools

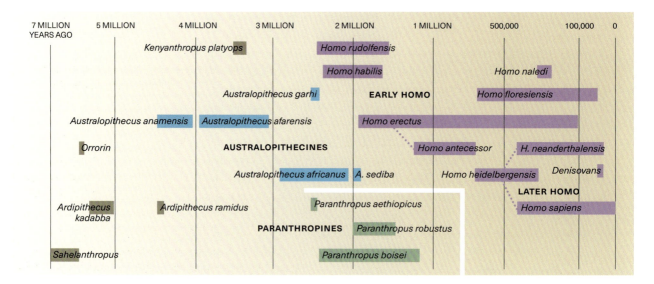

7 MILLION YEARS AGO	5 MILLION	4 MILLION	3 MILLION	2 MILLION	1 MILLION	500,000	100,000	0

Kenyanthropus platyops — Homo rudolfensis

Homo habilis — Homo naledi

Australopithecus garhi — EARLY HOMO — Homo floresiensis

Australopithecus anamensis — Australopithecus afarensis — Homo erectus

Orrorin — AUSTRALOPITHECINES — Homo antecessor — H. neanderthalensis

Australopithecus africanus — A. sediba — Homo heidelbergensis — Denisovans

Ardipithecus kadabba — Ardipithecus ramidus — Paranthropus aethiopicus — LATER HOMO — Homo sapiens

PARANTHROPINES — Paranthropus robustus

Sahelanthropus — Paranthropus boisei

(Right) This 2-million-year-old skull was discovered in South Africa in 2008. It has been tentatively assigned to a new species, *Australopithecus sediba*, possibly representing a transitional phase between the australopithecines and hominins.

(Below) Neanderthal woman. Recent work on Neanderthal DNA has shown that these hominins, and the ancestors of our own species, *Homo sapiens*, descended from a common ancestor who lived as recently as 700,000 years ago. We are close cousins.

(from Hadar, Ethiopia) date from about 2.5 million years ago, but it is not known which hominin made them because *Homo* fossils of this age have not yet been found. It is possible that australopithecines also had a tool culture before or during *Homo*'s time. The early toolkits, comprising flake and pebble tools, are called the **Oldowan industry**—after Olduvai Gorge, where they are particularly well represented.

By more than 1.6 million years ago, the next stage in human evolution, *Homo erectus*, had emerged in East Africa. These hominins had larger brains than *Homo habilis*, their probable ancestor, and were makers of the characteristic teardrop-shaped stone tools flaked on both sides called Acheulian hand-axes. These artifacts are the dominant tool form of the Lower Paleolithic. By the time *Homo erectus* became extinct (around 100,000 years ago, or possibly even as recently as 50,000 years ago), the species had colonized the rest of Africa, southern, eastern, and western Asia, and central and western Europe. Their remote descendants (now designated *Homo floresiensis*) seem to have survived in Indonesia to around 50,000 years ago, as discoveries on the island of Flores suggest.

The Middle Paleolithic period—from about 200,000 to 40,000 years ago— saw the emergence of modern *Homo sapiens*. Neanderthals, who used to be classified as a subspecies of *Homo sapiens* (*Homo sapiens neanderthalensis*) lived in Europe and western and central Asia from about 400,000 to 30,000 years ago. But as a result of analysis of ancient Neanderthal DNA they are now seen as more distant cousins, and again regarded as a different species, *Homo neanderthalensis*, although they may have made some contribution to *Homo sapiens* DNA through contact. As a result of DNA work it seems clear that *Homo sapiens* evolved in Africa, and that there was a major "Out of Africa" expansion between 60,000 and 50,000 years ago of humans ancestral to all present-day humans. Australia was colonized by humans some 50,000 years ago (the dates are still debated), and Europe and Asia by at least 40,000 years ago. There may have been an earlier dispersal of archaic modern humans who

First colonization of the world by modern humans, with very approximate dates—in years BP—and ice sheets (darker shading) and low sea levels (white areas outside present coastline) of *c.* 18,000 BP. Many scholars believe the Americas were settled as early as 30,000–15,000 BP.

SIBERIA
35,000–
25,000

EUROPE
40,000

CENTRAL ASIA

CHINA

JAPAN
30,000

SAHARA
DESERT

60,000

SOUTH
ASIA

SOUTHEAST
ASIA

NEW GUINEA
40,000

AFRICA

ANCESTRAL
MODERN HUMANS
200,000–150,000

INDIAN OCEAN

AUSTRALIA
50,000

Klasies River Mouth

TASMANIA

0   2000 miles

0   2000 km

180°   150°   120°   90°   60°

ARCTIC OCEAN

BERINGIA

ALASKA
15,000

NORTH AMERICA

PACIFIC OCEAN

ATLANTIC
OCEAN

CLOVIS SITES
13,500–13,000

HAWAII
1400

RONESIA

MARQUESAS ISLANDS
1500

PERU (COAST)
12,000

MELANESIA

SOCIETY ISLANDS
1500

SOUTH AMERICA

FIJI   TONGA
3000–2800

EASTER ISLAND
1300?

CHILE
14,000

NEW ZEALAND
800?

(Opposite) Monuments and sites constructed by state societies around the world (clockwise from top left): the ziggurat of Ur, in modern Iraq, c. 2000 BCE; a giant Olmec head, possibly a portrait of a ruler, Mexico, c. 1200–600 BCE; elaborate reliefs at Persepolis, Iran, c. 515 BCE; the Inca site of Machu Picchu, fifteenth century CE; the temple of Ramesses II (c. 1279–1213 BCE) at Abu Simbel, Egypt, with statues of the pharaoh.

reached the eastern Mediterranean some 100,000 to 90,000 years ago, but they probably have no surviving descendants.

It is uncertain when humans initially crossed from northeastern Asia into North America across the Bering Strait, and south to Central and South America. The earliest secure dates for the first Americans are around 14,000 years ago, but there is controversial evidence that the continent was populated before then. By 10,000 BCE, most of the land areas of the world, except the deserts and Antarctica, were populated. The most conspicuous exception is the Pacific, where Western Polynesia does not seem to have been colonized until the first millennium BCE, and Eastern Polynesia progressively from c. 300 CE. By around 1000 CE the colonization of Oceania was complete. The spread of humans around the world is summarized in the map on pp. 136–37.

Nearly all the groups of humans so far mentioned may be regarded as hunter-gatherer societies, made up of relatively small groups of people.

One of the most significant occurrences in world history at a global level is the development of food production, based on domesticated plant species and also (although in some areas to a lesser extent) of domesticated animal species. One of the most striking facts of world prehistory is that the transition from hunting and gathering to food production seems to have occurred independently in several areas, in each case after the end of the Ice Age, i.e. after c. 10,000 years ago.

In the Near East, we can recognize the origins of this transition even before this time, for the process may have been gradual, the consequence (as well as the cause) of restructuring in the social organization of human societies. At any rate, well-established farming, dependent on wheat and barley as well as sheep and goats (and later cattle), was underway there by about 8000 BCE. Farming had spread to Europe by 6500 BCE, and is documented in South Asia at Mehrgarh in Balochistan, Pakistan, at about the same time.

A separate development, based at first on the cultivation of millet, seems to have taken place in China, in the valley of the Huang He (Yellow River), by 5000 BCE or even earlier. Rice cultivation began at about the same time in the Yangtze Valley in China and spread to Southeast Asia. The position in Africa south of the Sahara is more complicated due to the diversity of environments, but millet and sorghum wheat were cultivated by the third millennium BCE. The Western Pacific (Melanesian) complex of root and tree crops had certainly developed by that

World Chronology
Key Events

Earliest stone tools	2.5 million years ago
Acheulian hand-axes	1.6 million years ago
Homo sapiens	at least 100,000 years ago
First Australians	50,000 years ago
First Americans	14,000 years ago or more
First farmers	at least 10,000 years ago in the Near East 9000 years ago in China 9000 years ago in the Americas 8500 years ago in Europe
First state societies	5500 years ago in the Near East 3500 years ago in China 3500 years ago in the Americas

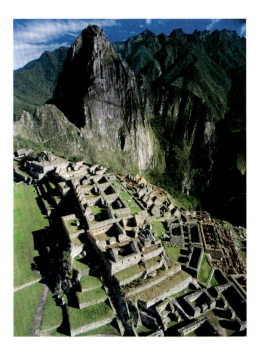

time: indeed, there are indications of field drainage for root crops very much earlier.

In the Americas, a different range of crops was available. Cultivation of beans, squash, peppers, and some grasses may have begun by 7000 or even 8000 BCE in Peru, and was certainly underway there and in Mesoamerica by the seventh millennium BCE. Other South American species, including manioc and potato, were soon added, but the plant with the greatest impact on American agriculture was maize, believed to have been brought into cultivation in Mexico by 5600 years ago, though possibly earlier in northwestern Argentina.

These agricultural innovations were rapidly adopted in some areas (e.g. in Europe), but in others, such as North America, their impact was less immediate. Certainly, by the beginning of the Common Era, hunter-gatherer economies were very much in the minority.

The urban revolution, the next major transformation that we recognize widely, is not simply a change in settlement type: it reflects profound social changes. Foremost among these is the development of **state** societies displaying more clearly differentiated institutions of government than do **chiefdoms**. Many state societies had writing. We see the first state societies in the Near East by about 3500 BCE, in Egypt only a little later, and in the Indus Valley by 2500 BCE. In the Near East, the period of the early Mesopotamian city-states was marked by the rise of such famous sites as Ur, Uruk, and later Babylon, and was followed in the first millennium BCE by an age of great empires, notably those of Assyria and Achaemenid Persia. In Egypt, it is possible to trace the continuous development of cultural and political traditions over more than 2000 years, through the pyramid age of the Old Kingdom and the imperial power of the New Kingdom.

On the western edge of the Near East, further civilizations developed: Minoans and Mycenaeans in Greece and the Aegean during the second millennium BCE, Etruscans and Romans in the first millennium BCE. At the opposite end of Asia, state societies with urban centers appeared in China before 1500 BCE, marking the beginnings of the Shang civilization. At about the same time, Mesoamerica saw the rise of the Olmec, the first in a long sequence of Central American civilizations including the Maya, Zapotec, Toltec, and Aztec. On the Pacific coast of South America, the Chavín (from 900 BCE), Moche, and Chimú civilizations laid the foundations for the rise of the vast and powerful Inca empire that flourished in the fifteenth century CE.

The remaining story is the more familiar one of literate history, with the rise of the Classical world of Greece and Rome as well as of China, and then of the world of Islam, the Renaissance of Europe, and the development of the colonial powers. From the eighteenth century to the present there followed the independence of the former colonies, first in the Americas, then in Asia and in Africa. We are talking now not simply of state societies but of nation states and, especially in colonial times, of empires.

Study Questions

1 How are absolute dating methods different from relative dating methods?
2 Why is an understanding of stratigraphy vital to most relative dating methods?
3 Why is tree-ring dating considered to be an absolute dating method?
4 Why is it necessary to calibrate radiocarbon dates?
5 What types of artifacts cannot be radiocarbon dated? Why?
6 What are some of the main sources of errors in the field of radiocarbon dating?

Summary

THE ANSWER to the question "When?" in archaeology has two main components. Relative dating methods allow us to determine that something is *relatively* older or younger than something else. Absolute methods make it possible to give a date in years. Archaeological dating is at its most reliable when the two methods are used together, e.g. when the relative order assigned to layers in an excavation can be confirmed by absolute dates for each layer. Wherever possible, results from one absolute method should be cross-checked by those from another.

IN AREAS WHERE ancient calendars and historical chronologies are available, such as Mesoamerica, these remain one of the most important methods of absolute dating. Elsewhere, the two methods most useful to the archaeologist are radiocarbon dating and tree-ring dating. Although many other absolute dating techniques exist, these tend to be reserved either for very specific applications or for sites that are beyond the range of radiocarbon, back in the Paleolithic period.

ULTIMATELY, THE PRECISION of dating attainable for each period helps determine the kinds of questions we ask about the past—for the Paleolithic, questions are about long-term change; for later periods, the questions are more usually concerned with the shorter-term variations in worldwide human development.

Further Reading

The following works provide a good introduction to the principal dating techniques used by archaeologists:

Aitken, M. J. 1990. *Science-based Dating in Archaeology*. Longman: London & New York.

Biers, W. R. 1992. *Art, Artefacts and Chronology in Classical Archaeology*. Routledge: London.

Brothwell, D. R. & Pollard, A. M. (eds). 2005. *Handbook of Archaeological Sciences*. Wiley: Chichester & New York.

Pollard, A. M. *et al.* 2007. *Analytical Chemistry in Archaeology*. Cambridge University Press: Cambridge.

Speer, J. H. 2010. *Fundamentals of Tree-Ring Research*. University of Arizona Press: Tucson.

Taylor, R. E. & Aitken, M. J. (eds). 1997. *Chronometric Dating in Archaeology*. Plenum: New York.

Taylor R. E. & Bar-Yosef, O. 2013. *Radiocarbon Dating: An Archaeological Perspective* (2nd ed.). Left Coast Press: Walnut Creek, CA.

Wintle, A. G. 1996. "Archaeologically relevant dating techniques for the next century." *Journal of Archaeological Science* 23, 123–38.

[See p. 345 for a list of useful websites]

5

How Were Societies Organized?
Social Archaeology

Some of the most interesting questions we can ask about early societies are social. They are about people and about relations between people, about the exercise of power, and about the nature and scale of organization. But the answers are not directly visible in the archaeological record: we have to ask the right questions of the data, and devise the means of answering them.

In this respect archaeology is very different from cultural or social anthropology, where the observer can actually visit the living society and rapidly form conclusions about its social and power structures before moving on to other more complex matters, such as the details of the kinship system or the minutiae of ritual behavior. The archaeologist has to work hard to gain even basic details of these kinds, but the prize is a rich one: an understanding of the social organization not just of societies in the present or very recent past (like cultural anthropology) but also of societies at many different points in time, with all the scope that that offers for studying change. Only the archaeologist can obtain that perspective, and hence seek some understanding of the processes of long-term change.

Different kinds of society need different kinds of questions, and the techniques of investigation will need to vary radically with the nature of the evidence. The questions we put, and the methods for answering them, must be tailored to the community we are dealing with. So it is all the more necessary to be clear at the outset about the general nature of that community, which is why the most basic social questions are always the first ones to ask.

We must first address the size or scale of the society. The archaeologist will often be excavating a single site. But was that an independent political unit, for example a Maya or Greek city-state, or a simpler unit, such as the base camp of a hunter-gatherer group? Or was it, on the other hand, a small cog in a very big wheel, a subordinate settlement in some far-flung empire, such as that of the Incas of Peru? Any site we consider will have its own hinterland, or catchment area, for the feeding of its population. But one of our interests is to go beyond that local area, and to understand how that site interacts with others. From the standpoint of the individual site—which is often a convenient perspective to adopt—that raises questions of dominance. Was the site politically independent or autonomous? Or, if it was part of a larger social system, did it take a dominant part (like the capital city of a kingdom) or a subordinate one?

If the scale of the society is a natural first question, the next is certainly its internal organization. What kind of society was it? Were the people forming it on a more-or-less equal social footing? Or were there instead prominent differences in status, rank, and prestige within the society—perhaps different social classes? And what of the professions: were there people who specialized in particular crafts? And if so, were they controlled within a centralized system, as in some of the palace economies of the Near East and Egypt? Or was this a freer economy, with flourishing free exchange, where merchants could operate at will in their own interest?

These questions, however, may all be seen as top-down, looking at the society from above and investigating its organization. But increasingly an alternative perspective is being followed, looking first at the individual, and at the way the identity of the individual in the society in question is defined—a bottom-up perspective. Archaeologists have come to realize that the way such important social constructs as gender, status, and even age are constituted in a society are not "givens," but are specific to each different society. These insights have led to new fields: the archaeology of the individual and the archaeology of identity.

Establishing the Nature and Scale of the Society

The first step in social archaeology is so obvious that it is often overlooked. It is to ask, what was the scale of the largest social unit, and what kind of society, in a very broad sense, was it? The largest social unit could be anything from a small and completely independent hunter-gatherer **band** to a great empire. In the case of a complex society it can comprise many lesser units.

In terms of research in the field, the question is often best answered from a study of settlement: both in terms of the scale and nature of individual sites and the relationships between them, through the analysis of settlement pattern. But we should not forget that written records, where a society is literate and uses writing, oral tradition, and **ethnoarchaeology**—the study from an archaeological point of view of present-day societies (see pp. 164–67)—can be equally valuable in assessing the nature and scale of the society under review.

First, however, we need a frame of reference, a hypothetical classification of societies against which to test our ideas.

Classification of Societies

Anthropologists have outlined broad patterns of social organization that can be applied to many human societies. The most famous (and now controversial) is that of American anthropologist Elman Service, who developed a four-fold classification of societies (mobile hunter-gatherer groups, **segmentary societies**, chiefdoms, and states), which can be associated with particular kinds of site and settlement pattern. Some archaeologists question the value of such broad classifications as "chiefdom." It is important to recognize that human culture presents a wide array of social organizational types that have been tried, altered, and abandoned. It would seriously misrepresent the diversity of human prehistory to suggest that people evolved from one classification to the next in a unilinear fashion. Yet, at a preliminary stage of analysis, and with a cautious eye, the classifications are useful in initially conceptualizing the size and complexity of a society.

MOBILE HUNTER-GATHERER GROUPS.   These are small-scale societies of hunters and gatherers (sometimes called "bands"), generally of fewer than 100 people, who move seasonally to exploit wild food resources. Most surviving hunter-gatherer groups today are of this kind, such as the San of southern Africa. Band members are generally kinsfolk, related by descent or marriage, and bands do not have formal leaders, so there are no marked economic differences or disparities in status among their members.

Because bands are mobile groups, their sites consist mainly of seasonally occupied camps, and other smaller and more specialized sites. These include kill or butchery sites—locations where large mammals are killed and sometimes butchered—and work sites, where tools are made or other specific activities carried out. Camps may show evidence of insubstantial dwellings or temporary shelters, along with the debris of residential occupation.

During the Paleolithic period (before 12,000 years ago) most archaeological sites seem to conform to one or other of these categories—camp sites, kill sites, work sites—and archaeologists usually operate on the assumption that most Paleolithic societies were organized into bands.

SEGMENTARY SOCIETIES.   These are generally larger than mobile hunter-gatherer groups, but their population rarely numbers more than a few thousand, and their diet or subsistence is based largely on cultivated plants and domesticated animals. They are sometimes referred to as "**tribes**." Typically, they are settled farmers, but they may be nomad pastoralists with a mobile economy based on the intensive exploitation of livestock. Segmentary societies generally consist of many individual communities integrated into the larger society through kinship ties. Although some have officials and even a capital or seat of government, such officials lack the economic base necessary for effective use of power.

The typical settlement pattern for segmentary societies is one of settled agricultural homesteads or villages. Characteristically, no one settlement dominates any of the others in the region. Instead, the archaeologist finds evidence for isolated, permanently occupied houses (a dispersed settlement pattern) or for permanent villages (a nucleated pattern). Such villages may be made up of a collection of free-standing houses, for example those of the first farmers of the Danube Valley in Europe, *c.* 4500 BCE. Or they may be clusters of buildings grouped together—so-called agglomerate structures—for example, the pueblos of the American Southwest.

CHIEFDOMS. "Chiefdom" is a controversial term, and can mean different things to different people. In general terms, these societies are characterized by ranking—differences in social status between people. Different **lineages** (a lineage is a group claiming descent from a common ancestor) are graded on a scale of prestige, and the senior lineage, and hence the society as a whole, is governed by a chief. Prestige and rank are determined by closeness of relationship to the chief. There is no true stratification into classes, and the role of the chief is crucial. Chiefdoms vary greatly in size, but the range is generally between about 5000 and 20,000 persons.

Often, there is local specialization in craft production, and surpluses of these and of foodstuffs are periodically paid as obligations to the chief. He uses these to maintain his close personal followers, and may use them for **redistribution** to his subjects.

The chiefdom generally has a center of power, often with temples, residences of the chief and his retainers, and craft specialists. It is a permanent ritual and ceremonial center that acts as a central focus for the entire group. This is not, however, a permanent urban center (such as a city) with an established bureaucracy, as we find in state societies. But chiefdoms do give indications that some sites were more important than others (or in other words, that there was a site hierarchy). An example is provided by the Mississippian-period site of Spiro in Oklahoma (see box, pp. 154–55).

The personal ranking characteristic of chiefdom societies is also visible in the very rich grave-goods that often accompany the burials of deceased chiefs.

EARLY STATES. These share many of the features of chiefdoms, but the ruler (perhaps a king or sometimes a queen) has explicit authority to establish laws and also to enforce them by the use of a standing army. Society no longer depends totally upon kin relationships: it is now stratified into different classes. Agricultural workers or serfs and the poorer urban dwellers form the lowest classes, with the craft specialists above, and the priests and kinsfolk of the ruler higher still. The functions of the ruler are often separated from those of the priest: palace is distinguished from temple. The territory is "owned" by the ruling lineage and populated by tenants who have an obligation to pay taxes. Taxes and other revenues are collected by officials based in the central capital, and then distributed to government, army, and craft specialists. Many early states developed complex redistributive systems to support these essential services.

Early state societies generally show a characteristic urban settlement pattern in which cities play a prominent part. The city is typically a large population center (often of more than 5000 inhabitants) with major public buildings, including temples and work places for the administrative bureaucracy. Often, there is a pronounced settlement hierarchy, with the capital city as the major center, and with subsidiary or regional centers as well as local villages.

Challenging Social Categories

The rather simple social typology presented here should not be used unthinkingly. For instance, there is some difference between the rather vague idea of the tribe and the more modern concept of the segmentary society. The term tribe, implying a larger grouping of smaller units, carries with it the assumption that these communities share a common ethnic identity and self-awareness, which is now known not generally to be the case. The term segmentary society refers to a relatively small and autonomous group, usually of agriculturalists, who regulate their own affairs: in some cases, they may join together with other comparable segmentary societies to form a larger ethnic unit or tribe; in other cases, they do not. For the remainder of this chapter, we shall therefore refer to segmentary societies in preference to the term tribe. And what in Service's typology were called bands are now more generally referred to as mobile hunter-gatherer groups.

Certainly, it would be wrong to overemphasize the importance of the four types of society given above, or to spend too long trying to decide whether a specific group should be classed in one category rather than another. It would also be wrong to assume that somehow societies inevitably evolve from hunter-gatherer groups to segmentary societies, or from chiefdoms to states. One of the challenges of archaeology is to attempt to explain why some societies become more complex and others do not. While a degree of categorization offers a framework to help organize our thoughts, it should not deflect us from focusing on what we are really looking for: changes over time in the different institutions of a society—whether in the social sphere, the organization of the food quest, technology, contact and exchange, or spiritual life. Archaeology has the unique advantage of being able to study processes of change over thousands of years, and it is these processes we are seeking to isolate. Fortunately there are sufficiently marked differences between simple and more complex societies for us to find ways of doing this.

As we saw above, in the description of Service's four types of society, complex societies show in particular an increased specialization in, or separation between, different aspects of their culture. In complex societies people no longer combine, say, the tasks of obtaining food, making tools, or performing religious rites, but become specialists at one or other of these tasks, either as full-time farmers, craftspeople, or priests. As technology develops, for example, groups of individuals may acquire particular expertise in pottery-making or metallurgy, and will become full-time craft specialists, occupying distinct areas of a town or city and thus leaving traces for the archaeologist to discover. Likewise, as farming develops and population grows, more food will be obtained from a given piece of land (food production will intensify) through the introduction of the plow or irrigation. As this specialization and intensification take place, so too does the tendency for some people to become wealthier and wield more authority than others— differences in social status and ranking develop.

It is the methods for looking at these processes of increasing specialization, intensification, and social ranking that help us identify the presence of more complex societies in the archaeological record. For simpler groups like hunter-gatherers, other methods are needed if we are to identify them archaeologically, as will become apparent.

Methods of Social Analysis

Different methods are suitable for investigating the social interactions and social structures of different kinds of societies. The principal source of data about early societies comes from settlement analysis and excavation. The study of burials with their associated artifacts is often a very good way of assessing the dress, possessions, and status of deceased individuals in a society. For some societies, the study of the monuments that they have built can also be very informative.

The data available from a hunter-gatherer camp are naturally very different from those from a city. For one thing, state societies are often literate societies, and written records may be available. For societies for which no written testimony is available, archaeologists have often relied upon ethnographic analogy, drawing upon what anthropologists have observed in more recent non-urban societies so as to suggest interpretations for what is found in the archaeological record. Ethnoarchaeology, as this field is known, seeks to use the experience derived from living societies to suggest interpretive and explanatory approaches to archaeological data.

Settlement Analysis and Site Hierarchy

One of the principal ways of answering the basic question "what is the scale of the society?" is through an understanding of settlement pattern, and this can come only from survey. Whatever the period in question, we should be interested in finding the major center or centers of settlement along with any smaller sites. We can use many of the survey, sampling, and remote sensing techniques described in Chapter 3 to do this, but the exact nature of the work will depend on the society in question—it is much harder to find the scanty traces that are left by mobile hunter-gatherers than it is to find an ancient city, so more intensive survey is needed.

Any survey will result in a map and a catalog of the sites discovered, together with details of each site including size, chronological range (as may be determined from such surface remains as pottery), architectural features, and possibly an approximate estimate of population. The aim is then to reach some classification of the sites on the basis of their relative importance—a site hierarchy. Possible categories for the different types of site encountered might include, for instance, regional center, local center, nucleated village, dispersed village, and hamlet.

Various techniques can be used to establish the site hierarchy of a region, but the simplest is based solely on site size. Sites are arranged in rank order by size and then displayed as a histogram (frequency distribution), which will usually show that the small sites are the most frequent. Such histograms allow comparisons to be made between the site hierarchies of different regions, different periods, and different types of society. In band societies, for example, there will usually be only a narrow range of variation in site size and all the sites will be relatively small. State societies, on the other hand, will have both hamlets and farmsteads, and large towns and cities. The degree to which a single site is dominant within a settlement system will also be evident from this type of analysis, and the organization of the settlement system will often be a direct reflection of the organization of the society that created it. In a general way, the more hierarchical the settlement pattern, the more hierarchical the society.

Work by Gregory Johnson on the Early Dynastic (c. 2800 BCE) settlement sites in a region of Mesopotamia showed this very clearly, as can be seen in the graph to the left. The sites ranged in size from 25 ha (60 acres) to just over one tenth of a hectare (0.25 acres), and could be divided into five categories based on their size: Johnson called these large towns, towns, large villages, small villages, and hamlets. The existence of a settlement hierarchy of this kind has been used by some archaeologists as an indicator of a state society.

The excavation of settlement remains, however, is the major source of information about social relations within a society. This applies for any level of complexity, but the methods used can vary greatly, the main distinction being between mobile and sedentary societies.

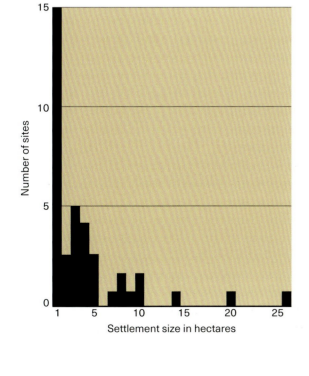

Site hierarchy for Early Dynastic settlements in a region of Mesopotamia.

Key Concepts
Methods of Social Analysis

Settlement Analysis: the main method of investigating past social organization. Data are collected by survey and excavation, but the specific methods used can vary greatly depending on the society in question

Burial Analysis: rank and social status are best revealed by the analysis of grave-goods within individual burials

Monuments and Public Works: the scale of monuments and public works, as well as their distribution, can be a good indicator of social organization

Written Records: an excellent source of information about the organization of early state societies

Ethnoarchaeology: the study of living societies in order to help interpret the past, with a specific emphasis on the use and significance of artifacts, buildings and structures, and how these material things might become incorporated into the archaeological record

MOBILE HUNTER-GATHERER SOCIETIES. In mobile hunter-gatherer societies organization is exclusively at a local level, with no permanent administrative centers. So having identified various sites, the first approach is to concentrate on the sites themselves, with the aim being to understand the nature of the activities that took place there, and of the social group that used them.

Among mobile communities of hunter-gatherers archaeologists draw a distinction between cave sites and open sites. Occupation deposits in cave sites tend to be deep, usually indicating intermittent human activity over thousands or tens of thousands of years, and meticulous excavation and recording are required to interpret the stratigraphy of the site accurately. Open sites may have been occupied for shorter periods of time, but the deposits, without the protection provided by a cave, may have suffered greater erosion.

If it proves possible to distinguish single short phases of human occupation at a hunter-gatherer site, we can then look at the distribution of artifacts and bone fragments within and around features and structures (hut foundations, remains of hearths) to see whether any coherent patterns can be observed. It is not always clear, however, whether the distribution is the result of human activity on the spot (or in situ) or whether the materials have been transported by flowing water and redeposited. In some cases, too, especially with bone debris, distribution may be the result of the action of predatory animals, not of humans.

The study of such questions requires sophisticated sampling strategies and very thorough analysis. The work of Glynn Isaac's team at the early Paleolithic site of Koobi Fora on the eastern shore of Lake Turkana, Kenya, gives an indication of the recovery and analytical techniques involved. The excavation procedure was highly controlled, with exact recording of the coordinates of every piece of bone or stone recovered, and careful analysis of the degree of post-depositional disturbance. Isaac's team was able to fit some fragments of bone and stone back together again. The team interpreted the network of joins (see diagram opposite) as showing areas where hominins broke open bones to extract marrow, and where stone tools were made—so-called activity areas.

For a wider perspective, we need to consider the entire territory in which the group or band operated, and the relationship between sites. Ethnoarchaeology has helped to establish a framework of analysis, so that we may think in terms of an annual home range (i.e. the whole territory covered by the group in the course of a year) and specific types of site within it, such as a home base camp (for a particular season), transitory camps, hunting blinds, butchery or kill sites, storage caches, and so on. These issues are basic to hunter-gatherer archaeology, and a regional perspective is essential to understand the annual life cycle of the group and its behavior. This means that, in addition to conventional sites (with a high concentration

Bones

Stones

Conjoining bones

Conjoining stones

0 — 30 ft.

0 — 10 m

Glynn Isaac's research at the early Paleolithic site of Koobi Fora, Kenya. (Top row) Location of bones and stone artifacts. (Second row) Lines joining bones and stones that could be fitted back together, perhaps indicating activity areas.

of artifacts), we need to look for sparse scatters of artifacts, consisting of perhaps just one or two objects in every 10-m survey square. We must also study the whole regional environment and the likely human use of it by hunter-gatherers.

A good example is provided by the work of the British anthropologist Robert Foley in the Amboseli region of southern Kenya. He collected and recorded some 8531 stone tools from 257 sample locations within a study area covering 600 sq. km (232 sq. miles). From this evidence he was able to calculate the rate of discard of stone tools within different environmental and vegetation zones, and interpret the distribution patterns in terms of the strategies and movements of hunter-gatherer groups. In a later study, he developed a general model of stone tool distribution based on a number of studies of hunter-gatherer bands in different parts of the world. One conclusion was that a single band of some 25 people might be expected to discard as many as 163,000 artifacts within their annual territory in the course of a single year. These artifacts would be scattered, but with significant

Robert Foley's model (left) of activities within the annual home range of a hunter-gatherer band, and the artifact scatters (right) resulting from such activities.

concentrations at home base camps and temporary camps. According to Foley's study, however, only a very small proportion of the artifacts discarded would be found by archaeologists working at a single site, and it is vitally important that individual site assemblages are interpreted as parts of a broader pattern.

SEDENTARY SOCIETIES. Investigation of the social organization of sedentary communities, which include segmentary societies, chiefdoms, and states, is best approached with an investigation of settlement (although, as we shall see below, cemeteries and public monuments evident in these societies also form useful areas of study).

Although much can be learned from survey, for effective analysis of the community as a whole some structures need to be excavated completely and the remainder sampled intensively enough to obtain an idea of the variety of different structures. The careful excavation of individual houses and of complete villages is standard procedure when dealing with smaller sedentary communities. This opens the way to the study of households, and of community structure, as well as to well-founded estimates of population.

Kent Flannery's excavation of Early Formative houses at Tierras Largas in Oaxaca, Mexico, offers a useful example. He was able to establish the first map showing the layout of a Formative village in Oaxaca. Evidence for differences in social status emerged. Residences, deduced to be of relatively high status, had not only a house platform built of higher-quality adobe and stone, but also a greater quantity of animal bone, imported obsidian, and imported marine shell than the area of wattle-and-daub houses deduced to be of lower status. Significantly, locally available (and therefore less prestigious) chert formed a higher proportion of the tools in the lower-status area.

Most of the techniques of analysis appropriate to less developed societies remain valid for the study of centralized chiefdoms and states, which incorporate within themselves most of the social forms and patterns of interaction seen in the simpler societies. Additional techniques are needed because of the centralization of society, the hierarchy of sites, and the organizational and communicational devices that characterize chiefdom and state societies. A wide-ranging example is provided by the work at the Mississippian site of Spiro, described in the box overleaf.

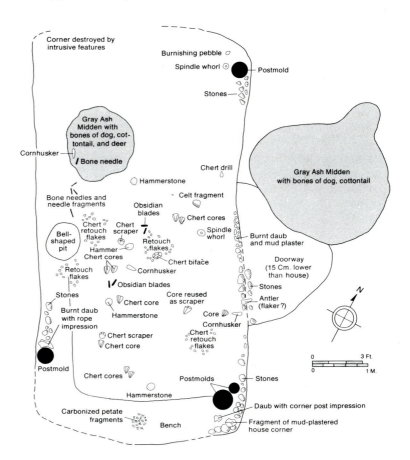

Plan of a house at Tierras Largas, c. 900 BCE, with certain artifacts plotted in position.

Conspicuous Ranking at Mississippian Spiro

Few sites in North America can match the abundance of finely crafted mortuary-related artifacts found at Spiro in eastern Oklahoma, and none of them has inspired as many ground-breaking studies of mortuary behavior and its relationship to social organization and belief systems. The Mississippian-period Spiro site first came to attention in 1935 when looters discovered a hollow chamber in the depths of the Craig Mound filled with human bones along with elaborate items heaped over a vast number of shell beads. Among the extraordinary artifacts were large engraved marine-shell cups, several big effigy pipes, wooden masks and human figures, copper axes, lidded baskets containing copper plates, and textiles. Tunneling in, the looters destroyed many of these items and their contextual relationships with one another.

The Great Mortuary

Subsequent controlled excavations brought a measure of order to the Craig Mound discoveries. They are now understood to be a collective deposit of bones and artifacts, referred to as the Great Mortuary, with a later tomb for a single individual on top. The cavity that excited so much initial interest has recently been interpreted as an intentional beehive-shaped cavity with a basal diameter and height each of about 4.5 m (15 ft.), within which was found one person accompanied by a rich array of symbolically significant and carefully arranged grave-goods.

Artifacts removed by the looters, dispersed to private and public collections, along with field notes and materials from later work have been the basis for a number of archaeological studies, most notably by James A. Brown. His work over forty years has clarified what went on in the Great Mortuary for well over a century up to the final burial event in the early fifteenth century CE. Interpretations of this remarkable deposit have changed as additional data have come to light, with funerary materials telling far more complex stories than once believed.

Social Organization

The first systematic study of the Craig Mound mortuary materials coincided with the recognition, around 1970, that burial areas provide perspectives on social organization that are

(Above) Craig Mound, Spiro.

(Right) Plan of the excavated Great Mortuary, with the later circular hollow chamber at the center.

difficult to obtain from other kinds of archaeological information. At the Great Mortuary, there was variation in skeletal articulation and completeness, with a wide array of artifacts, and bones were scattered across the floor and associated with cane baskets and cedar litters. Differences in how the skeletal remains were treated were equated to distinctions in rank. Demonstrating the existence of such a hierarchy was consistent with what was then a new interest in using burial contexts to reconstruct the social structure of past societies, in this instance a "chiefdom." The objects, especially elaborate engravings on marine-shell cups, emphasized several themes, with war prominent among them. These images underscored the centrality of being a successful warrior to the highest-ranking people.

Later the range of skeletal preservation, the presence of broken items, and soil adhering to bones and artifacts were recognized as indicating that much of the Great Mortuary deposit was formed by materials gathered from other places. It is as if the intent was to figuratively and literally create a genealogical history by gathering the remains of important people together. Altering ancestral connections to legitimize the positions of high-ranking lineages and the most important people within them is not at all uncommon in human societies. The deposit was not

a one-time event as it was cleaned out and reconstituted an unknown number of times.

Evidence for Social Change

Field records indicate that impressive and symbolically significant items, including massive pipes and wooden statues, were placed in ritually important locations within the hollow chamber. The overall arrangement of objects is indicative of cosmological principles that are as yet incompletely understood.

The much greater attention now being focused on the hollow chamber has clarified its relationship to the Great Mortuary. It appears that the cavity, located within a dome of hard clay lined by cedar poles, was a tomb built on top of the Great Mortuary deposit after the latter had been sealed. Within it an individual was richly furnished with numerous intact sacred objects. It signals a major social change from shared political leadership, represented by collective burial, to a more restricted authority structure late in the history of the Spiro community.

Thus, there has been a shift from a focus on the social identities of the people interred in the mound to what the group responsible for shaping the burial area was conveying to a broader audience about their place in the physical and supernatural worlds. The recent clarification of how the Great Mortuary and the later tomb

(Above left) Excavations in the 1930s, with upright cedar post and tunnels/hollows visible.

(Above) Elaborate cedar mask with deer antlers.

were related to one another underscores the differences that existed in the leadership structure of Mississippian societies, and in chiefdoms in general, and how that structure could change over time even within individual communities.

(Below) Soapstone effigy pipe depicting a warrior executing his victim.

One of the first steps when looking at a complex society is to identify one or more primary centers, and this is done by considering the size of a site, either in absolute terms, or in terms of the distances between major centers, so as to determine which are dominant and which subordinate. With this information a map can be created identifying the principal independent centers and the approximate extent of the territories surrounding them.

The reliance on size alone, however, can be misleading, and it is necessary to seek other indications of which are the primary centers. The best way is to try to find out how the society in question viewed itself and its territories. This might seem an impossible task until one remembers that, for most state societies at any rate, written records exist. These may name various sites, identifying their place within the hierarchy. The archaeologist's task is then to find those named sites, usually by the discovery of an actual inscription including the name of the relevant site—one might for example hope to find such an inscription in any substantial town of the Roman empire. The decipherment of Maya hieroglyphs in the second half of the twentieth century has opened up a whole new source of evidence of this sort.

Usually, however, site hierarchy must be deduced by more directly archaeological means, without relying on the written word. A highest-order center, such as the capital city of an independent state, can best be identified from direct indications of central organization, on a scale not exceeded elsewhere, and comparable with that of other highest-order centers of equivalent states.

One indication is the existence of an archive (even without understanding anything of what it says) or of other symbolic indications of centralized organization. For instance, many controlled economies used seals to make impressions in clay as indications of ownership, source, or destination. The finding of a quantity of such materials can indicate organizational activity. Indeed, the whole practice of literacy and of symbolic expression is so central to organization that such indications are valuable evidence.

A further indication of central status is the presence of buildings of standardized form known to be associated with central functions of high order. Examples of such buildings include palaces, such as those found in Minoan Crete; buildings of ritual function (since in most early societies the control of administration and control of religious practice were closely linked), for example a Maya temple complex; fortifications; and mints for producing coinage.

In a hierarchically organized society, it always makes sense to study closely the functions of the center, considering such possible factors as kinship, bureaucratic organization, redistribution and storage of goods, organization of ritual, craft specialization, and external trade. All of these offer insights into how the society worked.

Burial Analysis: The Study of Ranking from Individual Burials

In archaeology, the individual is seen all too rarely. One of the most informative insights into the individual and his or her social status is offered by the discovery of human physical remains—the skeleton or the ashes—accompanied by artifacts deposited in the grave. Examination of the skeletal remains will often reveal the sex and age at death of each individual, and possibly any dietary deficiency or other pathological condition (see Chapter 8). Communal or collective burials (burials of more than one individual) may be difficult to interpret, because it will not always be clear which grave-goods go with which deceased person. It is, therefore, from single burials that we can hope to learn most.

In segmentary societies, and others with relatively limited differentiation in terms of rank, a close analysis of grave-goods can reveal much about disparities in social status. It is important to remember, however, that what is buried with a deceased person is not simply the exact equivalent either of status or of material goods owned or used during life. Burials are made by living individuals, and are used by them to express and influence their relationships with others still alive as much as to symbolize or serve the dead. But there is nevertheless often a relationship between the role and rank of the deceased during life and the manner in which the remains are disposed of and accompanied by artifacts.

The analysis will seek to determine differences between male and female burials, and to assess whether these differences carry with them distinctions in terms of wealth or higher status. The other common factor involved with rank or status is age, and age differences may be systematically reflected in the treatment of the deceased. In relatively egalitarian societies, high status won through achievements (e.g. in hunting) in an individual's own lifetime is something commonly encountered, and often reflected in funerary practice.

But the archaeologist must ask, from the evidence available, whether such a burial really reflects status achieved by the individual or instead hereditary status through birth. To distinguish between the two is not easy. One useful criterion is to investigate whether children are in some cases given rich burial goods and other indications of preferential attention. If so, there may have been a system of hereditary ranking, because at so early an age the child is unlikely to have reached such a status through personal distinction alone.

Once the graves in the cemetery have been dated, the first step in most cases is simply to produce a histogram of the number of different artifact types in each grave. For further analysis, however, it is more interesting to seek some better indication of wealth and status so that greater weight can be given to valuable objects, and less weight to commonplace ones. This at once raises the problem of the recognition of value (for we cannot assume that past societies had the same ideas of value as we do). One answer might

Khok Phanom Di.

(Above left) The dead were buried individually, in neat, clustered rows.

(Above right) The Princess, who was accompanied by a set of shell jewelry, with more than 120,000 beads, a headdress, and a bracelet, as well as fine pottery vessels.

be to assume that valuable objects were those that took a long time to make, or were made of materials brought from a distance or difficult to obtain. We must also remember that ranking is not expressed solely in the grave-goods, but in the entire manner of burial.

A good example of the analysis of an entire cemetery is offered by the excavations of Charles Higham and Rachanie Thosarat at the site of Khok Phanom Di, a large mound inland from the Gulf of Siam in central Thailand. The settlement had been occupied for about 500 years from *c.* 2000 BCE, and left a cemetery containing 154 human burials with bone and shell ornaments intact. The graves occurred in clusters with spaces between them. A very detailed burial sequence was worked out that provided insights into the community's kinship system over about 20 generations. The ability to trace families down the generations in this way is extremely rare in prehistory. In the later phases there was a predominance of women, some of them, such as the so-called Princess, buried with considerable wealth. Also there was a clear link between the wealth of children and the adults with whom they were buried—poor children accompanied poor adults. The analysis of a complete cemetery in this way can yield many insights that are not available even from the very careful examination of a single grave.

Monuments and Public Works

Some societies invest a great deal of labor and considerable resources in the construction of monuments and public works. Such monuments were generally built with the intention of being conspicuous, and in some cases—such as the pyramids of Egypt—they remain conspicuous today. Many early state societies had at their center a major ceremonial site, and the monuments at such sites are informative not only about the religious beliefs of the society in question but also about aspects of their social organization.

The great plazas at the ceremonial centers of Mesoamerica are an excellent example. Monte Albán in Oaxaca, Mexico, became the principal center of the Zapotec state around 200 BCE. Its wonderfully situated central plaza, shown below, dominated the surrounding areas. From this time on, Monte Albán was the home of some 10,000 to 20,000 people, and the primary center of Oaxaca. Its monuments celebrate and reflect the power of the state and the city's central authority.

In some segmentary societies the surviving monuments were much more conspicuous than the settlements. In some cases the settlements are rarely recovered, while clear traces of the monuments remain. This is the case for the Neolithic period in the Wessex area of southern England, where earthen burial mounds, called long barrows, are the most evident trace of the farmers who lived there from *c.* 4000 BCE. With each cluster of mounds is associated a larger, circular monument with concentric ditches, termed a causewayed camp.

Despite the sparse remains of settlements, the analysis of the scale and distribution of the Wessex monuments does allow the reconstruction of important aspects of social organization. In the early phase of construction (*c.* 4000–3000 BCE), the spatial distribution and size of the long barrows suggests a possible interpretation: lines drawn between them divide the landscape into many possible territories, which are roughly equivalent in size. Each monument seems to have been the focal point for social activities and the burial place of the farming community inhabiting the local territory. A group of 20 people would have needed about 50 working days to construct a long barrow.

View south across the central plaza at Monte Albán, with the restored ruins of several temples visible. The site was founded on a mountain top in 500 BCE.

In Neolithic southern England, in the earlier long barrow/causewayed camp phase (near right), clusters of burial mounds establish a social landscape, each cluster with its causewayed enclosure. Analysis indicates that each mound was the territorial focus for a small group of farmers. This was a segmentary society, where no one group was dominant. In the later phase (far right), the causewayed enclosures were replaced by major henge monuments (see key, p. 161). Their scale indicates centralized organization, and hence perhaps a chiefdom society. At this time the two great monuments at Stonehenge and Silbury Hill were built.

(Above) West Kennet long barrow is one of the largest known monuments of its type.

In this early phase there is little suggestion of the ranking of sites or individuals: this was an egalitarian society. The causewayed enclosures may have served as a periodic meeting place for the larger group of people represented by one whole cluster of long barrows. (The 100,000 hours' labor required to construct one could be achieved in forty working days by 250 people.) This would have been a segmentary, or tribal, society.

In the later phase (*c.* 3000–2000 BCE), the long barrows and causewayed camps went out of use. In place of the latter, major ritual enclosures are seen. These were large circular monuments delimited by a ditch with a bank usually outside it: they are termed henges. Each would have required something in the order of 1 million hours of labor for its construction. The labor input suggests the mobilization of the resources of a whole territory. About 300 people working full time for at least a year would be needed: their food would have to be provided for them unless the process was spread over a very long period. At this time (*c.* 2800 BCE) the great earth mound at Silbury Hill was built. According to its excavator, it required 18 million hours of work, and was completed within two years. A few centuries later (*c.* 2500 BCE) the great monument at Stonehenge took final shape, with its circle of stones, representing an even greater labor investment—30 million hours if the transport of the stones is taken into account, amounting to a massive corporate endeavor. Although such labor calculations are very approximate they do show how some notion of the changing social organization can be formed through the study of the monuments, even at a time when the traces of domestic life are scanty.

The structures built at this early time can be very impressive. Stonehenge is certainly one of the largest, but it is not the oldest. Indeed over much of northwestern Europe there are stone monuments of the Neolithic period, mainly collective tombs, which are often termed "megalithic" (from the Greek *megas* (great) and *lithos* (stone)). Some of these go back as far as 4000 BCE, a millennium before the pyramids of Egypt. In the Orkney Islands, beyond the northern tip of Scotland, the local sandstone could readily be worked, even before the use of metal tools, and the surviving monuments, some of them well preserved, are sophisticated works of stone architecture. For instance, in the chambered tomb at Quanterness, dating to *c.* 3300 BCE, remains of a large number of individuals were found, perhaps as many

(Right) Analysis of the scale of the Wessex monuments in terms of labor hours needed for their construction suggests the emergence of a hierarchy in the later phase that may mirror a development in social relations and the emergence of a ranked society. Stonehenge, built at this time, is the greatest of the Wessex monuments. In the earlier Neolithic the scale of monuments is commensurate with an egalitarian, segmentary society.

(Below) Stonehenge, formed of huge sarsen stones and smaller bluestones, and the greatest of the Wessex monuments, had largely reached its current form by around 2500 BCE.

APPROX. WORK HOURS REQUIRED FOR CONSTRUCTION	
Late Neolithic	
	STONEHENGE 30,000,000
	HENGE 1,000,000
Early Neolithic	
	CAUSEWAYED CAMP 100,000
	LONG BARROW 10,000

KEY

■ Stonehenge
▲ Henge
◉ Causewayed camp
■ Long barrow

as 390. Males and females were about equally represented, and the age distribution could represent the pattern of deaths in the population at large; that is to say, that the age at death of the people buried in the tomb (46 percent below twenty years, 47 percent aged twenty–thirty years, and only 7 percent over the age of thirty years) could in proportional terms be the same as that of the whole population. The excavators concluded that this was a tomb equally available to most sectors of the community, and representative of a segmentary society rather than a hierarchical one, which the sophistication of its architecture might at first have suggested.

Written Records

For literate societies—those that use writing, for instance all the great civilizations in Mesoamerica, China, Egypt, and the Near East—historical records can answer many of the social questions set out at the beginning of this chapter. One of the main goals of the archaeologist dealing with these societies is therefore to find appropriate texts. Many of the early excavations at the great sites of the Near East, for example, concentrated on the recovery of archives of clay writing tablets. Major finds of this kind are still made today—for example, at the ancient city of Ebla (Tell Mardikh) in Syria in the 1970s, where an archive of 5000 clay tablets written in an early, probably provincial, dialect of Akkadian (Babylonian) was discovered.

In each early literate society, writing had its own functions and purposes. For instance, the clay tablets of Mycenaean Greece, dating from *c.* 1200 BCE, are almost without exception records of commercial transactions at the Mycenaean palaces. This gives us an impression of many aspects of the Mycenaean economy, and a glimpse into craft organization (through the names for the different kinds of craftspeople), as well as introducing the names of the offices of state. But here, as in other cases, accidents of preservation may be important. It could be that the Mycenaeans wrote on clay only for their commercial records, and used other, perishable materials for literary or historical texts now lost to us. It is certainly true that for the Classical Greek and Roman civilizations, it is mainly official decrees inscribed on marble that have survived. Fragile rolls of papyrus—the predecessor of modern paper—with literary texts on them, have usually only remained intact in the dry air of Egypt, or, for example, buried in the volcanic ash covering Pompeii. Coinage is also an important written source. The findspots of coins give interesting economic evidence about trade. But the inscriptions themselves are informative about the issuing authority—whether city-state (as in ancient Greece) or sole ruler (as in imperial Rome, or the kings of medieval Europe).

The decipherment of an ancient language transforms our knowledge of the society that used it. In recent times one of the most significant advances has been the decipherment of Maya glyphs. It had been widely assumed that Maya

Some of the 5000 clay tablets discovered in the royal palace at Ebla (Tell Mardikh) in modern Syria, dating from the late third millennium BCE. The tablets formed part of the state archives, recording more than 140 years of Ebla's history. Originally they were stored on wooden shelving, which collapsed when the palace was sacked.

The Inca had no writing system as such, but kept records of accounts and other transactions using knotted ropes called quipu.

inscriptions were exclusively of a calendrical nature, or that they dealt with purely religious matters, notably the deeds of deities. But the inscriptions can now in many cases be interpreted as relating to real historical events, mainly the deeds of the Maya kings. We can also now begin to deduce the likely territories belonging to individual Maya centers. Maya history has thus taken on a new dimension.

A more detailed example of the value of written sources for reconstructing social archaeology is Mesopotamia, where a huge number of records of Sumer and Babylon (c. 3000–1600 BCE), mainly in the form of clay tablets, have been preserved. The uses of writing in Mesopotamia may be summarized as follows:

Recording information for future use	• Administrative purposes
	• Codification of law
	• Formulation of a sacred tradition
	• Annals
	• Scholarly purposes
Communicating current information	• Letters
	• Royal edicts
	• Public announcements
	• Texts for training scribes
Communicating with the gods	• Sacred texts, amulets, etc.

(Right) Akkadian cylinder seal of *c.* 2400 BCE and its rollout impression, showing armed men, possibly hunters. The inscription, written, similarly to Hammurabi's law code (below), in the cuneiform script, reveals that the owner of the seal was Kalki, a servant of Ubilishtar, the brother of the king (who is not named, but was probably Sargon of Akkad). Such seals were used to mark ownership or authenticity. Many thousands have been recovered from Mesopotamian sites.

(Below) The famous law code of the Babylonian king Hammurabi, *c.* 1750 BCE.

Perhaps most evocative of all are the law codes, of which the most impressive example is the law code of Hammurabi of Babylon, written in the Akkadian language (and in cuneiform script) around 1750 BCE. The ruler is seen at the top of the stone, standing before Shamash, the god of justice. The laws were promulgated, as Hammurabi states, "so that the strong may not oppress the weak, and to protect the rights of the orphan and widow." These laws cover many aspects of life—agriculture, business transactions, family law, inheritance, terms of employment for different craftspeople, and penalties for such crimes as adultery and homicide.

Impressive and informative as it is, Hammurabi's law code is not straightforward to interpret, and emphasizes the need for the archaeologist to reconstruct the full social context that led to the drafting of a text. As the British scholar Nicholas Postgate has pointed out, the code is by no means complete, and seems to cover only those areas of the law that had proved troublesome. Moreover, Hammurabi had recently conquered several rival city states, and the law code was therefore probably designed to help integrate the new territories into his empire.

Ethnoarchaeology

Ethnoarchaeology is a fundamental method of approach for the social archaeologist. It involves the study of both the present-day use and significance of artifacts, buildings, and structures within living societies, and the way these material things become incorporated into the archaeological record—what happens to them when they are thrown away or (in the case of buildings and structures) torn down or abandoned. It is therefore an *indirect* approach to the understanding of any past society.

There is nothing new in the idea of looking at living societies to help interpret the past. In the nineteenth and early twentieth centuries European archaeologists frequently turned for inspiration to researches done by ethnographers among societies in Africa or Australia. But the so-called "ethnographic parallels" that resulted often simply and crudely likened past societies to present ones, stifling new thought rather than promoting it. In the United States archaeologists were confronted from the beginning with the living reality of complex Native American societies, which taught them to think rather more deeply about how **ethnography** might be used to aid archaeological interpretation. Nevertheless, full-fledged ethnoarchaeology is a development really of only the last forty years. The key difference is that now it is archaeologists themselves, rather than ethnographers or anthropologists, who carry out the research among living societies.

A good example is the work of Lewis Binford among the Nunamiut, a hunter-gatherer group of Alaska. In the 1960s Binford was attempting to interpret archaeological sites of the Middle Paleolithic in France (the Mousterian period, 180,000–40,000 years ago). He realized that only by studying how *modern* hunter-gatherers used and discarded bones and tools, or moved from site to site, could he begin to understand the mechanisms that had created the Mousterian archaeological record—itself almost certainly the product of a mobile hunter-gatherer economy. Between 1969 and 1973 he lived intermittently among the Nunamiut and observed their behavior. For instance, he studied the way bone debris was produced and discarded by men at a seasonal hunting camp (the Mask site, Anaktuvuk Pass, Alaska). He saw that, when sitting round a hearth and processing bone for marrow, there was a "drop zone" where small fragments of bone fell as they were broken. The larger pieces, which were thrown away by the men, formed a "toss zone," both in front and behind them (see illustration overleaf).

The Nunamiut might not provide an exact ethnographic parallel for Mousterian societies, but Binford recognized that there are certain actions or functions likely to be common to all hunter-gatherers because—as in the case of the processing of bone—the actions are dictated by the most convenient procedure when seated round a camp fire. The discarded fragments of bone then leave a characteristic pattern round the hearth for the archaeologist to find and interpret—indeed, Binford went on to use his model to reinterpret data from a Paleolithic camp site. From such analysis, it also proved possible to infer roughly how many people were in the group, and over what period of time the camp site was used. These are questions very relevant to our understanding of the social organization (including the size) of hunter-gatherer groups.

Ethnoarchaeology is not restricted to observations at the local scale. The British archaeologist Ian Hodder, in his study of the female ear decorations used by different tribes in the Lake Baringo area of Kenya, undertook a regional study to investigate the extent to which material culture (in this case personal decoration) was being used to express differences between the tribes. Partly as a result of such work, archaeologists no longer assume that it is an easy task to take archaeological assemblages and group them into regional "cultures," and then to assume that each "culture" so formed represents a social unit.

In the Lake Baringo area of Kenya, Ian Hodder studied the female ear decorations worn by the Tugen, Njemps, and Pokot (shown here) tribes, and showed how these ornaments were used to assert tribal distinctiveness.

Ethnoarchaeology: the work of Lewis Binford. (Right) The "drop zone" and "toss zones" model derived from observations of the Nunamiut. (Center) At the site of Pincevent, France, the excavator André Leroi-Gourhan interpreted three hearths as being evidence for a complex skin tent (plan and reconstruction shown). (Below left) Binford applied his "outside hearth model" to the three Pincevent hearths, and deduced from the distribution of bones that his model fitted the evidence better than that of Leroi-Gourhan: i.e. that the hearths lay outside, and not within a tent. (Below right) Classic semicircular arrangement around an outside hearth, as demonstrated by G/wi people at Ghanzi, Botswana, in the 1980s.

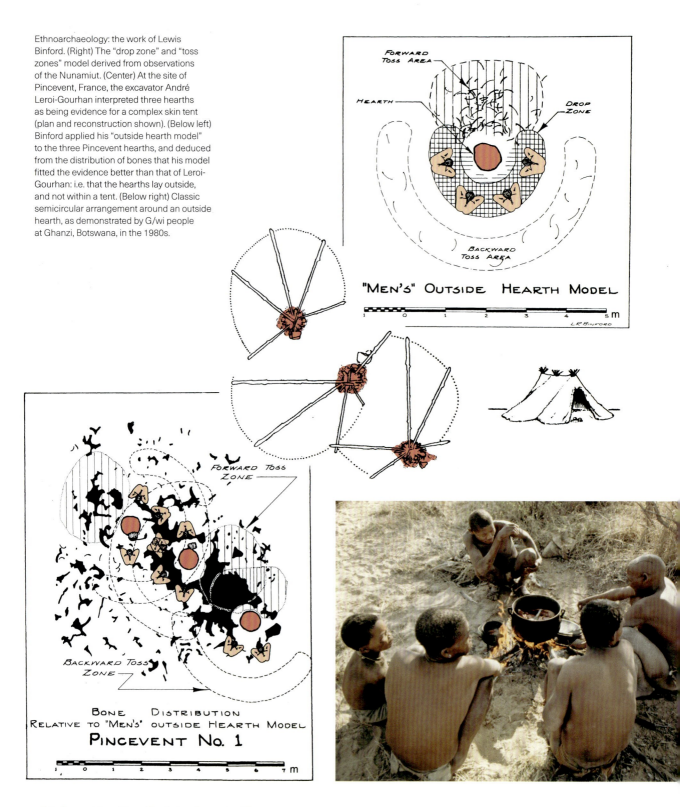

"MEN'S" OUTSIDE HEARTH MODEL

BONE DISTRIBUTION RELATIVE TO "MEN'S" OUTSIDE HEARTH MODEL
PINCEVENT No. 1

Such a procedure might, in fact, work quite well for the ear decorations Hodder studied, because the people in question chose to use this feature to assert their tribal distinctiveness. But, as Hodder showed, if we were to take other features of the material culture, such as pots or tools, the same pattern would not necessarily be followed. His example documents the important lesson that material culture cannot be used by the archaeologist in a simple or unthinking manner in the reconstruction of supposed ethnic groups.

The Archaeology of the Individual and of Identity

The discussion so far in this chapter has as its starting point the concept of the society and its organization. This is a deliberate feature of the structure of this book: before questions are asked about the variety of human experience it is necessary first to form some view about the scale of a society and its complexity. But at the same time this might be criticized as a top-down approach, beginning with questions of organization and of hierarchy, of power and of centralization, and only then turning to the individual who actually lives in society, to that person's role, gender, and status, and to what it was really *like* to live there at that time and in that social context.

It would be equally valid to start with the individual and with social relationships, including kinship relations, and to work outward from there: what one might term a bottom-up approach. This involves the consideration of such issues as social inequality, **ethnicity**, and gender.

One important aspect of the individual to remember is that most sides of our humanness and many of the concepts that we enshrine as human, including our schemes of perception, thought, gender, and sense of morals, our ways of moving our bodies around and communicating (such as standing, sitting, looking, speaking, and walking), and even the way we respond to our senses (such as our sense of smell and taste), are not natural "givens" but are in fact culturally specific: they are developed and adopted by humans within a society and vary through time and space. If we are really to know what it was like to live in a past society, we must be careful not to make assumptions based on our own experience of what it is to be human.

Social Inequality

The theme of the archaeology of social inequality has perhaps not been very comprehensively addressed yet, but in the field of historical archaeology there have been systematic studies of the material culture of some underprivileged groups, including some interesting studies of town areas known from documentary accounts to be considered poor.

The infamous Five Points slum area of Lower Manhattan, New York, described by early nineteenth-century writers including Charles Dickens, has been investigated through salvage excavations at the site of a new federal

A view of the rescue excavation of the nineteenth-century slum area of Five Points in lower Manhattan, New York (right). The cellar of a brothel was investigated and yielded much information concerning the daily lives of the inhabitants. While of a low social rank, the prostitutes enjoyed the use of Chinese porcelain (above).

Key Concepts
Finding the Individual

Many aspects of individual human behavior are not a cross-cultural "given" but are learned, and differ widely across both ancient and modern cultures

The existence of ethnic groups is difficult to recognize from the archaeological record: an affiliation to a particular style of material culture, for example, does not necessarily equate to ethnicity

It is important to recognize gender in the archaeological record (particularly the roles of women, which have traditionally been overlooked). There is also a distinction between sex and gender: sex is biologically determined, whereas gender roles in different societies vary greatly

courthouse at Foley Square. The excavated area included the site of a cellar brothel at 12 Baxter Street, historically documented (in the 1843 indictment of its keeper) as a "disorderly house—a nest for prostitutes and others of ill fame and name, where great numbers of characters are in the nightly practice of reveling until late and improper hours of the night." The excavations revealed insights based upon the material culture:

> The quality of the household goods found in the privy behind 12 Baxter [Street] far exceeded that of goods found anywhere else on the block. The prostitutes lived well, at least when they were at work. One attraction was the opportunity to live in a style that seamstresses, laundresses, and maids could not afford. Afternoon tea at the brothel was served on a set of Chinese porcelain that included matching teacups and coffee cups, saucers and plates, a slop bowl and a tea caddie. Meals consisted of steak, veal, ham, soft-shell clams, and many kinds of fish. There was a greater variety of artifacts from the brothel than from other excavated areas of the courthouse block.

Not far from Foley Square another excavation, that of the African Burial Ground, formerly known as the Negros Burial Ground, which was recorded on a plan of 1755, has proved highly informative and has had wide repercussions.

The rescue excavation of skeletons there in 1991 provoked outrage in the African-American community of today, which felt it had not been adequately consulted, and ultimately led to the establishment of a Museum of African and African-American History in New York City. There were no grave markers, and other than wood, coffin nails, and shroud pins, few

A Yoruba priestess and a Khamite priest perform a libation ceremony over the grave of a person buried in the African Burial Ground in Lower Manhattan, New York.

artifacts were found. Studies of the skeletons have combined DNA analysis with cranial metrics, morphology, and historical data, to discover where the people came from. The large size of the sample will allow study of nutrition and pathology. The remains of 419 individuals disinterred during the excavations were ceremonially reburied in October 2003, after being taken in a procession up Broadway.

Certainly the controversy and the excavation have proved a stimulus toward the development of African-American archaeology, already well-defined through the investigation of plantation sites.

Ethnicity and Conflict

Ethnicity (i.e. the existence of ethnic groups) is difficult to recognize from the archaeological record. For example, the idea that such features as pottery decoration are automatically a sign of ethnic affiliation has been questioned. This is a field where ethnoarchaeology is only now beginning to make progress.

The theme of ethnicity is a difficult one to approach archaeologically, unless with the help of written records, since ethnicity is based largely upon self-awareness. There is frequently a correlation between ethnic groups and language groups, which can offer further avenues for study. Questions of group self-identity, which is often much the same as ethnicity, often underlie conflict and warfare.

The role of warfare in early societies is one topic that merits further investigation. It has long been agreed that warfare is a recurrent feature of early state societies, but for prehistoric times it has been more common to think in terms of peace-loving "noble savages." There is, however, an increasing amount of evidence to suggest that warfare in prehistory was not so much the

Skeletons found in a pit at Talheim, Germany, dating to *c.* 5000 BCE, indicative of mass killing, contradict the notion of a peaceful early farming society (left to right, males, females, and children).

exception as the norm. A good example is provided by the Neolithic ditched enclosures (*c.* 5000 to 2000 BCE) of Talheim, Germany. Fieldwork suggested that they were not simply of symbolic significance, as many archaeologists had thought, but genuine fortifications. One pit contained the bodies of eighteen adults and sixteen children, all killed by blows from at least six different axes, contradicting the notion of a peaceful early farming society.

War need not be undertaken with the objective of permanently occupying the lands of the vanquished in a process of territorial expansion. The American archaeologist David Freidel made this point in his study of Maya warfare, based on the wall paintings at the site of Bonampak and also early written sources. According to his analysis, the function of Maya warfare was not to conquer, and thus enlarge the frontiers of the state in question, but instead to give Maya rulers the opportunity to capture kings and princes from neighboring states, many of whom were then later offered as sacrifices to the gods. Warfare thus allowed the Maya rulers to reaffirm their royal status: it had a central role in upholding the system of government, but that role was not one of territorial expansion.

Investigating Gender

An important aspect of the study of social archaeology is the investigation of gender. Initially this was felt to overlap with feminist archaeology, which often had the explicit objective of exposing and correcting the male bias (androcentrism) of archaeology. There is no doubt that in the modern world the role of women professionals, including archaeologists, has often been a difficult one. For instance, Dorothy Garrod, the first female professor of archaeology in Britain, was appointed in 1937, at a time when women at her university (Cambridge) were not allowed to take a degree at the end of their course, as male undergraduates did, but only a diploma. There was—and still is—an imbalance to be rectified in the academic world, and that was one of the early objectives of feminist archaeology. A second was to illuminate the roles of women in the past more clearly, where frequently they had been overlooked.

But the study of gender is much more than simply the study of women. An important central idea soon became the distinction between sex and gender. It was argued that sex—female or male—may be regarded as biologically determined and can be established archaeologically from skeletal remains. But gender—at its simplest woman or man—is a social construct, involving the sex-related roles of individuals in society. Gender roles in different societies vary greatly both from place to place and through time. Systems of kinship, of marriage, inheritance, and the division of labor are all related to biological sex but not determined by it. These perspectives permitted a good deal of profitable work in this second phase of gender studies in archaeology, but in turn were criticized by third-wave feminists, as emphasizing supposedly inherent differences between women and men, and emphasizing women's links to the natural world through reproduction.

The work of Marija Gimbutas on the prehistory of southeastern Europe, for example, is now criticized. She argued that the predominantly female figurines seen in the Neolithic and Copper Age of southeastern Europe and in Anatolia demonstrate the important status of women at that time. She had a vision of an Old Europe influenced by feminine values, which was to disappear in the succeeding Bronze Age with the dominance of a warlike male hierarchy, supposedly introduced by Indo-European warrior nomads from the east.

Different images symbolizing female power? (Top) A Neolithic vase from Romania; (above) a Zapotec figurine from Oaxaca, Mexico; and (right) a late Neolithic seated stone figure from Hagar Qim, Malta, originally with a removable head that could be manipulated with strings.

Marija Gimbutas became something of a cult figure in her own right, and her support for the concept of a great Mother Goddess representing a fertility principle has been embraced by modern "ecofeminist" and New Age enthusiasts. The current excavations by Ian Hodder at the early Neolithic site of Çatalhöyük in Turkey, where female figurines of baked clay have been found, are now visited regularly by devotees of the Goddess whose views are treated respectfully by the excavators, even though they do not share them. Hodder has argued instead that the figurines may represent the subordination of women as objects of ownership and male desires. Comparable figurines from the Aegean can often be shown to lack definite features diagnostic of sex or gender, and studies of rather similar baked clay figurines from Oaxaca, Mexico, have suggested that they were made by women for use in rituals relating to ancestors rather than deities. The notion that they represented a Mother Goddess lacks supporting evidence.

The third phase in the development of gender archaeology, in tune with the third wave of feminists of the 1990s, takes a different view of gender in two senses. First, in the narrower sense, and, as Lynn Meskell puts it, "led by women of color, lesbian feminists, queer theorists and postcolonial feminists," it recognizes that the field of gender and gender difference is more complex than a simple polarity between male and female, and that other kinds of difference have to be recognized. Indeed the very recognition of a simple structural opposition between male and female is itself, even in our own society, an oversimplification. In many societies children are not regarded as socially male or female until they reach the age of puberty—in the modern Greek language, for instance, while men and women are grammatically male and female in gender, the words for children generally belong to the third, neuter gender.

This leads on to the second point, that gender is part of a broader social framework, part of the social process—in Margaret Conkey's words, "a way in which social categories, roles, ideologies, and practices are defined and played out." While gender is, in any society, a system of classification, it is part of a larger system of social differences, including age, wealth, **religion**, ethnicity, and so forth. Moreover these are not static constructs but fluid and flexible, constructed and reconstructed in the practice of daily life.

The complexities in analyzing burial data with respect to gender are indicated by the study by Bettina Arnold of the so-called Princess of Vix burial from east-central France. The grave contained skeletal remains that analysis indicated were female, but included various **prestige goods** normally thought to be indicative of males. This exceptionally rich fifth-century BCE burial was initially interpreted as a transvestite priest because it was considered inconceivable that a woman could be honored in such a way. Arnold's careful reanalysis of the grave-goods supported the interpretation of the burial as an

(Above left) Reconstruction of part of the Princess of Vix burial. A woman's body adorned with jewelry lay on a cart, the wheels of which had been stacked against the wall of a timber chamber.

(Above right) This huge bronze krater, 1.64 m (5 ft. 4 in.) high, was among the grave-goods.

elite female. This may lead to a fresh assessment of the potentially powerful, occasionally paramount role that women played in Iron Age Europe. But this work may yet lead on to a wider consideration of gender distinctions in the Iron Age in a context that may reassess whether in individuals of very high status the traditional bipolar concept of gender is appropriate.

Study Questions

1 Societies are typically classified into what four main groups?
2 Why is the analysis of burials important to the study of segmentary societies?
3 How can the ethnoarchaeology of modern societies inform us about the past?
4 What are the key methods through which the structure of societies is analyzed?
5 Why is it hard to study ethnicity in the archaeological record?
6 What is the difference between sex and gender? Why is this difference important to archaeologists?

Summary

A FORMIDABLE BATTERY of techniques is available to archaeologists who wish to investigate the social organization of early societies. The potential for understanding the more complex and highly organized societies represented by states and chiefdoms is especially great.

WE CAN INVESTIGATE ranked societies through their site hierarchies and, in the case of state societies, through their urban centers. It should in this way be possible to identify the ruling center, and the extent of the area over which it held jurisdiction, using archaeological methods alone.

FOR RANKED OR STRATIFIED SOCIETIES (chiefdoms and states), the study of buildings and other evidence of administration at the center gives valuable information about social, political, and economic organization, as well as a picture of the life of the ruling elite. We can identify and analyze palaces and tombs, and studies of lower-order administrative centers give further information. Differences in the treatment accorded to different individuals at death, in both the size and wealth of grave offerings, can reveal the complete range of status distinctions in a society.

SIMILAR APPROACHES may be applied to segmentary societies, through the study of individual settlements, social ranking revealed by burials, and cooperative communal mechanisms for the construction of major monuments.

ON A SMALLER SCALE (and particularly important for the Paleolithic period), the camps of mobile hunter-gatherer societies and the seasonal movement between different sites may also be studied using the methods outlined in this chapter, especially when the insights provided by ethnoarchaeological research on living societies are used in conjunction with direct study of the archaeological record.

IN RECENT STUDIES a bottom-up perspective in social archaeologies has become important: the archaeology of individuals and of identity. Gender studies in particular are now adding new insight into the structure of society.

Further Reading

The following works illustrate some of the ways in which social organization can be reconstructed:

Binford, L. R. 2002. *In Pursuit of the Past*. University of California Press: Berkeley & London.
Hodder, I. 2009. *Symbols in Action*. Cambridge University Press: Cambridge & New York.
Janusek, J. W. 2004. *Identity and Power in the Ancient Andes*. Routledge: London & New York.
Meskell, L. 2006. *A Companion to Social Archaeology*. Wiley-Blackwell: Oxford.
Pyburn, K. A. (ed.). 2004. *Ungendering Civilization*. Routledge: London & New York.

[See p. 345 for a list of useful websites]

6

What Was the Environment and What Did They Eat?
Environment, Subsistence, and Diet

Environment and diet constitute two of the most fundamental and crucial factors of human life that the archaeologist needs to assess. The environment governs human life: latitude, altitude, landforms, and climate determine the vegetation, which in turn determines animal life, and both of these determine diet. And all these things taken together determine how and where humans have lived—or at least they did until very recently.

The reconstruction of the environment first requires an answer to very general questions of global climate change. What was the global climate like when the human activities under study took place? Does a context belong to a glacial or interglacial phase? These broad questions can be answered by relating the date of a context to evidence of long-term climatic fluctuations obtained from sea and ice cores, as well as from tree-rings.

More specific questions about past environments will follow, and these are particularly relevant for all postglacial contexts, after about 10,000 years ago. There are two main sources of evidence: plant and animal remains. Analysis of these will not only reveal the range of flora and fauna that people would have encountered at a particular time and place, but since many plants and animals are quite sensitive to climate change, we can also find out what the regional and local environment would have been like.

Unfortunately, owing to the poor preservation of many forms of organic evidence, and to the distorted samples we recover, we can never be certain about our conclusions. We simply have to aim for the best approximation available. No single method will give a full and accurate picture—all are problematic in one way or another—and so as many methods as data and funds will allow need to be applied to build up a composite image.

Once we know what the environment might have been like, as well as the kinds of plants and animals present, we can try to find out how people exploited those conditions and resources, and what they might have been eating. Subsistence, the quest for food, is one of the most basic of all necessities, and there is a variety of evidence for it to be found in the archaeological record. Plant and animal remains and the residues found on artifacts, such as pots or stone tools, can give indirect clues to diet, but the only direct evidence we have is from the study of actual human remains: stomach contents, fecal material, teeth, and bones.

Investigating Environments on a Global Scale

The first step in assessing previous environmental conditions is to look at them globally. Local changes make little sense unless seen against this broader climatic background. Tree-rings are a good source of information for the last 10,000 years or so, but since water covers almost three-quarters of the Earth, we should begin by examining evidence about past climates that can be obtained from this area, including data within glaciers and ice caps. We will then go on to look at what can be learned about past environments at a more local level, from plant and animal remains.

Evidence from Water and Ice

The sediments of the ocean floor accumulate very slowly, just a few centimeters every thousand years, but they can contain evidence of thousands or even millions of years of climate history. In some areas ocean sediments consist primarily of an ooze made up of microfossils, such as the shells of foraminifera—tiny one-celled marine organisms that live in the surface water of the oceans and sink to the bottom when they die. As in an archaeological stratigraphy, we can trace changes in environmental conditions through time by studying cores extracted from the seabed and fluctuations in the species represented and the physical form of single species through the sequence. Oxygen isotope analysis of foraminifera can also reveal changes in the environment (see box overleaf).

Thousands of deep-sea cores have now been extracted and studied, but cores can also be obtained from stratified ice sheets (some containing hundreds of thousands of annual growth layers), and here the oxygen isotopic composition also gives some guide to climatic oscillations. Results from cores in Greenland and the Antarctic, as well as Andean and Tibetan glaciers, are consistent with, and add detail to, those from deep-sea cores. It is also possible to analyze bubbles of ancient methane gas trapped in the ice (resulting from plant decomposition, which is sensitive to temperature and moisture variations).

ANCIENT WINDS. Isotopes can be used not merely for temperature studies but also for data on precipitation. And since it is the temperature differences between the equatorial and polar regions that largely determine the storminess of our weather, isotope studies can even tell us something about winds in different periods.

Sea and Ice Cores and Global Warming

The stratigraphy of sediment on the ocean floor is obtained from cores taken out of the seabed. Ships use a "piston corer" to extract a thin column of sediment, usually about 10–30 m (30–100 ft.) in length. The core can then be analyzed in the laboratory.

Dates for the different layers in the core are obtained by radiocarbon, archaeomagnetism, or the uranium-series method (see Chapter 4). Changing environmental conditions in the past are then deduced by two kinds of tests on microscopic fossils of tiny one-celled organisms, called foraminifera, found in the sediment. First, scientists study the simple presence, absence, and fluctuations of different foraminiferan species. Second, they analyze, by mass spectrometer, fluctuations in the ratio of the stable oxygen isotopes, oxygen-18 and oxygen-16, in the calcium carbonate of the foraminiferan shells. Variations discernible by these two tests reflect not simply changes in temperature, but also oscillations in the continental glaciers. For example, as the glaciers grew, water was drawn up into them, reducing sea levels and increasing the density and salinity of the oceans, and thus causing changes in the depths at

which certain foraminiferan species lived. At the same time the proportion of oxygen-18 in seawater increased. When the glaciers melted during periods of warmer climate, the proportion of oxygen-18 decreased.

Cores can also be extracted from present-day ice sheets in Greenland and Antarctica. Here too, variations in oxygen and also hydrogen isotopic composition at different depths reveal the temperature when the ice formed, and thus provide an indication of past climate; results coincide well with those from deep-sea cores. In addition, high carbon and methane levels (the so-called greenhouse gases) indicate periods of global warming.

The ice cores suggest that the next ice age is about 15,000 years away; however, the stability of our climate has been overturned by human

Microscopic fossils of the foraminiferan species *Globorotalia truncatulinoides*, which coils to the left during cold periods, and to the right during warm ones.

activity, and the ice shows that today's greenhouse gas concentrations in the atmosphere are the highest for at least 440,000 years. In the cores, even much smaller rises in the gas level have been followed by significant rises in global temperatures, but the current rate of increase in greenhouse gases is more than 100 times faster than anything recorded in the last half a million years. During that period, levels of carbon dioxide varied between 200 parts per million (ppm) in ice ages, and 280 ppm in interglacials—but since the industrial revolution, the levels have risen to 375 ppm, which alarms scientists.

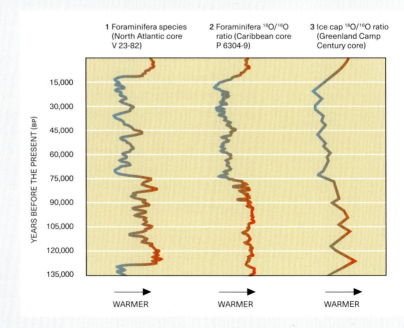

Three climate records compared. Left to right: proportions of different shell species in a deep-sea core; ratio of oxygen-18 to oxygen-16 in shells from a deep-sea core; and oxygen ratios from an ice core. The resemblance of the three records is good evidence that long-term climatic variation has been worldwide.

As air moves from low latitudes to colder regions, the water it loses as rain or snow is enriched in the stable isotope oxygen-18, while the remaining vapor becomes correspondingly richer in the other stable isotope of oxygen, oxygen-16. Thus from the ratio between the two isotopes in precipitation at a particular place, we can calculate the temperature difference between that place and the equatorial region.

Using this technique, the changing ratios found over the last 100,000 years in ice cores from Greenland and the Antarctic have been studied. The results show that during glacial periods the temperature difference between equatorial and polar regions increased by 20–25 percent, and thus wind circulation must have been far more violent. Confirmation has come from a deep-sea core off the coast of West Africa, analysis of which led to estimates of wind strength over the last 700,000 years. Apparently wind "vigor" was greater by a factor of two during each glacial episode than at the present; and wind speeds were 50 percent greater during glacial than interglacial phases. In future, analysis of the minute plant debris in these cores may also add to the history of wind patterns.

It has also been found that raindrops in hurricanes have more oxygen-16 than normal rain, and this leaves traces in layers of stalagmites—for example in caves in Belize—as well as in tree-rings. This method has pinpointed hurricane events of the past 200 years, and so it should also be possible to use older stalagmites to establish a record of hurricanes stretching back tens of thousands of years, thus revealing any changes in their patterns, locations, and intensity. So data from the past may clarify the possible linkage of modern global warming with such extreme weather.

Why should archaeologists be interested in ancient winds? The answer is that winds can have a great impact on human activity. For example, it is thought that increased storminess may have caused the Vikings to abandon their North Atlantic sea route at the onset of a cold period. Similarly, some of the great Polynesian migrations in the southwestern Pacific during the twelfth and thirteenth centuries CE seem to have coincided with the onset of a short period of slightly warmer weather, when violent storms would have been rare. These migrations were brought to an end a few centuries later by the Little Ice Age, which may have caused a sharp increase in the frequency of storms. Had the Polynesians been able to continue, they might conceivably have gone on from New Zealand to reach Tasmania and Australia.

Tree-rings and Climate

Tree-rings have a growth that varies with the climate, being strong in the spring and then declining to nothing in the winter; the more moisture available, the wider the annual ring. As we saw in Chapter 4, these variations in ring width have formed the basis of a major dating technique. Study of a

Evidence From Sea and Ice Cores:
analysis of isotopic ratios within dateable layers of ocean sediment and ice can give an accurate idea of climate. Studies from across the world are all in broad agreement about what global climate was like over the past few million years

Evidence From Tree-rings:
analysis of tree-rings gives a finer-scale idea of what the environment was like in different areas up to about 10,000 years ago

particular set of rings, however, can also reveal important environmental data, for example whether growth was slow (implying dense local forest cover) or fast (implying light forest). Tree growth is complex, and many other factors may affect it, but temperature and soil moisture do tend to be dominant.

Annual and decade-to-decade variations show up far more clearly in tree-rings than in ice cores, and tree-rings can also record sudden and dramatic shocks to the climate. For example, data from Virginia indicate that the alarming mortality and near abandonment of Jamestown, Virginia, the first permanent European settlement in the United States, occurred during an extraordinary drought, the driest seven-year episode in 770 years (1606–12 CE; see pp. 94–95).

The study of tree-rings and climate (dendroclimatology) has also progressed by using X-ray measurements of cell size and density as an indication of environmental productivity. More recently, ancient temperatures have been derived from tree-rings by means of the carbon isotope ratios preserved in their cellulose. Isotopic evidence preserved in the cellulose of timbers of the tamarisk tree, contained in the ramp that the Romans used to overcome the besieged Jewish citadel of Masada in 73 CE, have revealed to Israeli archaeologists that the climate at that time was wetter and more amenable to agriculture than it is today.

The role of tree-rings makes it clear that it is organic remains above all that provide the richest source of evidence for environmental reconstruction. We now take a look at the surviving traces of plants and animals and what these can tell us about ancient environments.

Reconstructing the Plant Environment

The prime goal in archaeological plant studies is to try to reconstruct what the vegetation was like in the past at any particular time or place. But we should not forget that plants lie at the base of the food chain. The plant communities of a given area and period will therefore provide clues to local animal and human life, and will also reflect soil conditions and climate. Some types of vegetation react relatively quickly to changes in climate (though less quickly than insects, for instance), and the shifts of plant communities in both latitude and altitude are the most direct link between climatic change and the terrestrial human environment, for example in the Ice Age.

Plant studies in archaeology have always been overshadowed by faunal analysis, simply because bones are more conspicuous than plant remains in excavation. Bones may sometimes survive better, but usually plant remains are present in greater numbers than bones. Thanks to the discovery that some of the constituent parts of a plant are much more resistant to decomposition than was previously believed, and that a huge amount of data survives that can tell us something about long-dead vegetation, plant studies have become very important. As with so many of the specializations on which archaeology can call, these analyses require a great deal of time and funds.

Some of the most informative techniques for making an overall assessment of plant communities in a particular period involve analysis not of the biggest remains but of the tiniest, microbotanical remains, especially pollen.

Microbotanical Remains

POLLEN ANALYSIS. **Palynology**, or the study of pollen grains (see box overleaf), was developed by a Swedish geologist, Lennart von Post, at the beginning of the twentieth century. It has proved invaluable to archaeology, since it can be applied to a wide range of sites and provides information on chronology as well as environment and forest clearance.

While palynology cannot produce an exact picture of past environments, it does give some idea of fluctuations in vegetation through time, whatever their causes may be (whether climatic or human), which can be compared with results from other methods. Pollen studies can also supply much-needed information for environments as ancient as those of the Hadar sediments and the Omo Valley in Ethiopia around 3 million years ago. It is usually assumed that these regions were always as dry as they are now, but **pollen analysis** has shown that they were much wetter and greener between 3.5 and 2.5 million years ago, with even some tropical plants present. The Hadar, which is now semi-desert with scattered trees and shrubs, was rich, open grassland, with dense woodland by lakes and along rivers. The change to drier conditions, around 2.5 million years ago, can be seen in the reduction of tree pollen in favor of more grasses.

Key Concepts
Reconstructing the Plant Environment

MICROBOTANICAL REMAINS

Pollen: most useful for the study of minor fluctuations in climate over the last 12,000 years, although pollen can be preserved for millions of years in some contexts

Phytoliths: survive very well in most archaeological sediments and can add to the picture of the environment built up from other sources

Diatoms: found in lake and shore sediments and thus useful for the analysis of past marine environments

MACROBOTANICAL REMAINS

Seeds and Fruits: can usually be identified to species, but interpretation can be difficult since they can be brought into a site from elsewhere

Plant Residues: can give some idea of what species were available

Wood: charcoal survives well in the archaeological record, and can be identified to species, but what is found tends to reflect human selection of wood rather than the full range of species growing around a site

Pollen Analysis

All hay fever sufferers will be aware of the pollen "rain" that can afflict them in the spring and summer. Pollen grains—the tiny male reproductive bodies of flowering plants—have an almost indestructible outer shell (exine) that can survive for tens of thousands of years. In pollen analysis the exines are extracted from the soil, studied under the microscope, and identified according to the distinctive exine shape and surface ornamentation of different families and genera of plants. Once quantified, these identifications are plotted as curves on a pollen diagram. Each plant category may then be studied for signs of climatic fluctuation, or forest clearance and crop planting.

Preservation

The most favorable sediments for preservation of pollen are acidic and poorly aerated peat bogs and lake beds, where biological decay is impeded and grains undergo rapid burial. Cave sediments are also usually suitable because of their humidity and constant temperature. Other contexts, such as

(Below left) Scanning electron micrograph of a selection of pollen grains.

sandy sediments or open sites exposed to weathering, preserve pollen poorly.

In wet sites, or unexcavated areas, samples are extracted in long cores, but in dry sites a series of separate samples can be removed from the sections. On an archaeological excavation, small samples are usually extracted at regular stratified intervals (great care must be taken to avoid contamination). Pollen can also be found in mud bricks, vessels, tombs, mummy wrappings, the guts of preserved bodies, ancient feces, and many other contexts.

Examination and Counting

A small portion of each sample is studied under the microscope in an attempt to identify a few hundred grains. Then the quantity of pollen for each plant type is calculated for each layer—usually as a percentage of the total number of grains in that layer—and then plotted as a curve. The curves can be seen as a reflection of climatic fluctuations through the sequence, using the present-day tolerances of these plants as a guide.

The curves can also show the human impact on past vegetation. The diagram shown below is based on a pollen core from Northern Ireland, and reveals the impact of the first farmers in the area. Forest clearance is indicated c. 4150 BCE with a fall in tree pollen (especially elm and oak) and a marked increase in open-country and field species, such as grass and sorrel. The subsequent regeneration of forest cover reflects the non-intensive nature of early farming in the area.

(Below right) Pollen data from Northern Ireland reveal the impact of the first farmers in the area.

Phytoliths are minute particles of silica in plant cells that survive after the rest of the plant has decomposed. Some are specific to certain parts of the plant (e.g. stem or leaf).

PHYTOLITHS.   A fast-developing branch of microbotanical studies concerns phytoliths, which were first recognized as components in archaeological contexts as long ago as 1908, but have only been studied systematically in the last few decades. These are minute particles of silica (plant opal) derived from the cells of plants, and they survive after the rest of the organism has decomposed or been burned. They are common in hearths and ash layers, but are also found inside pottery, plaster, and even on stone tools and the teeth of animals: grass phytoliths have been found adhering to herbivorous animal teeth from Bronze Age, Iron Age, and medieval sites in Europe.

These crystals are useful because, like pollen grains, they are produced in large numbers, they survive well in ancient sediments, and they have myriad distinctive shapes and sizes that vary according to type. They inform us primarily about the use people made of particular plants, but their simple presence adds to the picture of the environment built up from other sources.

In particular, a combination of phytolith and pollen analysis can be a powerful tool for environmental reconstruction, since the two methods have complementary strengths and weaknesses. The American scholar Dolores Piperno has studied cores from the Gatun Basin, Panama, the pollen content of which had already revealed a sequence of vegetation change from 11,300 years ago to the present. She found that the phytoliths in the cores confirmed the pollen sequence, with the exception that evidence for agriculture and forest clearance (i.e. the appearance of maize, and an increase in grass at the expense of trees) appeared around 4850 years ago in the phytoliths, about 1000 years earlier than in the pollen. This early evidence is probably attributable to small clearings that do not show up in pollen diagrams because grains from the surrounding forest overwhelm the samples.

Moreover, phytoliths often survive in sediments that are hostile to the preservation of fossil pollen (because of oxidation or microbial activity), and may thus provide the only available evidence for paleoenvironment or vegetational change. Another advantage is that, while all grass pollen looks the same, grass phytoliths can be assigned to ecologically different groups. It has recently been discovered that aluminum ions in phytoliths can be used to distinguish between forested and herbaceous vegetations, while oxygen and hydrogen isotope signatures in phytoliths will also provide important environmental data.

DIATOM ANALYSIS.   Another method of environmental reconstruction using plant microfossils is **diatom analysis**. Diatoms are single-cell algae that have cell walls of silica instead of cellulose, and these silica cell walls survive after the algae die. They accumulate in great numbers at the bottom of any body of water in which the algae live; a few are found in peat, but most come from lake and shore sediments.

A variety of diatoms, the microscopic single-cell algae, the silica cell walls of which survive in many sediments after death. Study of the changing species in a deposit can help scientists reconstruct fluctuations in past environments.

Diatoms have been recorded, identified, and classified for more than 200 years. The process of identifying and counting them is much like that used in palynology, as is the collection of samples in the field. Their well-defined shapes and ornamentations permit identification to a high level, and their assemblages directly reflect the types of algae present and their diatom productivity, and, indirectly, the water's salinity, alkalinity, and nutrient content. From the environmental requirements of different species (in terms of habitat, salinity, and nutrients), one can determine what their immediate environment was at different periods.

Since diatom assemblages can indicate whether water was fresh, brackish, or salt, they have been used to identify, for example, the period when lakes became isolated from the sea in areas of tectonic uplift, to locate past shorelines, and to reveal water pollution. For instance, the diatom sequence in sediments at the site of the former Lake Wervershoof in the Netherlands suggests that in around 800 CE seawater entered and overcame what had been a freshwater lake, causing a hiatus in human occupation of the immediate area.

All these microbotanical techniques mentioned—studies of pollen, phytoliths, and diatoms—can only be carried out by specialists. For archaeologists, however, a far more direct contact with environmental evidence comes from the larger, macrobotanical plant remains that they can actually see and conserve themselves in the course of excavation.

Macrobotanical Remains

A variety of bigger types of plant remains are potentially retrievable, and provide important information about which plants grew near sites, which were used or consumed by people, and so on. Here we shall focus on the valuable clues that macrobotanical remains provide regarding local environmental conditions.

Retrieval of vegetation from sediments has been made easier by the development of screening (sieving) and **flotation** techniques able to separate organic material from soil. In flotation, samples of soil from an excavation are poured into an overflowing tank, the lighter organic material floating to the top and spilling over the lip to be caught in sieves of different grades. This material is then dried and identified.

Sediments are by no means the only source of plant remains, which have also been found in the stomachs of frozen mammoths and preserved bog bodies; in ancient feces; on teeth; on stone tools; and in residues inside vessels. The remains themselves are varied.

SEEDS AND FRUITS. Ancient seeds and fruits can usually be identified to species, despite changes in their shape caused by charring or waterlogging. In some cases, the remains have disintegrated but have left their imprint behind—grain impressions are fairly common on pottery, leaf impressions are also known, and imprints exist on materials ranging from plaster to leather and corroded bronze. Identification, of course, depends on the type and quality of traces. Not all such finds necessarily mean that a plant grew locally: grape pips, for example, may come from imported fruit, while impressions on potsherds may mislead since pottery can travel far from its place of manufacture.

PLANT RESIDUES.   Chemical analysis of plant residues in vessels will be dealt with below in the context of human diet, but the results can give some idea of what species were available. Pottery vessels themselves may incorporate plant fibers (not to mention shell, feathers, or blood) as a tempering material, and microscopic analysis can sometimes identify these remains—for example, study of early pots from South Carolina and Georgia in the United States revealed the presence of shredded stems of Spanish moss, a member of the pineapple family.

REMAINS OF WOOD.   Study of charcoal (burnt wood) is making a growing contribution to archaeological reconstruction of environments and of human use of timber. A very durable material, charcoal is commonly found by the archaeologist during excavation. Fragments can be examined by the specialist under the microscope, and identified (thanks to the anatomy of the wood) normally at the genus level, and sometimes to species. Charcoal and charred seeds have also proved the most reliable material from which to take samples for radiocarbon dating (see Chapter 4).

Many charcoal samples are the remains of firewood, but others may come from wooden structures, furniture, and implements burnt at some point in a site's history. Samples therefore inevitably tend to reflect human selection of wood rather than the full range of species growing around the site. Nevertheless, the totals for each species provide some idea of one part of the vegetation at a given time.

Occasionally, charcoal analysis can be combined with other evidence to reveal something not only of the local environment but also of human adaptation to it. At Boomplaas Cave in South Africa, excavation has uncovered traces of human occupation stretching back 70,000 years. There is a clear difference between Ice Age and post-Ice Age charcoals: at times of extreme cold when conditions were also drier, between 22,000 and 14,000 years ago, the species diversity both in the charcoals and the pollen was low, whereas at times of higher rainfall and/or temperature the species diversity increased. A similar pattern of species diversity is seen also in the small mammals.

The vegetation around Boomplaas Cave at the time of maximum cold and drought was composed mainly of shrubs and grass with few plant resources that could be used by people; the larger mammal fauna was dominated by

Scanning electron micrograph of charcoal from the thorn tree *Acacia karroo* found at Boomplaas Cave.

grazers that included "giant" species of buffalo, horse, and hartebeest, which became extinct by about 10,000 years ago.

The Boomplaas charcoal directly reflects the gradual change in climate and vegetation that led to the disappearance of the large grazers, and to a corresponding shift in subsistence practices by the cave's occupants. The charcoal analysis also highlights more subtle changes that reflect a shift in the season of maximum rainfall. The woody vegetation in the Cango Valley— where the cave is located—is today dominated by the thorn tree, *Acacia karroo*, characteristic of large areas in southern Africa where it is relatively dry and rain falls mostly in summer. Thorn tree charcoal is absent in the Ice Age samples at Boomplaas, but it appears from about 5000 years ago and by 2000 years ago is the dominant species, indicating a shift to hot, relatively moist summers. As the number of species that enjoy summer rainfall increased, the inhabitants of the cave were able to make more use of a new range of fruits, the seeds of which can be found preserved at the site.

By no means all wood subjected to this kind of analysis is charred. Increasing quantities of waterlogged wood are recovered from wet sites in many parts of the world. And in some conditions, such as extreme cold or dryness, desiccated wood may survive without either burning or waterlogging.

OTHER SOURCES OF EVIDENCE. A great deal of information on vegetation in the less remote periods studied by archaeologists can be obtained from art, from texts (e.g. the writings of Pliny the Elder, Roman farming texts, accounts and illustrations by early explorers, such as Captain Cook), and even from early photographs.

No single category of evidence can provide us with a total picture of local or regional vegetation, of small-scale trends or long-term changes: each produces a partial version of past realities. Input is needed from every source available, and, as will be seen below, these must be combined with results from the other forms of data studied in this chapter in order to reconstruct the best approximation of a past environment.

In this section we have seen how we can use a variety of archaeological data to try to reconstruct the plant environment at any particular place or time in the past. But what evidence of animal life is there and what can this tell us about past environments?

Reconstructing the Animal Environment

Animal remains were the first evidence used by nineteenth-century archaeologists to characterize the climate of the prehistoric periods that they encountered in their excavations. It was realized that different species were absent, present, or particularly abundant in certain layers, and hence also in certain periods, and the assumption was that this reflected changing climate.

Today, in order to use faunal remains as a guide to environment, we need to look more critically at the evidence than did those nineteenth-century pioneers. For instance, we need to understand the complex relationship that exists between modern animals and their environment. We also need to investigate how the animal remains we are studying arrived at a site—either naturally, or through the activities of carnivores (including humans), and thus how representative they may be of the variety of animals in a particular period.

Microfauna

Small animals (microfauna) tend to be better indicators of climatic and environmental change than are large species, because they are much more sensitive to small variations in climate and adapt to them relatively quickly. In addition, since microfauna tend to accumulate naturally on a site, they reflect the immediate environment more accurately than larger animals, whose remains are often accumulated through human or animal predation. As with pollen, small animals, and especially insects, are also usually found in far greater numbers than larger ones, which improves the statistical significance of their analysis.

The remains of a wide variety of insectivores, rodents, and bats are found on archaeological sites, but it is necessary to ensure as far as possible that the bones were deposited at the same time as the layer in question, and that burrowing has not occurred. Certain small species can be indicative of fairly specific environmental conditions, but it should be remembered that, even if the remains are not intrusive, they will not always indicate the immediate environment—if they come from owl pellets, for example, they may have been caught up to a few kilometers from the site (the contents of bird pellets can nevertheless be of great value in assessing local environments).

Bones of birds and fish are particularly fragile, but are well worth studying. They can for example be used to determine the seasons in which particular sites were occupied. Birds are sensitive to climatic change, and the alternation of "cold" and "warm" species in the last Ice Age has been of great help in assessing environment. One problem is that it is sometimes difficult to decide whether a bird is present naturally or has been brought in by a human or animal predator.

The calcium carbonate shells of land molluscs (such as snails) are preserved in many types of sediment. They reflect local conditions, and can be responsive to changes in microclimate, particularly to changes in temperature and rainfall. But we need to take into account that many species have a very broad tolerance, and their reaction to change is relatively slow, so that they "hang on" in adverse areas, and disperse slowly into newly acceptable areas. The changing percentages of marine mollusc species through time can reveal something of the nature of the coastal microenvironment—such as whether

Key Concepts
Reconstructing the Animal Environment

Microfauna are better indicators of climatic and environmental change than macrofauna because they are much more sensitive to small variations in climate and adapt to them relatively quickly

Microfauna tend to accumulate naturally on a site and reflect the immediate environment more accurately than larger animals, whose remains are often accumulated through human or animal predation

Grasshopper engraved on a bone fragment from the late Ice Age (Magdalenian) site of Enlène, Ariège, France. Insects respond rapidly to climatic change, and are sensitive indicators of the timing and scale of environmental variations.

it was sandy or rocky—through study of the modern preferences of the species represented. The climatic change suggested by these alterations in the presence or abundance of different species can be matched with the results of oxygen isotope analysis of the shells.

A wide range of insects may also be found, in the form of adults, larvae, and (in the case of flies) puparia. The study of insects (**paleoentomology**) was rather neglected in archaeology until about thirty years ago, since when a great deal of pioneering work has been done. Insect exoskeletons can be quite resistant to decomposition, and some assemblages comprise thousands of individuals. Since we know the distribution and environmental requirements of their modern descendants, it is often possible to use insect remains as accurate indicators of the likely climatic conditions (and to some extent of the vegetation) prevailing in particular periods and local areas. Some species have very precise requirements in terms of where they like to breed and the kinds of food their larvae need. Rather than use single indicator species to reconstruct a microenvironment, however, it is safer to consider a number of species (the ancient climate lying within the area of overlap of their tolerance ranges).

Macrofauna

Remains of large animals found on archaeological sites mainly help us build up a picture of past human diet (see below, pp. 190–91). As environmental indicators they have proved less reliable than was once assumed, primarily because they are not so sensitive to environmental changes as small animals, but also because their remains will very likely have been deposited in an archaeological context through human or animal action. Bones from animals killed by carnivores, including humans, have been selected, and so cannot accurately reflect the full range of fauna present in the environment. The ideal is therefore to find accumulations of animal remains brought about by natural accident or catastrophe—animals caught in a flash flood perhaps, or buried by volcanic eruption, or that became frozen in permafrost. But such discoveries are rare—very different from the usual accumulations of animal bones encountered by archaeologists.

Assuming a suitable bone assemblage has been found and identified to species, what can the results tell us about the ancient environment?

The anatomy and especially the teeth of large animals tell us something about their diet and hence, in the case of herbivores, of the type of vegetation they prefer. Most information about range and habitat comes from studies of modern species, however, on the assumption that behavior has not changed substantially since the period in question. These studies also show that large animals will tolerate—that is, have the potential to withstand or exploit— a much wider range of temperatures and environments than was once thought. So the presence of such species as woolly rhinoceros in an Ice Age deposit should be regarded merely as proof of the ability of that species to tolerate low temperatures, rather than as evidence of a cold climate.

Large mammals are also not generally good indicators of vegetation, since herbivores can thrive in a wide range of environments and eat a variety of plants. Thus, individual species cannot usually be regarded as characteristic of one particular habitat, but there are exceptions. For example, reindeer reached northern Spain in the last Ice Age, as is shown not only by discoveries of their bones but also by cave art. Such major shifts clearly reflect environmental change. In the rock art of the Sahara, too, one can see clear evidence for the presence of species, such as giraffe and elephant, that could not survive in the area today, and thus for dramatic environmental modification.

As will be seen below, fauna can also be used to determine in which seasons of the year a site was occupied. In coastal sites, marine resources and herbivore remains may come and go through the archaeological sequence as changes in sea level extended or drowned the coastal plain, thus changing the sites' proximity to the shore and the availability of grazing.

We should remember that faunal fluctuations can have causes other than climate or people; additional factors may include competition, epidemics, or fluctuations in numbers of predators. Moreover, small-scale local variations in climate and weather can have major effects on the numbers and distribution of wild animals, so that despite its high powers of resistance a species may decline from extreme abundance to virtual extinction within a few years.

Subsistence and Diet

Having discussed methods for reconstructing the environment, we now turn to how we find out about what people extracted from it, in other words, how they subsisted. When reconstructing early subsistence, it is useful to make a distinction between meals—direct evidence of various kinds as to what people were eating at a particular time—and diet, which implies the pattern of consumption over a long period of time.

So far as meals are concerned, the sources of information are varied. Written records, when they survive, indicate some of the things people were eating, and so do representations in art. Even modern ethnoarchaeology helps indicate what they *might* have been eating by broadening our understanding of the range of options. The actual remains of the foodstuffs eaten can also be highly informative.

For the more difficult question of diet, there are several helpful techniques of investigation. Some methods focus on human bones. Isotopic analyses of the skeletal remains of a human population can indicate, for example, the balance of marine and terrestrial foods in the diet, and even show differences in nutrition between the more and less advantaged members of the same society.

These millet noodles, the earliest known (dating from around 4000 years ago) were found preserved in an overturned bowl at the Lajia site in northwestern China. Discovered in 2005, the remains indicate that routine millet-milling, including the repeated stretching of dough by hand to form a strand and its cooking in boiling water, was practiced in late Neolithic China.

Most of our information about early subsistence, however, comes directly from the remains of what was eaten. **Archaeozoology** (or **zooarchaeology**), the study of past human use of animals, is now big business in archaeology. There can be few excavations anywhere that do not have a specialist to study the animal bones found. The Paleo-Indian rockshelter of Meadowcroft, Pennsylvania, for example, yielded about a million animal bones (and almost 1.5 million plant specimens). On medieval and recent sites, the quantities of material recovered can be even more formidable. **Paleoethnobotany** (or **archaeobotany**), the study of past human use of plants, is likewise a growing discipline. In both areas, a detailed understanding of the conditions of preservation on a site is the first prerequisite to ensure that the most efficient extraction technique is adopted. In both areas, too, the focus of interest has developed to include not just the species eaten, but also the way these were managed. The process of domestication for both plants and animals is now a major research topic.

Interpretation of food remains can be problematic, and requires quite sophisticated procedures. We can initially reconstruct the range of food available in the surrounding environment (see above, pp. 186–89), but the only incontrovertible proof that a particular plant or animal species was actually consumed is the presence of its traces in stomach contents or in desiccated ancient fecal matter. If such evidence is not available, the archaeologist must try to determine whether a foodstuff was actually eaten from the context or condition of the finds. For instance, if bones are cut or burned they may have been butchered and cooked.

Plants that were staples in the diet may be underrepresented thanks to the generally poor preservation of vegetable remains; fish bones likewise may not survive well. The archaeologist therefore has to consider how far a site's food remains are representative of total diet. Here we need to assess a site's function, and whether it was inhabited once or frequently, for short or long periods, irregularly or seasonally (season of occupation can sometimes be deduced from plant and animal evidence as well). A long-term settlement is likely to provide more representative food remains than a specialized camp or kill site. Ideally, however, archaeologists should sample remains from a variety of contexts or sites before making judgments about diet.

We will now look at some of the main forms of evidence for human subsistence, as well as some of the different types of interpretations that can be made.

What Can Plant Foods Tell Us about Diet?

We can learn something of diet from the study of microbotanical remains, particularly through the study of phytoliths, which can, for example, help in differentiating between wild and domestic species of plant. But the vast majority of plant evidence that reaches the archaeologist is in the form of macrobotanical remains, and these are much more useful when trying to reconstruct diet.

Macrobotanical Remains

Macrobotanical remains may be desiccated (only in absolutely dry environments, such as deserts or high mountains), waterlogged (only in environments that have been permanently wet since the date of deposition), or preserved by charring. In exceptional circumstances, volcanic eruption can preserve botanical remains, such as at Cerén in El Salvador, where a wide variety has been found carbonized, or as impressions, in numerous vessels. Plant remains preserved in several different ways can sometimes be encountered within the same site, but in most parts of the world charring is the principal or only cause of preservation on habitation sites.

Occasionally, a single sample on a site will yield very large amounts of material. More than 27 kg (60 lb) of charred barley, wheat, and other plants came from one storage pit on a Bronze Age farm at Black Patch, southern England, for example. This can sometimes give clues to the relative importance of different cereals and legumes and weed flora, but the sample nevertheless simply reflects a moment in time. What the archaeologist really needs is a larger number of samples (each of preferably more than 100 grains) from a single period on the site, and, if possible, from a range of types of deposit, in order to obtain reliable information about what species were exploited, their importance, and their uses during the period of time in question.

When we have obtained enough samples we need to quantify the plant remains: for example by weight or by number of remains. Some archaeologists

Macrobotanical Remains: these can give us a good idea of what plants were present at a site, but there are problems of quantification and interpretation. It is important to understand how a plant might have been processed and used

Plant Residues on Artifacts: chemical traces of plants can be found on some artifacts (often pots and tools) and these can be tested and compared against a reference collection in order to identify a species

Domestication of Wild Plant Species: various techniques can help to answer the crucial question of whether plant remains found in the archaeological record are from wild or domesticated species

simply arrange samples in order of abundance. But this can be misleading, as was shown by the British archaeobotanist Jane Renfrew in her study of the material from the Neolithic settlement of Sitagroi, Greece. She noted that the most abundant plants may have been preserved by chance (such as an accident in the course of baking). Similarly, species that produce large quantities of seeds or grains may appear more important in the archaeological record than they actually were: at Sitagroi 19,000 seeds of knotgrass barely filled a thimble.

INTERPRETING THE CONTEXT AND THE REMAINS. It is crucial for the archaeologist or specialist to try to understand the archaeological context of a plant sample, as this can reveal more about exactly how the plant was being used. In the past, attention used to be focused primarily on the botanical history of the plants themselves, their morphology, place of origin, and evolution. Now, however, archaeologists also want to know more about the human use of plants in hunting-and-gathering economies, and in agriculture—which plants were important in the diet, and how they were gathered or grown, processed, stored, and cooked. This means understanding the different stages of traditional plant processing; recognizing the effect different processes have on the remains; and identifying the different contexts in the archaeological record. In many cases it is the plant remains that reveal the function of the location where they are found, and thus the nature of the context, rather than vice versa.

In a farming economy, for instance, there are many different stages of plant processing, summed up in the illustration opposite: cereals have to be threshed, winnowed, and cleaned before consumption, in order to separate the grain from the chaff, straw, and weeds; but seed corn also has to be stored for the next year's crop; and food grain might also be stored unthreshed in order to get the harvested crop out of the rain, and would then be threshed only when needed. From ethnoarchaeological and experimental observations it is known that certain of these activities leave characteristic residues with which archaeological samples can be compared, whether they are from ovens, living floors, latrines, or storage pits.

CHEMICAL RESIDUES IN PLANT REMAINS. Various chemicals survive in plant remains themselves, which provide an alternative basis for their identification. These compounds include proteins, fatty lipids, and even DNA. The analysis of lipids has so far proved the most useful method for distinguishing different cereal and legume species, but always in combination with other non-chemical identification techniques. DNA offers the prospect of eventually resolving identification at an even more detailed level and of perhaps tracing family trees of plants and patterns of trade in plant products.

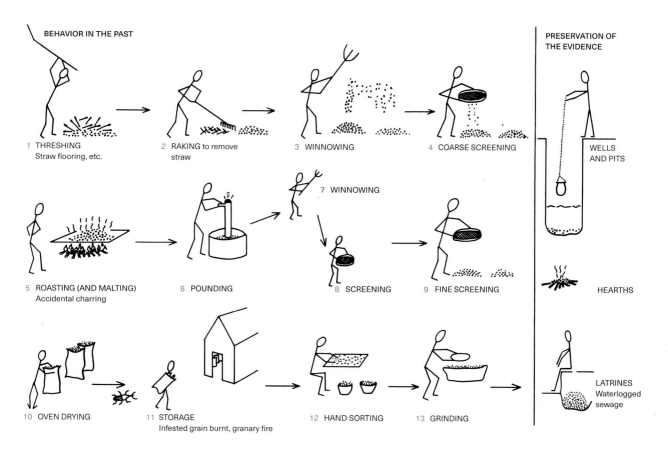

1 THRESHING
Straw flooring, etc.

2 RAKING to remove
straw

3 WINNOWING

4 COARSE SCREENING

5 ROASTING (AND MALTING)
Accidental charring

6 POUNDING

7 WINNOWING

8 SCREENING

9 FINE SCREENING

10 OVEN DRYING

11 STORAGE
Infested grain burnt, granary fire

12 HAND SORTING

13 GRINDING

PRESERVATION OF
THE EVIDENCE

WELLS
AND PITS

HEARTHS

LATRINES
Waterlogged
sewage

Cereal crop processing: waste products from many of these stages may survive as charred or waterlogged remains.

PLANT IMPRESSIONS. Impressions of plant remains are quite common in fired clay, and do at least prove that the species in question was present at the spot where the clay was worked. Such impressions, however, do not necessarily prove that the plant was important in the economy or diet, since they constitute a very skewed sample and only seeds or grains of medium size tend to leave imprints. One has to be particularly careful with impressions on potsherds, because pottery can be discarded far from its point of manufacture, and in any case many pots were deliberately decorated with grain impressions, thus perhaps overemphasizing the importance of a species.

Analysis of Plant Residues on Artifacts

As we shall see in Chapter 7, **microwear analysis** of a tool edge can identify broadly whether the tool was used to cut meat, wood, or some other material. Discovery of phytoliths can show what type of grasses were cut by a tool. Microscopic study can also reveal and identify plant fibers. Another method is chemical analysis of residues on tool edges: certain chemical reagents can provide a means of proving whether plant residues are present on tools or in vessels—thus, potassium iodide turns blue if starch grains are present, and yellow-brown for other plant materials. Starch grains can also be detected by microscope and, for example, have been extracted with a needle from crevices in the surfaces of prehistoric grinding stones from Aguadulce Shelter in the humid tropics of Panama. The species of the grains can be identified, and show that such tubers as manioc and arrowroot—which do not usually leave recoverable fossilized remains—were being cultivated here *c.* 5000 BCE, the earliest recorded occurrence of manioc in the Americas.

The site also yielded maize starch, and this technique is thus important for proving the presence of maize in structures or sites without charred remains: for example, at the Early Formative village of Real Alto (Ecuador), maize starch grains and phytoliths from maize cobs have been retrieved from stone tools and sediments dating to 2800–2400 BCE. Starch grains have even been recovered from a large flat piece of basalt in a hut at Ohalo II, Israel, dating to about 23,000 years ago. This was clearly a grindstone, and the grains from barley, and perhaps wheat, show that wild cereals were already being processed at this early date. Recently, in Mozambique, starch grains retrieved from the surfaces of Middle Stone Age stone tools showed that early *Homo sapiens* was consuming grass seeds at least 105,000 years ago.

Chemical investigation of fats preserved in vessels is also making progress, because it has been found that fatty acids, amino acids (the constituents of protein), and similar substances are very stable and preserve well. Samples are extracted from residues, purified, concentrated in a centrifuge, dried, and then analyzed by means of a spectrometer, and by a technique known as chromatography, which separates the major constituent components of the fats. Interpretation of the results is made by comparison with a reference collection of "chromatograms" (readouts) from different substances.

For example, the German chemist Rolf Rottländer has identified mustard, olive oil, seed oils, butter, and other substances on potsherds, including specimens from Neolithic lake dwellings. In work on sherds from the German Iron Age hillfort of the Heuneburg, he was able to prove that some amphorae—storage vessels usually associated with liquids—did indeed contain olive oil and wine, whereas in the case of a Roman amphora the charcoal-like black residue proved to be not liquid but wheat flour. This important technique not only provides dietary evidence, but also helps to define the function of the vessels with which the fats are associated. Ever more refined techniques are currently being developed for identifying food species from protein, lipid, and DNA biochemical analysis of small fragments of plant material. Indeed, DNA extracted from two 2400-year-old amphorae from a shipwreck off the Greek island of Chios has revealed that they probably contained olive oil flavoured with herbs.

Wild and domestic cereals. Clockwise from top left: wild einkorn, domestic einkorn, extinct wild maize, and domestic maize. The wild einkorn sheds its grain easily. But the tougher domestic form does so only when threshed: a real advantage for the early farmer, since if grains fall off before threshing, they are lost.

The Domestication of Wild Plant Species

One of the major areas of debate in modern archaeology concerns the question of human management of plants, and particularly whether some species that we find were wild or domesticated, since this sheds light on one of the most crucial aspects of human history: the transition from a mobile (hunter-gatherer) to a settled (agricultural) way of life. It can often be difficult, impossible, or irrelevant to try to distinguish between wild and domesticated varieties, since many types of cultivation do not change the form of the plant, and even in cases where such change occurs we do not know how long it took to appear. Experimental evidence suggests that the transition from wild to domestic could have been complete within only 20 to 200 years—without conscious intervention on the farmers' part—but in practice it seems to have taken about a millennium. Any line drawn between wild and domestic plants does not necessarily correspond to a distinction between gathering and agriculture.

There are nevertheless cases where a clear distinction can be made between wild and fully domestic forms. Macrobotanical remains are of most use here. For example, the American archaeologist Bruce Smith found that 50,000 charred seeds of *Chenopodium* (goosefoot), nearly 2000 years old from Russell Cave, Alabama, exhibited a set of interrelated characteristics reflecting domestication. He was thus able to add this starchy-seed species to the brief list of cultivated plants—including bottle gourd, squash, marsh elder, sunflower, and tobacco—available in the garden plots of the Eastern Woodlands before the introduction of maize by about 200 CE.

There has been some debate in recent years about whether wild and domestic legumes can be differentiated by their structure, but archaeobotanical work by the British scholar Ann Butler suggests that there is no foolproof way to do this, even in a scanning electron microscope. Cereals, on the other hand, where well preserved, are more straightforward, and domestication can be identified by clues, for example the loss of anatomical features, such as the brittle rachis, which facilitate the dispersal of seeds by natural agents. In other words, once people began to cultivate cereals, they gradually developed varieties that retained their seeds until they could be harvested.

Plant Evidence from Literate Societies

Archaeologists studying the beginnings of plant cultivation, or plant use among hunter-gatherers, have to rely on the kind of scientific evidence outlined above, coupled with the judicious use of ethnoarchaeological research and modern experiments. For the student of diet among literate societies, however, particularly the great civilizations, there is a wealth of evidence for the domestication of plants, as well as for farming practices, cookery, and many other aspects of diet to be found written in documents and in art.

Harvesting and processing a cereal crop: scenes depicted on the walls of a New Kingdom tomb at Thebes in Egypt.

The Greek writer Herodotus, for example, gives us plenty of information about eating habits in the fifth century BCE, notably in Egypt, a civilization for which there is extensive evidence about food and diet. Much of the evidence for the pharaonic period comes from paintings and foodstuffs in tombs, so it has a certain upper-class bias, but there is also information to be found about the diet of humbler folk, from plant remains in workers' villages, such as that at Tell el-Amarna, and from hieroglyphic texts. In the later Ptolemaic period there are records of corn allowances for workers, such as the third-century BCE accounts concerning grain allotted to workers on a Faiyum agricultural estate. Models are also instructive about food preparation: the tomb of Meketre, a nobleman of the 12th dynasty (2000–1790 BCE), contained a set of wooden models, including women kneading flour into loaves, and others brewing beer. Three newly deciphered Babylonian clay tablets from Iraq, 3750 years old, present cuneiform texts containing 35 recipes for a wide variety of rich meat stews, and thus constitute the world's oldest cookbook.

In the New World, we owe much of our knowledge of Aztec food crops, fishing practices, and natural history to the invaluable writings of the sixteenth-century Franciscan scholar Bernardino de Sahagún, based on his own observations and on the testimony of his Native American informants.

It should be remembered, however, that written evidence and art tend to give a very short-term view of subsistence. Only archaeology can look at human diet with a long-term perspective.

Investigating Diet, Seasonality, and Domestication from Animal Remains

Although plant foods may always have constituted the greater part of the human diet—except in special circumstances or high latitudes such as the Arctic—meat may well have been considered more important, either as food or as a reflection of the prowess of the hunter or the status of the herder. Animal remains are usually better preserved on archaeological sites too so that, unlike plant remains, they have been studied since the very beginnings of archaeology.

The first question the archaeologist must face when interpreting animal remains is to decide whether they are present through human actions rather than through natural causes or the activities of other predators (as in the case of carnivore debris, owl pellets, burrowing animals, etc.). Animals may also have been exploited at a site for non-dietary purposes (skins for clothing, bone and antler for tools).

As with plant remains, therefore, one must be particularly careful to examine the context and content of faunal samples. This is usually straightforward in sites of recent periods, but in the Paleolithic, especially the Lower Paleolithic, the question is crucial.

PROVING HUMAN EXPLOITATION OF ANIMALS IN THE PALEOLITHIC.
In the past, association of animal bones and stone tools was often taken as proof that humans were responsible for the presence of the faunal remains, or at least exploited them. We now know, however, that this is not always a fair assumption, and since in any case many used bones are not associated with tools, archaeologists have sought more definite proof from the marks of stone tools on the bones themselves. A great deal of work is currently aimed at proving the existence of such marks, and finding ways of differentiating them from other traces, such as scratches and punctures made by animal teeth, etching by plant roots, abrasion by sedimentary particles or post-depositional weathering, and damage by excavation tools. This is also part of the search for reliable evidence in the current major debate in Paleolithic studies as to whether early humans were genuine hunters, or merely scavenged meat from carcasses of animals killed by other predators.

Much attention has been directed to bones from the famous Lower Paleolithic sites of Olduvai Gorge and Koobi Fora, in East Africa, that are more than 1.5 million years old. Archaeologists used a scanning electron microscope to examine suspected toolmarks on the bones, comparing their results with marks produced by known processes on modern bones. The diagnostic feature of a toolmark produced by a slicing action, for example, was a V-shaped groove with a series of longitudinal parallel lines at the

Key Concepts
Information from
Animal Resources

Animal remains are often well-preserved on archaeological sites

It is important to establish whether animal remains are present on a site through human agency or through other causes

We can sex and age animal bones, study their seasonality, and deduce whether the animals were wild or domesticated, all of which helps us to understand how humans were exploiting the animal environment

Carnivore marks or toolmarks? (Above left) Round-bottomed groove made on a modern bone by a hyena. (Above right) V-shaped groove made on a modern bone by a sharp stone flake. (Right) Fossil bone from Olduvai Gorge that may show two slicing marks (s) made by a stone flake, and carnivore tooth marks (t) made later.

(Below) Bones of contention: marks on two animal bones from Dikika, Ethiopia, are thought by some specialists to have been made by australopithecines with stone tools— at 3.4 million years ago, this corresponds to the date of the earliest known stone tools from Lomekwi in Kenya (see p. 210) and also pushes back the date for butchery and meat eating. The marks were examined by microscopy and chemical analysis, and were clearly made before the bones fossilized; their morphology fits tools far better than teeth.

(see p. 210)

bottom; marks made by carnivores were much more rounded (see illustration above). They found that many bones had both toolmarks and carnivore scratches, suggesting some competition for the carcass. In some cases, the carnivore marks were clearly superimposed on the toolmarks, but in most cases the carnivores seem to have got there first!

Recent work, however, suggests that very similar marks can be produced by other causes, such as when bones are damaged by trampling. Thus microscopic features alone are not sufficient evidence to prove human intervention. The context of the find and the position of the marks need to be studied too.

More work still needs to be done before we can be sure of proving early human activity in this way, and also of identifying episodes where our early ancestors were hunters rather than scavengers. There are other types of evidence, however, that can provide proof of human processing of bones. These include artificial concentrations of bones in particular places, such as the use of mammoth bones for the construction of huts in the Paleolithic of Central and Eastern Europe. Burning of bones is another clear indication of human processing.

Having demonstrated so far as possible that animal remains were indeed produced by human action, the archaeologist then can move on to try to answer the interesting questions, such as what people ate, in which seasons they ate particular foods, how they hunted and butchered the animals, and whether the animals were domesticated.

The most abundant and informative residues of animals are the macroremains—bones, teeth, antlers, shells, etc. Numerous techniques are now available to help extract information from data of this type. In analyzing an assemblage of bones, we have first to identify them and then quantify them, both in terms of numbers of animals and of meat weight. The amount of meat represented by a bone will depend on the sex and age of the animal, the season of death, and geographical variation in body size and in nutrition. But if factors of age, sex, and season of death need to be allowed for, how are they established?

Strategies of Use:
Deducing Age, Sex, and Seasonality from Large Fauna

Sexing is easy in cases where only the male has antlers (most deer), or large canines (pig), or where a penis bone is present (dog), or where the female has a different pelvic structure. Measurements of certain bones, such as the foot bones of some animals, can sometimes provide two distinct clusters of results, interpreted as male (large) and female (small).

The age of an animal can be assessed from such features as the degree of closure of sutures in the skull, or, to a certain extent, from the stage of development of limb bones. Age is then estimated by comparison with information on these features in modern populations. Estimates of the age at which mammals were killed, however, are usually based on the eruption and wear patterns of the teeth.

The season of death is also a crucial factor. There are many ways of studying seasonality from animal remains—for example, the identification of species

Bison-drive Sites

The driving of bison over bluff or cliff edges was an important periodic hunting method for thousands of years in North America. Much was known from accounts by Native American informants recorded in the first decades of this century, but the picture needed filling out through archaeological investigation of actual drive sites.

The Boarding School Site

One of the first of such excavations was undertaken by Thomas Kehoe in the 1950s at the Boarding School site, Montana. The work was carried out with the help of the local Blackfoot tribe. Boarding School was not a cliff, but one of the more common, lower but abrupt drops that led to a natural enclosure. In a deep stratigraphy, three main bone layers were found, with well-preserved bison remains that gave insights into the size and composition of the herd, and hence into the seasons of the drives. Bison numbers were assessed using the "minimum number of individuals" technique. Ages of the animals came from the eruption sequence and degree of wear on the teeth, and from bone fusion, while sex was established on the basis of size and pelvic shape.

The site proved to have been used intermittently for a long period as a temporary camp. Then *c.* 1600 CE (according to radiocarbon dating of charred bone) a herd of about 100 bison was driven over the bluff. Their remains

formed the "3rd bone layer," which included a fetal bone but no mature bulls, implying a late fall or winter drive of a herd composed of cows, calves, and young bulls. A season or two later, another herd of 150 were driven over, forming the "2nd bone layer." This had remains of mature bulls, and together with the lack of fetal or newborn calves it indicated a drive of a "cow and bull" herd in the rutting season, between July and September, when pemmican (dried meat) had to be prepared for the winter.

A much later drive (probably just before historic contact), produced the "1st bone layer." Here the remains of thirty bison were subjected to light butchering, probably for transport to

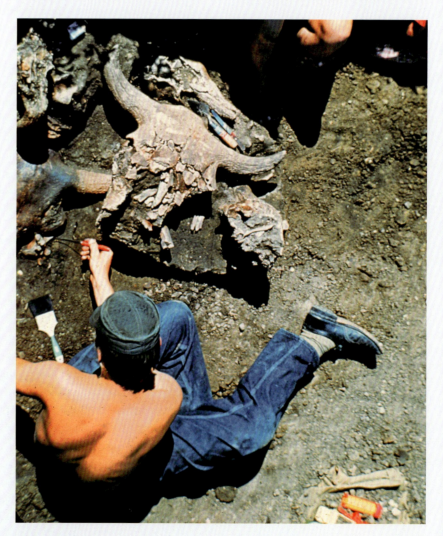

Excavation of a group of bison skulls at Gull Lake.

a distant camp: much of what was left behind was in articulated units. In the earlier two layers, butchery techniques were similar but far more of each animal was utilized, and much was processed on the spot. Clearly, the distance to the home base was shorter than in the case of the later drive. The lack of pottery at Boarding School emphasized its role as strictly a kill site and meat-processing station. Traces of corral poles were found and the total of 440 projectile points suggested an average of 4 or 5 arrows used on each animal.

The Gull Lake Site

In the early 1960s Kehoe carried out a similar excavation at the Gull Lake site, over the border in southwestern Saskatchewan, Canada. Here, too, bison had been driven over a bluff into a depression serving as a corral. Five bone layers were encountered, one of them (*c.* 1300 CE) perhaps representing the remains of as many as 900 bison. The drives began in the late second century CE, and show little processing of bone: many limb bones and even spinal columns are intact. In the later

(Above left) Gull Lake bison drive.

(Above right) Excavating the densely packed bone layers at Gull Lake.

drives, however, processing was far more thorough, with few articulated bones, and extensive scattering and burning of scrap, indicating a utilization for grease and pemmican.

only available at certain times of year, or which shed their antlers in specific seasons. If it is known at what time of year the young of a species were born, then remains of fetuses, or bones of the newly born, can pinpoint a season of occupation (see box opposite and above).

The Question of Animal Domestication

An entirely different set of methods is required to assess the status of the animals—i.e. whether they were wild or domesticated. Like the study of plant domestication described earlier (see p. 195), this is a crucial question about one of the most important developments in human history: the transition from a mobile to a settled, agricultural way of life. In some cases the answer can be obvious, such as where non-indigenous animals have been introduced onto islands by humans—for example, the appearance of cattle, sheep, goat, dog, and cat on Cyprus.

One criterion of animal domestication is human interference with the natural breeding habits of certain species, which has led to changes in the physical characteristics of such species from their wild state. But there are other definitions, and specialists disagree about which physical changes in animals are diagnostic of domestication. Too much emphasis on the wild/domestic dichotomy may also mask a whole spectrum of human-animal relationships, such as herd management without selective breeding. Nevertheless, domestication, by any definition, clearly occurred separately in many parts of the world, and archaeologists therefore need to differentiate fully wild from fully domestic animals, and to investigate the process of domestication.

Among a number of other possible lines of evidence, certain tools may indicate the presence of domesticated animals—for example, plows, yokes, and horse trappings. Deformities and disease can also provide convincing evidence for domestication. When used for traction, horses, cattle, and camels can all sometimes suffer osteoarthritis or strain deformities on their lower limbs. Work is also progressing on tracing the history of domestication through DNA.

Remains of Individual Meals

One of the most direct kinds of evidence of what people ate comes from occasional finds of actual meals. At Pompeii, for example, meals of fish, eggs, bread, and nuts were found intact on tables, as well as food in shops. Food is often preserved in funerary contexts, as in the desiccated corncobs and other items in Peruvian graves, or at Saqqara, Egypt, where the 2nd-dynasty tomb of a noblewoman contained a huge variety of foodstuffs, constituting a rich and elaborate meal that, to judge by the tomb paintings, was not unusual. The Han period in China (206 BCE–220 CE) had tombs stocked with food: that of the wife of the Marquis of Dai held a unique collection of provisions, herbal medicines, and prepared dishes in containers of lacquer, ceramic, and bamboo, with labels attached, and even inventory slips giving the composition of the dishes! It is unlikely, however, that such magnificent remains are representative of everyday diet. Even the meals found so wonderfully preserved at Pompeii are merely a tiny sample from a single day. The only way in which we can really study what people ate habitually is to examine actual human remains.

Assessing Diet from Human Remains

The only incontrovertible evidence that something was actually consumed by humans is its presence in either stomachs or feces. Both kinds of evidence give us invaluable information about individual meals and short-term diet. The study of human teeth also helps us to reconstruct diet, but the real breakthrough in recent years in understanding long-term diet has come from the analysis of bone collagen. What human bones can reveal about general health will be examined in Chapter 8.

A meal as a funerary offering: elaborate food remains, more than 3000 years old, found in Egyptian New Kingdom tombs at Thebes, including (front left) unleavened bread on a woven palm leaf dish; (front center) a bowl of figs; (front right) a bowl containing sun-dried fish. The wicker stand holds cooked duck and loaves of bread.

Individual Meals

STOMACH CONTENTS.   Stomachs survive only rarely in archaeological contexts, except in bog bodies. Some mummies also provide dietary evidence: the overweight wife of the Marquis of Dai from second-century BCE China, mentioned above, seems to have died of a heart attack caused by acute pain from her gallstones an hour or so after enjoying a generous helping of watermelon (138 melon seeds were discovered in her stomach and intestines).

When stomachs survive in bog bodies, the dietary evidence they provide can be of the greatest interest. Pioneering studies of the stomach contents of Danish Iron Age bogmen showed that Grauballe Man, for instance, had consumed more than sixty species of wild seeds, together with one or two cereals and a little meat (as shown by some small bone splinters), while Tollund Man had eaten only plants. But we should keep in mind that these results, while fascinating, do not necessarily indicate everyday diet, since these victims were possibly executed or sacrificed, and thus their last meal may have been out of the ordinary.

FECAL MATERIAL.   Experiments have been done to assess the survival properties of different foodstuffs relevant to the study of ancient diet, and it has been found that many organic remains can survive surprisingly well after their journey through the human digestive tract. Feces themselves survive only rarely, in very dry sites, such as caves in the western United States and Mexico, or very wet sites (these feces are often wrongly called **coprolites**, which means fossilized/petrified excrement). But, where they are preserved, they have proved to be a highly important source of information about what individuals ate in the past.

Macroremains can be extremely varied in human excrement, in fact this variety is an indication of human origin. Bone fragments, plant fibers, bits of charcoal, seeds, and the remains of fish, birds, and even insects are known. Shell fragments—from molluscs, eggs, and nuts—can also be identified. Hair can be assigned to certain classes of animals by means of its scale pattern, visible under the microscope, and it can thus help us to know which animals were eaten.

Exceptional conditions at Lovelock Cave, Nevada, have preserved 5000 feces dating from 2500 to 150 years ago, and Robert Heizer's study of their contents yielded remarkable evidence about diet, which seems to have comprised seeds, fish, and birds. Feather fragments were identified from waterfowl, such as the heron and grebe; fish and reptile scales, which pass through the alimentary canal unaltered, also led to identification of several species. Fish remains were abundant in some of the feces; one, for example, from 1000 years ago, contained 5.8 g (0.2 oz) of fish bone, which, it was calculated, came from 101 small chubs, representing a total live weight of 208 g (7.3 oz)—the fish component of a meal for a single person.

Excrement and fecal residues represent single meals, and therefore provide short-term data on diet, unless they are found in great quantities, as at Lovelock Cave, and even there the feces represent only a couple of meals a year. For human diet over whole lifetimes, we need to turn to the human skeleton itself.

Human Teeth as Evidence for Diet

Teeth survive in extremely good condition, made as they are of the two hardest tissues in the body, and microscopic examination of the abrasions on certain dental surfaces can provide evidence for the sort of food that their owners enjoyed. Abrasive particles in food leave striations on the enamel, the orientation and length of which are directly related to the meat or vegetation in the diet and its process of cooking. Modern meat-eating Greenland Inuit, for instance, have almost exclusively vertical striations on their lateral tooth surfaces, while largely vegetarian Melanesians have both vertical and horizontal striations, with a shorter average length.

When these results are compared with data from fossil teeth hundreds of thousands of years old, it has been found that there is an increase in horizontal and a decrease in vertical striations, and a decrease in average striation length over time. In other words, less and less effort was needed to chew food, and meat may have decreased in importance as the diet became more mixed: early people crushed and broke down their food with their teeth, but less chewing was required as cooking techniques developed and improved.

Tooth decay as well as wear will sometimes provide us with dietary information. Remains of the California Native Americans display very marked tooth decay, attributed to their habit of leaching the tannin out of acorns, their staple food, through a bed of sand, which caused excessive tooth abrasion. Decay and loss of teeth can also set in thanks to starchy and sugary foods. Dental caries became abundant on the coast of Georgia, United States, in the twelfth century CE, particularly among the female population. It was in this period that the transition occurred from hunting, fishing, and gathering to maize agriculture. Anthropologist Clark Larsen believes that the rise in tooth decay over this period, revealed by a study of hundreds of skeletons, was caused by the carbohydrates in maize. Since the women of the group were more subject to the caries than were the men, it is probable that they were growing, harvesting, preparing, and cooking the corn, while the men ate more protein and less carbohydrate.

Isotopic Methods: Diet over a Lifetime

A revolution has been taking place in dietary studies through the realization that **isotopic analysis** of human tooth enamel and bone collagen can reveal a great deal about long-term food intake. The method relies on reading the chemical signatures left in the body by different foods—we are what we eat.

Plants can be divided into three groups—temperate land plants, tropical land plants, and marine plants—based on their differing ratios of two carbon isotopes. As animals eat plants, these different chemical signatures are passed along the food chain and are eventually fixed in human and animal bone tissue. They can show whether diet was based on land or marine plants. Only archaeological evidence, however, can provide more detail about precisely which species of plants or animals contributed to past diet. Recently, for example, isotopic analysis of tooth enamel from four *Australopithecus africanus* individuals from Makapansgat, South Africa, revealed that they ate not only fruits and leaves, as had been thought, but also large quantities of grasses or sedges, or the animals that ate those plants, or both. In other words, they regularly exploited fairly open environments (woodlands or grasslands) for food; and since their tooth wear lacks the characteristic scratches of grass-eaters, it is possible that they were indeed already consuming meat, by hunting small animals or scavenging larger ones.

Isotope studies have been used to shed light on the disappearance of the first Norse settlement in Greenland in the fifteenth century. The Norse settled Greenland from Iceland during a warm period around 1000 CE. The traditional view was that as the climate became colder, the Norse remained committed to raising livestock while squandering natural resources like soil and timber. Meanwhile, the seal-hunting Inuit survived in the very same environment. Over the last decade, archaeologists have revised this

In a recent study of the bones of Norse settlers in Greenland, the carbon isotopes showed clearly the shift to a more marine-based diet through time, as conditions worsened between 950 and 1450 CE. The temperature data here come from studies of oxygen isotopes in ice cores, and the level of "storminess" is based on the measurement of salt particles in ice cores.

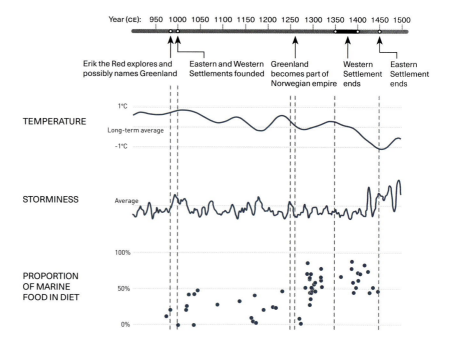

view, drawing on isotopic analysis. By studying the ratio of carbon and nitrogen isotopes in human remains, it was possible to see how the Norse settlers shifted towards a more marine-based diet between 950–1450 CE, as environmental conditions worsened. These findings challenge the traditional view that the Norse were inflexible in their subsistence practices, and suggests that the cause for the collapse of the Greenland settlement is far more complex than first speculated.

Study Questions

1 What techniques do scientists use to study the environment on a global scale?
2 How are plant remains used to reconstruct past environments?
3 Why is the question of plant and animal domestication important to archaeologists?
4 What is the difference between meals and diet?
5 What are some of the complications in determining if humans have processed animal bones?
6 How can human teeth aid in the study of diet?

Summary

HUMANKIND HAS DEVELOPED from being an inconsequential species at the mercy of the environment and the latter's food resources to one with a huge influence over its surroundings. The environment is of crucial importance to archaeology. During every period of the past it has played a vital role in determining where and how people could live, and on what. Archaeologists now have a battery of techniques, largely based on the analysis of plant and animal remains, to help reconstruct such past environments.

WHERE FOOD IS CONCERNED, the evidence available varies from botanical and animal remains, large and microscopic, to tools and vessels, plant and animal residues, and art and texts. We can discover what was eaten, in which seasons, and sometimes how it was prepared. We need to assess whether the evidence arrived in the archaeological record naturally or through human actions, and whether the resources were wild or under human control. Occasionally we encounter the remains of individual meals left as funerary offerings, or the contents of stomachs or feces. Finally, the human body itself contains a record of diet in its tooth wear and in the chemical signatures left in bones by different foods.

MANY OF THE TECHNIQUES must be carried out by specialists, particularly biochemists, but archaeologists should know how to interpret the results, because the rewards are enormous for our knowledge of what the environment was like, what people ate, how they exploited their resources, and in what proportions.

Further Reading

General introductions to environmental archaeology and the subject of diet can be found in:

Barker, G. 2006. *The Agricultural Revolution in Prehistory*. Oxford University Press: Oxford & New York.

Bellwood, P. 2004. *First Farmers: The Origins of Agricultural Societies*. Blackwell: Oxford.

Brothwell, D. & P. 1997. *Food in Antiquity: A Survey of the Diet of Early Peoples*. Johns Hopkins University Press: Baltimore.

Dincauze, D. F. 2000. *Environmental Archaeology*. Cambridge University Press: Cambridge & New York.

Gilbert, R. I. & Mielke, J. H. (eds). 1985. *The Analysis of Prehistoric Diets*. Academic Press: New York & London.

O'Connor, T. 2000. *The Archaeology of Animal Bones*. Sutton: Stroud.

O'Connor, T. & Evans, J. G. 2005. *Environmental Archaeology: Principles and Methods* (2nd ed.). Tempus: Stroud.

Pearsall, D. M. 2015. *Paleoethnobotany: A Handbook of Procedures* (3rd ed.). Left Coast Press: Walnut Creek, CA.

Reitz, E. & Shackley, M. 2012. *Environmental Archaeology*. Springer: New York.

Reitz, E. J. & Wing, E. S. 2008. *Zooarchaeology* (2nd ed.). Cambridge University Press: Cambridge & New York.

Smith, B. D. 1998. *The Emergence of Agriculture* (2nd ed.). Scientific American Library: New York.

[See p. 345 for a list of useful websites]

7

How Were Artifacts Made, Used, and Distributed?

Technology, Trade, and Exchange

It is the physical remains of humanly made artifacts that form the bulk of the archaeological record. We have seen how archaeologists can find and date artifacts, but in this chapter we will start by addressing two questions of fundamental importance: how were artifacts made, and what were they used for? There are several approaches to these two questions—the purely archaeological, the scientific analysis of objects, the ethnographic, and the experimental.

When assessing ancient technologies, the archaeologist always needs to bear in mind that the sample preserved may well be biased. During the long Paleolithic period, for instance, wood and bone artifacts must surely have rivaled those of stone in importance—as they do in hunting-and-gathering societies today—but stone tools dominate the archaeological record.

Once made, artifacts usually move around as they are acquired or passed on between individuals or groups—a phenomenon that can tell us a great deal about the frequency and extent of contacts between different groups, as well as about transportation, economics, and so forth. By analyzing where the materials used to make an artifact came from, as well as the distribution of artifacts as found by archaeologists, we can reconstruct something of these trading relationships: who was exchanging goods with whom, and by what method?

When an archaeologist investigates an object, it must first be decided whether it was actually made or used by people in the past. For most periods the answer will be obvious (although we have to beware of fakes and forgeries), but for the Paleolithic, and especially the Lower Paleolithic, judgment can be more difficult. Where the very earliest tools are concerned, on which we would expect the traces of human work to be minimal, the question is not easy to resolve, since the crudest human working may be indistinguishable from damage caused by nature.

We will make a convenient distinction in the next section on ancient technology between two classes of raw material used in creating objects—between those that are largely unaltered, such as flint, and those that are synthetic, the product of human activities, such as pottery or metal. Of course, even supposedly unaltered materials have often been treated by heat or by chemical reactions in order to assist the manufacturing process. But synthetic materials have undergone an actual change in state, usually through heat treatment. The human use of fire—**pyrotechnology**—is a crucial factor here.

Unaltered Materials

Stone

From the first recognizable tools, dating back about 3.3 million years at Lomekwi, Kenya, up to the adoption of pottery-making, dated to 20,000 BCE in China, the archaeological record is dominated by stone. How were stone artifacts, from the smallest stone tools to the greatest stone monuments, extracted, manufactured, and used?

Much of the stone used for making early tools was probably picked up from streambeds or other parts of the landscape, but the sources most visible archaeologically are the mines and quarries. The best-known mines are the Neolithic and later flint mines in various parts of northern Europe, such as Grime's Graves in England, where multiple 15-m- (50-ft.-) deep shafts were sunk into the chalk to reach the best-quality flint layers; rough estimates suggest that the site could have produced 28 million flint axes. Quarries were a common source of larger stones for building or monuments. The job of the archaeologist is sometimes made easier by the discovery of unfinished or abandoned stones within or near ancient quarry sites. One of the most impressive examples is the statue quarry on Easter Island, where many statues lie in various stages of manufacture.

A combination of archaeological investigation and modern experimentation can give us valuable insights into how stones were worked. Here we will concentrate on stone tool manufacture, although much archaeological and experimental work is also done on larger stones and how they were moved, dressed, and fitted.

STONE TOOL MANUFACTURE AND FUNCTION.
Most stone tools are made by removing material from a pebble or **core** until the desired shape has been attained. The first flakes struck off (primary flakes) bear traces of the outer surface (cortex). Trimming flakes are then struck off to achieve the final shape, and certain edges may then be retouched by further removal of tiny secondary

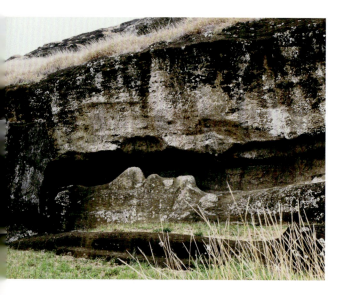

Stone quarry on Easter Island: a giant statue lies flat on its back, unfinished and still attached to the rock face, but at an advanced stage of manufacture—yielding clues as to how it was made.

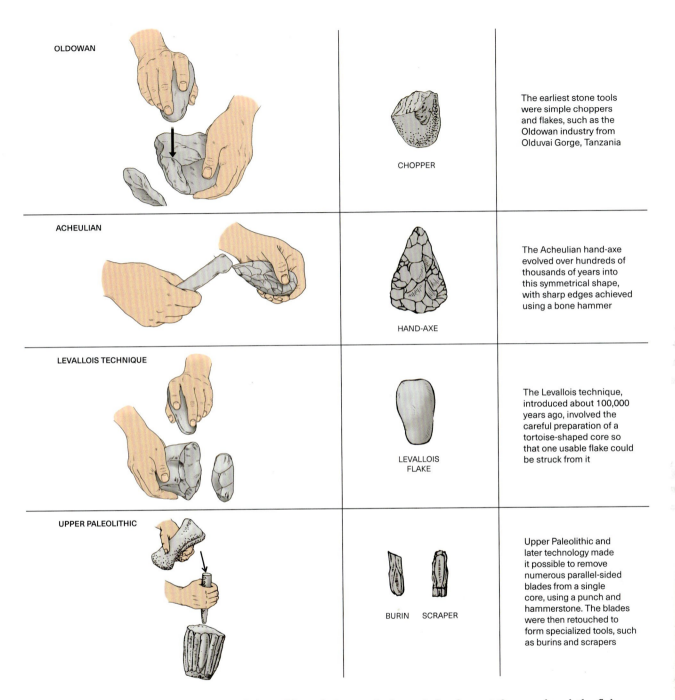

OLDOWAN

CHOPPER

The earliest stone tools were simple choppers and flakes, such as the Oldowan industry from Olduvai Gorge, Tanzania

ACHEULIAN

HAND-AXE

The Acheulian hand-axe evolved over hundreds of thousands of years into this symmetrical shape, with sharp edges achieved using a bone hammer

LEVALLOIS TECHNIQUE

LEVALLOIS FLAKE

The Levallois technique, introduced about 100,000 years ago, involved the careful preparation of a tortoise-shaped core so that one usable flake could be struck from it

UPPER PALEOLITHIC

BURIN   SCRAPER

Upper Paleolithic and later technology made it possible to remove numerous parallel-sided blades from a single core, using a punch and hammerstone. The blades were then retouched to form specialized tools, such as burins and scrapers

The evolution of stone tools, from the earliest, Oldowan technology to the refined methods of the Upper Paleolithic onward.

flakes. Although the core is the main implement thus produced, the flakes themselves may well be used as knives, scrapers, etc. The toolmaker's work will have varied in accordance with the type and amount of raw material available.

The history of stone tool technology (illustrated above) shows a sporadically increasing degree of refinement. The first recognizable tools are simple choppers and flakes made by knocking pieces off pebbles to obtain sharp edges. The best-known examples are the so-called Oldowan tools from Olduvai Gorge, Tanzania, the earliest of which date back some 2.6 million years. After hundreds of thousands of years, people progressed to flaking both surfaces of the tool, eventually producing the symmetrical Acheulian hand-axe shape. The next improvement, dating to around 100,000 years ago, came with the introduction of the Levallois technique—named after the site in a Paris suburb where it was first identified—where the core was knapped in such a way that large flakes of predetermined size and shape could be removed.

Around 35,000 years ago, during the Upper Paleolithic period, blade technology became dominant in some parts of the world. Long, parallel-sided blades were systematically removed with a punch and hammerstone from a cylindrical core. This was a great advance, not only because it produced large numbers of blanks that could be further trimmed and retouched into a wide range of specialized tools (scrapers, burins, borers), but also because it was far less wasteful of the raw material, obtaining a much greater total length of working edges than ever before from a given amount of stone. This trend toward greater economy reached its peak around 10,000 years ago, with the rise to dominance of microliths, tiny stone tools, many of which were probably used as barbs on composite implements.

To find out how a stone tool was made we must try to reconstruct the sequence of manufacturing steps, and there are two principal approaches to doing this: replication and refitting. Stone tool replication is a type of experimental archaeology that involves making exact copies of different types of stone tool—using only the technology available to the original makers—in order to assess the processes entailed, and the amount of time and effort required. Many years of patient practice are required to become proficient at tool replication.

One specific problem that expert knapper Donald Crabtree was able to solve through trial and error was how the Paleo-Indians of North America had made their fluted stone tools known as Folsom points, dating to some 11,000–10,000 years ago. In particular, how had they removed the "flute" or channel flake? This had remained a mystery and experiments with a variety of techniques met with disappointing results, until the decisive clue was found in a seventeenth-century text by a Spanish priest who had seen Aztecs make long knife blades from obsidian. The method, as experiments proved, involves pressing the flake out, downward, by means of a T-shaped crutch placed against the chest; the tip of the crutch is forced down against a precise point on the core, which is clamped firm.

Replication cannot usually prove conclusively which techniques were used in the past, but it does narrow the possibilities and often points to the most likely method, as in the Folsom example above. Refitting, on the other hand,

(Above) How were Paleo-Indian Folsom points made? Experiments by Donald Crabtree showed that the flakes were pressed from the core using a T-shaped crutch.

(Below) Flintknappers have produced almost perfect replica points.

Stone: the archaeological record is dominated by stone artifacts. A combination of archaeological investigation, modern experimentation, and ethnographic observation can tell us a great deal about how stone artifacts were made and used

Wood: wood does not survive well, apart from in very dry or waterlogged conditions, but was almost certainly as important a resource as stone

Plant and Animal Fibers: containers, fabrics, and cords made from plant and animal fibers would also have been common objects in the past, but, again, they rarely survive in the archaeological record

Other Materials: bone, antler, shell, and leather are also often found by archaeologists, but, along with most other artifacts made from unaltered materials, we must be careful to establish whether an object is actually humanly made, or whether it has been created by natural processes

involves working with the original tools and demonstrates clearly the precise chain of actions of the knapper. This entails attempting to put tools and flakes back together again, like a 3D jigsaw puzzle. The work is tedious and time-consuming, but when successful can allow us to follow the stages of the knapper's craft.

But how can we discover the function of a stone tool? Ethnographic observation of the use of similar tools in living societies often gives valuable clues, as do the minute traces of organic residues that can sometimes be found on tool surfaces; experimentation can also determine which uses are feasible or most probable. A single tool, however, can be used for many different purposes—an Acheulian hand-axe could be used for hacking wood from a tree, for butchering, smashing, scraping, and cutting—and conversely the same task can be done by many different tools. The only direct proof of function is to study the minute traces, or microwear patterns, that remain on the original tools. These minute polishes and marks, only properly visible using a scanning electron microscope, can be compared against evidence from modern experiments, and we can deduce the type of material a tool was used to work (such as wood, bone, hide, or meat) and the type of action used (such as piercing, cutting, or scraping).

Wood

Wood is one of the most important organic materials, and must have been used to make tools for as long as stone and bone. Indeed, many prehistoric stone tools were employed to obtain and work timber. If wood survives in good condition, it may preserve toolmarks to show how it was worked. A wide range of wooden tools can survive under special conditions. In the dry environment of ancient Egypt, for instance, numerous wooden implements for farming (rakes, hoes, grain scoops, sickles), furniture, weapons, and toys,

In 1954 the dismantled parts of a cedarwood boat were found buried in a pit on the south side of the Great Pyramid of Cheops (Khufu) at Giza, Egypt. One important clue to the reconstruction proved to be the four classifying signs, marked on most of the timbers, that indicated to which of the four quarters of the ship the timbers belonged. After fourteen years of work, the 1244 pieces of the ship were finally reassembled.

such carpentry tools as mallets and chisels, and even whole ships have come down to us. Egyptian paintings, such as those in the tomb of the nobleman Rekhmire at Thebes, sometimes depict carpenters using drills and saws. But it has been waterlogged wood (including the remains of ships and boats) that has yielded the richest information about woodworking skills.

Plant and Animal Fibers

The making of containers, fabrics, and cords from skins, bark, and woven fibers probably dates back to the very earliest archaeological periods, but these fragile materials rarely survive. As we saw in Chapter 2, however, they do survive in very dry or wet conditions. In arid regions, such as Egypt or parts of the New World, such perishables have come down to us in some quantity, and the study of basketry and cordage there reveals complex and sophisticated designs and techniques that display complete mastery of these organic materials. Waterlogged conditions can also yield a great deal of fragile evidence.

Where textiles are concerned, the most crucial question is how they were made, and of what. In the New World, information on pre-Columbian weaving methods is available from ethnographic observation, as well as from colonial accounts and illustrations, from depictions on Moche pottery, and from actual finds of ancient looms and other objects found preserved in the Peruvian desert. The richest New World evidence, however, comes from Peruvian textiles themselves, which have survived well in the dry conditions. The Andean cultures mastered nearly every method of textile weaving or decoration now known, and their products were often finer than those of today—indeed, they were some of the best ever made.

Other Unaltered Materials

Artifacts made from bone, antler, shell, and leather are also commonly found on archaeological sites. Microwear analysis—combined with experimental archaeology—is the most successful means of determining firstly whether the find really is humanly made (sharp bone points or pierced shells, for instance, can easily be created by natural processes), as well as reconstructing manufacturing techniques and deducing function.

Synthetic Materials

It is possible to consider the whole development of technology, as far as it relates to synthetic materials, in terms of the control of fire: pyrotechnology. Until very recent times, nearly all synthetic materials depended upon the control of heat, and the development of new technologies has often been largely dependent upon achieving higher and higher temperatures under controlled conditions.

Clearly the first step along this path was the mastery of fire, possible evidence for which already occurs in the Swartkrans Cave, South Africa, in layers dating to 1.5 million years ago. Cooked food and preserved meat then became a possibility, as did the use of heat in working flint, and in hardening wooden implements, such as the yew spear from the Middle Paleolithic site of Lehringen, Germany.

A significant development of the Early Neolithic period in the Near East, around 8000 BCE, was the construction of special ovens used both to parch cereal grains (to facilitate the threshing process) and to bake bread. These ovens consisted of a single chamber in which the fuel was burnt. When the oven was hot the fuel was raked out and the grain or unbaked bread placed inside. This represents the first construction of a deliberate facility to control the conditions under which the temperature was raised. We may hypothesize that it was through these early experiences in pyrotechnology that the possibility of making pottery by firing clay was discovered. Initially pottery was made by firing in an open fire, but the introduction of the potter's kiln meant higher temperatures could be achieved, which also spurred on the development of metallurgy.

Pottery

Throughout the earlier periods of prehistory, containers made of light, organic materials were probably used. This does not mean, as has often been assumed, that Paleolithic people did not know how to make pottery: every fire lit on a cave floor will have hardened the clay around it, and terracotta figurines were sometimes produced. The lack of pottery vessels before the Neolithic period is mainly a consequence of the mobile way of life of Paleolithic hunter-gatherers, for whom heavy containers of fired clay would have been of limited utility.

The introduction of pottery generally seems to coincide with the adoption of a more sedentary way of life, for which vessels and containers that are durable and strong are a necessity. The almost indestructible potsherd is as common in later periods as the stone tool is in earlier ones— and just as some sites yield thousands of stone tools, others contain tons of pottery fragments.

HOW WERE POTS MADE?   The making or "throwing" of pots on a wheel or turntable was only introduced after 3400 BCE at the earliest (in Mesopotamia), but in the New World only after European contact. The previous method, still used in some parts of the world, was to build the vessel up by hand in a series of coils or slabs of clay. A simple examination of the interior and exterior

---

Key Concepts
Artifacts Made from Synthetic Materials

Many of the developments in pottery and metalworking technology can be linked to developments in pyrotechnology—the ability to control fire, and attain and maintain ever higher temperatures

Pottery: pottery is very hard-wearing and potsherds are a common find on archaeological sites. We can learn through simple observation how pottery was made (either by hand or on a wheel) and through experiment and ethnographic studies how it was fired

Metals: we can identify what metal or combination of metals an artifact is made from with simple laboratory techniques. The examination of the microscopic structure of the metal can give clues as to how an artifact was manufactured

Evidence for pot-making using a wheel. An Egyptian potter shapes a vessel on a turntable-type wheel in this limestone portrait of *c.* 2400 BCE.

surfaces of a pot usually allows us to identify the method of manufacture. Wheel-thrown pots generally have a telltale spiral of ridges and marks that is absent from handmade wares. These marks are left by the fingertips as the potter draws the vessel up on the turntable.

The firing technique can be inferred from certain characteristics of the finished product. For example, if the surfaces are vitrified or glazed (i.e. have a glassy appearance), the pot was fired at more than 900°C (1652°F) and probably in an enclosed kiln. The extent of oxidization in a pot (the process by which organic substances in the clay are burnt off) is also indicative of firing methods. Complete oxidization produces a uniform color throughout the paste. If the core of a sherd is dark (gray or black), the firing temperature was too low to oxidize the clay fully, or the duration of the firing was insufficient, factors that often point to the use of an open kiln. Experimental firing of different pastes at different temperatures and in various types of kiln provides a guide to the colors and effects that can be expected.

Unlike the making of stone tools, the production of pottery by traditional methods is still widespread in the world, so a good deal can be learned from ethnoarchaeological studies not only about the technological aspects but also about the use and trade of pottery.

Metals

The study of ancient metal artifacts and manufacturing processes is known as archaeometallurgy. Many of the advances in metalworking techniques made in the past were dependent on the ability to achieve and control ever higher temperatures.

NON-FERROUS METALS.   The most important non-ferrous metal—that is, one not containing iron—used in early times was copper. In due course people learned that a harder, tougher product could be made by **alloying** the copper with tin to produce bronze. Other elements, notably arsenic and antimony, were sometimes used in the alloying process; and in the later Bronze Age of Europe it was realized that a small amount of lead would improve the casting qualities. Gold and silver were also important, as was lead itself.

The techniques of manufacture of artifacts made from these materials can be investigated in several ways. The first point to establish is composition. Traditional laboratory methods readily allow the identification of major constituents. For instance, the alloys present in bronze may be identified in this way. In practice, however, it is now more usual to utilize the techniques of **trace-element analysis** (see pp. 221–22). The other essential approach is **metallographic examination**, when the structure of the material is examined microscopically. This will determine whether an artifact has been formed by cold-hammering, **annealing**, casting, or a combination of these methods.

IRON.   Iron was not used in the New World during pre-Columbian times, and made its appearance in quantity in the Old World with the beginning in the Near East of the Iron Age around 1000 BCE. Once the technique of smelting iron was well understood, it became very important, since iron is more widely found in nature than is copper. But it is much more difficult to reduce—i.e. to separate from oxygen, with which it is found combined in nature in the form of iron oxides—requiring temperatures of about 800°C (1472°F).

It is clearly important and interesting to identify what an artifact is made of, how it was made, and what it was used for. But once an artifact has been created, it takes on a life of its own—not only in terms of being used, broken, or discarded, but also in terms of being transported, bought, or exchanged. The study of these processes teaches us a great deal about past human societies and how they operated. In the next section we will discuss what can be learned from the study of trade and exchange, and examine some methods for investigating the movements of different kinds of materials.

Trade and Exchange

Societies and economies depend upon exchanges—of information and of actual goods—between individuals and between organizations. Every social transaction implies some interaction between people, and the study of the movement and flow of goods in the course of exchange transactions is often the most direct way for the archaeologist to monitor such interactions.

In many exchanges the relationship is more important than what is exchanged. In the Christian tradition, for instance, when presents are exchanged within a family at Christmas, the giving of presents between relatives is generally more important than the actual objects: "it's the thought that counts." There are also different kinds of exchange relationship: some where generosity is the order of the day (as in the family Christmas); others where the aim is profit, and the personal relationship is not emphasized. Moreover, there are different kinds of goods: everyday commodities that are bought and sold; and special goods, valuables (see box overleaf), that are suitable as gifts.

When **diffusionist explanations** were popular in archaeology, some fifty years ago, the presence of objects of foreign type or material at an archaeological site was often thought to indicate significant "influence"

Materials of Prestige Value

Nearly all cultures have valuables. Although some of these are useful (e.g. pigs in Melanesia, which can be eaten), most of them have no use at all, other than display. They are simply prestige objects.

Valuables tend to be in a limited range of materials to which a particular society ascribes a high value. For instance, in our own society gold is so highly valued as to be a standard against which all other values are measured.

We tend to forget that this valuation is entirely arbitrary, speaking of gold's intrinsic value, as if in some way it were inherent. But gold is not a very useful material (although it is bright, and does not tarnish), nor is it the product of any special skills of the craftsperson. Intrinsic value is a misnomer: the Aztecs valued feathers more highly, unlike the Conquistadors, who craved gold; both were following subjective systems of value. When we survey the range of materials to which different societies have ascribed intrinsic value we can see that many of them had the qualities of rarity, of durability, and of being visually conspicuous:

- The bright feathers favored by the Aztecs and by tribes of New Guinea fulfill two of these qualities.

- Ivory: elephant and walrus tusks have been valued since Upper Paleolithic times.

- Shell, especially of large marine molluscs, has been highly prized in many cultures for millennia.

- The very special organic material amber was valued in Upper Paleolithic times in northern Europe.

- Jade is a favored material in many cultures, from China to Mesoamerica, and was valued as long ago as 4000 BCE in Neolithic Europe.

- Other naturally hard and colorful stones (e.g. rock crystal, lapis lazuli, obsidian, quartz, and onyx) have always been valued.

- Gemstones have taken on a special value in recent centuries, when the technique of cutting them to a faceted, light-catching shape was developed.

- Gold has perhaps pride of place (certainly in European eyes) among "intrinsically" valuable commodities, followed by silver.

- Copper and other metals have taken a comparable role: in North America copper objects had a special value.

- With the development of pyrotechnology, artificial materials such as faience and glass came into full prominence.

- The finest textiles and other clothing materials (e.g. tapa, bark cloth, in Polynesia) have also always been highly valued, for prestige often means personal display.

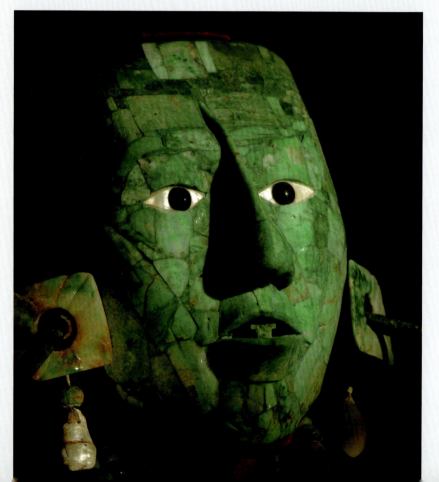

(Left) A jade mask from Palenque, Mexico, found in Lord Pakal's tomb.

Prestige objects (clockwise from above right): woven silk robe from the reign of the Chinese Qianlong Emperor (1735–96), bearing the imperial dragon; sculpted ivory bison from Zaraisk in Russia, colored with red ocher, c. 22,000 years old; gold mask thought by Schliemann to represent King Agamemnon, from a shaft grave at Mycenae, late sixteenth century BCE; Mississippian shell pendant (c. 14 cm) from Texas, showing a panther and bird of prey; embossed copper face, with typical forked-eye motif, from North America's Mississippian culture (c. 900–1450 CE); the Portland vase, a superb example of first-century CE Roman glassworking; feathered headdress of the Aztec emperor Motecuhzoma (Moctezuma) II.

from other, perhaps more advanced, cultures. Today, however, we are more interested in finding out what those objects can tell us about social and economic interactions between distant groups. But the mere resemblance in the form of an artifact with those found elsewhere is not usually enough to be sure an exchange has occurred or that there is a definite link between two groups. We must show that the actual material the artifact is made from *must* have come from a distant source, and we can do this by **characterization**.

Discovering the Sources of Traded Goods: Characterization

The discovery of an artifact at a particular location does not mean that it originated in that place: it may, in fact, have been brought over hundreds or even thousands of miles. The study of where artifacts originated is not simple: artifact forms can be imitated, or can resemble each other by chance. So it is not always safe to recognize an import in an archaeological context just because it resembles objects that are known to have been made elsewhere. Much more reliable evidence for trade can be provided if the raw material from which the object is made can be reliably shown to have originated elsewhere. Characterization, or sourcing, refers to those techniques of examination by which characteristic properties of the constituent material may be identified, and so allow the source of that material to be determined. Some of the main methods for sourcing of materials by characterization are described below.

For characterization to work, there must obviously be something about the source of the material that distinguishes its products from those coming from other sources. Of course, sometimes a material is so unusual and distinctive in itself that it can at once be recognized as deriving from a given source. But in practice, there are very few materials for which the different sources can be distinguished by eye. Usually, it is necessary to use scientific techniques that allow a much more precise description of the material. During the past forty years there have been striking advances in the ability to analyze very small samples with accuracy. A successful characterization, however, does not just depend on analytical precision: sources of some materials (e.g. flint, or some metals) are often very similar and so cannot be distinguished whatever the precision of the testing. For other materials (e.g. obsidian), the sources are all quite different and can be distinguished relatively easily.

An important point to note is that the sourcing of materials by characterization studies depends crucially on our knowledge of the distribution of the raw materials in nature. This comes mainly from the fieldwork of such specialists as geologists. For example, we might have a good knowledge of the exact kinds of rock a whole range of stone axes were made from, but this would not help us unless we could match those particular kinds of rock with their specific occurrences in nature (i.e. the quarries). Thus, good geological mapping is a necessary basis for a sound sourcing study.

MICROSCOPIC THIN-SECTION ANALYSIS. Since the middle of the nineteenth century techniques have existed for cutting a thin section of a sample taken from a stone object or a potsherd to determine the source of the material. It is made thin enough to transmit light, and then, by means of petrological examination (studying the rock or mineral structure) with a light microscope, it is usually possible to recognize specific minerals that may be characteristic of a specific source. This part of the work has to be done by someone with petrological training.

This method has been applied to stone objects in different parts of the world—to pinpoint the sources of building stones (e.g. the special colored stones used by the ancient Greeks and Romans), monuments (e.g. Olmec heads, Stonehenge), and portable artifacts, such as stone axes (e.g. in Australia and New Guinea). One of the success stories of characterization studies is the analysis of the patterns of trade in stone axes in Neolithic times in Britain, which started before 3000 BCE.

With pottery, the clay itself may be distinctive, but more often it is the inclusions—particles of minerals or rock fragments—that are characteristic. Sometimes the inclusions are naturally present in the clay. In other cases, the inclusions are deliberately added as **temper** to improve drying and firing qualities, and this can complicate characterization studies, since the pottery fabric may then consist of material from two or more separate sources. Fossil constituents, such as diatoms (see pp. 183–84) can also be an aid to identification of the source of the raw materials.

The picture of the prehistoric trade in pottery in Britain that such work has documented is quite surprising. Until the **thin-section analysis** of David Peacock and his associates it was simply not realized that pottery bowls and other vessels might be traded over quite long distances (of the order of 100 km (62 miles)) in Neolithic times, before 3000 BCE. Now that we know the extent of this exchange of pottery, and that of stone axes discussed above, it is clear that many individuals and settlements were linked by quite far-flung exchange systems.

TRACE-ELEMENT ANALYSIS. The basic composition of many materials is very consistent. Obsidian, a volcanic glass used in the manufacture of chipped stone tools in the same manner as flint, is a good example of this. The concentration of the main elements of which obsidian is formed (silicon, oxygen, calcium, etc.) is broadly similar whatever the source of the material. The trace elements (elements present only in very small quantities, measured

Key Concepts
Characterization

Characterization allows archaeologists to discover the source of the material from which an artifact was made

Successful characterization depends on all the sources of a material being sufficiently different so as to be distinguishable through scientific analysis

The main methods for sourcing materials by characterization are microscopic thin-section analysis, trace-element analysis, and isotopic analysis in just a few parts per million) do vary according to the source, however, and there are a variety of useful methods for measuring their concentration.

When obsidian from New Britain and the Admiralty Islands in the Pacific was examined using trace-element analysis, it was found that obsidian from one source in New Britain (Talasea) was being traded as far as Fiji to the east and Sabah (northern Borneo) to the west, a distance of 6500 km (4000 miles), about 3000 years ago. This is surely the widest distribution of any commodity in the global Neolithic record.

ISOTOPIC ANALYSIS.   Atoms of the same element, but with different numbers of neutrons in the nucleus, are called isotopes. Most elements occurring in nature consist of a number of isotopes. Particularly when we are investigating metal sources, we can analyze the sources (as well as the artifacts we are investigating) for the presence of different proportions of lead isotopes in order to characterize them. Sometimes more than one source can have the same isotope ratios, but this can usually be resolved by consideration of trace-element data.

Lead isotope analysis is of direct use not only for lead artifacts, but also for those of silver, in which lead is usually present as an impurity. Copper sources also contain at least a trace of lead, and it has been shown by experimentation that a large proportion of that lead passes into the copper metal produced during smelting. Here, then, is a characterization method applicable to lead, silver, and copper artifacts. It has been used successfully for the determination of mineral sources of Classical and medieval silver coins, Bronze Age copper and bronze tools, lead weights, as well as lead in pigments of glasses and glazes, and lead-based white paint.

Oxygen isotope ratios have also proved useful for the characterization of marine shell. The shell of *Spondylus gaederopus* was widely traded in the form of bracelets and decorations during the Neolithic in southeastern Europe. Archaeologists needed to know whether it came from the Aegean, or possibly from the Black Sea. As discussed in the section on deep-sea cores in Chapter 6, the oxygen isotopic composition of marine shell is dependent on the local temperature of the sea. The Black Sea is much colder than the Mediterranean, and analysis confirmed that the shells in question came from the Aegean.

The Study of Distribution

The study of the traded goods themselves, and the identification of their sources by means of characterization, are the most important procedures in the investigation of exchange. But it is the study of distribution, or the movement of goods, that allows us to get to the heart of the matter—how societies operated and how they interrelated socially and economically.

(Left) A distribution study. Roman storage containers (amphorae) bearing the stamp of the potter Sestius (above) have been found in northern Italy and widely throughout central and southern France. They and their contents (probably wine) were probably made on an estate near Cosa. The distribution map thus indicates the general pattern of the export from the Cosa area of this commodity.

In the absence of written records it is not easy to determine what were the mechanisms of distribution, or what was the nature of the exchange relationship. Where such records exist they can be most informative. Earlier evidence from pre-literate societies—societies without written records—can, however, give some clear idea of ownership and of the managed distribution of goods. For example, clay sealings, used to stopper jars, to secure boxes, and to seal the doors of storehouses, and distinguished by the impression of a carved seal, are widely found in the pre-literate phases in the Near East, and in the Aegean Bronze Age.

In some cases, however, the traded goods themselves were marked by their owner or producer. For instance, the potters who produced storage containers (amphorae) in Roman times used to stamp their name on the rim. The general pattern of export can be made clear by the production of a distribution map.

But a distribution map must be interpreted if we are to understand the processes that lay behind it. At this point it is useful to consider how the spatial distribution of finds may depend on the exchange mechanism— or in other words, what can the pattern of distribution of finds tell us about the type of exchange that was occurring? The different mechanisms can be summarized as follows:

- "Direct access": the user goes directly to the source of the material, without the intervention of any exchange mechanism.
- "Down-the-line" exchange: repeated exchanges characterized by **reciprocity**, so that a commodity travels across successive territories through successive exchanges.

- "Freelance (middleman)" trading: traders operate independently and for gain. Usually the traders work by bargaining, but instead of a fixed marketplace they are travelers who take goods to the consumer.
- "Emissary" trading: the "trader" is a representative of a central organization based in the home country.

Not all of these types of transaction can be expected to leave clear and unmistakable indications in the archaeological record, although, as we shall see, down-the-line trading apparently does. And a former port of trade ought to be recognizable if the materials found there come from a wide range of sources, and it is clear that the site was not principally an administrative center, but was specialized in trading activities.

Spatial Analysis of Distribution

Several formal techniques are available for the study of distribution. The first and most obvious technique is naturally that of plotting the distribution map for finds, as in the case of the stamped Roman amphorae mentioned on the previous page. Quantitative studies of distributions are also helpful; the size of the dot or some other feature can be used as a simple device to indicate the number of finds on the map. This kind of map can give a good indication of important centers of consumption and of redistribution. Direct use of distribution maps, even when aided by quantitative plotting, may not, however, be the best way of studying the data, and more thorough analysis may be useful.

Recently, there has been a considerable focus of interest in **fall-off analysis**. The quantity of a traded material usually declines as the distance from the source increases. This is not really very surprising, but in some cases (such as when a particular type of trade is happening) there are regularities in the way in which the decrease occurs. If the quantities of material are plotted against the distance from source on a graph, a fall-off curve is created. Although different mechanisms of distribution sometimes produce comparable end results, down-the-line trading, for instance, produces a quite distinctive exponential curve (which on a logarithmic scale is represented by a straight line, as in the example opposite).

DISTRIBUTION STUDIES OF OBSIDIAN.   A good example is the obsidian found at early Neolithic sites in the Near East (see illustration opposite). Characterization studies pinpointed two sources in central Anatolia and two in eastern Anatolia. Samples were obtained from most of the known early Neolithic sites in the Near East, dating from the seventh and sixth millennia BCE. A rather clear picture emerged with the central Anatolian obsidians being traded in the Levant area (down to Palestine), while those

Key Concepts
Distribution

Analysis of the spatial distribution of finds can help us to understand the exchange mechanisms that were operating in the past

The main different exchange mechanisms can be summarized as: direct access; down-the-line exchange; freelance trading; and emissary trading

Quantitative studies, for example fall-off analysis, can give a statistical indication of which method was in use

The obsidian trade in the Near East. Characterization studies revealed that early Neolithic villages in Cyprus, Anatolia, and the Levant obtained their obsidian from two sources in central Anatolia, while such villages as Jarmo and Ali Kosh depended on two sources in Armenia (eastern Anatolia). At sites relatively close to the sources (e.g. Çatalhöyük), obsidian formed 80 percent of the chipped stone tools, suggesting that within this "supply zone" (inner lines on the distribution map below) people collected obsidian directly from the source. Beyond this zone the fall-off curves (right) were indicative of down-the-line trade.

of eastern Anatolia were mostly traded down the Zagros mountain range to sites in Iran, such as Ali Kosh.

A quantitative distributional study revealed a pattern of fall-off that indicated down-the-line trade. It could therefore be concluded that obsidian was being handed on down from village settlement to village settlement. Only in the area close to the sources (within 320 km (200 miles))—termed the supply zone—was there evidence that people were going direct to the source to collect their own obsidian. Outside that area—within what has been termed the contact zone—the exponential fall-off indicates a down-the-line system. There is no indication of specialist middleman traders at this time, nor does it seem that there were central places that had a dominant role in the supply of obsidian.

SHIPWRECKS AND HOARDS: TRADE BY SEA AND LAND. A different approach to distribution questions is provided by the study of transport. Travel by water was often much safer, quicker, and less expensive than travel by land. The best source of information, both for questions of transport and for the crucial question of what commodity was traded against what, and on which scale, is offered by shipwrecks. From earlier times, for instance, complete cargoes of the Roman amphorae discussed on p. 223 have been recovered. Our knowledge of marine trade has been greatly extended by George Bass's investigations of two important Bronze Age shipwrecks off the south coast of Turkey, at Cape Gelidonya and Uluburun (see box overleaf).

The terrestrial equivalent of the shipwreck is the trader's cache or hoard. When substantial assemblages of goods are found in archaeological deposits, it is not easy to be clear about the intentions of those who left them there: some hoards evidently had a votive character, left perhaps as offerings to deities, but those with materials for recycling, such as scrap metal, may well have been buried by itinerant smiths who intended to return and retrieve them.

In such cases, particularly with a well-preserved shipwreck, we come as close as we shall ever do to understanding the nature of distribution.

Exchange and Interaction: The Complete System

The archaeological evidence is rarely sufficient to permit the reconstruction of a complete exchange system. It is extremely difficult, for example, to establish without written records what was traded against what, and which particular values were ascribed to each commodity. Furthermore, exchange in perishable materials will have left little or no trace in the archaeological record. In most cases, all we can hope to do is to fit together the evidence about sources and distribution that can be established archaeologically. A good example of such a project is the work of Jane Pires-Ferreira in Oaxaca, Mexico.

AN EXCHANGE SYSTEM IN ANCIENT MEXICO. Pires-Ferreira studied five materials used in Oaxaca during the Early and Middle Formative periods (1450–500 BCE). The first was obsidian, of which some nine sources were identified. These were characterized and the relevant networks were established. Pires-Ferreira then proceeded to consider exchange networks for another material, mother-of-pearl shell, and concluded that two different networks were in operation here, one bringing marine material from the Pacific coast, the other material from freshwater sources in the rivers draining into the Atlantic.

For her next study she considered the iron ore (magnetite) used to manufacture mirrors in the Formative period. Finally, she was able to bring

The complete system: Jane Pires-Ferreira's map, which shows some of the commodities that linked regions of Early Formative Mesoamerica from the study of five different materials.

into consideration two classes of pottery, the area of manufacture of which (in Oaxaca and in Veracruz, respectively) could be determined stylistically. These results were then fitted together onto a single map, showing some of the commodities that linked regions of Mesoamerica in the Early Formative period into several exchange networks. The picture is evidently incomplete, and it does not offer any notion of the relative values of the traded goods. But it does make excellent use of the available characterization data, and undertakes a preliminary synthesis of the area's exchange networks that is securely based on the archaeological evidence.

SYMBOLIC EXCHANGE AND INTERACTION. Interaction involves the exchange not only of material goods but also of information, which includes ideas, **symbols**, inventions, aspirations, and values. Modern archaeology has been able to learn quite a lot about material exchanges, using characterization studies and spatial analyses, but it has been more difficult to identify and explain the more symbolic aspects of interaction.

While similar innovations separated by long distances should not be used as indicators of contact in the absence of other evidence, the development of a striking new technology, making its appearance at a number of locations over a limited area, usually indicates the flow of information and hence contact.

In the past archaeologists talked of "diffusion" when they discussed interactions between neighboring areas. The term implied that one area was dominant over the other, and that new technologies passed down to the

Distribution: The Uluburun Wreck

It is difficult for the archaeologist to learn what commodity was traded against what other commodity, and to understand the mechanics of trade. The discovery of the shipwreck of a trading vessel, complete with cargo, is thus of particular value.

In 1982, just such a wreck, dating from close to 1300 BCE, was found at Uluburun, near Kaş, off the south Turkish coast in 43 m (141 ft.) to 60 m (198 ft.) of water. It was excavated between 1984 and 1994 by George Bass and Cemal Pulak of the Institute of Nautical Archaeology in Texas.

The ship's cargo contained about 10 tons of copper in the form of more than 350 of the four-handled ingots already known from wall paintings in Egypt and from finds in Cyprus, Crete, and elsewhere. The copper for these ingots was almost certainly mined on the island of Cyprus (as suggested by lead-isotope analysis, and trace-element analysis). Also of particular importance are nearly a ton of ingots and other objects of tin found on the seafloor in the remains of the cargo. The source of the tin used in the Mediterranean at this time is not yet clear. It seems evident that at the time of the shipwreck, the vessel was sailing westward from the east Mediterranean coast, and taking with it tin, from some eastern source, as well as copper from Cyprus.

The pottery included Canaanite amphorae, so called because they were made in Palestine or Syria (the land of Canaan). Most held turpentine-like resin from the terebinth tree, but several contained olives, and another glass beads. Similar jars have been found in Greece, Egypt, and especially along the Levantine coast.

The exotic goods included lengths of a wood resembling ebony, which grew in Africa south of Egypt. Then there were Baltic amber beads, which came originally from northern Europe (and that probably reached the Mediterranean overland). There was also ivory in the form of elephant and hippopotamus tusks, possibly from the eastern Mediterranean,

(Above) Three striking objects from the wreck (clockwise from left): a bronze statuette of a female deity, partly clad in gold foil, that may have been the ship's protective goddess; a boxwood diptych (object with folding plates) with ivory hinges, and with recesses to hold beeswax writing surfaces; and a gold pendant showing an unknown goddess with a gazelle in each upraised hand.

(Left) The map shows the probable route of the ill-fated ship found at Uluburun. Also indicated are likely sources of materials for the various artifacts found on board the wreck.

and ostrich eggshells that probably came from North Africa or Syria. Bronze tools and weapons from the wreck show a mixture of types that include Egyptian, Levantine, and Mycenaean forms. Among other important finds were several cylinder seals of Syrian and Mesopotamian types, ingots of glass (at that time a special and costly material), and a chalice of gold.

This staggering treasure gives a glimpse into Bronze Age trade in the Mediterranean. Bass and Pulak consider it likely that the ship started its final voyage on the Levantine coast. Its usual circuit probably involved sailing across to Cyprus, then along the Turkish coast, past Kaş and west to Crete, or, more likely, to one of the major Mycenaean sites on the Greek mainland, or even further north, as hinted by the discovery on the wreck of spears and a ceremonial scepter/mace from the Danube region of the Black Sea. Then, profiting from seasonal winds, it would head south across the open sea to the coast of North Africa, east to the mouth of the Nile and Egypt, and, finally, home again to Phoenicia. On this occasion, however, the crew lost their ship, their cargo, and possibly their lives at Uluburun.

(Right) Divers working on the four-handled ingots.

subordinate area. The opposite approach would be to consider different areas as completely autonomous and independent. But it seems unrealistic to exclude the possibility of significant interactions between different groups.

The solution is to seek ways of analyzing interactions, including their symbolic components, that do not make assumptions about dominance and subordination, core and periphery, but consider different areas as on a more or less equal footing. When discussing such interactions between independent societies of equal status, it has been found useful to speak of **interaction spheres**.

One major interaction sphere is competition. Neighboring areas compete with one another in various ways, judging their own success against that of their neighbors. This often takes a symbolic form in periodic meetings at some major ceremonial centers where representatives of the various areas meet, celebrate rituals, and sometimes compete in games and other enterprises.

Such behavior is seen among hunter-gatherer bands, which meet periodically in larger units (at what in Australia are called corroborees). It is seen also in the pilgrimages and rituals of state societies, most conspicuously in ancient Greece at the Olympic Games and at other Panhellenic assemblies, when representatives of all the city states would meet.

At such gatherings there is a tendency for one society to try to outdo its neighbors in conspicuous consumption, such as in the expensive

Potlatch ceremony at Sitka, Alaska, on December 9, 1904, with Tlingit chiefs dressed in their ceremonial finery. Such occasions involved the elaborate display of wealth and the public destruction of valuable items to manifest the high status of their owners.

public feasts of the Northwest Coast Native Americans, the institution of the potlatch. Very similar in some ways is the erection of magnificent monuments at regional ceremonial centers, each outdoing its neighbor in scale and grandeur. Something similar may have occurred in the ceremonial centers of Maya cities, and the same phenomenon is seen in the magnificent cathedrals in the capital cities of medieval Europe.

Warfare is, of course, an obvious form of competition. But the object of the competition is not necessarily to gain territory—for example, it might also be used to capture prisoners for sacrifice. It operated under well-understood rules, and was as much a form of interaction as the others listed here.

Innovations can also be transmitted—naturally a technical advance made in one area will soon spread to other areas. And there may also be a ceremonial exchange of valuables: although we have emphasized non-material (i.e. symbolic) interactions here, it is certainly the case that between the elites of different societies there may also be a series of material exchanges—the transfer of marriage partners and of valuable gifts. At the same time, large-scale exchanges between participating societies of everyday commodities should not, of course, be overlooked. Economies in some cases became linked together.

Such concepts, where as much emphasis is laid on symbolic aspects as on the physical exchange of material goods, can profitably be used to analyze interactions in most early societies and cultures. Systematic analysis of this kind has, however, so far been rare in archaeology.

Study Questions

1 What are some of the differences between unaltered and synthetic materials?
2 How is experimental archaeology used in the study of stone tools?
3 What is characterization and how does it aid in the study of ancient trade?
4 What are the four main types of exchange mechanisms and how do they differ?
5 What are some of the common qualities of valuables?
6 What is fall-off analysis and how does it relate to the study of distribution?

Summary

IN THIS CHAPTER we have highlighted some basic questions about early technology, and considered how to find answers to them. First, one must assess whether an object is indeed an artifact, and then of what material—unaltered (primarily stone, wood, fibers) or synthetic (pottery, metals). Ethnography and archaeological context may suggest the function of a tool; but only analysis of its microwear or residues can demonstrate its likely use. Nevertheless, ethnoarchaeology is proving extremely valuable.

STUDIES OF CHARACTERIZATION—i.e. the sources of the raw materials that make up artifacts—have been of enormous importance in archaeology, by shedding light on technological processes, and contact and trade between different regions and cultures. Thin-section analysis, as well as trace-element analysis and isotopic analysis, have played a major role in these investigations.

ONCE AN UNDERSTANDING of the whole process of making and using the artifacts has been attained, we can turn to their distribution—the spatial analysis of their places of manufacture and discovery, and hence the exchange and transportation systems that have caused these distribution patterns to come about.

Further Reading

Broad surveys of ancient technology, trade, and exchange include:

Cuomo, S. 2007. *Technology and Culture in Greek and Roman Antiquity*. Cambridge University Press: Cambridge & New York.

Earle, T. K. & Ericson, J. E. (eds). 1977. *Exchange Systems in Prehistory*. Academic Press: New York & London.

Ericson, J. E. & Earle, T. K. (eds). 1982. *Contexts for Prehistoric Exchange*. Academic Press: New York & London.

Fagan, B. M. (ed.). 2004. *The Seventy Great Inventions of the Ancient World*. Thames & Hudson: London & New York.

Forbes, R. J. (series). *Studies in Ancient Technology*. E. J. Brill: Leiden.

Lambert, J. B. 1997. *Traces of the Past: Unraveling the Secrets of Archaeology Through Chemistry*. Helix Books/Addison-Wesley Longman: Reading, MA.

Nicholson, P. & Shaw, I. (eds). 2009. *Ancient Egyptian Materials and Technology*. Cambridge University Press: Cambridge & New York.

Scarre, C. & Healy, F. (eds). 1993. *Trade and Exchange in Prehistoric Europe*. Oxbow Monograph 33: Oxford.

Torrence, R. 2009. *Production and Exchange of Stone Tools: Prehistoric Obsidian in the Aegean*. Cambridge University Press: Cambridge & New York.

[See p. 345 for a list of useful websites]

8

What Were They Like?
The Bioarchaeology of People

One of archaeology's principal aims is to recreate the lives of the people who produced the archaeological record, and what more direct evidence can there be than the physical remains of past humanity? In the next chapter we will see how archaeology can help us to understand the ways in which ancient people thought, but we have much more tangible evidence—complete skeletons, bones, bone fragments, and sometimes corpses that have been preserved in special circumstances—that enables us to reconstruct the physical attributes of past individuals and groups. If sufficient remains have survived, archaeologists can determine, for example, the sex and age of an individual, perhaps how that person died, and even his or her physical appearance. The study of such human remains is known as **bioarchaeology**; the topic also raises ethical issues, and these are examined in Chapter 11.

The Variety of Human Remains

How does the archaeologist know that human remains are present? This is relatively easy where intact bodies, complete skeletons, or skulls are found. Individual bones and large fragments can usually be reliably identified as human. In cases of fragmentary multiple burials or cremations, the minimum number of individuals can be assessed from the part of the body that is most abundant. Even small fragments may include diagnostic features. In some recent, careful excavations, individual hairs have been recovered that can be identified under the microscope as human.

Even where the physical remains of a body have disappeared, evidence may sometimes survive. The best-known examples are the hollows left by the bodies of the people of Pompeii as they disintegrated inside their hardened casing of volcanic ash. Modern plaster casts of these bodies show not only the general physical appearance, hairstyles, clothing, and posture, but also even such fine and moving detail as the facial expression at the moment of death.

Nevertheless the vast majority of human remains are in the form of actual skeletons and bone fragments, which yield a wide range of information, as we

Plaster, poured into the cavity left by the body, recreates the shape of a Pompeiian struck down in flight.

shall see. Indirect physical evidence about people also comes from ancient art, and provides important clues about what people looked like.

Identifying Physical Attributes

Once the presence and abundance of human remains have been established, how can we attempt to reconstruct physical characteristics—sex, age at death, build, appearance, and relationships? A good example of what we can learn

Bones of the human skeleton, with salient differences between the sexes.

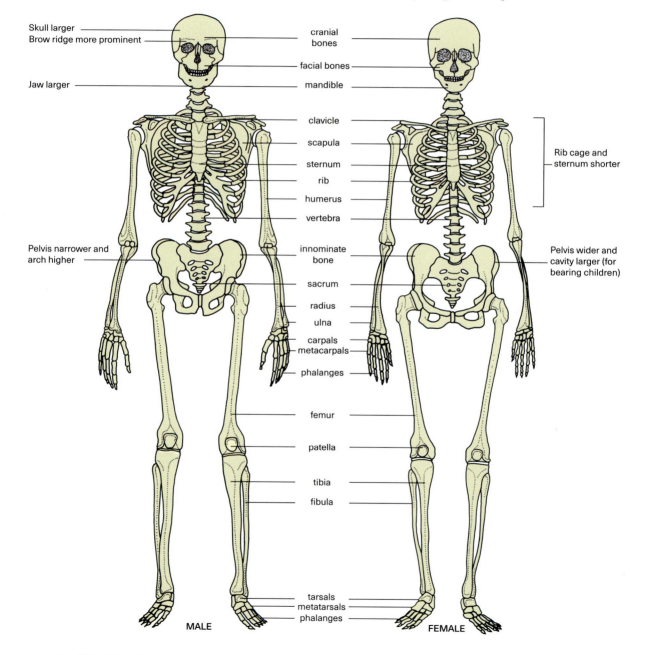

Skull larger
Brow ridge more prominent

cranial bones

facial bones

Jaw larger

mandible

clavicle

scapula

sternum

rib

humerus

vertebra

Rib cage and sternum shorter

Pelvis narrower and arch higher

innominate bone

sacrum

radius

ulna

carpals
metacarpals

phalanges

Pelvis wider and cavity larger (for bearing children)

femur

patella

tibia

fibula

tarsals
metatarsals
phalanges

MALE

FEMALE

The variety of human remains.

(Above left) The well-preserved 2000-year-old body of a girl, drowned in a bog at Windeby, northern Germany.

(Left) Early medieval burials at Sutton Hoo, eastern England, could be recovered only as outlines in the acid sandy soil.

(Above right) The 8500-year-old skeleton of a child from Çatalhöyük in Turkey.

from human remains is provided by the Grauballe Man bog body (see box overleaf). The techniques for assessing each different physical characteristic are described below.

Which Sex?

Where intact bodies and artistic depictions are concerned, sexing is usually straightforward from the genitalia. If these are not present, secondary characteristics, such as breasts and facial hair, provide fairly reliable indicators. Where human skeletons and bone remains without soft tissue are concerned, however, there are lots more sources of evidence, owing to differences between the sexes in the size and shape of various bones, known as sexual dimorphism.

The best indicator of sex is the shape of the pelvis, since this is visibly different in males and females (see diagram opposite). Other parts of the skeleton can also be used in sex differentiation: male bones are generally bigger, longer, more robust, and have more developed muscle markings than those of females, which are slighter.

Grauballe Man: The Body in the Bog

Grauballe

In 1952, peat cutters at Grauballe, Denmark, encountered a beautifully preserved bog body. It was lying in a prone position, with the left leg extended and the right leg and arm flexed. The various studies made of the body by multidisciplinary teams both in 1952 and, with new techniques, a few years ago have yielded remarkable insights into the life and death of this individual, now radiocarbon dated to 400–200 BCE, most likely c. 290 BCE.

Age and Sex
The body is that of a man, aged about thirty. When found, he had a 1-cm- (0.4-in.-) long beard and moustache, but these fell off during conservation. As facial hair grows c. 2.5–3.5 mm (0.1–0.14 in.) per week, and post-mortem skin shrinkage causes beard hair to stick out by 4–5 mm (0.16–0.2 in.), his beard was thus about two weeks old when he died.

Physique
Grauballe Man appears to have been of average build for the period. His height has been estimated at between 1.65 and 1.7 m (5 ft. 6 in. and 5 ft. 8 in.), but this is uncertain due to shrinkage of the remains.

Appearance
There were no traces of clothing or artifacts with the body. His hair is 15 cm (6 in.) long. Its relatively straight-cut ends suggest it was cut by scissors. It is now reddish-brown, but this may be due to its immersion in the bog, so one cannot be sure what color it was originally. The hands have well-preserved fingerprints, and the rounded-off nails, like the clear lines on the palms, indicate that he had not been involved in heavy manual work—the same seems to be true of many other male bog bodies in northwestern Europe.

State of Health
Grauballe Man was apparently fit and healthy—his body displays no sign of illness or disease—but he did

(Above) Grauballe Man's beautifully preserved feet, shortly after excavation.

have incipient arthritis in the thoracic vertebrae, which rarely occurs before the age of thirty. He still had twenty-one teeth, though several had fallen out since his death. They were worn, due to a coarse diet, and dental analysis revealed periods of starvation or poor health during his early childhood. The existence of periodontitis and cavities here and there showed that he had endured terrible toothache at times. Analysis of his hair shows that in his final months he had a terrestrial-based diet, with most protein coming from animal sources. His last meal was a gruel, a kind of poor muesli—it was dominated (80 percent) by seeds from a very small number of weed species, but there was also cereal bran. Small fragments of bone, including some from a pig, showed the presence of meat. The food would have been nutritious but not palatable—it is not known if

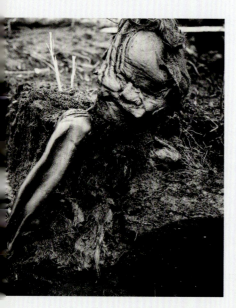
(Left) The body of Grauballe Man during excavation in 1952.

(Near left) This deep throat wound, severing the jugular vein and carotid arteries, was the cause of Grauballe Man's death.

(Left) Grauballe Man's body, as displayed in the Moesgaard Museum, Denmark.

it was typical of the everyday diet or not. The absence of fruit and greens suggests that he died in the winter.

How Did He Die?

The cause of his death was a deep cut to the throat from ear to ear while his head was bent sharply backwards—it was so deep that the jugular vein and carotid arteries were severed by a large sharp blade. It was originally thought that a blow to the head in the temple area had been inflicted by a blunt instrument, but a recent CT scan has proved it to be post-mortem damage. An oblique fracture on the left tibia, however, was clearly caused by a heavy blow—perhaps to bring him to his knees so that his throat could be cut more easily. We do not know why he, or any other bog body, died—perhaps as a sacrifice, or as an executed criminal—but we have been able to learn a great deal about the life and death of Grauballe Man thanks to the very wide variety of tests and analyses that have been applied to him.

For children it is worth noting that, with the exception of preserved bodies and artistic depictions showing genitalia, their remains cannot be sexed with the same degree of reliability as adults, although analysis of teeth can provide some evidence. When we examine subadult skeletal remains we can often only guess—though the odds of being right are 50:50. Recently, a new technique has been developed for determining the sex of fragmentary or infant skeletal remains from DNA analysis.

How Long Did They Live?

Some scholars feel able to assign exact age at death to particular deceased human beings, but it should be stressed that what we can usually establish with any certainty is biological age at death—young, adult, old—rather than any accurate measurement in years and months. The best indicators of age, as with animals, are the teeth. We can study the eruption and replacement of the milk teeth; the sequence of eruption of the permanent dentition; and finally the degree of wear, allowing as best one can for the effects of diet and method of food preparation.

A timescale for age at death derived from this kind of dental information in modern people works reasonably well for recent periods, despite

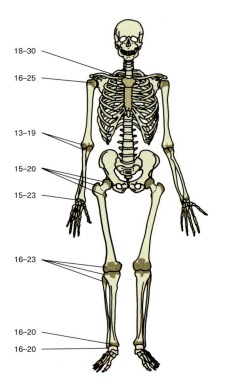

18–30

16–25

13–19

15–20

15–23

16–23

16–20
16–20

Assessing age: the years at which bone ends fuse.

much individual variation. But can it be applied to the dentition of our remote ancestors? New work on the microstructure of teeth suggests that old assumptions may not be correct. Tooth enamel grows at a regular, measurable rate, and its microscopic growth lines form ridges that can be counted from epoxy resin replicas of the tooth placed in a scanning electron microscope. In modern populations a new ridge grows approximately each week, and analysis of molar structure in Neanderthals has shown that they had a very similar rate of growth to that of modern humans. By measuring tooth growth ridges in fossil specimens, Tim Bromage and Christopher Dean have concluded that previous investigators overestimated the age at death of many early **hominins**. The famous 1–2 million-year-old australopithecine skull from Taung, South Africa, for example, belonged to a child who probably died at just over three years of age, not at five or six as had been believed. This suggests that our earliest ancestors grew up more quickly than we do, and that their development into maturity was more like that of the modern great apes.

Bones are also used in assessing age. The sequence in which the articulating ends of bones become fused to the shafts gives a timescale that can be applied to the remains of young people. One of the last bones to fuse is the inner end of the clavicle (collar bone) at about twenty-six; after that age, different criteria are needed to age bones. Skull thickness in immature individuals also bears a rough relationship to age—the thicker the skull the older the person—and in old age all bones usually get thinner and lighter, although skull bones actually get thicker in about 10 percent of elderly people.

But what if the bone remains are small fragments? The answer lies under the microscope, in bone microstructure. As we get older, the architecture of our bones changes in a distinct and measurable way. A young longbone, at about twenty, has rings around its circumference, and a relatively small number of circular structures called osteons. With age the rings disappear, and more and smaller osteons appear. By this method, even a fragment can provide an age. Putting a thin section of a femur (thigh bone) under the microscope and studying the stage of development is a technique that, in tests with documented known skeletons, has achieved accuracy to within five years.

Assessing age: changes in bone structure are visible under the microscope as humans grow older. The circular osteons become more numerous and extend to the edge of the bone.

INTERPRETING AGE AT DEATH.   It must be stressed that we can only calculate average age at death for the bodies and skeletons that have survived and been discovered. Many scholars used erroneously to believe that to dig up a cemetery, and assess the age and sex of its occupants, provided an accurate guide to the life expectancy and mortality pattern of a particular culture. This entails the considerable assumption that the cemetery contains all members of the community who died during the period of its use—that everyone was buried there regardless of age, sex, or status; that nobody died elsewhere; and that the cemetery was not reused at another time. This assumption cannot realistically be made. A cemetery provides a sample of the living population, but we do not know how representative that sample might be. Figures on life expectancy and average age should therefore be looked at critically before they are accepted and used by archaeologists.

What Did They Look Like?

Once again, it is preserved bodies that provide us with our clearest glimpses of faces. Tollund Man, one of the remarkable Iron Age bog bodies from Denmark, is the best-known prehistoric example. Discoveries at Thebes in Egypt in 1881 and 1898 of two royal burial caches have given us a veritable gallery of mummified pharaohs, their faces still vivid, even if some shrinkage and distortion has taken place.

Thanks to artists from the Upper Paleolithic onward, we also have a huge array of portraits. Some of them, such as images painted on mummy cases, are directly associated with the remains of their subject. Others, such as Greek and Roman busts, are accurate likenesses of well-known figures whose remains may be lost for ever. The extraordinary life-size terracotta army found near Xi'an, China, is made up of thousands of different models of soldiers of the third century BCE. Even though only the general features of each are represented, they constitute an unprecedented "library" of individuals, as well as providing invaluable information on hairstyles, armor, and weaponry. From later periods we have many life- or death-masks, sometimes used as the basis for life-size funerary effigies or tomb figures, such as those of European royalty and other notables from medieval times onward.

Attempts to reconstruct faces were carried out in the nineteenth century by German anatomists in order to produce likenesses from the skulls of such celebrities as Schiller, Kant, and Bach. But the best-known exponent of the technique in the twentieth century was the Russian Mikhail Gerasimov, who worked on remains ranging from fossil humans to Ivan the Terrible. It is now felt that much of his work represented "inspired interpretation," rather than factual reconstruction. The process is now more accurate.

One of the most intriguing facial reconstructions has been of the best-preserved Etruscan skeleton known today, that of a noblewoman called

Seianti Hanunia Tlesnasa, who died about 2200 years ago in central Italy. Since 1887 her remains have been housed in the British Museum inside a splendid painted terracotta sarcophagus that bears her engraved name (illustrated opposite). The lid of this sarcophagus features a life-size image of the dead woman, reclining on a soft pillow, with a bronze mirror in her jeweled hand. This is perhaps the earliest identifiable portrait in western art, but is it really Seianti?

Anthropologists deduced from the skeleton that the woman was about 1.5 m (4 ft. 11 in.) tall, and middle-aged at death. Damage and wear on her bones, and the fact that she was almost toothless, had at first suggested old age, but in fact she had incurred severe injuries, most likely a riding accident that had crushed her right hip and knocked out the teeth of her right lower jaw. The bone was damaged where the jaw joins the skull, and opening her mouth wide would have been painful. This prevented her from eating anything but soups and gruels, and from keeping her remaining teeth clean—most of them subsequently fell out. Seianti would also have had painful arthritis and increasing disabilities.

Faces from the past.

(Left) Bronze head of the Roman emperor Hadrian (reigned 117–138 CE), from the Thames River.

(Below left) An old man with a wrinkled face is portrayed (with an accompanying duck) on this 1000-year-old Tiwanaku-period (500–1100 CE) vase from the island of Pariti in Lake Titicaca, Bolivia.

(Right) Tutankhamun's mummy was unwrapped in 1923, revealing a shrunken body. The young king's original height was estimated by measuring the longbones.

(Below center) Tutankhamun's facial features have recently been reconstructed using CT scans of his skull as a base—three teams separately produced very similar reconstructions, one of which is shown here.

(Right) The terracotta sarcophagus of Seianti Hanunia Tlesnasa, which contained her bones; the lid takes the form of a life-size image of the dead woman—but how accurately did it represent her appearance?

(Above) The reconstruction made from the skull found in the sarcophagus.

Two of the surviving teeth confirmed, from analysis of the dentine, that she was about fifty when she died. And radiocarbon dating of the bones produced a result of 250–150 BCE, which proved that the skeleton was genuinely ancient and of the right period. The facial reconstruction showed a middle-aged woman who had grown rather obese. How did it compare with the coffin image?

From the side, there were differences, since the artist had given Seianti a prettier nose, but from the front the resemblances were clearer. The final confirmation came from a computerized technique for matching facial proportions and features—the computer photocomparison of the reconstruction and the portrait left no doubt that this was the same person. The sarcophagus image showed her as some years younger, with fewer chins, and a smaller, more girlish mouth. In other words, the sculptor had made flattering improvements to the portrait of this short, portly, middle-aged woman, but also captured Seianti's likeness extremely well.

How Were They Related?

In certain cases it is possible to assess the relationship between two individuals by comparing skull shape or analyzing the hair. There are other methods of achieving the same result, primarily by study of dental morphology. Some dental anomalies (such as enlarged or extra teeth, and especially missing wisdom teeth) run in families. Blood groups, which are inherited in a simple fashion from parents, can also sometimes help clarify physical relationships between different bodies.

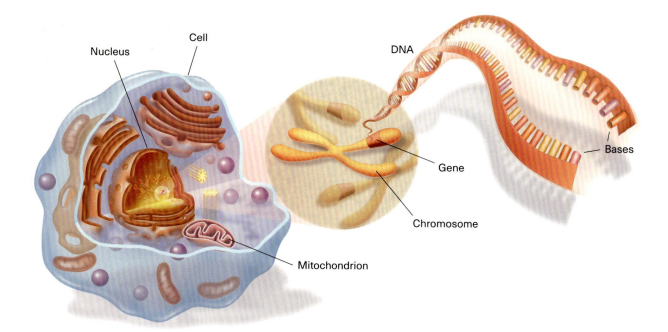

Cell

Nucleus

DNA

Gene

Bases

Chromosome

Mitochondrion

Genes, the organizers of inheritance, are composed of DNA (deoxyribonucleic acid), which carries the hereditary instructions needed to build a body and make it work. Genes are copied or "replicated" with every new generation of living cells; nuclear DNA forms the blueprint for the cells, and is copied every time a new cell is produced. The mitochondria (small organelles) within the cell contain relatively small loops of DNA (mitochondrial DNA; abbreviated mtDNA) that have been intensively studied.

Family relationships can also be worked out through DNA analysis (see illustration above). In 1985 the Swedish scientist Svante Pääbo first succeeded in extracting and cloning mitochondrial DNA from the 2400-year-old mummy of an Egyptian boy. Over such a long time period, the DNA molecules are broken up by chemical action, so there is no question of reconstituting a functioning gene, far less a living body. But information on the DNA sequences of, for example, Egyptian mummies may determine whether members of a dynasty did indeed practice incest, as is commonly believed: an analysis of DNA from six mummies of 2200 BCE found at Hagasa, Egypt, has proved that they were a family group. Recent advances in genetic engineering have opened up fascinating possibilities for future work in human evolution, past human relationships, and the origin and evolution of disease.

Where Did They Come from?

People moved from one region to another in the past, as we do today. The best information on early population movements is the genetic material we all carry ourselves. Mitochondrial DNA (mtDNA), which is contained not in the cell nucleus but in other bodies in our cells (mitochondria), and is passed on only by females, has proved very important in tracing populations in the past. Since mtDNA is inherited only through the mother, unlike nuclear DNA, which is a mixture of both parents' genes, it preserves a family record that is altered over the generations only by mutations.

In 1987 Rebecca Cann, Mark Stoneking, and Allan Wilson wrote an influential paper that analyzed mtDNA from 147 present-day women from

Africa, Asia, Europe, Australia, and New Guinea and concluded that people of sub-Saharan African descent showed the most differences among themselves, which implied that their mtDNA had had the most time to mutate, and hence that their ancestors must be the earliest. This would imply that our species, *Homo sapiens*, originated in sub-Saharan Africa. This important result, which is now widely accepted, argued against the alternative view, the multiregional hypothesis, in which there would have been an evolutionary process in different parts of the world involving the transition from our ancestor *Homo erectus* to *Homo sapiens*. It seems instead that the lineages derived from *Homo erectus* and living outside of Africa became extinct, being replaced by the new *sapiens* humans some 60,000 years ago. This view has been supported by the study of Y-chromosome DNA, which is inherited in the male line (and which likewise does not recombine as the genetic material is passed on to the next generation).

The archaeology of our own cells has started to tell us much about ourselves and our past. It must be noted, however, that genetics based upon living populations can only tell us about past populations that left descendants; it can tell us nothing about people who died out. For that we have to turn to ancient DNA.

ANCIENT DNA.   The recent contribution of ancient DNA, from the remains of ancient burials and other human remains, has proven highly important. The Neanderthal genome project led by Svante Pääbo published the entire draft sequence of the Neanderthal genome, using Neanderthal bones from the Vindija Cave in Croatia, between 44,000 and 38,000 years old. This is the most ambitious project so far based on ancient DNA, and indicates that the date of divergence between modern humans and Neanderthals is estimated to lie between 440,000 and 270,000 years ago. They also observed that the Neanderthals are significantly closer to living Europeans and Asians than to modern Africans. It was concluded that there must have been significant gene flow from Neanderthals into modern humans, which may be, "explained by mixing of early modern humans ancestral to present-day non-Africans with Neanderthals in the Middle East before their expansion into Eurasia." This conclusion has proved a controversial one. The work of the Neanderthal genome project represents nonetheless a significant step forward in our understanding of the human past.

The picture has been complicated by the DNA analysis of another fossil fragment from the Denisova Cave in Siberia, revealing that the individual in question there is neither human nor Neanderthal, but a hominin of a species that split from the human and Neanderthal lineage some 1 million years ago. The whole-genome sequencing of the tooth and finger bone in question suggests that the Denisovans have an evolutionary history distinct both from

Sex: intact bodies can be sexed from the genitalia; skeletons and bone remains, much more common in the archaeological record, are sexed from size and form differences between male and female bones. Children are difficult to sex

Age: the main methods of establishing the age of a skeleton are by examinations of the growth patterns of bones and teeth, and of bone microstructure

Appearance: it is now possible to make accurate facial reconstructions of ancient individuals, as long as their skull or fragments of it survive

Relationships: examinations of skull shape, hair type, teeth, blood group, and DNA can help to establish whether two individuals were related

DNA: the rapidly developing field of genetics offers many possibilities for archaeologists studying evolution and the past movements of humans. Much information is stored in our own DNA, but new developments are increasingly making the study of ancient DNA feasible

western Eurasian Neanderthals and from modern humans, although the claim for a new species would traditionally be supported by some more impressive parts of the cranium and skeleton.

ANCIENT DNA OF "MODERN" HUMANS.   New developments are allowing genetic work on anatomically modern humans of our own species to be undertaken on human remains from the Upper Paleolithic period, and indeed also on prehistoric human remains from more recent times.

Cold conditions are favorable to the preservation of ancient DNA, and so most of the positive results so far come from samples found in northern Europe, Siberia, or North America. The pace of research in the ancient DNA field is illustrated by the 2014 whole-genome analysis by Morten Rasmussen and his colleagues in Copenhagen of a male infant from the Anzick burial site in western Montana, radiocarbon dated to about 12,500 years ago. Found associated with tools of the Clovis industry, it is the only human burial directly linked with the Clovis culture. His mtDNA is of a lineage already thought to be one of the founder lineages carried by the First Americans, and his Y-chromosome lineage is also common to Native Americans. Comparison of his nuclear genome with that of Eurasians and Native Americans shows that he is more genetically similar to Siberians than to other Eurasians.

In Europe, ancient DNA has shown that the position is more complicated than one might appreciate if relying simply on DNA from living populations. An early European farmer cluster, with origins in Anatolia or the Near East, can now be recognized in samples taken from early Neolithic burials in Germany and Sweden. A west European hunter-gatherer cluster can be recognized from samples from hunter-gatherer (Mesolithic) contexts in Spain and Luxembourg, as can an ancient north Eurasian cluster from sites in Siberia, including Mal'ta. Technical difficulties are being overcome in this rapidly developing field, allowing documentation of a migration of people from the Eurasian steppe into central Europe around 2500 BCE, implicated in the formation of the Corded Ware culture and in the subsequent occupation of southern Britain by a beaker-using culture in the following centuries.

Disease, Deformity, and Death

In addition to the basic physical attributes described above, it is also necessary to look at the other, often more negative aspects of the picture: What was people's quality of life? What was their state of health? We may know how long they lived, but how did they die? Where we have intact bodies, the precise cause of death can sometimes be deduced—indeed, in some cases, such as the asphyxiated people of Pompeii and Herculaneum, it is obvious from the circumstances (the effect of the eruption of the volcano Vesuvius). For the more numerous skeletal remains that come down to us, however, cause of death can be ascertained only rarely, since most afflictions leading to death leave no trace on bone. Paleopathology (the study of ancient disease) tells us far more about life than about death, a fact of great benefit to the archaeologist.

In parallel, biological and forensic anthropologists are increasingly using techniques developed within archaeology to assist them with the recovery and study of human remains. Indeed, a new subdiscipline has now developed—forensic archaeology—which helps in the recovery and interpretation of murder victims, as well as trying to identify individuals within mass burials, as encountered in Rwanda and the former Yugoslavia.

Evidence in Soft Tissue

Since most infectious diseases rarely leave detectable traces in bones, a proper analysis of ancient diseases can only be carried out on surviving soft tissue, which rarely survives except in specific environments. The surface tissue sometimes reveals evidence of illness, such as eczema. It can also reveal some causes of violent death, such as the slit throats of several bog bodies.

The coffin of Meresamun, an ancient Egyptian singer-priestess of *c.* 800 BCE, in the temple at Karnak, was acquired by the Oriental Institute in Chicago in 1920 and has remained unopened. It has been CT-scanned three times as technology has improved—most recently in 2008 when a state-of-the-art 256-slice scanner was used. The data can be rendered in 3D and manipulated in different ways, effectively allowing one to strip away successive layers, and to isolate particular bones or features of interest for analysis; movie sequences can also be created. Many details missed in the previous scans were uncovered, from items of jewelry and dental features to degenerate spinal changes and minor post-mortem fractures.

Richard III Rediscovered

In 2012 the world was startled to learn that a skeleton, believed to belong to England's King Richard III (1452–85), had been uncovered in Leicester, in the Midlands. Immortalized by Shakespeare as a villainous hunchback, the last of the Plantagenet kings was killed in battle at Bosworth Field in 1485, and it is known that he was buried in Leicester's Greyfriars church. There was also a story, however, that his body was later exhumed and thrown into the nearby river; in any case the church was demolished in the sixteenth century.

Excavations in the Leicester parking lot where Richard III's burial was found. The grave cut can be made out at the bottom center of the photo. Richard's remains were reinterred inside Leicester Cathedral in a formal ceremony in March 2015.

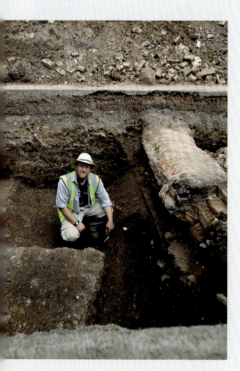

The project was an unusual collaboration between professional and academic archaeologists, an amateur group (the Richard III Society), and the City of Leicester. Excavation began in August 2012, in what had become a parking lot, and rapidly revealed the foundations of part of the church. The skeleton in question was found on day one, in a location that turned out to be a high-status position beneath the choir. The body was in an irregularly cut grave that was too short for it, whereas other graves in the choir were neatly rectangular and of the correct length. The lower limbs were fully extended, but torso was twisted to the north, and the head was propped up against a corner of the hole: in other words, it seemed the body had been crammed feetfirst into this small hole, which implies great haste and/or a lack of respect. There was no evidence of a coffin or shroud.

If the skeleton is indeed Richard, the haste may have been caused by the fact that his body had been on public display for several days, in the height of summer. The hands were crossed at the wrist, which may indicate that they were bound. The feet had been lost to some digging by nineteenth-century workmen, but otherwise the skeleton is in good condition—with 135 bones and 29 teeth. It is that of an adult male of gracile build, aged, according to bone growth and tooth development, in his late twenties to late thirties (Richard was 32 when he died). The most remarkable feature is a severe scoliosis, i.e. a spine badly curved to the side (as opposed to the hunched back of legend).

The scoliosis developed around the age of ten to thirteen. The progressive condition would have put a strain

The proposed skeleton of Richard III, showing pronounced curvature of the spine.

on his heart and lungs, possibly causing shortness of breath and pain. Without scoliosis, his thigh bones indicate that he would have stood c. 1.73 m (5 ft. 8 in.) tall, above average for the period, but the disability would have reduced this to perhaps 1.42 m (4 ft. 8 in.), and his right shoulder would have stood higher than the left. In other words, this man had a squat torso and uneven shoulders, which fits the few contemporary accounts of Richard's appearance. Radiocarbon dating of the remains produced a result of 1456– 1530 CE, which is consistent with the battle of 1485.

The teeth were a little worn, but had no cavities, and he was infected with roundworms. Analysis of nitrogen and carbon in the ribs by different laboratories revealed a high protein diet, including about 25 percent seafood, which implies high status. Oxygen and strontium isotopes from fluids he ingested as a child reflect the geology of the water source, and are consistent with Richard's origins in Northamptonshire. It then seems the person moved farther west by the age of seven, possibly to the Welsh Marches (Richard resided at Ludlow

The facial reconstruction of the Leicester skeleton bears a remarkable likeness to the few portraits of Richard III, but the sculptor did know in advance which skull was involved.

Castle in 1459). On the other hand, there is a significant increase in the oxygen isotope composition in the last few years of his life, which analysts claim cannot be accounted for by beer and food, so they have attributed it to grape juice, in the form of wine—the equivalent of a modern bottle a day would lead to such a raised signature!

The skeleton displays at least eleven wounds, all of them peri-mortem (i.e. inflicted round the time of death), since none shows signs of healing. Two large wounds under the back of the skull are consistent with blows from a halberd and sword, and would probably have caused almost instant death. There is a third, smaller penetrating wound to the top of the skull, possibly from a dagger.

None of the skull wounds could have been inflicted on someone wearing a fifteenth-century helmet. Two other wounds—a cut on a right rib, and one on the right pelvis (probably caused by a thrust through the right buttock)—are also unlikely on someone wearing armour. So these may be "humiliation injuries", delivered after death. In short, this person almost certainly died in battle, and the nearest battle in this time range was that of Bosworth, 24 km

(15 miles) west of Leicester. Finally, initial genetic analysis has been carried out on the body's mitochondrial DNA, and a link has been claimed with two modern-day descendants of Anne of York, Richard's sister. The researchers therefore believe that they have proven the identity of this skeleton "beyond reasonable doubt." Whether or not they are correct, the project has displayed archaeology's occasional and unique potential for mass appeal to the world's media.

Where inner tissue is involved, a number of methods are at the analyst's disposal. X-rays can provide much information, and have been used on Egyptian mummies, but newer, more powerful methods, such as **Computed Tomography** (**CT**) **scanning** and Magnetic Resonance Imaging (MRI), are also now available (see illustration, p. 245).

Skeletal Evidence for Deformity and Disease

Skeletal material is far more abundant than preserved soft tissue, and can reveal a great deal of paleopathological information. Effects on the outer surface of bone can be divided into those caused by violence or accident, and those caused by disease or congenital deformity. Where violence or accidents resulting in skeletal trauma are concerned, observations can often reveal how the damage was caused, and how serious its consequences were. The small number of diseases that affect bone do so via either erosion, growths, or an altered structure. Furthermore, the bony lesions associated with various illnesses can differ in terms of their number and location. Some afflictions leave quite clear signs (see box opposite and above), whereas others do not. The former include several infections, nutritional deficiencies, and cancers. It is also possible to detect growth disorders by the overall size and shape of bones.

Diet and Nutrition

Nutrition can be described as the measure of a diet's ability to maintain the human body in its physical and social environment. We are of course interested to be able to learn whether a particular group of people in the past enjoyed good nutrition. Furthermore, comparison of nutrition at different periods may significantly add to our understanding of fundamental changes to the pattern of life, as in the transition from hunting and gathering to farming.

Malnutrition

What are the skeletal signs of malnutrition? So-called Harris lines, detected by X-rays on bones, indicate periods of arrested growth during development, and these are sometimes caused by malnutrition. A similar phenomenon occurs in teeth, where patches of poorly mineralized enamel, which a specialist can detect in a tooth section, reflect growth disturbance brought about by a diet deficient in milk, fish, oil, or animal fats (or sometimes by such childhood diseases as measles). A lack of vitamin C produces scurvy, an affliction that causes changes in the palate and gums, and has been identified in an Anglo-Saxon individual from Norfolk, England, as well as in Peru, North America, and elsewhere.

The general size and condition of a skeleton's bones can provide an indication of aspects of diet. Sand in food, or the grit from grindstones, can have drastic effects on teeth. The excessive abrasion of teeth among certain California Native Americans can be linked to their habit of leaching the tannins out of acorns (their staple food) through a bed of sand, leaving a residue in the food.

Additional evidence for malnutrition can be obtained from art and literature. Vitamin B deficiency (beriberi) is mentioned in the *Su Wen*, a Chinese text of the third millennium BCE, and Strabo also refers to a case among Roman troops. Egyptian art provides such scenes as the well-known famine depicted at Saqqara, dating to around 2350 BCE.

Evidence for malnutrition: detail of a wall relief from the complex surrounding the pyramid of Unas, at Saqqara in Egypt, depicting famine victims, *c.* 2350 BCE.

Chemical analysis of bone allows further insights. Much has been done with the stable isotopes of carbon and nitrogen (see Chapter 6), which vary among individuals according to what they ate. The carbon isotopes incorporated in bone—the stable ones, not the ^{14}C that is used for dating purposes—can be used to detect a diet high in certain plants or in marine resources. The consumption of maize, in particular, can be identified, so the method has been used to investigate subsistence strategies in parts of the prehistoric New World. In eastern North America, for example, a shift in the stable carbon isotope signature of human bones about 1000 years ago corresponds nicely to a marked change in the representation of maize in the plant remains from habitation sites. This is one example where independent lines of evidence—the composition of bones and the kinds of carbonized plant remains—complement one another, increasing confidence in the inferences one makes about the past.

Cannibalism

Cannibalism—the eating of human flesh by humans—has often been claimed to exist in different periods of the past, usually on the flimsiest of evidence. Early scholars simply assumed that cannibalism was a "primitive" trait and must therefore have existed in prehistory, but the traditional urge to uncover cannibalism suffered a massive jolt with the appearance more than thirty years ago of a ground-breaking work by anthropologist William Arens that, for the first time, showed that the vast majority of claims for cannibalism in the ethnographic or ethnohistorical record were untrustworthy. In recent decades, a better understanding of taphonomy, greater familiarity with the huge variety of funerary rituals around the world, and a more objective assessment of the facts, have helped to weed out many claims for prehistoric cannibalism. Meanwhile new claims have been put forward that rely on more plausible evidence.

At Atapuerca in northern Spain (see box, p. 131), the bones of a human ancestor called *Homo antecessor*, dating to perhaps 1 million years ago and found in the Gran Dolina site, bear abundant cutmarks that, in the absence of any evidence for funerary rituals or other secondary treatment of the dead, are most likely butchery marks, which have therefore been interpreted as evidence for cannibalism, and it is difficult to disagree with this inference. However, a later site at Atapuerca, the Sima de los Huesos, also presents the earliest evidence in the world for some kind of funerary ritual, perhaps some 600,000 years ago. We know from recent times that a huge variety of often bizarre funerary practices exists, some involving cutting, smashing, and burning of bones, either shortly after death or long afterwards. The archaeological record contains many instances from different periods, stretching back into prehistory, that can plausibly be attributed to such practices.

Cutmarks on this human bone from Gran Dolina were almost certainly caused by butchering.

In order to decide whether human remains were produced by cannibalism or by funerary activities (or warfare, etc.), there are two main categories of evidence: the presence of human bones with marks of cutting, smashing, or burning, and the presence of human bones mixed with animal bones (i.e. the remains of food), with similar marks and treatment. However, one must avoid jumping to simplistic and "obvious" conclusions. The data are always ambiguous, and must be assessed carefully and objectively.

Dramatic claims have been made for cannibalism among the Ancestral Pueblo of the American Southwest, around 1100 CE, including supposed human fecal material containing human tissue; but once again alternative explanations are available, involving not only funerary practices but also the extreme violence and mutilation inflicted on enemy corpses in warfare. The fecal material may actually be from a scavenging coyote.

The possibility remains that cannibalism may have existed occasionally, but even if that were true, the contribution of human flesh to diet must have been minimal and sporadic, paling into insignificance beside that of other creatures, especially the big herbivores.

Study Questions

1 Which physical attributes can be determined from human remains?
2 How can archaeologists determine if two individuals are related?
3 How are teeth used to assess how old an individual was at death?
4 What are some of the methods archaeologists use to determine what people in the past looked like?
5 What can human remains tell us about the lives of people living in the past?
6 What is the evidence for prehistoric cannibalism? How valid is it?

Summary

THE PHYSICAL REMAINS of past peoples provide direct evidence about their lives. Bioarchaeology is the study of human remains from archaeological sites. Though whole human bodies can be preserved in a variety of ways, including mummification and freezing, the vast majority of human remains recovered by archaeologists are in the form of skeletons and bone fragments.

AN IMPORTANT PART of the analysis of human remains is the identification of physical attributes. The gender of skeletal remains, for example, can be determined through observing the shape of the pelvis as well as other bones. Teeth and bones can help establish an individual's relative age at death, namely whether they were young, adult, or old. It is even possible to reconstruct what an individual looked like through careful analysis of skull features, or to assess the relationship between two individuals.

EXAMINATION OF HUMAN REMAINS can also shed light on the more negative aspects of past lives—the diseases and deformites suffered, and sometimes an individual's cause of death. Study of bones and the chemical signatures within them provides evidence of ancient diet and nutrition (or malnutrition), and can even give clues as to whether early humans might have eaten each other.

Further Reading

The following works provide an introduction to the study of the physical remains of humans:

Aufderheide, A. C. 2003. *The Scientific Study of Mummies*. Cambridge University Press: Cambridge & New York.

Blau, S. & Ubelaker, D. H. 2008. *Handbook of Forensic Archaeology and Anthropology*. World Archaeological Congress Research Handbooks in Archaeology. Left Coast Press: Walnut Creek, CA.

Brothwell, D. 1986. *The Bog Man and the Archaeology of People*. Harvard University Press: Cambridge, MA.

Chamberlain, A. T. & Parker Pearson, M. 2004. *Earthly Remains. The History and Science of Preserved Human Bodies*. Oxford University Press: New York.

Donnan, C. B. 2003. *Moche Portrait Vessels from Ancient Peru*. University of Texas Press: Austin.

Larsen, C. S. 2002. *Skeletons in Our Closet: Revealing Our Past Through Bioarchaeology*. Princeton University Press: Princeton.

Matisoo-Smith, E. & Horsburgh, K. A. 2012. *DNA for Archaeologists*. Left Coast Press: Walnut Creek, CA.

Mays, S. 2010. *The Archaeology of Human Bones*. Routledge: London.

Reich, D. 2018. *Who We Are and How We Got Here: Ancient DNA and the New Science of the Human Past*. Pantheon Books: New York.

Waldron, T. 2001. *Shadows in the Soil: Human Bones and Archaeology*. Tempus: Stroud.

[See p. 345 for a list of useful websites]

9

What Did They Think?
Cognitive Archaeology

The mental attributes of our ancestors are covered in this chapter. In Chapter 8 we examined their physical attributes, but of course the lives of ancient people who produced the archaeological record were not just about the physical aspects of existence: they had mental abilities, thoughts, and spiritual lives, just as we do today.

We will begin this chapter by looking at **cognitive archaeology**—the study of past ways of thought from material remains—which is in many respects one of the newer branches of modern archaeology. Rather than simply "imagining" what people in the past must have thought or believed, it is possible to use the more disciplined techniques of cognitive archaeology to gain insights into these important aspects of the past: we can analyze the concepts people had and the way they thought.

We can, for example, investigate how people went about describing and measuring their world: as we shall see, the system of weights used in the Indus Valley civilization can be understood very well today. We can investigate which material goods people valued most highly, and perhaps viewed as symbols of authority or power. And we can also investigate the manner in which people conceived of the supernatural, and how they responded to these conceptions in their ritual practice.

Cognitive Archaeology

It is generally agreed today that what most clearly distinguishes the human species from other life forms is our ability to use symbols. A symbol may be defined as the representation of an idea or of a concept, whether in verbal or in visual form. All intelligent thought and indeed all coherent speech are based on symbols, for words are themselves symbols, where the sound or the written letters stand for and thus represent (or symbolize) an aspect of the real world. Usually, however, meaning is attributed to a particular symbol in an arbitrary way. And that meaning is specific to a particular cultural tradition. It is usually impossible to infer the meaning of a symbol within a given culture from the symbolic form of the image or object alone. We have to see how that form is used, and to try to understand its meaning from the context in which it is used. Cognitive archaeology has thus to be very careful about specific contexts of discovery. There are very few symbols that have a universal meaning cross-culturally. It is the assemblage that matters, not the individual object in isolation.

Investigating How Human Symbolizing Faculties Evolved

The field of cognitive archaeology is concerned primarily with the cognitive behavior of our own species, *Homo sapiens*. Modern genetic studies suggest that we are all closely related, and that the innate cognitive abilities within any one regional group of our species, along with other behavioral attributes, are much like those in another. For instance, all human groups today have the capacity of complex speech, a capacity that in all probability we share with our ancestors of 80,000 to 60,000 years ago, the time of the first human dispersals out of Africa. Clearly, however, as we go back much further in time and consider earlier hominin species, whether *Homo habilis* or *Homo erectus*, we are dealing with creatures of more limited cognitive abilities. Their study represents an important subdivision of cognitive archaeology—the development of hominin cognitive abilities up to the emergence of our own species. It presents special problems, since for these earlier ancestors we cannot make the assumption that they had innate cognitive facilities much like our own. That is something that has to be investigated.

LANGUAGE AND SELF-CONSCIOUSNESS.   Most biological anthropologists agree that modern human abilities have been present since the emergence of *Homo sapiens* some 200,000–150,000 years ago. But as we look earlier, scholars are less united. Some archaeologists and biological anthropologists consider that an effective language may have been developed by *Homo habilis* around 2 million years ago, along with the first chopper tools, but others think that a full language capability developed very much more recently, with the emergence of *Homo sapiens*. This would imply that the tools made by hominins in the Lower and Middle Paleolithic periods were produced by beings without true linguistic capacities.

The origins of self-consciousness have been debated by scientists and philosophers, but with few definite conclusions. There is little evidence available to clarify the matter, but one philosopher, John Searle, has argued that there is no sudden transition, but rather a gradual development: he asserted, for example, that his dog Ludwig had a significant degree of self-consciousness.

Key Concepts
Early Human Symbolizing Faculties

The development of language and self-consciousness

Evidence of design in tool manufacture

Evidence of the procurement of materials and planning

The deliberate burial of human remains

Representations and "art"

There are several lines of approach to other aspects of early human abilities. One way that we can try to assess early human cognitive ability is by examining the way stone tools and other artifacts were made.

DESIGN IN TOOL MANUFACTURE.   Whereas the production of simple pebble tools—for instance by *Homo habilis*—may perhaps be considered a simple, habitual act, not unlike a chimpanzee breaking off a stick to poke at an ant hill, the fashioning by *Homo erectus* of so beautiful an object as an Acheulian hand-axe seems more advanced.

So far, however, that is just a subjective impression. How do we investigate it further? One way is to measure, by experiment, the amount of time taken in the manufacturing process. A more rigorous quantitative approach, as developed by Glynn Isaac, is to study the range of variation in an assemblage of artifacts. For if the toolmaker has, within his or her **cognitive map**, some enduring notion of what the end product should be, one finished tool should be much like another. Isaac distinguished a tendency through time to produce an increasingly well-defined variety or assemblage of tool types. This implies that each person making tools had a notion of different tool forms, no doubt destined for different functions. Planning and design in tool manufacture thus become relevant to our consideration of the cognitive abilities of early hominins, abilities that moreover distinguish them from higher apes, such as the chimpanzee.

The production of a stone tool, a pot, a bronze artifact, or any product of a well-defined manufacturing process involves a complicated and often highly standardized sequence of events. For early periods, such as the Paleolithic, the study of the processes involved in making artifacts offers one of the few insights available into the way cognitive structures underlay complex aspects of human behavior. French prehistorians Claudine Karlin and Michèle Julien analyzed the sequence of events necessary for the production of blades in the Magdalenian period of the French Upper Paleolithic; many other production processes can be investigated along similar lines.

PROCUREMENT OF MATERIALS AND PLANNING TIME.   Another way of investigating the cognitive behavior of early hominins is to consider planning time, defined as the time between the planning of an act and its execution. For instance, if the raw material used to manufacture a stone tool comes from a specific rock outcrop, but the tool itself is produced some distance away (as documented by waste flakes produced in its manufacture), that would seem to indicate some enduring intention or foresight by the person who transported the raw material. Similarly, the transport of natural or finished objects, whether tools, seashells, or attractive fossils, as has been documented, indicates at least a continuing interest in them, or the intention of using

Deliberate burial of the dead: a young girl (left, aged nine to ten) and an adolescent boy (right, aged twelve to thirteen) buried head to head at Sungir, northeast of Moscow, c. 27,000 years ago. They wore a variety of pendants, bracelets, and other ornaments, their clothes were covered with thousands of ivory beads, and the boy wore a belt of fox teeth. The entire burial was covered in red ocher.

them, or a sense of "possession." The study of such objects, by the techniques of characterization discussed in Chapter 7 and other methods, has now been undertaken in a systematic way.

DELIBERATE BURIAL OF HUMAN REMAINS. From the Upper Paleolithic period onward there are many well-established cases of human burial, where the body or bodies have been deliberately laid to rest within a dug grave, sometimes accompanied by ornaments of personal adornment. Evidence is emerging, however, from even earlier periods. The act of burial itself implies some kind of respect or feeling for the deceased individual, and perhaps some notion of an afterlife (although that point is less easy to demonstrate). Adornment seems to imply the existence of the idea that objects of decoration can enhance the individual's appearance, whether in terms of beauty or prestige or otherwise. A good Upper Paleolithic example is the discovery made at Sungir, some 200 km (125 miles) northeast of Moscow, Russia, and dating from c. 27,000 years ago: burials of a man and two children together with mammoth ivory spears, stone tools, ivory daggers, small animal carvings, and thousands of ivory beads.

In assessing such finds, we must be sure to understand the formation processes—in particular what may have happened to the burial after it was made. For example, animal skeletons have been discovered alongside human remains in graves. Traditionally this would have been taken as proof that animals were deliberately buried with the humans as part of some ritual act. Now, however, it is thought possible that in certain cases animals scavenging for food found their way into these burials and died accidentally—thus leaving false clues to mislead archaeologists.

REPRESENTATIONS. Any object, and any drawing or painting on a surface that can be unhesitatingly recognized as a depiction—that is, a representation of an object in the real world (and not simply a mechanical reproduction of one, as a fossil is)—is a symbol. General questions about representations and depictions for all time periods are discussed later (see pp. 260–72). For the Paleolithic period, there are two issues of prime importance: evaluating the date (and hence in some cases the authenticity), and confirming the status as a depiction. Although it has long been believed that the earliest depictions are of Upper Paleolithic date and produced by *Homo sapiens*, increasing numbers of earlier examples are forcing us to reexamine this supposition.

So far the earliest well-dated product that might securely be described as "art," or at least as "graphic design" is a zigzag engraving on a freshwater mussel shell from Trinil, Java, dating to at least 430,000 years ago. Such a date suggests it was created by *Homo erectus*. An incised network pattern has also been found on a piece of red ocher from the Blombos Cave, South Africa, dating to 77,000 years ago. It is believed to be the work of our own species *Homo sapiens*.

(Right) Mussel shell from Trinil, Java, with engraved zigzags, at least 430,000 years old.

(Below right) Piece of red ocher with abstract engravings, from the Blombos Cave, South Africa, dating to *c.* 77,000 years ago.

Paleolithic Art

Cave Art

Much has been written about the Ice Age caves of western Europe, decorated with images of animals and abstract markings. Clustered in specific regions—most notably the Périgord and Pyrenees in southwestern France and Cantabria in northern Spain—they span the whole of the Upper Paleolithic, from about 30,000 BCE onward. The majority of the art, however, dates to the latter part of the Ice Age, to the Solutrean and especially the Magdalenian period, ending around 10,000 BCE.

The cave artists used a great range of techniques, from simple finger tracings and modeling in clay to engravings and bas-relief sculpture, and from hand stencils to paintings using two or three colors. Much of the art is unintelligible—and therefore classified by scholars as "signs" or abstract marks—but of the

figures that can be identified, most are animals. Very few humans and virtually no objects were drawn on cave walls. Figures vary greatly in size, from tiny to more than 5 m (16.5 ft.) in length. Some are easily visible and accessible, while others are carefully hidden in recesses of the caves.

The first systematic approach to the study of cave art ("parietal art") was that of the French archaeologist André Leroi-Gourhan, working in the 1960s. Following the lead of Annette Laming-Emperaire, Leroi-Gourhan argued that the pictures formed compositions. Previously they had been seen as random accumulations of individual images, representing simple "hunting magic" or "fertility magic." Leroi-Gourhan studied the positions and associations of the animal figures in each cave. He established that horse and bison are by far the most commonly depicted animals, accounting for about 60 percent of the total, and that they are concentrated on what seem to be the central panels

(Above) Principal locations of Paleolithic cave art in western Europe.

of caves. Other species (e.g. ibex, mammoth, and deer) are located in more peripheral positions, while less commonly drawn animals (e.g. rhinoceroses, felines, and bears) often cluster in the cave depths. Leroi-Gourhan therefore felt sure

(Left) The spectacular paintings of Chauvet Cave, southern France, discovered in 1994, depict more than 440 animals.

(Below) An engraving of a mammoth from Cussac Cave in the Dordogne, France.

Portable art. (Above) Engraving of three lions on a bone from the cave of La Vache in southwestern France. (Left and below) Three bone carvings from the cave of La Garma, northern Spain. (Right) A recently discovered "Venus figurine" in mammoth ivory from the open-air site of Zaraisk, near Moscow, Russia.

he had found the "blueprint" for the way each cave had been decorated.

We now know that this scheme is too generalized. Every cave is different, and some have only one figure, whereas others (e.g. Lascaux in southwestern France) have hundreds. Nevertheless, Leroi-Gourhan's work established that there is a basic thematic unity—profiles of a limited range of animals—and a clearly intentional layout of figures on the walls. Currently, research is exploring how each cave's decoration was adapted to the shape of its walls, and even to the areas in the cave where the human voice resonates most effectively.

New finds continue to be made— an average of one cave per year, including major discoveries in France, such as Cosquer Cave (1991) near Marseille, the Ice Age entrance of which is now drowned beneath the sea, and the spectacular Chauvet Cave (1994) in the Ardèche, with its unique profusion of depictions of rhinoceroses and big cats.

In the 1980s and 1990s, however, a series of discoveries also revealed that "cave art" was produced in the open air. Indeed this was probably the most common form of art production in the Ice Age, but the vast majority of it has succumbed to the weathering of many millennia, leaving us with the heavily skewed sample of figures that survived more readily inside caves. Only a dozen sites are known so far, in Spain, Portugal, and France, but they comprise hundreds of figures, mostly pecked into rocks, which by their style and content are clearly Ice Age in date.

Portable Art

Ice Age portable ("mobiliary") art comprises thousands of engravings and carvings on small objects of stone, bone, antler, and ivory. The great majority of identifiable figures are animals, but perhaps the most famous pieces are the so-called "Venus figurines," such as the limestone Venus of Willendorf, from Austria. These depict females of a wide span of ages and types, and are by no means limited to the handful of obese specimens that are often claimed to be characteristic.

Venus figurine from the Balzi Rossi caves at Grimaldi, northern Italy.

We should, however, note the enormous cognitive significance of the act of depiction itself, in all the vividness seen in the art of Chauvet or Lascaux in France, or Altamira in Spain. We do not yet understand very well, however, why such representation was rare in the Pleistocene (Ice Age) period, or what the significance to their creators of the remarkable depiction of animals in the painted caves of France and Spain may have been (see box, pp. 258–59).

Working with Symbols

We are interested in studying how symbols were used. Perhaps we cannot fully understand their meaning, if that implies the full meaning they had for the original users (without going into a profound analysis, we can define "meaning" as "the relationship between symbols"). We can, however, hope to establish some—but by no means all—of the original relationships between the symbols observed.

In the pages that follow we shall consider cognitive archaeology in terms of five different uses to which symbols are put.

- A basic step is the establishment of place by marking and delimiting territory and the territory of the community, often with the use of symbolic markers and monuments, thereby constructing a perceived landscape, generally with a sacred as well as a secular dimension (a land of memories).
- A fundamental cognitive step is the development of symbols of measurement—as in units of time, length, and weight—which help us organize our relationships with the natural world.
- Symbols allow us to cope with the future world, as instruments of planning. They help us define our intentions more clearly, by making models for some future intended action, for example plans of towns or cities.
- Symbols are used to regulate and organize relations between human beings. Money is a good example of this, and with it the whole notion that some material objects have a higher value than others. Beyond this is a broader category of symbols, such as the badges of rank in an army, that have to do with the exercise of power in a society.
- Symbols are used to represent and to try to regulate human relations with the Other World, the world of the supernatural or the transcendental—which leads on to the archaeology of religion and cult.

No doubt there are other kinds of uses for symbols, but this rather simplistic listing will help us in our discussion of how we should set about analyzing them.

Key Concepts
Working with Symbols

The human species is distinguished from other life forms by its use of symbols

Symbols are used by humans for a variety of purposes, some of which can be recognized in the archaeological record:

- The marking of place and the definition of territory
- The construction of systems of measurement
- Design, mapping, and the planning of future actions
- Shaping and reflecting social realities, including identity and power relationships
- Communicating with supernatural powers in the Other World

Establishing Place: The Location of Memory

One of the fundamental aspects of the cognition of the individual is the establishment of place, often through the establishment of a center, which in a permanent settlement is likely to be the hearth of the home. For a community another significant place is likely to be the burial place of the ancestral dead, whether within the house or at some collective tomb or shrine. For a larger community, whether sedentary or mobile, there may be some communal meeting place, a sacred center for periodic gatherings.

These various features, some of them deliberate symbolic constructions, others more functional works that nonetheless are seen to have meaning—the home, the tilled agricultural land, the pasture—together constitute a constructed landscape in which the individual lives. As some archaeologists have pointed out, this landscape structures the experience and the worldview of that individual. These observations are just as relevant to small-scale societies as to state societies. Many great cities from China to Cambodia and from Sri Lanka to the Maya lowlands and Peru are laid out on cosmological principles, allowing the ruler to ensure harmony between his subjects and the prevailing sacred and supernatural forces. But the sacred center can be important in smaller societies also, and many of those that appear to have had a corporate structure rather than a powerful central leader were capable of major public works—the temples of Malta and the megalithic centers of Carnac, in Brittany, and Orkney, off the north coast of Scotland, are good examples, as well as Stonehenge and Chaco Canyon. Such monuments can also be used to structure time and can operate to facilitate access to the other, sacred world.

But these aspects of life operate also at a local level, not only at great centers. So the entire countryside becomes a complex of constructed landscapes, with meaning as well as of practical use. The landscape is composed of places bringing memories, and the history of the community is

The ceremonial center of Orkney, off the north coast of Scotland, a ritual landscape in which individuals lived and which in turn shaped their experience and worldview. The Ring of Brodgar (below left) was one element of a complex and rich sacred landscape (below right), which demonstrates that it was not only large, organized state societies that were capable of creating major public works.

told with reference to its significant places. Landscape archaeology thus has a cognitive dimension, which takes it far beyond the preoccupation with productive land use characteristic of a purely materialist approach: the landscape has social and spiritual meaning as well as utility.

Measuring the World

One aspect of an individual's cognition we can readily reconstruct is the way in which it copes with measurement or quantitative description. The development of units was a fundamental cognitive step. In many cases, they can be recovered archaeologically—especially units of time, length, and weight.

The measurement of time is implied whenever a calendrical system can be documented. It is implied also when an alignment is evident that preserves the direction of the sun (or moon) at one of the major turning points. That is well known to be the case for the major axis of Stonehenge, the great Neolithic monument in England, which is oriented toward the midsummer sunrise, and also for the stone tomb of Newgrange in Ireland, dating from c. 3200 BCE, the entrance passage of which is oriented toward the midwinter sunrise.

The existence of measurements of weight can be demonstrated by the discovery of objects of standard form that prove to be multiples of a recurrent quantity (by weight), which we can assume to be a standard unit. Such finds are made in many early civilizations. Sometimes the observations are reinforced by the discovery of markings on the objects themselves, which accurately record how many times the standard the piece in question weighs. Systems of coinage are invariably graded using measurement by weight, as well as by material (gold, silver, etc.), although their purpose is to measure differences in value. More directly relevant here are discoveries of actual weights.

An excellent example comes from the site of Mohenjodaro, a major city of the Indus Valley civilization around 2500–2000 BCE. Attractive and carefully worked cubes of colored stone were found there. They proved to be multiples of what we may recognize as a constant unit of mass (namely 0.836 g, or 0.03 oz), multiplied by such integers as 1, 4, or 8, up to 64, then 320 and 1600.

It can be argued that this simple discovery indicates that:

1 the society in question had developed a concept equivalent to our own notion of weight or mass;
2 the use of this concept involved the operation of units of measure;
3 there was a system of numbering, involving hierarchical numerical categories (e.g. tens and units), in this case apparently based on the fixed ratio of 16:1;
4 the weight system was used for practical purposes (as the finding of scale pans indicates);

Units of weight: stone cubes from Mohenjodaro, Pakistan, were produced in multiples of 0.836 g (0.03 oz). Scale pans indicate the practical use to which the cubes were put.

5 there probably existed a notion of equivalence, on the basis of weight among different materials, and hence, it may follow, a ratio of value between them;

6 this inferred concept of value may have entailed some form of constant rate of exchange between commodities.

Items 5 and 6 are more hypothetical than the others in the list. But it seems a good example of the way that superficially simple discoveries can, when subjected to analysis, yield important information about the concepts and procedures of the communities in question.

Planning: Maps for the Future

The cognitive map that each one of us carries in our mind's eye allows us to conceive of what we are trying to do, to formulate a plan, before we do it. Only rarely does the archaeologist find direct material evidence of this, but sometimes the product is so complex or so sophisticated that a plan prepared in advance, or a formalized procedure, can be postulated.

It is, of course, difficult to demonstrate purposive planning, if by that is meant the prior formulation of a conscious plan in the construction of some work. At first sight, a settlement like Çatalhöyük in Turkey (c. 6500 BCE), or a sector of such an early Sumerian town as Ur (c. 2300 BCE), suggest prior planning. But when we look at the operation of various natural processes we can see that effects of very high regularity can occur simply by repetition within a well-defined scheme. There is no need to suggest that the polyps in a coral reef, or the worker bees in a beehive, are operating according to

(Below left) The regularity in layout of the Indus Valley city of Mohenjodaro—with main streets approximately at right angles—hints at conscious town planning.

(Below right) The Çatalhöyük village layout (bottom) may have been no more consciously planned than the cells in a beehive (top).

a conscious plan: they are simply getting on with the job, according to an innate procedure. The layouts of Çatalhöyük and Ur may be no more sophisticated than that. To demonstrate prior planning it is necessary to have some clear evidence that the scheme of construction was envisaged at the outset. Such proof, however, is rarely forthcoming. A few actual maps have come down to us from prehistoric or early historic times; but most probably represent depictions or representations of existing features, not the planning of future ones. Just occasionally, however, we find models of buildings that may have been constructed before the building itself. There are five or six models of Neolithic temples on the Mediterranean island of Malta that might represent planning in this way: they certainly show close attention to architectural detail.

Such direct projections in symbolic form of the cognitive map of the designer are rare. Sculptors' trial pieces and models, such as have been found at the ancient Egyptian city of Tell el-Amarna, are likewise unusual discoveries.

An alternative strategy is to seek ways of showing that regularities observed in the finished product are such that they could not have come about by accident. That seems to be the case for the passage grave of Newgrange in Ireland, dating from *c.* 3200 BCE. At sunrise on midwinter's day the sun shines directly down the passage and into the tomb chamber. There is only a low probability that the alignment would be by chance in the approximate direction of the sun's rising or setting at one of its two major turning points on the horizon. But it is unlikely also that, in terms of altitude, the passage of such a tomb would be aligned on the horizon at all. In fact, there is a special "roof box" with a slit in it, over the entrance, which seems to have been made to permit the midwinter sun to shine through.

Deliberate alignment: the rays of the midwinter sun illuminate the passage and chamber at Newgrange, Ireland.

End recess

Roof box

Light

Entrance stone

Often, careful planning can be deduced from the methods used in a particular craft process. Any metal objects produced by the lost-wax method undoubtedly represent the result of a complex, controlled, premeditated sequence, where a version of the desired shape was modeled in wax before the clay mold was constructed round it, which then allowed the shape in question to be cast in bronze or gold. Another example is the standardization in many early metal-using communities of the proportions of different metals in objects made of alloyed metal. The constant level of ten percent tin found in the bronze objects of the early Bronze Age in Europe is not fortuitous: it is evidently the result of carefully controlled procedures that must themselves have been the result of generations of trial and experiment. The use of a unit of length will also document some measure of planning.

Complete regularity in layout, where there is a grid of streets at right angles, evenly spaced, is also a convincing indication of town planning. Traditionally, it is claimed that the Greek architect Hippodamus of Miletus (in the sixth century BCE) was the first town planner. But ancient Egypt furnishes much earlier examples—for instance, in the town built by the pharaoh Akhenaten at Tell el-Amarna, which dates from the fourteenth century BCE. The cities of the Indus Valley civilization around 2000 BCE also show some very regular features. They are not laid out on an entirely rectilinear grid, but the main thoroughfares certainly intersect approximately at right angles. How much of this was deliberate prior planning, and how much was simply unplanned urban growth, are questions that have not yet been systematically investigated.

A stronger case for deliberate town planning can be made when the major axis of a city is aligned on an astronomically significant feature, as discussed earlier (see pp. 262–63), for example the great Mesoamerican and Andean centers. Paul Wheatley, in his influential book *The Pivot of the Four Quarters* (1971), has emphasized how the desire to harmonize the urban order with the cosmic order influenced town planning. This seems to be true not just for American civilizations but also for Indian, Chinese, and Southeast Asian ones as well. The argument is reinforced when the urban order is supplemented by a rich cosmic iconography, as in such cities as Angkor, capital of the Khmer empire, in modern Cambodia.

Symbols of Organization and Power

Symbols are used for regulating and organizing people as well as the material world. They may simply convey information from one person to another, as with language or, as in the case of archival records, from one point in time to another. But sometimes they are symbols of power, commanding obedience and conformity, such as the giant statues of rulers found in many civilizations.

Power relations are sometimes documented graphically, as in the statues of the Egyptian pharaohs, or on the splendid stelae and reliefs of the Maya. For example, Lintel 24 from Yaxchilan, illustrated below, shows the ruler ("Shield Jaguar III") and his wife during a bloodletting ritual. The glyphs that frame their images give details of their names, the calendar date (October 25, 709 CE), and a description of the rite. The images do of course have religious significance, but they also emphasize the role of the ruler and his family in subjecting themselves to this painful ritual for the good of the community. Shield Jaguar holds aloft a flaming torch. He has a magnificent headdress, with feathers at the rear and the shrunken head of a past sacrificial victim tied to the top of his head by a headband.

More often, however, power relations are not documented pictorially but have to be inferred from the association of prestigious artifacts made, often with beautiful craftsmanship, from exotic materials.

Archaeological evidence on its own can in fact yield evidence of scales of value, as work on the analysis of finds from the late Neolithic cemetery

				Shield Jaguar III the captor of
5 Eb 15 Mac 9.13.17.15.12 (October 25, 709 CE)	It is his image in penance	with a fiery spear	It is the penance of the 4 Katun Lord	captive's name (undeciphered)
				Divine Pa'chan Lord (name of local dynasty)

It is her image in penance

Lady ? Xook

Lady K'abal Xook

Ix Kaloomte' (title)

Lintel 24 from Yaxchilan, showing Shield Jaguar III and his wife, Lady K'abal Xook, during a sacred ritual. The glyphs that frame their images give details of their names and titles, the calendar date, and a description of the rite.

Deducing scales of value: the great worth of the gold from Varna, Bulgaria, is suggested by, among other things, its use to decorate significant parts of the body.

at Varna in Bulgaria, dating from *c*. 4000 BCE, has shown. Numerous golden artifacts were discovered in the cemetery, constituting what is the earliest known major find of gold anywhere in the world. But it cannot simply be assumed that the gold is of high value (its relative abundance in the cemetery might imply the opposite).

Three arguments, however, can be used to support the conclusion that the gold here was indeed of great worth:

1. Its use for artifacts with evidently symbolic status: e.g. to decorate the haft of a perforated stone axe that, through its fine work and delicate nature, was clearly not intended for use.
2. Its use for ornaments at particularly significant parts of the body: e.g. for face decorations, for a penis sheath.
3. Its use in simulation: sheet gold was used to cover a stone axe to give the impression of solid gold. Such a procedure normally indicates that the material hidden is less valuable than the covering material.

The demonstration that gold objects were highly valued by society at this time in ancient Bulgaria also implies that the individuals with whom the gold finds were associated had a high social status. The importance of burials as sources of evidence for social status and ranking was discussed in Chapter 5. Here we are more interested in the use of grave-goods, such as the Varna gold-covered axes, and other discoveries, as symbols of authority and power. The display of such authority is not very pronounced in such a society as the one excavated at Varna, but it becomes more blatant the more hierarchical and stratified the society becomes.

The Archaeology of Religion

One leading English dictionary defines religion as: "Action or conduct indicating a belief in, or reverence for, and desire to please, a divine ruling power." Religion thus involves a framework of beliefs, and these relate to supernatural or superhuman beings or forces that go beyond the everyday material world. In other words superhuman beings are conceptualized by humans, and have a place in the shared cognitive map of the world.

One problem that archaeologists face is that these belief systems are not always given expression in material culture. And when they are—in what can be termed the **archaeology of cult**—there is the problem that such actions are not always clearly separated from the other actions of everyday life: cult can be embedded within everyday functional activity, and thus difficult to distinguish from it archaeologically. The first task of the archaeologist is to recognize the evidence of cult for what it is, and not make the old mistake of classifying as religious activity every action in the past that we do not understand.

RECOGNITION OF CULT.   If we are to distinguish cult from other activities, such as the largely secular ceremonial that may attend a head of state (which can also have very elaborate symbolism), it is important not to lose sight of the transcendent or supernatural object of the cult activity. Religious ritual involves the performance of expressive acts of worship toward the deity or transcendent being. In this there are generally at least four main components (we will see below how these may then help us draw up a list of aspects that are identifiable archaeologically):

- *Focusing of attention.* The act of worship both demands and induces a state of heightened awareness or religious excitement. In communal acts of worship, this invariably requires a range of attention-focusing devices, including a sacred location, architecture (e.g. temples), light, sounds, and smell, to ensure that all eyes are directed toward the crucial ritual acts.
- *Boundary zone between this world and the next.* The focus of ritual activity is the boundary area between this world and the Other World. It is a special and mysterious region with hidden dangers. There are risks of pollution and of failing to comply with the appropriate procedures: ritual washing and cleanliness are therefore emphasized.
- *Presence of the deity.* For ritual to be effective, the deity or supernatural force must in some sense be present. It is divine as well as human attention that needs to be heightened. In most societies, the deity is symbolized by a material form or image: this need be no more than a very simple symbol—for instance, the outline of a sign or container, the contents of which are not seen—or it may be a three-dimensional cult image, such as a statue.
- *Participation and offering.* Worship makes demands on the celebrant. These include not only words and gestures of prayer and respect, but also often active participation involving movement, and perhaps eating and drinking. Frequently, it involves also the offering of material things to the deity, both by sacrifice and gift.

An excellent example of cult activity visible in the archaeological record is offered by the site of Göbekli Tepe in Turkey (see box overleaf). Another is the great ceremonial center at Chavín de Huantar in north-central Peru, which flourished from 850 to 200 BCE. The most immediately obvious feature of the site is its imposing architecture, comprising a complex of stone-faced platforms built in the earliest phase on a U-shaped plan and set apart from living areas at the site. Ritual involving both conspicuous public display and hidden mysteries is implied by the presence of an open circular sunken plaza that could hold 300 participants, and hidden underground passageways, the most important of which led to a narrow chamber dominated by a 4.5-m- (14-ft.-9-in.-) high granite shaft known as the Lanzón (Great Image).

SOUTH AMERICA
• Chavín de Huantar

(Above) Perspective and plan views of the early U-shaped platforms at Chavín, with a section through the central passageway showing the narrow chamber dominated by the Lanzón or Great Image.

(Above left) Two views of the Lanzón or Great Image (center, complete image; above, rollout drawing), depicting a fanged anthropomorphic being.

(Right) Transformation of a masked shaman (near) into a jaguar (far). These sculptures were displayed on the outer wall of the temple, and hint at drug-induced rituals.

The World's Oldest Sanctuary: Göbekli Tepe

The site of Göbekli Tepe, near the town of Urfa in southeastern Turkey, can lay claim to be the world's oldest sanctuary. Dating from between 9000 and 8000 BCE, it is a large mound 300 m (1,000 ft.) in diameter, containing a series of enclosures, perhaps as many as twenty, of which four are under excavation by a team of the German Archaeological Institute in Istanbul. Although radiocarbon dates set it contemporary with the very earliest Neolithic of the Levant, Pre-Pottery Neolithic A, there are no traces of cultivated plants at the site, and the fauna includes only wild species, such as gazelle, wild cattle, wild ass, red deer, and wild pig. The society that built and used the site was effectively one of hunter-gatherers. But this was not a settlement site.

Carved Pillars

The most characteristic feature of Göbekli Tepe are the pillars, arranged to create oval structures including up to twelve such pillars, interconnected by stone benches. Each is a T-shaped monolith of limestone standing several meters high and weighing up to 12 tons. The largest, not yet fully excavated, seems to be 5 m (16 ft.) high.

Upon these pillars are carvings in relief of animals—lions, foxes, gazelle, wild boar, wild asses, aurochs, snakes, birds, insects, and spiders. Its previous excavator, the late Klaus Schmidt, suggested that the pillars themselves represent stylized humans, the horizontal and vertical elements representing the head and body, for

A view of the excavations at Göbekli Tepe. Large T-shaped stone pillars connected by walls and benches form enclosures.

A wild boar and other animals carved in relief on one of the pillars at Göbekli Tepe.

when those areas are excavated. Certainly it seems reasonable to suggest that Göbekli Tepe was a special central place, a ritual focus for the regional population. Contemporary villages are known nearby: Nevali Çori, also excavated by Schmidt, was one such. In it was a small enclosure, likewise containing T-shaped megalithic pillars and life-size limestone sculptures of humans and animals, which may be regarded as a small sanctuary.

But Göbekli Tepe was much larger and more specialized, lacking the residential accommodation of the village. Ritual practice at this special site seems highly likely. As we have seen, funerary ritual is possible, but not yet documented. Nor is there yet evidence of "deities" (in the sense of beings with transcendent powers)— there is no iconography to suggest supernatural beings. It is possible, of course, that the rituals at the site involved veneration for ancestors. So it might be premature to speak of "cult" if that is taken to imply the worship of deities.

What is remarkable, however, is that the use of Göbekli Tepe seems to precede the development of farming in this area—although the site lies close to the region where einkorn wheat was first domesticated. It may have been visited seasonally and need not document a sedentary population. But for the archaeologist interested in the origins of farming in this very area, it is a notable and intriguing site.

the pillars sometimes show arms and hands in low relief. There are also three-dimensional sculptures of animals, mainly boar, that seem to have been placed on the tops of walls.

Analysis

These enclosures certainly suggest the practice of ritual, with their special architectural forms, meeting the "focusing of attention" criteria discussed in this chapter. Moreover they are rich in animal symbolism. Klaus Schmidt suggested that funerary rituals were practiced there, which he suggested would account for the very considerable labor involved in the construction of each of the enclosures. But no burials have yet been found: Schmidt predicted that they will be discovered beneath the benches or behind the walls of the enclosures

The carving on this shaft of a fanged anthropomorphic being, its location in a central chamber facing east along the temple's main axis, and its size and workmanship all suggest that this was the principal cult image of the site. Moreover, some 200 other stone sculptures, dominated by images of caymans, jaguars, eagles, and snakes, were found in and around the temple. A cache of more than 500 broken high-quality pots containing food found in an underground gallery may have been offerings (though the excavator believes they were used for storage). There is some evidence for drug-induced rituals and the possibility that canals beneath the site were used for ritual washing and to create roaring sounds to heighten the impact of ceremonies.

The study of Chavín thus demonstrates that a careful archaeological and art-historical analysis of different kinds of evidence can produce sound proof of cult activity—even for a site and society concerning which there are no written records whatsoever.

The Impact of Literacy

Symbols of depiction provide us with perhaps our most direct insight into the cognition of an individual or a society for pre-literate periods. Among literate communities, however, written words—those deceptively direct symbols used to describe the world—inevitably dominate the evidence. The earliest writing systems around the world are summarized on the map below.

Ancient literature in all its variety, from poems and plays to political statements and early historical writings, provides rich insights into the cognitive world of the great civilizations. But, to use such evidence accurately

Map showing locations of the world's earliest writing systems.

Runic alphabet 2nd century CE

Aegean scripts: Linear A (Crete) 18th century BCE
Linear B (Crete & Greece) c. 1450 BCE
Greek alphabet (Crete, Greece, & Western Turkey) c. 750 BCE

Hittite hieroglyphs c. 1450 BCE

Etruscan alphabet c. 700 BCE

Mesopotamian cuneiform c. 3100 BCE

Japanese script 5th century CE

Zapotec/Mixtec script c. 600 BCE

Chinese characters c. 1200 BCE

Brahmi alphabet c. 350 BCE

Maya hieroglyphs c. 350 BCE

Egyptian hieroglyphs c. 3000 BCE

Phoenician alphabet c. 1000 BCE

Indus Valley script c. 2500 BCE

Easter Island script (rongorongo) c. 1500 CE

and effectively, we need to understand something of the social context of the use of writing in different societies.

The very existence of writing implies a major extension of human cognitive processes. Written symbols have proved the most effective system ever devised by humans not only to describe the world around them, but also to communicate with and control people, to organize society as a whole, and to pass on to posterity the accumulated knowledge of a society.

Literacy in Classical Greece

The importance of literacy is well illustrated by the case of Classical Greece. In several ancient civilizations writing was practiced only by a small segment of the population, notably scribes—for instance in ancient Egypt or Mesopotamia, and the same was probably true in Mesoamerica. In Greece, however, it is likely that many who had the status of citizens were able to read.

For extended texts, whether works of literature or accounts, the Greeks wrote on papyrus. Examples of such texts have been found at Pompeii and in the very dry conditions of the Faiyum depression in Egypt. For public inscriptions, the Greeks used stone or bronze, although notices that were not of permanent interest were put on display on whitened boards (the simple alphabetic script of the Greeks favored such relatively casual use). Among the functions of Greek inscriptions carved on stone or bronze were:

- Public decrees by the ruling body (council or assembly)
- Awards of honors by the ruling body to an individual or group
- Treaties between states
- Letters from a monarch to a city
- Lists of taxes imposed on tributary states
- Inventories of property and dedications belonging to a deity
- Rules for divination (understanding omens), e.g. from the flight of birds
- Building accounts, records of specifications, contracts, and payments
- Public notices: e.g. lists for military service
- Boundary stones and mortgage stones
- Epitaphs
- Curses laid on whomever might disturb a particular tomb

It is clear from this list what an important role writing had within the democratic government of the Greek states. A better indication of literacy and of the role of writing in Greek daily life, however, is given by the various objects bearing inscriptions, and by comments scrawled on walls (graffiti). One type of object, the *ostrakon*, was a voting ticket in the form of a fragment of pottery with the name of the individual—for (or against) whom the vote was being cast—incised on it. Many have been found in Athens where

Potsherds (*ostraka*) inscribed with two famous Greek names: Hippokrates (above) and Themistokles (below).

(by the system of "ostracism") public men could, by a vote of the assembly, be driven into exile. Other Greek uses of writing on a variety of objects were:

- On coins, to show the issuing authority (city)
- To label individuals shown in scenes on wall paintings and painted vases
- To label prizes awarded in competitions
- To label dedications made to a deity
- To indicate the price of goods
- To give the signature of the artist or craftsperson
- To indicate jury membership (on a jury ticket)

These simple inscriptions enable us to glimpse aspects of everyday life and even to identify and learn things about individuals. The British Museum has a black-figure drinking cup of c. 530 BCE, made in Athens and imported to Taranto, Italy, bearing the inscription: "I am Melousa's prize: she won the maiden's carding contest." The cognitive archaeology of ancient Greece thus inevitably draws to a great extent on the insights provided by such literary evidence. But we should not imagine that cognitive archaeology is thus necessarily dependent on literary sources to generate or test its theories.

Textual evidence is indeed of paramount importance in helping us understand ways of thought among literate societies, but there are in addition purely archaeological sources that may be used to create theories about the thought processes of ancient individuals and peoples, and purely archaeological criteria to judge their validity. Moreover, literary sources may themselves be biased in ways that need to be fully assessed before any attempt can be made to match such sources with evidence from the archaeological record.

Study Questions

1   What are symbols and how do they relate to cognitive archaeology?
2   What are some of the ways in which humans use symbols?
3   How do archaeologists and anthropologists investigate the cognitive abilities of our hominin ancestors?
4   What are some of the ways in which past people measured their world?
5   How do archaeologists recognize religion or cult in the archaeological record?
6   What was the role of writing in Classical Greek daily life?

Summary

IN THIS CHAPTER we have shown how archaeological evidence can be used to provide insights into the way of thinking of cultures and civilizations long dead.

WHETHER IT BE EVIDENCE for measurement, means of organization and power, or cult activity, there are good archaeological procedures for analyzing and testing cognitive hypotheses about the past. An archaeological project may focus on one aspect of the way ancient people thought (for example, in the search for a possible standard unit of measurement), or it may be much broader (for example, the work at Chavín). While textual evidence may be of crucial importance in supporting or helping to assess cognitive claims—as in Mesoamerica or Mesopotamia—cognitive archaeology does not depend on literary sources for its validity.

Further Reading

The following works provide an introduction to the study of the attitudes and beliefs of ancient humans:

Arsuaga, J. L. 2003. *The Neanderthal's Necklace: In Search of the First Thinkers*. Four Walls Eight Windows: New York.

Aveni, A. F. (ed.). 2008. *People and the Sky: Our Ancestors and the Cosmos*. Thames & Hudson: London & New York.

Bahn, P. G. 2016. *Images of the Ice Age*. Oxford University Press: Oxford.

Johnson, M. 2010. *Archaeological Theory*. Blackwell: Oxford.

Lorblanchet, M. & Bahn, P. G. 2017. *The First Artists: In Search of the World's Oldest Art*. Thames & Hudson: London & New York.

Renfrew, C. & Zubrow E. B. W. (eds). 1994. *The Ancient Mind: Elements of Cognitive Archaeology*. Cambridge University Press: Cambridge & New York.

Renfrew, C. 2009. *Prehistory: The Making of the Human Mind*. Modern Library: New York.

[See p. 345 for a list of useful websites]

10

Why Did Things Change?
Explanation in Archaeology

To answer the question "why?" is the most difficult task in archaeology. We must go beyond simply describing the appearance of things and try to *understand* the pattern of events.

This is the goal motivating many who take up the study of the human past. There is a desire to learn something from the study of what is dead and gone that is relevant for the conduct of our own lives and our societies today. Archaeology, which allows us to study early and remote prehistoric periods as well as the more recent historical ones, is unique among the human sciences in offering a considerable time depth. Thus, if there are patterns to be found among human affairs, the archaeological timescale may reveal them.

There is no agreed and accepted way of setting out to understand the human past. A chapter such as this is therefore bound to be inconclusive, and certain to be controversial. But it is a chapter worth writing and worth thinking about, for it is in this area of inquiry that archaeological research is now most active. The main debates have developed over the past forty years or so.

Traditional explanations of change in the past focused on the concepts of **diffusion** and migration—they assumed that changes in one group must have been caused either by the influence or influx of a neighboring and superior group. But in the 1960s the development of the processual approach of the so-called New Archaeology exposed the shortcomings of the earlier explanations. It was realized that there was no well-established body of theory to underpin archaeological inquiry (to a large extent this is still true, although there have been many attempts).

The early New Archaeology involved the explicit use of theory and of models, and above all of generalization. It was criticized, however, as being too much concerned with ecological aspects of adaptation and with efficiency, and with the purely utilitarian and functional aspects of living (in other words, it was too "functionalist"). Meanwhile, an alternative perspective, inspired by Marxism, was laying more stress on social relations and the exercise of power.

From the 1970s, in reaction to the processual "functionalists," some archaeologists favored a **structuralist archaeology** and then a postprocessual one. These approaches stressed that the ideas and beliefs of past societies should not be overlooked in archaeological explanation.

Since that time archaeologists have given more systematic attention to the way humans think, how they make and use symbols, and to what may be described as cognitive issues. One approach, today termed "cognitive archaeology," seeks to work in the tradition of processual archaeology while stressing social and cognitive aspects.

So far there is no single, widely agreed approach.

Migrationist and Diffusionist Explanations

The New Archaeology made the shortcomings of traditional archaeological explanations much more apparent. These shortcomings can be made clearer in an example of the traditional method—the appearance of a new kind of pottery in a given area and period, the pottery being distinguished by shapes not previously recognized and by new decorative motifs. The traditional approach will very properly require a closer definition of this pottery style in space and time. The archaeologist will be expected to draw a distribution map of its occurrence, and also to establish its place in the stratigraphic sequence at the sites where it occurs. The next step is to assign it to its place within an archaeological culture.

Using the traditional approach, it was argued that each archaeological culture is the manifestation in material terms of a specific people—that is, a well-defined ethnic group, detectable by the archaeologist by the method just outlined. This is an ethnic classification, but of course the "people," being prehistoric, were given an arbitrary name. Usually, they were named after the place where the pottery was first recognized (e.g. the Mimbres people in the American Southwest), or sometimes after the pottery itself (e.g. the Beaker Folk).

Next it was usual to see if it is possible to think in terms of a folk migration to explain the changes observed. Could a convenient homeland for this group of people be located? Careful study of the ceramic assemblages in adjoining lands might suggest such a homeland, and perhaps even a migration route.

Alternatively, if the migration argument did not seem to work, a fourth approach was to look for specific features of the cultural assemblage that have parallels in more distant lands. If the whole assemblage cannot be attributed to an external source, there may be specific features of it that can. Links may be found with more "civilized" lands. If such parallels can be discovered, the traditionalist would argue that these were the points of origin for the features in our assemblage, and were transmitted to it by a process of cultural diffusion. Indeed, before the advent of radiocarbon dating, these parallels could also be used to date the pottery finds in our hypothetical example, because the features and traits lying closer to the "civilized" heartlands would almost certainly already be dated through comparison with the latter's historical chronology.

It would be easy to find many actual examples of such explanations. For instance, in the New World, the very striking developments in architecture and other crafts in Chaco Canyon in New Mexico have been explained by comparisons of precisely this kind with the more "advanced" civilizations of Mexico to the south.

Recently it has in some cases been possible to document prehistoric migrations by establishing the arrival of a new population using ancient DNA obtained from human remains (see pp. 243–44). If, within a given area, burials at a specific time show identifiable characteristics in their DNA that are known to have existed earlier in a neighboring area, then it is clear that there has been a movement of population. A now well-documented example is the so-called "Kurgan migration," which Marija Gimbutas suggested on traditional archaeological grounds (mainly pottery styles) had brought nomads from the steppe lands north of the Black Sea westward into Central Europe at the onset of the early Bronze Age. Recent ancient DNA work gives strong support to her Kurgan hypothesis.

Traditional explanations rest, however, on assumptions that are easily challenged today. First, there is the notion among traditionalists that archaeological "cultures" can somehow represent real entities rather than merely the classificatory terms devised for the convenience of the scholar. Second is the view that ethnic units or "peoples" can be recognized from the archaeological record by equation with these notional cultures. It is in fact clear that ethnic groups do not always stand out clearly in archaeological remains. Third, it is assumed that when resemblances are noted between the cultural assemblages of one area and another, this can be most readily explained as the result of a migration of people. Of course, migrations did indeed occur (see below), but they are not so easy to document archaeologically as has often been supposed.

Finally, there is the principle of explanation through the diffusion of culture. Today, it is felt that this explanation has sometimes been overplayed, and nearly always oversimplified. For although contact between areas, not least through trade, can be of great significance for the developments in each area, the effects of this contact have to be considered in detail: explanation simply in terms of diffusion is not enough.

Nevertheless it is worth emphasizing that migrations did take place in the past, and on rare occasions this can be documented archaeologically. The colonization of the Polynesian islands in the Pacific offers one example. A complex of finds—especially pottery with incised decoration—known as the

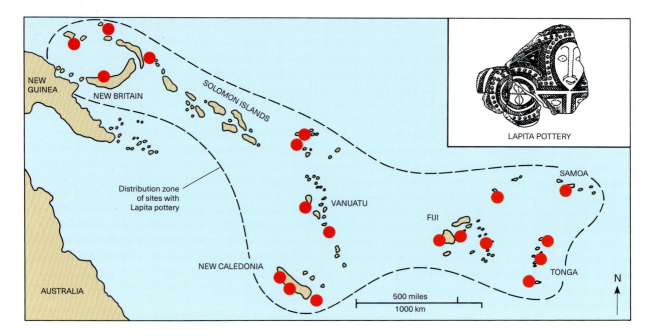

Distribution zone
of sites with
Lapita pottery

NEW GUINEA

NEW BRITAIN

SOLOMON ISLANDS

VANUATU

NEW CALEDONIA

AUSTRALIA

FIJI

SAMOA

TONGA

N

500 miles
1000 km

LAPITA POTTERY

(Above) Migration: a positive example. The question of the first settlement of the Polynesian islands has apparently been resolved by the discovery of the Lapita culture, which is characterized in particular by pottery with incised decoration. Lapita sites provide a record of the rapid movement of islanders by boat, eastward from the northern New Guinea region to as far as Samoa in western Polynesia, between 1600 and 1000 BCE.

Lapita culture provides a record of the rapid movement of islanders eastward across a vast uninhabited area, from the northern New Guinea region to as far as Samoa, between 1600 and 1000 BCE (see map above). Also, innovations are frequently made in one place and adopted in neighboring areas, and it is still perfectly proper to speak of the mechanism as one of diffusion (see illustration of the origins of the Roman alphabet below). A good example of what was first a migrationist explanation, and then became a diffusionist explanation, until it was subsequently rejected, is offered by the case of Great Zimbabwe (see box opposite).

(Right) Diffusion: a positive example. One instance where an innovation in one place is known to have spread widely elsewhere through diffusion is that of the alphabet. Around the twelfth century BCE, on the Levantine coast, the Phoenicians developed a simplified phonetic script to write their Semitic language. By the early first millennium BCE, the script had been adapted by the Greeks to write their own language. Then the Greek alphabet was modified in Italy, to write Etruscan and Latin, the Roman language. It was through Latin that our own alphabet (known as the Roman alphabet) came to much of Europe, and later the rest of the world.

N

REST OF EUROPE

ETRUSCAN
LATIN

GREEK

PHOENICIAN SCRIPT

200 miles
300 km

Explaining Great Zimbabwe

AFRICA

Great Zimbabwe

The remarkable monument of Great Zimbabwe, near Masvingo in modern Zimbabwe, has been the subject of intense speculation ever since the region was first explored by Europeans in the nineteenth century. For here was an impressive structure of great sophistication, with beautifully finished stonework.

Early scholars ascribed the site to builders from "more civilized" lands to the north. During a visit by the British colonialist Cecil Rhodes, the local Karanga chiefs were told that "the Great Master" had come "to see the ancient temple which once upon a time belonged to white men." This was thus a migrationist view.

Systematic excavations were undertaken by Gertrude Caton-Thompson (see p. 34), and she concluded her report in 1931: "Examination of all the existing evidence, gathered from every quarter, still can produce not one single item that is not in accordance with the claim of Bantu origin and medieval date." But despite this, other archaeologists continued to offer diffusionist explanations in speaking of "influences" from "higher centers of culture." Portuguese traders were one favored source of inspiration.

Subsequent research has backed up the conclusions of Caton-Thompson. Great Zimbabwe is now seen as the most notable of a larger class of monuments in this area.

(Below) Carved soapstone bird found at Great Zimbabwe in 1903, and one of eight from the site. The motif adorns the modern Zimbabwean flag, banknotes, and coinage.

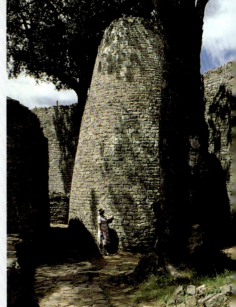

(Above) The conical tower is one of the most impressive features at the site.

Archaeologists are now able to give a coherent picture of the economic and social conditions in the area in the thirteenth to fifteenth centuries CE that made the great achievement of the construction of the monument possible. Significant influence—diffusion—from more "advanced" areas is no longer part of that picture.

(Right) Site plan: the Elliptical Building, with its series of enclosed areas, platforms, and the conical tower.

Northeast entrance

North entrance

Passage

Enclosure 1

Enclosure 15

Platforms

Enclosure 4

Platform

Monoliths (restored)

West entrance

Enclosure 5

Enclosure 7

Enclosure 6

Conical tower

N

150 ft.

50 m

The Processual Approach

The processual approach attempts to isolate and study the different processes at work within a society, and between societies, placing emphasis on relations with the environment, on subsistence and the economy, on social relations within the society, on the impact that the prevailing ideology and belief system have on these things, and on the effects of the interactions taking place between the different social units.

It is a characteristic of processual explanations that they have usually focused on ecological and social factors the operation of which can be analyzed in some detail. Sometimes a systems model is used, looking at the interaction of what may be defined as the subsystems of the culture system. A good early example of a processual explanation, even though today it is regarded as incomplete, is offered by Lewis Binford's explanation for the origins of sedentary society and of a farming economy.

In 1968, Binford published an influential paper, "Post-Pleistocene Adaptations," in which he set out to explain the origins of farming, or food production. Attempts to do this had been made by earlier scholars. But Binford's explanation had one important feature that distinguished it from earlier explanations and made it very much a product of the New Archaeology: its generality. For he was setting out to explain the origins of farming not just in the Near East or the Mediterranean—although he focused on these areas— but also worldwide. He drew attention to global events at the end of the last Ice Age (i.e. at the end of the Pleistocene epoch, hence the title of his paper).

Binford centered his explanation on demography: he was concerned with population dynamics within small communities, stressing that once a formerly mobile group becomes sedentary—ceases to move around—its population size will increase markedly. For in a settled village the constraints no longer operate that, in a mobile group, severely limit the number of small children a mother can rear. There is no longer the difficulty, for instance, of carrying children from place to place. Crucial to the question was the fact that in the Near East some communities (of the Natufian culture around 9000 BCE) did indeed become sedentary before they were food-producing. He could see that, once settled, there would be considerable population pressure, in view of the greater number of surviving children. This would lead to increasing use of such locally available plant foods as wild cereals, which had hitherto been considered marginal and of little value. From the intensive use of cereals, and the introduction of ways of processing them, would develop the regular cycle of sowing and harvesting, and thus the course of plant-human involvement leading to domestication would be well underway.

But why did these pre-agricultural groups become sedentary in the first place? Binford's view was that rising sea levels at the end of the Pleistocene (caused by the melting of polar ice) had two significant effects. First, they reduced the extent of the coastal plains available to the hunter-gatherers. And second, the new habitats created by the rise in sea level offered to human groups much greater access to migratory fish and to migrant fowl. Using these rich resources, rather as the inhabitants of the Northwest Coast of North America have done in more recent times, the hunter-gatherer groups found it possible for the first time to lead a sedentary existence. They were no longer obliged to move.

In some respects Binford's explanation is seen today as rather too simple. Nevertheless, it has many strengths. Although the focus was on the Near East, the same arguments can equally be applied to other parts of the world. Binford avoided migration or diffusion, and analyzed the origins of farming in processual terms.

Marxist Archaeology

Following the upsurge in theoretical discussion that followed the initial impact of the New Archaeology, there was a reawakening of interest in applying to archaeology some of the implications of the earlier work of Karl Marx. Marx was an extremely influential nineteenth-century philosopher and political economist. Although his work covered a wide range of issues, he is most famous for his analysis of history in terms of conflicts between social classes.

The key feature of **Marxist archaeology**, then, is that change within a past society was caused mainly by the contradictions that arise between the forces of production and social organization. Characteristically these contradictions emerge as a struggle between classes (if this is a society where distinct social classes have already developed). Emphasis on class struggle and internal differences is a feature of most Marxist explanations: this is a view of the world where change comes about through the resolution of internal dissent. It may be contrasted with the "functionalist" view favored by the early New Archaeology, where selective pressures toward greater efficiency are seen to operate and changes are often viewed as mutually beneficial.

In traditional Marxism the ideology of a society—the whole system of knowledge and belief—is seen as largely determined by the nature of the economic base. This point is disputed by the "neo-Marxists" who regard ideology and economics as interrelated and mutually influential, rather than one as dominant and the other subordinate.

There are many positive features that Marxist analyses share with processual archaeology, but, in comparison with the processual studies of the New Archaeologists, many such Marxist analyses seem rather short on the handling of concrete archaeological data. The gap between theoretical archaeology and field archaeology is not always effectively bridged, and the critics of Marxist archaeology sometimes observe that since Karl Marx laid

Karl Marx has influenced the interpretations of many archaeologists, especially concerning how change occurs in a society.

down the basic principles more than a century ago, all that remains for the Marxist archaeologists to do is to elaborate them: research in the field is superfluous. Despite these differences, processual archaeology and Marxist archaeology have much in common.

Evolutionary Archaeology

Evolutionary archaeology explores the notion that the processes responsible for biological evolution (as set out by Charles Darwin in the nineteenth century) also drive culture change.

Proponents see the modern mind as the product of biological evolution, and argue that the only way so complex an entity can have arisen is by natural selection. In particular they argue that the human mind evolved under the selective pressures faced by hunter-gatherers during the Pleistocene period, and that our minds remain adapted to that way of life. Several writers have followed this lead, seeking to place the evolution of mind in an explicitly evolutionary framework. These are fascinating insights, but they have not yet been supported by any neurological analysis of the hardware of the brain and of its evolution.

Evolutionary archaeologists in the United States advocate the application of Darwinian evolutionary theory to the archaeological record. They can justifiably point to longstanding cultural traditions in different parts of the world that reflect the inheritance of cultural traits from generation to generation. It could be argued that they have shown how the transmission of human culture can validly be seen in Darwinian evolutionary terms. It is less clear, however, that to analyze culture change in those terms offers fresh insights not already available to archaeologists. Evolutionary archaeology has not yet produced case studies of culture change that explain its processes more coherently or persuasively than other approaches: that is the challenge that it currently faces.

The Form of Explanation: Specific or General?

To understand these debates within archaeology it is useful to consider what exactly we mean by "explanation." The different things we try to explain might require different kinds of explanation.

There are two completely opposite forms of explanation. The first approach is specific: it seeks to know more and more of the details surrounding an event. It assumes that if we can establish enough of what led up to the event we hope to explain, then that event itself will become much clearer for us. Such explanation has sometimes been called "historical."

Some historical explanations lay great stress on any insights we can gain into the ideas of the historical people in question, and for that reason are sometimes termed idealist. If you want to know why an action was taken it is necessary to get inside the mind of the decision maker, and thus to know as many of the surrounding details, and as much about his or her life, as possible.

The second form of explanation, that of the New Archaeology, lays much more stress on generalization. The early New Archaeologists sought "regularities," patterns in the data, and turned to the philosophy of science (of the time) for help. Unluckily, perhaps, they turned to the German-American philosopher Carl Hempel, who argued that all explanations should be framed in terms of natural laws. A lawlike statement is a universal statement, meaning that in certain circumstances (and other things being equal) X always implies Y, or that Y varies with X according to a certain definite relationship. Hempel argued that the events we might be seeking to explain could be accounted for by bringing together two things: the detailed circumstances leading up to the event, and the "law" that would allow us to forecast what actually happened.

A few New Archaeologists tried to write archaeology in the form of universal laws. Most, however, saw that it is very difficult to make universal laws about human behavior that are not either very trivial, or untrue. Some archaeologists, such as Kent Flannery, saw that when Hempel's approach was applied to archaeology, it produced only "Mickey Mouse laws" of little conceivable value. Flannery's favorite example was: "As the population of a site increases, the number of storage pits will go up."

One of the positive contributions of the New Archaeology, however, was in fact to follow the scientific convention of making specific and explicit, as far as is possible, the assumptions on which an argument rests. It makes very good sense to formulate a hypothesis, establish by deduction what would follow from it if it were true, and then to see if these consequences are in fact found in the archaeological record by testing the hypothesis against fresh data. Processual archaeologists argued that it is this willingness to test our beliefs and assumptions against real data that separates a scientific approach from mere uncontrolled speculation.

Explanation: One Cause or Several?

As soon as we start to address the really big questions in archaeology, explanation becomes a very complicated matter: many of the big questions refer not to a single event, but to a class of events.

One of the biggest questions, for example, is the development of urbanization and the emergence of state societies. This process apparently happened in different parts of the world independently. Each case was, in a sense, no doubt unique. But each was also a specific instance of a more general process. In just the same way, a biologist can discuss (as Darwin did) the process by which the different species emerged, without denying the uniqueness of each species, or the uniqueness of each individual within a species.

If we focus now on the origins of urbanization and the state as an example, we shall see that this is a field where many different explanations have been offered. Broadly speaking, we can distinguish between explanations that concentrate largely on one cause (**monocausal explanations**) and those that consider a number of factors (**multivariate explanations**).

Monocausal Explanations: The Origins of the State

If we look at different monocausal explanations in turn, we shall find that some of them are in their way very plausible. Often, however, one explanation works more effectively than another when applied to a particular area—to the emergence of the state in Mesopotamia, for instance, or in Egypt, but not necessarily in Mexico or in the Indus Valley. Each of the following examples today seems incomplete. Yet each makes a point that remains valid.

THE HYDRAULIC HYPOTHESIS. The historian Karl Wittfogel, writing in the 1950s, explained the origin of the great civilizations in terms of large-scale irrigation of the alluvial plains of the great rivers. It was, he suggested, this alone that brought about the fertility and the high yields that led to considerable density of population in the early civilizations, and hence to the possibility of urbanism. At the same time, however, irrigation required effective management—a group of people in authority who would control and organize the labor needed to dig and maintain irrigation ditches, etc. So irrigation and "hydraulic organization" had to go together, and from these, Wittfogel concluded, emerged a system of differentiated leadership, greater productivity and wealth, and so on.

Wittfogel categorized the system of government characteristic of those civilizations founded on irrigation agriculture as one of "oriental despotism." Among the civilizations to which this line of thinking has been applied are:

- Mesopotamia: the Sumerian civilization from *c.* 3000 BCE onward and its successors
- Ancient Egypt: the Valley of the Nile from *c.* 3000 onward BCE
- India/Pakistan: the Indus Valley civilization from *c.* 2500 onward BCE
- China: the Shang civilization, *c.* 1500 BCE, and its successors

INTERNAL CONFLICT. In the late 1960s the Russian historian Igor Diakonoff developed a different explanation for state origins. In his model, the state is seen as an organization that imposes order on class conflict, which itself arises from increased wealth. Internal differentiation within the society is here seen as a major causative element, from which other consequences follow.

WARFARE.   Warfare between adjacent groups is increasingly seen as an agent of change. While in some cases there were cyclical conflicts with little long-term effect, in others the result was conquest and the formation of larger, inclusive state societies. Kent Flannery has emphasized the historically documented role of individual military leaders in the initial formation of state societies (an example of the "agency" of the individual, see pp. 294–95).

POPULATION GROWTH.   An explanation much favored by many archaeologists focuses on the question of population growth. The eighteenth-century English scholar Thomas Malthus argued that human population tends to grow to the limit permitted by the food supply. When the limit or "carrying capacity" is reached, further population increase leads to food shortage, and this in turn leads to an increased death rate and lower fertility (and in some cases to armed conflict). That sets a firm ceiling on population.

population growth ⟶ food shortage ⟶ increased death rate and lower fertility

Ester Boserup, in her influential book *The Conditions of Agricultural Growth* (1965), effectively reversed the position of Malthus. He had viewed food supply as essentially limited. She argued that agriculture will intensify—farmers will produce more food from the same area of land—if population increases. In other words, by shortening the periods during which land is left to lie fallow, or by introducing the plow, or irrigation, farmers can increase their productivity. Population growth can then be sustained to new levels.

population growth ⟶ introduction of new farming methods ⟶ increase in agricultural production

So increase of population leads to intensification of agriculture, and to the need for greater administrative efficiencies and economies of scale, including the development of craft specialization. People work harder because they have to, and the society is more productive. There are larger units of population, and consequent changes in the settlement pattern. As numbers increase, any decision-making machinery will need to develop a hierarchy. Centralization ensues, and a centralized state is the logical outcome.

ENVIRONMENTAL CIRCUMSCRIPTION.   A different approach, although one that uses some of the variables already indicated, is offered by Robert Carneiro. Taking as his example the formation of state society in Peru, he developed an explanation that stressed the constraints imposed by the environment, and on the role of warfare (**environmental circumscription**). Population increase is an important component of his model, but it is put together in a different way, and the development of strong leadership in time of war is a key factor.

EXTERNAL TRADE.   The importance of trading links with communities outside the homeland area has been stressed by several archaeologists seeking explanations for the formation of the state. One of the most elaborate of these is the model put forward by the American archaeologist William Rathje for the emergence of state societies in the Maya lowlands. He argued that in lowland areas lacking basic raw materials there will be pressure for the development of more integrated and highly organized communities able to ensure the regular supply of those materials. He used this hypothesis to explain the rise of the Classic Maya civilization in the lowland rainforest.

Multivariate Explanations: The Classic Maya Collapse

All the preceding explanations for the origins of the state primarily emphasize one chief variable, a principal strand in the explanation, even though there are several strands involved. In reality, when there are so many factors at work, there is something rather too simplified about such monocausal explanations. It is necessary somehow to be able to deal with several factors at once: that is why such explanations are termed multivariate. Of course, none of the explanations summarized above is so naive as to be truly monocausal: each involves a number of factors. But these factors are not systematically integrated. Several scholars have therefore sought ways of coping with a large number of variables that simultaneously vary.

One example of a multivariate explanation has been developed for the collapse of Classic Maya society in the ninth century CE (see box overleaf).

Postprocessual or Interpretive Explanation

After the mid-1970s, the early New Archaeology (or **functional-processual archaeology**) came under criticism from several quarters. For example, early on it was criticized by Bruce Trigger in his book *Time and Traditions* (1978), who found the approach, which sought to formulate explanatory laws, too constraining. He preferred the broadly descriptive method of the traditional historian. It was also criticized by Kent Flannery, who was scornful of the trivial nature of some of the so-called laws proposed and felt that more attention should be focused on the ideological and symbolic aspects of societies. Ian Hodder, likewise, felt that archaeology's closest links were with history, and wanted to see the role of the individual in history more fully recognized.

Hodder also very validly stressed what he called "the active role of material culture," emphasizing that the artifacts and the material world we construct are not simply reflections of our social reality that become embodied in the material record. On the contrary, material culture and actual objects are a large part of what makes society work: wealth, for instance, is what spurs many to work in a modern society. Hodder goes on to assert that material culture is "meaningfully constituted," or in other words that it is the result of deliberate actions by individuals whose thoughts and actions should not be overlooked.

Discussions of these issues led some archaeologists in Britain and in the United States to create the postprocessual archaeology of the 1990s, overcoming some of what they saw as the limitations of processual archaeology (and indeed much of traditional Marxist archaeology also). These debates are now largely over, but the result is a series of interesting approaches that together will shape the "interpretive archaeologies" of the early twenty-first century, operating alongside continuing processual or **cognitive-processual archaeology**.

Structuralist Approaches

Several archaeologists have been influenced by the structuralist ideas of the French anthropologist Claude Lévi-Strauss, and by the advances in linguistics of the American Noam Chomsky. Structuralist archaeologists stress that human actions are guided by beliefs and symbolic concepts, and that the proper object of study is the structures of thought—the ideas—in the minds of human actors who made the artifacts and created the archaeological record. These archaeologists argue that there are recurrent patterns in human thought in different cultures, many of which can be seen in such polar opposites as: cooked/raw; left/right; dirty/clean; man/woman, etc. Moreover, they argue that thought categories seen in one sphere of life will be seen also in other spheres, so that, for example, a preoccupation with boundaries in the field of social relations is likely to be detectable in other areas, such as "boundaries" visible in pottery decoration.

Critical Theory

Critical Theory is the term given to the approach developed by the so-called "Frankfurt School" of German social thinkers, which came to prominence in the 1970s. This stresses that any claims to seek "objective" knowledge are illusory. By their interpretive approach these scholars seek a more enlightened view, which will break out of the limitations of existing systems of thought. They see researchers (including archaeologists) who claim to be dealing in a scientific way with social matters as tacitly supporting the "ideology of control" by which domination is exercised in modern society.

This overtly political critique has serious implications for archaeology. For the philosophers of this school stress that there is no such thing as an objective fact. Facts only have meaning in relation to a view of the world, and in relation to theory. Followers of this school are critical of the criterion

The Classic Maya Collapse

Contrary to widespread belief, Maya civilization did not suffer a single, sudden, and total collapse. When the Spaniards reached northern Yucatan in the early sixteenth century they found dense populations of Maya-speaking people living in hundreds of thriving local polities.

Archaeologists now know that cycles of collapse and recovery were common in Maya society for 1500 years. The earliest "big" collapse occurred in the Mirador Basin of northern Guatemala, where huge centers thrived in the Middle and Late Preclassic. By around 150 CE this region was largely abandoned (and never substantially recovered) and there is evidence that ecosystems there and elsewhere were increasingly degraded.

The Classic period (250–900 CE) southern Maya lowlands also saw many local collapses, as Maya capitals and their dynastic lines waxed and waned, as well as a final collapse in the tenth century.

Collapse in the Southern Lowlands

The final collapse in the southern lowlands has long been the most celebrated and difficult to explain because of its scale and because there was no recovery in that region. In 750 CE this vast area supported a population of at least several million people divided among forty to fifty major kingdoms. But eight centuries later, when Europeans arrived, it was almost deserted. Explorers in the nineteenth century told of imposing and overgrown ruins, creating romanticized impressions of a catastrophic collapse. By the beginning of the twentieth century scholars could decipher dates carved on Maya monuments. These suggested a steady expansion of, and vigor in, Maya civilization beginning in the third century CE, peak activity around 790 CE, and then a precipitous decline in monument building over the next 120 years, which signaled the collapse of centralized rulership. Although only elite activity was directly reflected in these data, in the absence of other information it was presumed that each Classic political system and population suffered a catastrophic collapse in one or two generations.

We now know that the collapse process was much more complicated and protracted. Most scholars agree that the decline began at least as early as 760 CE, when centers in the west of the region were abandoned during well-documented cycles of destructive warfare. Centers elsewhere continued

Temple I at Tikal, Guatemala, built around 740–750 CE. Tikal was one of the great Maya centers, but was almost completely deserted after 950 CE.

to erect monuments for some time, the last in about 909 CE. Royal building projects ceased—sometimes very suddenly—and no more royal burials were interred. Although some polities and capitals collapsed abruptly and with clear signs of violence, others were abandoned more gradually (and apparently peacefully). If our perspective is the whole southern lowlands, the disintegration of centralized political institutions thus occurred over a period of roughly 150 years (although some imposing centers did somehow survive the troubles).

What happened to the populations associated with the defunct Classic capitals is a more controversial issue. Many regions do appear to have suffered abrupt demographic declines, but others did not. At Copan, for example, elite activity continued in some sub-royal palace compounds until about 1000 CE, and the overall population dwindled away over some four centuries.

Explaining the Collapse

Most archaeologists agree that no single cause can explain what happened. Instead, a set of interlocked stresses, such as overpopulation, deterioration of the agricultural landscape, famine, disease, warfare, internal social unrest, climate change, and ideological fatigue increasingly afflicted the Late Classic Maya (see diagram opposite). Some causes were certainly more important than others. Most recently, paleoclimatologists have postulated a series of droughts in the interval between 770 and 1100 CE. Some believe this was the single most important trigger of the collapse, affecting food production in an increasingly damaged and vulnerable landscape. This stress, however, was probably exacerbated by social and ideological components. Kingship, the central institution of Maya political life, stressed the supernatural potency of rulers. Kings projected themselves as the great guarantors of prosperity and stability, and manifestly were unable to

The interactions that may have helped trigger the Classic Maya collapse.

deliver on these promises during the critical eighth and ninth centuries.

of testing as used by processual archaeologists, seeing this procedure as merely the importing into archaeology and history of "positivistic" approaches from the sciences. They call into question most of the procedures of reasoning by which archaeology has operated.

The processualists' response to these ideas is to point out that to follow them seems to imply that one person's view of the past is as good as another's (so-called "relativism"), without any hope of choosing systematically between them. This would open the way to the "fringe" or "alternative" archaeologies discussed in Chapter 11, where explanations can be offered in terms of flying saucers, or extraterrestrial forces, or any other fantasy. It is not entirely clear how the Critical Theorists can answer this criticism.

Neo-Marxist Thought

Neo-Marxist thought places a much greater emphasis on the significance of ideology in shaping change in societies than does traditional Marxism (which treats ideology as subordinate to economy). One example of a neo-Marxist approach is offered by the work of Mark Leone at Annapolis in Maryland, as part of a research project concerned with establishing a deeper historical identity for the area. His example is the eighteenth-century garden of William

Paca, a wealthy landowner: the garden has been studied archaeologically and has now been reconstructed.

Leone examined the Annapolis garden in detail, and emphasized the contradiction represented between a slave-owning society and one proclaiming independence in order to promote individual liberty, a contradiction seen also in Paca's life. "To mask this contradiction," Leone writes, "his position of power was placed in law and in nature. This was done both in practicing law and in gardening."

This neo-Marxist outlook has its echo in the emerging local archaeologies of some countries in the developing world, where there is an understandable desire to construct a history (and an archaeology) that lays stress on the local population and its achievements before the colonial era (see Chapter 11).

Cognitive Archaeology

During the 1980s and 1990s a new perspective emerged, which transcends some of the limitations of the functional-processual archaeology of the 1970s. This new synthesis, known as cognitive archaeology (or "cognitive-processual" archaeology), while willingly learning from any suitable developments in postprocessual archaeology, remains in the mainstream of processual archaeology. It still wishes to explain rather than merely describe. It also still emphasizes the role of generalization within its theoretical structure, and stresses the importance not only of formulating hypotheses but also of testing them against the data. It rejects the total relativism that seems to be the end point of Critical Theory, and it is suspicious of structuralist (and other) archaeologists who claim privileged insight into "meaning" in ancient societies, or proclaim "universal principles of meaning."

Cognitive-processual archaeology differs from its functional-processual predecessor in several ways:

- It seeks to incorporate information about the cognitive and symbolic aspects of early societies into its formulations (see below, pp. 293–94).
- It recognizes that ideology is an active force within societies and must be given a role in many explanations, as neo-Marxist archaeologists have argued, and that ideology acts on the minds of individuals.
- Material culture is seen as an active factor in constituting the world in which we live. Individuals and societies construct their own social reality, and material culture has an integral place within that construction, as effectively argued by Ian Hodder and his colleagues.
- The role of internal conflict within societies is a matter to be more fully considered, as Marxist archaeologists have always emphasized.
- The rather limited view of historical explanation being entirely related to the human individual should be revised.

Cognitive archaeology is the study of the ways of thought and structures of belief of past societies on the basis of their material remains

It attempts to use the more rigorous and explicit methods of the processual approach

It applies rigorous methods to symbolic and ideological issues, many of which were first addressed by postprocessual or interpretive approaches (e.g. questions of identity, gender, and religious belief in the past)

It shows willingness to address the symbolizing and reasoning abilities of hominins before the emergence of *Homo sapiens*, sometimes within an evolutionary framework

It accepts the postprocessual emphasis on the active role of material culture

It recognizes that cognitive developments are also social developments

- It can take account of the creative role of the individual without relying on intuition or becoming extremely subjective.
- "Facts" can no longer be viewed as having an objective existence independent of theory.

This last point needs further discussion. Philosophers of science have long contrasted two approaches to the evaluation of the truth of a statement. One evaluates the statement by comparing it with relevant facts, to which, if true, it should correspond. The other evaluates the statement by judging whether or not it is consistent with the other statements that we believe to be true within our framework of beliefs. Although it might be expected that the scientist would follow the first of these two procedures, in practice any assessment is based on a combination of the two. For it is accepted that facts have to be based on observations, and observations themselves cannot be made without using some framework of inference, which itself depends on theories about the world. It is more appropriate to think of facts modifying theory, yet of theory being used in the determination of facts.

Cognitive-processual archaeologists, like their functional-processual predecessors, believe that theories must be tested against facts. They reject the relativism of the Critical Theory and postprocessual archaeology of the 1990s. They do, however, accept that the relationship between fact and theory is more complicated than some philosophers of science forty years ago recognized.

Symbol and Interaction

The point has already been made that the early New Archaeology aspired to investigate social structures. But it was slow to explore symbolic aspects of culture, which is why cognitive-processual archaeology is a recent development.

The role of religious ritual within society has been investigated in a new way over the past thirty years by the cultural anthropologist Roy Rappaport. Instead of seeking to immerse himself in the agricultural society in New Guinea under study, becoming totally familiar with the meanings of its symbolic forms, he followed instead a strategy of distancing himself—of looking at the society from the outside, at what it actually does (not what it says it does) in its ritual behavior. This position is a convenient one for the archaeologist who is always outside the society under study, and unable to discuss issues of meaning with its participants. Rappaport has studied the way ritual is used within society and his focus is on the functioning of symbols rather than on their original meaning.

His work influenced Kent Flannery, one of the few of the original generation of New Archaeologists to concern himself in detail with symbolic questions.

The book written by Joyce Marcus and Kent Flannery, *Zapotec Civilization* (1996), is one of those rare archaeological studies where symbolic and cognitive questions are integrated with subsistence, economic, and social ones to form an integrated view of society.

Quite clearly religion and such other ideologies as modern communism have brought about great changes, not just in the way societies think but also in the way they act and behave—and this will leave its mark in the archaeological record. The whole field of official symbolism, and of religious symbolism within it, is now the focus of archaeological research in several parts of the world.

Postprocessual archaeology has not shown itself adept at explaining classes of events or general processes, since the focus in postprocessual thought is upon the specific conditions of the context in question, and the validity of wider or cross-cultural generalizations is not accepted. Cognitive-processual archaeology on the other hand is very willing to generalize, and indeed to integrate the individual into the analysis as an active agent.

Two studies in the mainstream processual tradition exemplify well the emphasis that is now placed upon the cognitive dimension. Timothy Earle in *How Chiefs Come to Power* (1997) devotes successive chapters to economic power, military power, and ideology as a source of power, utilizing three widely separated case studies situated in Denmark, Hawaii, and the Andes.

And, likewise treating the subject within a comparative perspective, Richard Blanton has examined the sources of power in early states, contrasting the "cognitive-symbolic base of power" with what he terms the "objective base of power." The study fully integrates the cognitive dimension into the analysis, alongside economic issues. In such works the limitations of the earlier processual archaeology have been transcended and the roots of change are investigated with full weight being given to the cognitive and the symbolic dimensions.

Agency and Material Engagement

In the past decade or so archaeologists working in different conceptual traditions have sought in various ways to integrate the cognitive and symbolic on the one hand with the practical and productive on the other. One aim is to reconcile the short-term intentions or agency of the individual with the long-term and often unintended consequences of cumulative actions. Archaeologists who take this approach hope to combine a broad outline of processes of change with the finer texture of specific culture histories.

Agency

The concept of agency has been introduced to permit discussion of the role of the individual in promoting change, but the scope of the term is not always clear, particularly when used, as by some anthropologists, as a quality that can be assigned to artifacts as well as to people. The various discussions of agency attempt to illuminate the role of the individual, but it is very difficult to determine clearly how the actions of one individual had a wider and longer-term impact.

Material Engagement

A related notion, that change arises from conscious and often purposeful human activities, is associated with the recently developed concepts of material engagement or materialization. These seek to overcome the duality in discussions of human affairs between the practical and the cognitive, the material and the conceptual. Indeed most innovations and long-term changes in human societies, even technical ones, have a symbolic dimension as well as a material one, involving what the philosopher John Searle terms "institutional facts," which are themselves social creations.

The material engagement approach is one of several that gives greater attention to things and the material properties of things, and the different interactions between humans and the material world that come about through developing technologies and changing social and economic relations.

There is still a tension also between those using archaeology to write culture history (usually of a single society) and those using evolutionary thinking to analyze long-term change. Each perspective has clear coherence and validity, but the two rarely seem to mesh together.

In these different approaches to the explanation of change there is some commonality of aspiration and this may yet lead to interesting new developments. But there is no single theoretical perspective that commands universal or even widespread respect.

Study Questions

1 Why is archaeology unique among the human sciences?
2 What are the key differences between processual and postprocessual archaeology?
3 What is Marxist archaeology and how is it different from the New Archaeology?
4 What are some monocausal explanations for the origins of the state?
5 What is Critical Theory and what are its implications for archaeology?
6 Is there a correct way to explain change in the past?

Summary

IT IS DIFFICULT to explain why things happened in the past, yet this must be one of the key tasks of archaeology.

EXPLANATIONS IN TERMS of the migrations of people or using the rather vague idea of the "diffusion" of culture used to be very popular: today they are less frequent.

THE PROCESSUAL APPROACH has consistently tried to see broader patterns and general explanations. In general, multivariate (multiple-factor) explanations work better than monocausal (single-factor) explanations for such complex outcomes as the origins of state societies.

INTERPRETIVE EXPLANATIONS, on the other hand, usually emphasize the specific context. Both approaches converge toward a cognitive archaeology that acknowledges the role of human intelligence, creativity, and initiative.

YET THERE REMAIN several different approaches to the difficult task of explanation. Some scholars advocate the notion of human agency, others analyze the knowledgeable engagement between humans and the material world. This remains an underdeveloped area of archaeological theory.

Further Reading

The broad topics covered in this chapter are explored in:

DeMarrais, E., Gosden, C., & Renfrew, C. (eds). 2004. *Rethinking Materiality: The Engagement of Mind with the Material World*. McDonald Institute: Cambridge.

Gamble, C. 2007. *Origins and Revolutions: Human Identity in Earliest Prehistory*. Cambridge University Press: Cambridge & New York.

Haak W. *et al*. 2015. "Massive migration from the steppe was a source for Indo-European languages in Europe." *Nature* 522, 207–11.

Hodder, I. 2004. *Reading the Past* (3rd ed.). Cambridge University Press: Cambridge & New York.

Malafouris, L. 2013. *How Things Shape the Mind: A Theory of Material Engagement*. MIT Press: Cambridge, MA.

Reich, D. 2018. *Who We Are and How We Got Here: Ancient DNA and the New Science of the Human Past*. Pantheon Books: New York.

Renfrew, C. 2009. *Prehistory: The Making of the Human Mind*. Modern Library: New York.

Shennan, S. 2002. *Genes, Memes and Human History*. Thames & Hudson: London & New York.

Webster, D. L. 2002. *The Fall of the Ancient Maya*. Thames & Hudson: London & New York.

[See p. 345 for a list of useful websites]

11

Whose Past?
Archaeology and the Public

This book is concerned with the way that archaeologists investigate the past, with the questions we can ask, and our means of answering them. But the time has come to address much wider questions: Why, beyond reasons of scientific curiosity, do we want to know about the past? What does the past mean to us? What does it mean to others with different viewpoints? Whose past is it anyway?

These issues lead us to questions of responsibility, public as well as private. For surely a national monument, such as the Parthenon in Athens, means something special to the modern descendants of its builders. But does it not also mean something to all humankind? If so, should it not be protected from destruction, in the same way as endangered plant and animal species? If the looting of ancient sites is to be deplored, should it not be stopped, even if the sites are on privately owned land? Who owns, or should own, the past?

These very soon become ethical questions—of right and wrong, of appropriate action and reprehensible action. The archaeologist has a special responsibility because excavation itself entails destruction. Future workers' understanding of a site can never be much more than our own, because we will have destroyed the evidence and recorded only those parts of it we considered important and had the energy to publish properly.

The past is big business—in tourism and in the auction rooms. But by their numbers tourists threaten the sites they seek to enjoy; and the plunder of looters and illegal excavators finds its way into private collections and public museums. The past is politically highly charged, ideologically powerful, and significant. And the past, as we shall see in the next chapter, is subject to increasing destruction through unprecedented commercial, industrial, and agricultural exploitation of the Earth's surface, and through damage in war.

The Meaning of the Past: The Archaeology of Identity

When we ask what the past means, we are asking what the past means for us, for it means different things to different people. An Australian Aborigine, for example, may attach a very different significance to fossil human remains from such an early site as Lake Mungo, or to paintings in the Kakadu National Park, than a white Australian. Different communities have very different conceptions about the past that often draw on sources well beyond archaeology.

At this point we go beyond the question of what actually happened in the past, and of the explanation of why it happened, to issues of meaning, significance, and interpretation. And it is at this point, therefore, that many of the concerns that have become explicit in archaeology over the past couple of decades become entirely relevant. How we interpret the past, how we present it (for instance in museum displays), and what lessons we choose to draw from it are to a considerable extent matters for subjective decision, often involving ideological and political issues.

For in a very broad sense the past is where we came from. Individually we each have our personal, genealogical past: our parents, grandparents, and earlier kinsfolk from whom we are descended. Increasingly in the Western world there is an interest in this personal past, reflected in the enthusiasm for family trees and for "roots" generally. Our personal identity, and generally our name, are in part defined for us in the relatively recent past, even though those elements with which we choose to identify are largely a matter of personal choice. Nor is this inheritance purely a spiritual one. Most land tenure in the world is determined by inheritance, and much other wealth is inherited: the material world in this sense comes to us from the past, and is certainly, when the time comes, relinquished by us to the future.

Nationalism and Its Symbols

Collectively our cultural inheritance is rooted in a deeper past: the origins of our language, our faith, and our customs. Increasingly archaeology plays an important role in the definition of national identity. This is particularly the case for those nations that do not have a very long written history, though many consider oral histories of equal value to written ones. The national emblems of many recently emerged nations are taken from artifacts seen as typical of some special and early local golden age: even the name of the state of Zimbabwe comes from the name of an archaeological site.

Yet sometimes the use of archaeology and of images recovered from the past to focus and enhance national identity can lead to conflict. In the 1990s a major crisis related to the name and national emblems adopted by the then newly independent Former Yugoslav Republic of Macedonia. For in Greece, immediately to the south, the name Macedon refers not only to contemporaneous provinces within Greece, but also to the ancient kingdom of that famous Greek leader, Alexander the Great. The affront that the name

Either Philip II of Macedon, father of Alexander the Great, or Philip III, Alexander's half-brother, was buried in a gold casket decorated with an impressive star (bottom). This was adopted as the national symbol of the Former Yugoslav Republic of Macedonia, as seen on one of their stamps (top).

The larger of the colossal Buddhas of Bamiyan (top), carved from the cliff face in perhaps the third century CE, and now destroyed (above).

caused in Greece was compounded by the FYR Macedonia's use of a star as a national symbol, using the image on a gold casket found among the splendid objects in a tomb from the fourth century BCE at Vergina, a tomb located well within modern Greek territory, thought to have belonged either to Philip II of Macedon, the father of Alexander, or to Philip III, Alexander's brother. Territorial claims can sometimes be based on contentious histories, and some Greeks thought that the FYR Macedonia was seeking not only to appropriate the glorious history of Macedonia but perhaps also to incorporate Greece's second city, Thessaloniki, within its territorial boundaries. Riots ensued, based, however, more on inflamed ethnic feelings than upon political reality.

Archaeology and Ideology

The legacy of the past goes beyond sentiments of nationalism and ethnicity. Sectarian sentiments often find expression in major monuments, and many Christian churches were built on the site of deliberately destroyed "pagan" temples. In just a few cases they actually utilized such temples—the Parthenon in Athens is one example—and one of the best-preserved Greek temples is now the cathedral in Syracuse in Sicily.

Religious extremism is responsible for many acts of destruction. The senseless demolition in March 2001 by the Taliban of the two giant Buddhas carved into the sandstone cliffs at Bamiyan, in the Hindu Kush, perhaps in the third century CE, shocked the world. The only motivation seems to have been that these were religious images not in accordance with the faith of the Taliban. Despite a delegation from the Organization of the Islamic Conference, at which fifty-five Islamic nations were represented, the destruction went ahead. Standing 53 and 36 m (174 and 118 ft.) high, these were the tallest standing Buddhas in the world; explosive charges destroyed them almost totally.

With a video released in February 2015 the regime of the so-called Islamic State (IS) in Iraq and the Levant announced the most conspicuous acts of fanatical destruction in recent years. These included the use of a power drill to erase the face of a well-preserved, man-faced winged bull at the Nergal Gate at Nineveh near Mosul in northern Iraq, dating to Neo-Assyrian times, from the seventh century BCE. The video also showed the deliberate destruction in the Mosul Museum of life-size statues of rulers from the caravan city of Hatra in Iraq's western desert, dating from Parthian times in the second and third centuries CE. Ironically these are among the first Arab rulers in recorded history and Hatra is the best-preserved Arab site from the pre-Islamic era. Or rather it was the best preserved, since there are reports of systematic destruction at the site by IS forces. Similar destruction is also documented at numerous other sites, most notably at the ancient city of Palmyra in Syria. From May to September 2015, IS demolished statues, temples, tower tombs, and the Roman Arch of Triumph (see p. 100).

The Temple of Bel at Palmyra, Syria, before and after being blown up by IS forces. This substantial building, completed in 32 CE, was almost entirely destroyed—only its entrance arch remains. Syrian forces retook Palmyra in March 2017, and while there are various plans to restore the site, clearly much has been lost forever.

Archaeological Ethics

Ethics is the science of morals—i.e. what it is right or wrong—and increasingly most branches of archaeology are seen to have an ethical dimension. Precisely because archaeology relates to identity (as reviewed in the last section), and to the existence of communities, nations, and indeed humankind itself, it touches upon urgent practical problems of an ethical nature. These are often difficult problems because they deal in conflicting principles.

The Latin author Terence is quoted as saying: "Homo sum: humani nihil a me alienum puto"—"I am a human being, so consider nothing human alien to me." Such thinking is central to the Universal Declaration of Human Rights. Many anthropologists feel that "the proper study of (hu)mankind is (hu)man(ity)," to update the seventeenth-century English poet Alexander Pope. The implication is that the entire field of human experience should be our study. Such sentiments encourage the study of fossil hominins, for instance, and clearly make the study of Australian aboriginal remains (see pp. 308–9) or those of Kennewick Man (see p. 308) a necessary part of the work of the biological anthropologist. So there is one principle. But, on the other hand, it is usual to have a decent respect for the earthly remains of our own relatives and ancestors. In many tribal societies such respect imposes obligations, which often find recognition in the law, for instance in the Native American Graves Protection and Repatriation Act (NAGPRA: see pp. 307–8). This then is a second principle, which has led to the reburial (and consequent destruction) of ancient human remains whose further study could have been of benefit to science. Which of the two principles is right? That is what one may term an ethical dilemma. It is one that is difficult to resolve, and that underlies several of the sections in this chapter and the next.

The right to property is another such principle. But the legitimate rights of the individual property owner (including the collector) can come into conflict with the very evident rights of wider communities. So it is that the commercial property developer can disagree with the conservationist. The ethical tensions between conservation and development are dealt with in the next chapter. Similar difficulties arise when the purchasing power of the private collector of antiquities leads to the destruction of archaeological sites through illicit excavation (looting). Increasingly the importance of material culture as something with significant social meaning is appreciated in our society. There are problems here that will not go away, because they are the product of the conflict of principles. That is why archaeological ethics is now a growth subject.

Popular Archaeology vs Pseudoarchaeology

The purpose of archaeology is to learn more about the past, and archaeologists believe that it is important that everyone should have some knowledge of the human past—of where we have come from, and how we have come to be where we are. Archaeology is not just for archaeologists. For that reason it is crucially important that we communicate effectively with the wider public. But there are several ways in which this important mission can be subverted. The first is the development of **pseudoarchaeology**, often for commercial purposes—that is to say the formulation of extravagant but ill-founded stories about the past. Sometimes those telling these stories may actually believe them, but often, as with Dan Brown's popular novel *The Da Vinci Code* (2003), it is suspected that the primary motive of the author is to make money. Archaeology can be subverted, also, when people actually manufacture false evidence, and perpetrate archaeological fraud.

ARCHAEOLOGY AT THE FRINGE.   In the later years of the twentieth century "other" archaeologies grew up at the fringe of the discipline, offering alternative interpretations of the past. To the scientist these seem fanciful and extravagant—manifestations of a postmodern age in which horoscopes are widely read, New Age prophets preach alternative lifestyles, and when many members of the public are willing to believe that "corn circles" and megalithic monuments are the work of aliens. Many archaeologists label such populist approaches as "pseudoarchaeology," and place them on a par with such archaeological frauds as Piltdown Man, where deliberate deception can be demonstrated or inferred.

Stonehenge has generated innumerable theories about its origins and meaning. Several groups, including Druids and New Agers, claim it as a monument central to their beliefs.

But how does an archaeologist persuade the self-styled Druids who perform their rituals at Stonehenge at the summer solstice that their beliefs are not supported by archaeological evidence? This brings us back to the central question of this chapter: "Whose Past?" It is not clear that we should question the reality of the Dreamtime of the Australian Aborigines, even if aspects of their belief effectively clash with current scientific interpretations. Where do we distinguish between respect for deeply held beliefs and the role of the archaeologist to inform the public and to dismiss credulous nonsense?

One of the most popular and durable myths concerns a "lost Atlantis," a story narrated by the Greek philosopher Plato in the fifth century BCE, and attributed by him to the Greek sage Solon, who had visited Egypt and consulted with priests, the heirs to a long religious and historical tradition. They told him of a legend of the lost continent beyond the Pillars of Hercules (the modern Straits of Gibraltar), hence in the Atlantic Ocean, with its advanced civilization, which vanished centuries earlier "in a night and a day." In 1882 Ignatius Donnelly published *Atlantis: The Antediluvian World*, elaborating this legend. His work was one of the first to seek a simple explanation of all ancient civilizations of the world by a single marvellous means. Such theories often share characteristics:

1 They celebrate a remarkable lost world, the people of which possessed many skills surpassing those of the present.
2 They account for most of the early accomplishments of prehistoric and early state societies with a single explanation: all were the work of the skilled inhabitants of that lost world.
3 That world vanished in a catastrophe of cosmic proportions.
4 Nothing of that original homeland is available for scientific examination, nor are any artifacts surviving.

The basic structure of Donnelly's argument was repeated with variants by Immanuel Velikovsky (meteors and astronomical events) and recently by Graham Hancock (who sites his lost continent in Antarctica). A popular alternative, elaborated with great financial profit by Erich von Däniken, is that the source of progress is outer space, and that the advances of early civilizations are the work of aliens visiting Earth. Ultimately, however, all such theories trivialize the much more remarkable story that archaeology reveals— the history of humankind.

FRAUD IN ARCHAEOLOGY. Fraud in archaeology is nothing new and takes many forms—from the manipulation of evidence by Heinrich Schliemann to such infamous cases of fakery as Britain's Piltdown Man. It has been

A cluster of hand-axes at Kamitakamori faked by Japanese archaeologist Shinichi Fujimura.

suggested that more than 1200 fake antiquities are displayed in some of the world's leading museums. A particularly serious example came to light as recently as 2000, when a leading Japanese archaeologist admitted planting artifacts at excavations. Shinichi Fujimura—nicknamed "God's hands" for his uncanny ability to uncover ancient objects—had been videotaped burying his "discoveries" before digging them up again as new finds. He admitted having buried dozens of artifacts in secret, claiming that it was the pressure of having to discover older sites that forced him to fake them by using artifacts from his own collections.

Of 65 pieces unearthed at the Kamitakamori site north of Tokyo, Fujimura admitted to having faked 61, together with all 29 pieces found in 2000 at the Soshinfudozaka site in northern Japan. He later admitted having tampered with evidence at 42 sites; but in 2004 the Japanese Archaeological Association declared that all of the 168 sites he dug had been faked. Japanese archaeological authorities are understandably worried about the potential impact on evidence for the early Paleolithic period in Japan unearthed since the mid-1970s.

It seems that this phenomenon may currently be on the rise. Some of this can be blamed on the increased "mediatization" of the field, where, as in Japan, it can be important to generate publicity to further one's career, and scientific publication often takes a back seat to press conferences where the latest finds are trumpeted. Spectacular discoveries are now sometimes seen as more important than scholarly debate or critical review. Nevertheless, the actual fabrication or planting of fake objects is an extreme form of fraud. Japanese archaeologists are worried that there may be other fraudulent artifacts, yet to be unearthed, a situation that has been likened to "archaeological landmines," ready to wreak havoc on future generations of scholars.

THE WIDER AUDIENCE.   Although the immediate aim of most research is to answer specific questions, the fundamental purpose of archaeology must be to provide people with a better understanding of the human past. Skillful popularization—using site and museum exhibits, books, television, and increasingly the Internet—is therefore required, but not all archaeologists are prepared to devote time to it, and few are capable of doing it well.

Excavators often regard members of the public as a hindrance to work on-site. More enlightened archaeologists, however, realize the financial and other support to be gained from encouraging public interest, and they organize information sheets, open days, and on long-term projects even fee-paying daily tours, as at the Bronze Age site of Flag Fen in eastern England. In Japan, on-the-spot presentations of excavation results are given as soon as a dig is completed. Details are released to the press the previous day, so that the public can obtain information from the morning edition of the local paper before coming to the site itself.

(Below) Part of the "Elgin Marbles" in the British Museum: a horseman from the frieze of the Parthenon in Athens, *c.* 440 BCE.

(Bottom) The New Acropolis Museum in Athens, built to house the Parthenon marbles that are still in Athens and, one day (it is hoped), the "Elgin Marbles" too.

Clearly, there is an avid popular appetite for archaeology. In a sense, the past has been a form of entertainment since the early digging of burial mounds and the public unwrapping of mummies in the nineteenth century. The entertainment may now take a more scientific and educational form, but it still needs to compete with rival popular attractions if archaeology is to thrive.

Who Owns the Past?

Until recent decades, archaeologists gave little thought to the question of the ownership of past sites and antiquities. Most archaeologists themselves came from Western, industrialized societies, the economic and political domination of which seemed to give an almost automatic right to acquire antiquities and excavate sites around the world. Since World War II, however, former colonies have grown into independent states eager to uncover their own past and assert control over their own heritage. Difficult questions have therefore arisen. Should antiquities acquired for Western museums during the colonial era be returned? And should archaeologists be free to excavate the burials of groups whose modern descendants may object on religious or other grounds?

Museums and the Return of Cultural Property

At the beginning of the nineteenth century Lord Elgin, a Scottish diplomat, removed many of the marble sculptures that adorned the Parthenon, the great fifth-century BCE temple that crowns the

Acropolis in Athens. Elgin did so with the permission of the then Turkish overlords of Greece, and later sold the sculptures to the British Museum, where they still reside, displayed in a special gallery. The Greeks now want the "Elgin Marbles" back.

The Greek claim for the return of the Acropolis marbles from the British Museum has been given greater force by the construction of the new Acropolis Museum. Plaster casts of all the "Elgin Marbles" now take their places in the appropriate positions in the original sculptural scheme, along with those sculptures that remained in Athens. These now sit there, patiently awaiting the hoped-for return of their long-lost relatives. That in essence is the story so far of perhaps the best-known case where an internationally famous museum is under pressure to return cultural property to the country of origin.

But there are numerous other claims directed at European and North American museums. The Berlin Museum, for example, holds the famous bust of the Egyptian queen Nefertiti, which was shipped out of Egypt illegally. The Greek government has officially asked France for the return of the Venus de Milo, one of the masterworks of the Louvre, bought from Greece's Ottoman rulers. And Turkey has recently been successful in recovering art treasures, including the "Lydian Hoard," from New York's Metropolitan Museum of Art (which has also returned the now infamous "Euphronios Krater" to Italy, see p. 312), and may now pursue Turkish statuary and objects in European countries, including the British Museum.

Excavating Burials: Should We Disturb the Dead?

The question of excavating burials can be equally complex. For prehistoric burials the problem is not so great, because we have no direct written knowledge of the relevant culture's beliefs and wishes. For burials dating from historic times, however, religious beliefs are known to us in detail. We know, for example, that the ancient Egyptians and Chinese, the Greeks, Etruscans, and Romans, and the early Christians all feared disturbance of the dead. Yet it has to be recognized that tombs were falling prey to the activities of robbers long before archaeology began. Egyptian pharaohs in the twelfth century BCE had to appoint a commission to inquire into the wholesale plundering of tombs at Thebes. Not a single Egyptian royal tomb, including that of Tutankhamun, escaped the robbers completely. Similarly, Roman carved gravestones became building material in cities and forts; and at Ostia, the port of ancient Rome, tomb inscriptions have even been found serving as seats in a public latrine!

THE NATIVE AMERICANS.   For some Native Americans in North America, archaeology has become a focal point for complaints about wrongdoings of the past. They have expressed their grievances strongly in recent years, and their political influence has resulted in legal mechanisms that sometimes restrict or prevent archaeological excavations, or provide for the return to Native American peoples of some collections now in museums. Apart from the question of returning and/or reburying material, sometimes there have been vehement objections to new excavations. The Chumash, for example, refused permission for scientists to remove what may be the oldest human remains in California, even though an offer was made to return and rebury the bones after a year's study. The bones, thought to be about 9000 years old, were eroding out of a cliff on Santa Rosa Island, 100 km (62 miles) west of Los Angeles. Under California's state laws the fate of the bones lay with their most likely descendants—and the Chumash were understandably angry about past treatment of their ancestors' skeletons, with hundreds of remains scattered in various universities and museums. They preferred to see the bones destroyed "in accordance with nature's law" than to have other people interfere with them. In other cases, however, Native American communities have provided for the systematic curation of such remains once they have been returned to them.

As in Australia (see overleaf), there is no single, unified indigenous tradition. Native Americans have wide-ranging attitudes toward the dead and the soul. Nonetheless demands for reburial of ancestral remains are common. The solution to the problem has been found to lie in acquiescence, compromise, and collaboration. Often archaeologists have supported the return of remains of fairly close ancestors of living people. Material has also been returned that had no archaeological context and was thus of minimal value to science.

Repatriation of older and more important material is a difficult issue. The longstanding position of the Society for American Archaeology (SAA) is that scientific and traditional interests in archaeological materials must be balanced, weighted by the closeness of relationship to the modern group making a claim and the scientific value of the remains or objects requested. With the society's support, in 1990 the Native American Graves Protection and Repatriation Act (NAGPRA) was passed. It requires some 5000 federally funded institutions and government agencies to inventory their collections and assess the "cultural affiliation" of Native American skeletons, funerary and sacred objects, and items of cultural patrimony. If cultural affiliation can be shown, the human remains and objects must, on request, be returned to the affiliated Native American tribe or Native Hawaiian organization. Difficult problems lie in interpreting key terms in the law, such as "cultural affiliation," and in weighing diverse forms of evidence in the context of prehistoric material. In addition to archaeological and historical information, the law explicitly recognizes the validity of oral traditions. This has led to broad expectations by tribes that prehistoric remains can be claimed if their oral traditions say that its people were created in the same region where the remains were found. However, when these expectations were tested

Seminole bones from Florida are reburied in 1989 by archaeologists and Native Americans at Wounded Knee.

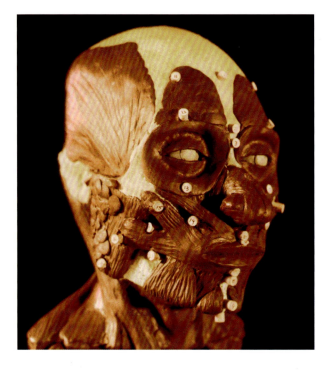

Facial features of Kennewick Man during reconstruction, with muscles added in clay.

in court it was found that the law requires a balanced consideration of oral tradition with scientific evidence.

An amendment to the NAGPRA regulations in 2010 extended rights to culturally unaffiliated remains as long as these were found on tribal lands or areas of aboriginal occupation. This means that US museums will now have to relinquish control of many more human remains to tribal groups.

Controversy and a legal battle dogged the bones of "Kennewick Man," found in 1996 in Washington State, and radiocarbon dated to 9300 BP. Eight prominent anthropologists sued the Army Corps of Engineers, which has jurisdiction over the site, for permission to study the bones, but the Corps wanted to hand the skeleton to the local Native American Umatilla tribe for reburial, in accordance with NAGPRA. The scientists were extremely anxious to run tests, since preliminary examination had suggested that Kennewick Man was a nineteenth-century settler; its early date raises complex, important, and fascinating questions about the peopling of the Americas. The Umatilla, on the other hand, were adamantly against any investigation, insisting that their oral tradition says their tribe has been part of this land since the beginning of time, and so all bones recovered from here are necessarily their ancestors—and must not be damaged for dating or genetic analysis. In 2002 a magistrate affirmed the right of the scientists to study the bones and, despite subsequent legal appeals, in June 2005 the battle (which cost millions of dollars in legal fees) was finally won, and analysis began in earnest. In 2015, DNA testing proved that Kennewick Man was closely related to the Colville tribe of northeastern Washington State, the region where the remains were found. In 2016 legislation was passed to return the bones to a coalition of tribes, and they were reburied in February 2017.

THE AUSTRALIAN ABORIGINES.   In Australia, the present climate of Aboriginal emancipation and increased political power has focused attention on wrongdoings during the colonial period, when anthropologists had little respect for Aboriginal feelings and beliefs. Sacred sites were investigated and published, burial sites desecrated, and cultural and skeletal material exhumed, to be stored or displayed in museums. The Aborigines were thus, by implication, seen as laboratory specimens. Inevitably, the fate of all this material, and particularly of the bones, has assumed great symbolic significance. Unfortunately, here as in other countries, archaeologists are being blamed for the misdemeanors of the non-archaeologists who obtained most of the human remains in question.

The view of Aborigines in some parts of Australia is that all human skeletal material (and occasionally cultural material too) must be returned to them, and then its fate will be decided. In some cases they themselves wish the remains to be curated in conditions that anthropologists would consider to be satisfactory, usually under Aboriginal control. Since the Aborigines have an unassailable moral case, the Australian Archaeological Association (AAA) is willing to return remains that are either quite modern or of "known individuals where specific descendants can be traced," and for these to be reburied. Such remains, however, are somewhat the exception. The University of Melbourne's Murray Black Collection consists of skeletal remains from more than 800 Aborigines, ranging in date from several hundred years to at least 14,000 years old. They were dug up in the 1940s without any consultation with local Aborigines. Owing to a lack of specialists the collection has still by no means been exhaustively studied—but nevertheless it has been returned to the relevant Aboriginal communities. In 1990 the unique series of burials from Kow Swamp, 19,000 to 22,000 years old, were handed back to the Aboriginal community and reburied; more recently the first skeleton found at Lake Mungo, the world's oldest known cremation (26,000 years BP), was returned to the custody of the Aborigines of the Mungo area; and Aboriginal elders have announced they may rebury all the skeletal material (up to 30,000 years old) from Mungo.

Archaeologists are understandably alarmed at the prospect of having to hand over material many thousands of years old. Some also point out that the Aborigines—like indigenous peoples elsewhere—tend to forget that not all of their recent forebears took pious care of the dead. But, not least in the light of Aboriginal sufferings at European hands, their views are entitled to respect.

The Responsibility of Collectors and Museums

It has become clear in recent years that private collectors and even public museums, for centuries regarded as guardians and conservators of the past, have become (in some cases) major causative agents of destruction. The market in illegal antiquities—excavated illegally and clandestinely with no published record—has become a major incentive for the looting of archaeological sites. The looting is funded, whether directly or indirectly, by unscrupulous private collectors and by unethical museums. All over the world looters are continuing their destructive work. Several languages have a word for them: in Greece they are *archaiokapiloi*, in Latin America *huaqueros*, and in Italy *tombaroli*. They unearth beautiful, salable objects. But deprived of their archaeological context, these objects no longer have the power to tell us much

Destruction and Response: Mimbres

UNITED STATES
• Mimbres

The Mimbres potters of the American Southwest created a unique art tradition in the prehistoric period, painting the inside of hemispherical bowls with vigorous animal and human forms. These bowls are now much admired by archaeologists and art lovers. But this fascination has led to the systematic looting of Mimbres sites on a scale unequaled in the United States, or indeed anywhere in the world.

The Mimbres people lived along a small river (also called the Mimbres) in mud-built villages, similar in some respects to those of the later Puebloans. Painted pottery began, as we now know, around 550 CE, and reached its apogee in the Classic Mimbres period, from about 1000 to 1130 CE.

Systematic archaeological work on Mimbres sites began in the 1920s, but it was not in general well published. Looters soon found, however, that with pick and shovel they could unearth Mimbres pots to sell on the market for primitive art. Nor was this activity necessarily illegal. In United States law there is nothing to prevent excavation of any kind by the owner on private land, and nothing to prevent the owner permitting others to destroy archaeological sites in this way (although some state laws, in New Mexico and Arizona, for example, now protect human burials on both private and state land).

In the early 1960s, a method of bulldozing Mimbres sites was developed that did not destroy all the pottery. The operators found that by controlled bulldozing they could remove a relatively small depth of soil at a time and extract many of the pots unbroken. In the process, sites were of course completely destroyed, and all hope of establishing an archaeological context for the material was lost.

Since 1973 there has at last been a concerted archaeological response. The Mimbres Foundation, under the direction of Steven LeBlanc, was able to secure funding from private sources to undertake excavations in the remains of some of the looted sites. It also made good progress in explaining to the owners of those sites how destructive this looting process was to any hope of learning about the Mimbres' past. From 1975 to 1978 a series of field seasons at several partially looted sites succeeded in establishing at least the outlines of Mimbres archaeology, and in putting the chronology upon a sure footing.

Animalian forms were a popular Mimbres subject. The "kill" hole allowed the object's spirit to be released.

The Mimbres Foundation also reached the conclusion that archaeological excavation is an expensive form of conservation, and decided to purchase a number of surviving (or partially surviving) Mimbres sites in order to protect them. Moreover, this is a lesson that has been learned more widely. Members of the Mimbres Foundation have joined forces with other archaeologists and benefactors to form a national organization, the Archaeological Conservancy. Several sites in the United States have now been purchased and conserved in this way. The story thus has, in some sense, a happy ending. But nothing can bring back the possibility of really understanding Mimbres culture and art, a possibility that did exist at the beginning of the twentieth century before the devastating looting.

Unfortunately, in other parts of the world there are similar stories to tell.

Mimbres bowl from the Classic period, showing a ritual decapitation.

that is new about the past. Many of them end up on display in some of the less scrupulous museums of the world. When a museum fails to indicate the context of discovery, including the site the exhibit came from, it is often a sign that the object displayed has come via the illicit market.

One such *tombarolo*, Luigi Perticarari, a robber in Tarquinia, Italy, published his memoirs in 1986 and makes no apology for his trade. He has more first-hand knowledge of Etruscan tombs than any archaeologist, but his activity destroys the chance of anyone sharing that knowledge. He claims to have emptied some 4000 tombs dating from the eighth to the third centuries BCE in thirty years. So it is that, while the world's store of Etruscan antiquities in museums and private collections grows larger, our knowledge of Etruscan burial customs and social organization does not.

The same is true for the remarkable marble sculptures of the Cycladic islands of Greece, dating to around 2500 BCE. We admire the breathtaking elegance of these works in the world's museums, but we have little idea of how they were produced or of the social and religious life of the Cycladic communities that made them. Again, the contexts have been lost.

In the American Southwest, 90 percent of the Classic Mimbres sites (*c*. 1000 CE) have now been looted or destroyed (see box opposite). In southwestern Colorado, 60 percent of prehistoric Ancestral Pueblo sites have been vandalized. Pothunters work at night, equipped with two-way radios, scanners, and lookouts. It is very difficult to prosecute them under the present legislation unless they are caught red-handed, which is almost impossible.

The *huaqueros* of Central and South America, too, are interested only in the richest finds, in this case gold—whole cemeteries are turned into fields of craters, with bones, potsherds, mummy wrappings, and other objects smashed and scattered. The remarkable tombs excavated between 1987 and 1990 at Sipán, northwestern Peru, of the Moche civilization, were rescued from the plunderers only by the persistence and courage of the local Peruvian archaeologist, Walter Alva.

So far as illicit antiquities are concerned, the spotlight has indeed turned upon museums and private collectors. Many of the world's great museums, following the lead of the University of Pennsylvania Museum (the Penn Museum) in 1970, now decline to purchase or receive by gift any antiquities that cannot be shown to have been exported legally from their country of origin. But others, such as the Metropolitan Museum of Art, New York, have in the past had no such scruples: Thomas Hoving, at that time director of the museum, stated: "We are no more illegal in anything we have done than Napoleon was when he brought all the treasures to the Louvre." The J. Paul Getty Museum, with its great wealth, has a heavy responsibility in this, and has recently adopted a much more rigorous acquisition policy.

Such museums as the Metropolitan Museum of Art, which in 1990 put on display the collection of Shelby White and the late Leon Levy, and the Getty Museum, which in 1994 exhibited (and then acquired) that of Barbara Fleischman and the late Lawrence Fleischman—both collections with a high proportion of antiquities of unknown provenience—must share some responsibility for the prevalence of collecting in circumstances where much of the money paid inevitably goes to reward dealers who are part of the ongoing cycles of destruction, and thus ultimately the looters. The responsibility borne by collectors who, in buying such works, indirectly fund the looting process, is also now being recognized. It has been argued that "collectors are the real looters." Peter Watson, in his revealing survey *The Medici Conspiracy* (2006), has outlined the surprising events that led the Italian government to bring criminal charges against the former curator of antiquities at the Getty, and to recover from the Metropolitan Museum of Art one of their most celebrated antiquities, the "Euphronios Krater," for which they had in 1972 paid a million dollars, but without obtaining secure evidence of its provenience. As the Romans had it: "caveat emptor" ("buyer beware").

It remains a real paradox that collectors, who often have a genuine feeling for the antiquities that they amass, are ultimately funding the looting that is the main threat to the world's archaeological heritage.

There are signs that things may be improving, however. The Dealing in Cultural Objects (Offences) Act was approved by the United Kingdom Parliament in 2003. For the first time it is now a criminal offence in the UK knowingly to deal in illicitly excavated antiquities, whether from the UK or overseas. And in New York in June 2003 the United States Court of Appeals upheld the conviction of the antiquities dealer Frederick Schultz for conspiring to deal in antiquities stolen from Egypt. Schultz is a former president of the National Association of Dealers in Ancient, Oriental, and Primitive Art and has in the past sold antiquities to some leading museums in the United States. A jail term for so prominent a dealer will send a clear message to some conspicuous collectors and museum directors that they should be more attentive in future in the exercise of "due diligence" when acquiring unprovenienced antiquities.

Recent cases include:

The "Weary Herakles": the lower part, excavated in Turkey in 1980, and the upper part, which was exhibited in the Boston Museum of Fine Arts, are now reunited in Turkey.

- *The "Weary Herakles."* Two parts of a Roman marble statue of the second century CE are now separate. The lower part was excavated at Perge in Turkey in 1980 and is in the Antalya Museum, while the joining upper part was purchased by the late Leon Levy and was for some years exhibited at the Boston Museum of Fine Arts, to which Levy gave a half share. The museum and Levy's widow Shelby White initially resisted Turkish claims to the piece, but it has now been returned to Turkey.

A splendid silver dish from the looted Sevso Treasure, one of the major scandals in the recent story of illicit antiquities.

- *The Sevso Treasure.* A splendid late Roman assemblage of silver vessels was acquired as an investment by the Marquess of Northampton, but was subsequently claimed in a New York court action by Hungary, Croatia, and Lebanon. Possession was awarded to the marquess, who then found the treasure unsalable and sued his former legal advisors in London for their poor advice at the time of purchase; an out-of-court settlement, reportedly in excess of £15 million, was agreed on confidential terms in 1999. Hungary is now seeking to obtain this material, and perhaps Lord Northampton will sell his treasure after all. It was exhibited at a private viewing at Bonham's, the London auctioneers, in 2006, and nothing has been heard of it since.

- *The Getty Affair.* The J. Paul Getty Museum in Los Angeles found itself in the spotlight of publicity in 2005 when its Curator of Antiquities, Marion True (subsequently fired), went on trial in Italy on charges relating to the purchase by the Getty of antiquities allegedly illegally excavated in Italy. The trial ran out of time, without verdict, but the Getty Museum meanwhile by agreement returned many looted antiquities to Italy. The Getty Museum has also now adopted a strict acquisition policy fully in line with the 1970 UNESCO Convention against the illicit trade in artifacts.

- *The UCL Aramaic Incantation Bowls.* In 2005 University College London established a committee of inquiry into the provenience of 654 Aramaic incantation bowls (dating to the sixth to seventh centuries CE, and believed to come from Iraq) that had been lent for purposes of study by a prominent Norwegian collector, Martin Schøyen. It did so following claims that the bowls had been illegally exported from their country of origin. UCL received

Aramaic incantation bowl from the sixth to seventh century CE with a text, written in black ink, intended to bind demons, deities, and other hostile forces who might harm the owner.

the report of the committee in July 2006, but subsequently returned the bowls to Schøyen, with whom it had concluded a confidential out-of-court settlement preventing publication of the report, and agreeing to pay an undisclosed sum to Schøyen. This episode highlights the need for "due diligence" when antiquities are accepted, on loan as well as through gift or purchase, by public institutions. The full story of the UCL Aramaic incantation bowls remains to be told.

It is ironic that a love and respect for the past and for the antiquities that have come down to us should lead to such destructive and acquisitive behavior. "Who owns the past?" is indeed the key issue if the work of archaeology is to continue, and to provide us with new information about our shared heritage and about the processes by which we have become who we are. In that sense we may well ask "Does the past have a future?" That is the theme addressed in our final chapter.

Study Questions

1 Who owns the past?
2 What are some ways in which symbols from the past have led to conflict?
3 What are ethics? What sorts of ethical issues do archaeologists encounter?
4 Why are many archaeologists critical of "pseudoarchaeology"?
5 What are illicit antiquities?

Summary

THE PAST HAS DIFFERENT meanings for different people, and often personal identity is defined by the past. Increasingly archaeology is playing a role in the definition of national identity, where the past is used to legitimize the present by reinforcing a sense of national greatness. Ethnicity, which is just as strong a force today as in earlier times, relies upon the past for legitimization as well, sometimes with destructive consequences.

ETHICS IS THE SCIENCE of what is right and wrong, or morality, and most branches of archaeology are seen to have an ethical dimension. Until recent decades archaeologists gave little thought to such questions as "who owns the past?" Now every archaeological decision should take ethical concerns into account.

WE CANNOT SIMPLY dismiss the alternative theories of fringe archaeology as farcical, because they have been so widely believed. Anyone who understands how archaeology proceeds will already see why such writings are a delusion. The real antidote is to ask "where is the evidence?" Knowledge advances by asking questions and looking skeptically at the answers.

THE ARCHAEOLOGY of every land has its own contribution to make to the understanding of the human past. Although earlier scholars behaved with flagrant disregard for the feelings and beliefs of indigenous peoples, interest in these matters today is not an attempt further to appropriate the indigenous past.

PERHAPS THE SADDEST type of archaeological destruction comes from the looting of sites. Through this act, all information is destroyed in the search for highly salable artifacts. Museums and collectors bear some of the responsibility for this. Museums are also under increasing pressure to return antiquities to their lands of origin.

Further Reading

General introductions to the topics covered in this chapter include:

Brodie, N., Kersel, M., Luke, C., & Tubb, K. W. (eds). 2008. *Archaeology, Cultural Heritage, and the Antiquities Trade.* University Press of Florida: Gainsville.

Feder, K. 2008. *Frauds, Myths, and Mysteries: Science and Pseudoscience in Archaeology*. McGraw-Hill: New York.

Greenfield, J. 2007. *The Return of Cultural Treasures* (3rd ed.). Cambridge University Press: Cambridge & New York.

Jenkins, T. 2016. *Keeping Their Marbles: How the Treasures of the Past Ended Up in Museums and Why They Should Stay There*. Oxford University Press: Oxford.

Renfrew, C. 2009. *Loot, Legitimacy and Ownership*. Duckworth: London.

Watson, P. & Todeschini, C. 2006. *The Medici Conspiracy*. PublicAffairs: New York.

[See p. 345 for a list of useful websites]

12

The Future of the Past
Managing Our Heritage

What is the future of archaeology? Can our discipline continue to produce new information about the human past, the evolution of our species, and the achievements of humankind? This is one of the dilemmas that currently confront all archaeologists, and indeed all those concerned to understand the human past. For just as global warming and increasing pollution threaten the future ecology of our planet, so the record of the past is today faced by forces of destruction that demand a coherent and energetic response.

Some of those forces of destruction have been discussed earlier, and others are confronted here. The big question continues to be: What can be done? That is the problem that faces us, the solution to which will determine the future both of our discipline and of the material record that it seeks to understand. Here we review two parallel approaches: conservation (protection) and mitigation. The two, working together, have generated in recent years new attitudes toward the practice of archaeology.

The Destruction of the Past

There are two main agencies of destruction, both of them human. One is the construction of roads, quarries, dams, office blocks, etc. These are conspicuous and the threat is at least easily recognizable. The other, agricultural intensification, is slower but much wider in its extent, thus in the long term far more destructive. Elsewhere, reclamation schemes are transforming the nature of the environment, so that arid lands are being flooded and wetlands, such as those in Florida, are being reclaimed through drainage. The result is the loss of remarkable archaeological evidence. A third agent of destruction is conflict, the most obvious current threat being in the war zones of the Middle East.

There are two further human agencies of destruction that should not be overlooked. The first is tourism, which, while economically having important effects on archaeology, makes the effective conservation of archaeological sites more difficult. The second, as we have seen in Chapter 11, is not new, but has grown dramatically in scale: the looting of archaeological sites by those who

The Warka Vase (below) was looted from the National Museum of Iraq, Baghdad, during the invasion of Iraq in 2003. Fortunately it was recovered (bottom) and though in pieces, these were probably ancient breaks.

dig for monetary gain, seeking only salable objects and destroying everything else in their search. More ancient remains have been lost in the last two decades than ever before in the history of the world.

AGRICULTURAL DAMAGE.   Ever increasing areas of the Earth, once uncultivated or cultivated by traditional non-intensive methods, are being opened up to mechanized farming. In other areas, forest plantations now cover what was formerly open land, and tree roots are destroying archaeological sites.

Although most countries keep some control over the activities of developers and builders, the damage to archaeological sites from farming is much more difficult to assess. The few published studies make sober reading. One shows that in Britain even those sites that are notionally protected—by being listed on the national Schedule of Ancient Monuments—are not, in reality, altogether safe. The position may be much better in Denmark and in certain other countries, but elsewhere only the most conspicuous sites are protected. The more modest field monuments and open settlements are not, and these are the sites that are suffering from mechanized agriculture.

DAMAGE IN WAR.   Among the most distressing outrages of recent years has been the continuing destruction, sometimes deliberate, of monuments and artifacts in the course of armed conflict. Already, during World War II, historic buildings in England were deliberately targeted in German bombing raids.

In war the sentiments are sometimes national or ethnic, rather than religious. Such was the case in the civil war in Yugoslavia, although it also had religious overtones. The bridge at Mostar in Bosnia, built by the Ottoman Turks in 1566 and a symbol of Bosnian identity, was destroyed by Croatian forces in 1993. Although it has now been rebuilt, the loss of the original structure was one of the most tragic acts in Europe since World War II: the deliberate destruction of cultural heritage on purely ethnic grounds.

The failure of Coalition forces in the invasion of Iraq in 2003 to secure the National Museum of Iraq in Baghdad allowed the looting of the collections, including the celebrated Warka Vase, one of the most notable finds from the early Sumerian civilization—although, like many other important antiquities, this was later returned to the museum. The failure was all the more shocking since archaeologists in the United States had met with representatives of the Defense Department some months prior to the war to warn of the risk of looting in museums and at sites, and archaeologists in Britain had similarly indicated the dangers to the British government months before the war began. Only parts of the collection were taken, and it seems that it was the work both of looters from the street, who smashed cases, decapitated statues, and trashed offices, but also perhaps some well-informed individuals who knew what they were looking for and who

Objects from Tutankhamun's tomb looted from the Cairo Museum in 2011, and subsequently recovered by Egyptian authorities.

had access to storeroom keys. It is these who are likely to have taken the museum's collection of Mesopotamian cylinder seals, the finest in the world, for sale to collectors overseas.

In 2011, during the "Arab Spring" in Egypt, civil unrest gave the opportunity for thieves to break into the Cairo Museum and steal a number of significant antiquities, although the authorities rapidly restored order. Continuing conflict in Syria and Egypt is having a devastating effect on archaeology, with widespread looting of sites as well as thefts from museums. The effects are especially serious for Egypt, which relies so heavily upon archaeological tourism. In August 2013 the archaeological museum in Malawi, in Egypt's Minya region, was destroyed and looted—sarcophagi and statues were damaged, and curators revealed that 1040 of 1080 objects in the collection were missing, presumably now heading for the burgeoning trade in illicit antiquities.

It seems all the more extraordinary that the United States and the United Kingdom only ratified the 1954 Hague Convention for the Protection of Cultural Property in the Event of Armed Conflict in 2009 and 2017 respectively.

The Response: Survey, Conservation, and Mitigation

In many countries of the world where the material remains of the past are valued as an important component of the national heritage, the response has been the development of a public archaeology: the acceptance that the public and therefore both national and regional governments have a responsibility to avoid unnecessary destruction of that heritage. And of course there is an international dimension also. This acceptance implies that steps should be taken to conserve what remains, often with the support of protective legislation. And when development is undertaken, which is often necessary and inescapable—to build freeways for instance, or to undertake commercial development, or to bring land into cultivation—steps need to be taken to research and record any archaeological remains that in the process are likely to be destroyed. In this way the effects of development can be mitigated.

These approaches have highlighted the need, in advance of any potential development, for reliable information concerning whatever archaeological remains may be present. This puts crucial emphasis on one of the key developments in the archaeological methodology of the late twentieth century: site location and survey. The actions undertaken in response to a threat need a logical and natural order: survey, conservation, and mitigation.

Within the United States, what are termed "preservation" laws to protect heritage resources do not guarantee that archaeological remains will be preserved. The laws mandate a weighing of options and dictate the process by which the value of the resource is assessed against the value of the development. In rare cases, the value of a site is so great that it will be preserved and a project canceled or rerouted. In the vast majority of cases, though, sites are excavated, recorded, and destroyed: a compromise between development and heritage needs.

Survey

Before major developments are undertaken, a key part of the planning phase must be a survey or assessment of the likely effects of such development upon what may be termed the archaeological resource. Such an assessment extends beyond archaeology to more recent history and other aspects of the environment, including threatened plant and animal species. The cultural heritage, and especially its material remains, needs to be carefully assessed.

Such assessment today will often involve the use of satellite imagery as well as aerial photography. It requires mapping with the aid of GIS. And it also needs to involve field survey, using on-the-ground evaluation through field walking (sometimes called "ground truthing") so that unknown archaeological sites—and extant historical buildings and infrastructure, historic landscapes, and traditional cultural properties—can be located and evaluated before development begins.

Conservation and Mitigation

Most nations today ensure a degree of protection for their major monuments and archaeological sites. In the United Kingdom, as early as 1882, the first Ancient Monuments Protection Act was passed and the first Inspector of Ancient Monuments appointed: the energetic archaeologist and pioneer excavator General Pitt-Rivers (see pp. 22–23). A "schedule" of ancient monuments was drawn up, which were to be protected by law. Several of the most important monuments were taken into "guardianship," whereby they were conserved and opened to the public under the supervision of the Ancient Monuments Inspectorate.

In the United States, the first major federal legislation for archaeological protection, the American Antiquities Act, was signed into law in 1906 by Theodore Roosevelt. The act set out three provisions: that the damage, destruction, or excavation of historic or prehistoric ruins or monuments on federal land without permission would be prohibited; that the president would have the authority to establish national landmarks and associated reserves on federal land; and that permits could be granted for the excavation or collection of archaeological materials on federal land to qualified institutions that pursued such excavations for the purpose of increasing knowledge of the past and preserving the materials.

The American Antiquities Act set the foundation and fundamental principles for archaeology in the United States. These include that federal protection is limited to federal land (although some individual states and local governments have their own laws); that excavation is a permitted activity for those seeking to learn and conduct research in the public interest; that unpermitted archaeological activities and vandalism are criminally punishable; and that archaeological resources are important enough that the president may create reserves for protection independent of the other branches of government. These principles continue through the many other federal laws that followed. Today, the principal laws that practicing archaeologists must know and follow include the National Historic Preservation Act of 1966, the National Environmental Policy Act of 1969, the Archaeological Resources Protection Act of 1979, the Abandoned Shipwrecks Act of 1987, and the Native American Graves Protection and Repatriation Act of 1990. These laws, and a host of others, updated and expanded the basic principles and practices of protecting, preserving, and managing archaeological resources on federal lands in the United States (see the following section on Cultural Resource Management, pp. 324–25).

Similar provisions hold for the major monuments of many nations. But in the field of heritage management it is with the less obvious, perhaps less important sites that problems arise. Above all, it is difficult or impossible for sites to be protected if their existence is not known or recognized; this is why the role of survey is so crucial.

The conservation of the archaeological record is a fundamental principle of heritage management. It can be brought about by partnership agreement with the landowner—for instance to avoid plowing on recognized sites. Measures can be taken to mitigate the effects of coastal erosion (although this can be very difficult) or inappropriate land use. And above all, effective planning legislation can be used to prevent commercial development in sensitive archaeological areas. Indeed, increasingly, the approach is to think of entire landscapes and their conservation, rather than focusing upon isolated archaeological sites.

Conservation in Mexico City

MEXICO
Mexico City

(Right) Skeleton of a jaguar with a greenstone ball in its mouth, found in the Great Temple.

When the Spanish Conquistadors under Hernán Cortés occupied the Aztec capital, Tenochtitlan, in 1521, they destroyed its buildings and established their own capital, Mexico City, on the same site.

In 1790 the now-famous statue of the Aztec mother goddess Coatlicue was found, and also the well-known Calendar Stone, but it was not until the twentieth century that more systematic archaeological work took place.

Various relatively small-scale excavations were carried out on remains within the city as they came to light in the course of building work. But in 1975 a more coherent initiative was taken: the institution by the Department of Pre-Hispanic Monuments of the Basin of Mexico Project. Its aim is to halt the destruction of archaeological remains during the continuing growth of the city. In 1977, the Museum of Tenochtitlan Project was begun, with the aim of excavating the area where remains of what appeared to be the Great Temple of the Aztecs had been found in 1948. The project

was radically transformed early in 1978 when electricity workers discovered a large stone carved with a series of reliefs. The Department of Salvage Archaeology of the National Institute of Anthropology and History took charge. Within days, a huge monolith, 3.25 m (10 ft. 7 in.) in diameter, was revealed, depicting the dismembered body of the Aztec goddess Coyolxauhqui who, according to myth, had been killed by her brother, the war god Huitzilopochtli.

(Below) The Great Temple excavation site, with stairways visible of successive phases of the monument. The building was originally pyramidal in form, surmounted by twin temples to the war god Huitzilopochtli and the rain god Tlaloc.

(Above) The Great Stone, found in 1978, provided the catalyst for the Great Temple excavations. The goddess Coyolxauhqui is shown decapitated and dismembered—killed by her brother, the war god Huitzilopochtli.

The Museum of Tenochtitlan Project, under the direction of Eduardo Matos Moctezuma, became the Great Temple Project, which over the next few years brought to light one of the most remarkable archaeological sites in Mexico.

No one had realized how much would be preserved of the Great Temple. Although the Spaniards had razed the standing structure to the ground in 1521, this pyramid was the last of a series of rebuildings. Beneath the ruins of the last temple the excavations revealed those of earlier temples.

In addition to these architectural remains was a wonderful series of offerings to the temple's two gods, Huitzilopochtli and the rain god Tlaloc—objects of obsidian and jade, terracotta and stone sculptures, and other special dedications, including rare coral and the remains of a jaguar buried with a ball of greenstone in its mouth.

A major area of Mexico City has now been turned into a permanent museum and national monument.

(Above) This massive stone slab depicting the god Tlaltecuhtli ("Lord of the Earth") was found at the site in 2006. The monolith was moved to the Templo Mayor Museum in 2010.

Mexico has regained one of its greatest pre-Columbian buildings, and the Great Temple of the Aztecs is once again one of the marvels of Tenochtitlan.

When considering the impact of commercial or industrial development, one aspect of mitigation is the carefully planned avoidance of damage to the archaeological record. A well-considered strategy in advance of development will usually favour this approach. In some cases, however, the development necessarily involves damage to the archaeological record. It is at this point that rescue or **salvage archaeology** becomes appropriate. Rarely, when particularly important archaeological remains are unexpectedly uncovered, development may be halted entirely (for an example, see box opposite and above).

It is inevitable in the case of major developments, such as the construction of a freeway, that many archaeological sites will be encountered. In the survey stage of the planning process, most of these will have been located, observed, noted, and evaluated. A mitigation plan addresses what steps are required to protect the archaeological record or recover significant information if destruction cannot be avoided. In some cases it may be possible to alter the route of the freeway: that is one aspect of mitigation. But usually, if the project is to go ahead, the "preventive" archaeology will involve the investigation of the site by appropriate means of sampling, including excavation.

In many countries a significant proportion of the budget available for archaeological research is now deliberately assigned to these projects, where damage to the archaeological record seems inevitable and where it can be mitigated in this way. There is a growing presumption that sites that are not threatened should not be excavated if there is a potentially informative site that can provide comparable excavation, the future of which is threatened by development. It is increasingly realized that important research questions can be answered in the course of such mitigation procedures.

The Practice of CRM in the United States

Over the past four decades American archaeology has become embedded in Cultural Resource Management (CRM), a complex of laws, regulations, and professional practice designed to manage historic buildings and sites, cultural landscapes, and other cultural and historic places. The practice of CRM is often known as "applied archaeology."

The National Historic Preservation Act and the National Environmental Policy Act are the major legal bases for CRM. These laws require US government agencies to consider the environmental impacts of their actions (through an "environmental assessment," which may lead to an "environmental impact statement"), including effects on historical, archaeological, and cultural values. The role of State Historic Preservation Officer (SHPO) was created in each US state. Each agency runs its own compliance program.

Projects in which US government agencies are involved—whether on federal land or on other lands but federally funded or requiring a federal permit—must be reviewed to determine their effects on environmental, cultural, and historical resources. CRM programs in state and local governments, federal agencies, academic institutions, and private consulting firms have grown out of this requirement. The SHPOs coordinate many CRM activities, and keep files on historic and prehistoric sites, structures, buildings, districts, and landscapes.

Section 106 of the National Historic Preservation Act requires federal agencies to identify historic places of all kinds (archaeological sites, historic buildings, Native American sites, etc.) that may be affected by their actions, in consultation with SHPOs, tribes, and others. This identification and evaluation is organized into three phases. The goal of Phase I is to *identify* all structures or features that may be historic and could be placed onto the National Register of Historic Places. This often requires both field survey and the examination of published material. Phase II *evaluation* is needed when a historic structure, feature, or archaeological site needs to be assessed to determine whether it is eligible for inclusion on the National Register of Historic Places. Often this process is called a Determination of Eligibility, or "DOE."

If it is found that significant sites are present and that they will be adversely affected, ways to mitigate any negative effects are sought. Often this involves redesigning the project to prevent damage. If avoidance is not possible or feasible, Phase III, *data recovery*, is required. For archaeological sites, this often

Key Concepts
CRM in the USA

CRM (Cultural Resource Management) or "applied archaeology" accounts for more than 90 percent of the field archaeology carried out in the USA today

Legal Basis: under Section 106 of the National Historic Preservation Act, archaeological investigation is often carried out in advance of projects on federal land, using federal funds, or requiring a federal permit. The assessment of historic places stipulated in Section 106 follows three phases; identification, evaluation, and, if measures cannot be taken to avoid damage, data recovery

Funding: generally speaking, the proponent of the construction or land-use project pays for the work, whether that party is a federal, state, or local agency, or a private developer

Compliance: project proponents fund legally required compliance work that includes inventory (survey), evaluation of a resource's importance, assessment of impacts to important resources, and mitigation (which may include avoidance, excavation, and conservation)

Outcome: the fieldwork typically results in at least a report filed with the SHPO and data entered in government and other databases. Many CRM projects also result in published journal articles, monographs, and books

---

includes excavations to recover significant data before they are destroyed. If the parties cannot agree on what to do, an independent body known as the Advisory Council on Historic Preservation makes a recommendation and then the responsible federal agency makes its final decision.

Most surveys and data recovery projects in the USA are carried out by private firms—sometimes companies that specialize in CRM work, but otherwise by branches of large engineering, planning, or environmental impact assessment companies. Some academic institutions, museums, and non-profit organizations also carry out CRM work. CRM-based surveys and excavations now comprise at least 90 percent of the field archaeology carried out in the USA.

The review system under Section 106 can produce excellent archaeological research, but research interests must be balanced with other public interests, especially the concerns of Native American tribes and other communities. The quality of work depends largely on the integrity and skill of the participants—agency employees, SHPOs, tribal and community representatives, and private-sector archaeologists. Among the recurring problems are quality control in fieldwork, applying the results of fieldwork to important research topics, publication and other dissemination of results, and the long-term preservation and management of recovered artifacts.

One good example of this process is the Metro Rail Project (see box overleaf), although not all CRM projects are so well managed. Particularly in the case of small projects, which are carried out by the thousands, it is easy for very shoddy work to be done and little useful data to be produced. But on the other hand, large excavation projects find huge numbers of artifacts, and these have to be carefully stored—and this becomes more and more of a problem as time passes and new excavations are conducted. Large-scale CRM excavations also tend to be underfunded. Since Tennessee-Tombigbee and other similar projects in the 1970s and 1980s, the emphasis has shifted toward remote sensing and planning for the management of archaeological resources in ways that minimize the need for excavations. The Society for American Archaeology (SAA) has also helped to fund a Register of Professional Archaeologists in an attempt to improve standards. Professional requirements and qualifications have been established by the Department of the Interior, various land-managing agencies, and even some local governments. Permits to undertake archaeological work require credentials, experience, and acceptable past performance.

International Protection

Since world government is currently based upon the effective autonomy of the nation states of the United Nations, measures of conservation and mitigation likewise operate at the level of the nation states. Only in a few cases does some broader perspective prevail, often through UNESCO (the United Nations Educational, Scientific, and Cultural Organization).

CRM in Practice: The Metro Rail Project

Work conducted by Archaeological Consulting Services (ACS) in 2005–8 along the 31.5-km (19.6-mile) Central Phoenix/East Valley Light Rail corridor in Arizona discovered nine new sites, and greatly increased knowledge of twenty known sites in this busy urban area. Most of the work was carried out at the Hohokam site of Pueblo Grande in the City of Phoenix, and that of La Plaza in the City of Tempe. The project confirmed that the area was home to several different peoples during 1500 years of occupation.

The Light Rail Transit Project was constructed by Valley Metro Rail Inc. (METRO) and, as with any project that receives federal funding, METRO was legally required to undertake archaeological investigations before and during construction. More than 1000 features were encountered, and over a quarter of a million artifacts,

(Right) Excavations in progress at the Pueblo Grande site.

since the rail route traversed numerous prehistoric villages occupied by the Hohokam. It was already known that the important site of Pueblo Grande was occupied for about 1000 years, from c. 450/500 to 1450/1500 CE.

Native American Involvement
The work involved early and continuous consultation with a wide range of groups, including local Native American communities, the City of Phoenix Archaeologist, and the Four Southern Tribes Cultural Resources Working Group. Trust and respect was built with all such bodies, especially with regard to burials, and the project certainly met this aim, since an excellent working relationship was developed and maintained with all consulting parties.

For example, the Salt River Pima-Maricopa Indian Community expressed its appreciation for being contacted in a respectful manner regarding all discoveries, and more generally for ACS's informative and cooperative nature. Other groups involved included the Gila River Indian Community, the Fort McDowell Yavapai Nation and the Hopi Tribe. It was agreed that, if tribal consultations concluded that excavation was appropriate, any human remains and associated objects found would be repatriated to the communities.

Map of the Phoenix metropolitan area, showing the course of the new rail corridor in red.

Artifacts found by the Metro Rail Project at La Plaza included (clockwise from left): stone axe heads; stone palettes; a shell dog pendant; and a "three orifice" red-on-buff jar.

Archaeological Investigation

Four "sensitivity zones" were defined, each of which required different monitoring. Zone 1 comprised prehistoric habitation sites with known human remains. In these areas all ground disturbance was monitored by archaeologists. If any features or artifacts were found, construction would be stopped briefly so that archaeologists could evaluate whether further investigation was needed.

Zone 2 was defined as prehistoric habitation sites with the potential for human remains. Once again, all ground disturbance was closely watched, and the procedure was the same as for Zone 1, except that a single archaeologist monitored the excavations. Zone 3 comprised areas outside known site locations that were considered to have moderate sensitivity for cultural resources—most likely to be historic and prehistoric canal alignments. Excavations here required spot checking. Finally, Zone 4 was defined as locations where there were no known archaeological resources, with no systematic monitoring required. Contractors were merely instructed to notify archaeologists if any cultural materials were found. Sensitivity training of construction crews was carried out, and contact was maintained with them throughout, with occasional spot checks of open trenches.

THE WORLD HERITAGE LIST. Under the World Heritage Convention of 1972, the World Heritage Committee can place sites on the World Heritage List. At the time of writing there are 759 cultural sites on the list (some of which are illustrated overleaf), along with more than 200 natural and mixed sites. Although being on the list does not in itself afford protection, and certainly does not bring additional international resources to assist in conservation, it does act as an incentive for the responsible nation state to ensure that recognized standards are met.

There is in addition a World Heritage in Danger List that highlights the needs of specific threatened sites. The ancient city of Bam in Iran, seriously damaged by an earthquake in December 2003, is a case in point, as is the Bamiyan Valley in Afghanistan, which has suffered sadly through war and unrest (see p. 300). The walled city of Baku in Azerbaijan is another major site, damaged by an earthquake in November 2000 and now receiving support.

COUNTERING THE TRAFFIC IN ILLICIT ANTIQUITIES. The principal international measure against the traffic in illicit antiquities is the 1970 UNESCO Convention on the Means of P Preventing the Illicit Import, Export, and Transfer of Ownership of Cultural Property. But its principles are not directly enforced by international law, and depend rather on national legislation and on bilateral agreements between nations. The responsibilities

UNESCO World Heritage Sites.

(Clockwise from above left) Twelfth-century minaret at Jam, Afghanistan, decorated with stucco and glazed tile; one of 500 statues of Buddha at the eighth-century Buddhist temple at Borobudur, Indonesia; Fatehpur Sikri, India, capital city of the sixteenth-century Mughal emperor Akbar; spiral minaret, part of the great ninth-century mosque at Samarra, Iraq; the oval "pyramid" at the wonderfully preserved Maya city of Uxmal, Mexico; twelfth-century rock-cut Ethiopian orthodox church at Lalibela.

of collectors and museums were reviewed in Chapter 11. There are signs that it is becoming more difficult to sell recently looted antiquities on the open market, at any rate in some countries, but the problem remains a massive one.

PROTECTING THE CULTURAL HERITAGE IN TIMES OF WAR. The 1954 Hague Convention for the Protection of Cultural Property in the Event of Armed Conflict and its protocols in principle offer a degree of protection. In practice, however, they have not been effective and, as noted earlier, have only recently been ratified by the United Kingdom and by the United States. Both nations were criticized for their shortcomings during the invasion of Iraq in 2003.

These international initiatives are all important, and potentially significant. But at present they are very limited in their effectiveness. In the future they may be better supported, but most of the effective measures safeguarding the future of the past still work primarily at a national level.

Publication, Archives, and Resources

The pace of discovery through the surveys conducted to assess environmental impact and the excavation procedures undertaken in mitigation is remarkable. But the results are often not well published or otherwise made available either to specialists or to the public. In the United States there is an obligation that environmental impact statements and a summary of any measures taken in mitigation should be lodged with the state archive, but not that they should be published. In Greece the government has for some years failed to fund publication of the *Archaiologikon Deltion*, the official record of nationally funded excavations. The record is better in France and to some extent in Germany. But few countries can boast effective publication of the quite considerable activities undertaken, generally with a measure of state funding.

In some countries this has led to a division between the practice of academic archaeologists (working in universities and museums) and of those undertaking **contract archaeology**, whether funded by the developer or by the state, but in both cases working to mitigate the impact of development. The work of the former is supposed to be problem-oriented and often does indeed lead to publication in national or international archaeological journals and in detailed monographs. The work of the contract archaeologist is sometimes carefully coordinated, leading to informative regional and national surveys. But in too many instances its publication is not well coordinated at all.

The solution to these problems is not yet clear. But one possibility is certainly emerging: online publication. In this respect some of the major museums have led the way, making the catalogs of their collections available online. Few contract archaeologists currently make their environmental impact statements or mitigation reports available in that way, but this may one day become a requirement: a condition for funding in the first place. In the United Kingdom an important initiative has been taken by the national archaeological Portable Antiquities Scheme. There the practice of metal detecting in the search for archaeological artifacts is not prohibited by law, as it is in many countries, and this has been a concern to professional archaeologists. But at least state funding has been established for a scheme whereby metal detectorists can voluntarily report their finds to a reporting officer, and many in fact do so. In particular the results are being made available online, with a significant increase in information about the distributions of particular classes of artifact. Thus some of the traditional barriers between professional researchers and the wider public are breaking down. It is likely that in the future excavation data will also become available online and thus more rapidly accessible than is often currently the case. The obligation to inform the public, who ultimately provide the resources for much of the research, is being met.

What Use Is the Past?

The popularity of archaeology has markedly grown in recent years, if television programs and magazine articles are used as a measure. Certainly the number of archaeology students in university courses has increased greatly in many countries. And the world's great museums have ever-increasing visitor numbers. As we have seen, in many countries public resources are invested in conservation, and developers are obliged to ensure that proper measures are undertaken in mitigation of their impact upon the cultural environment. But are these resources expended simply to satisfy the idle curiosity of the world's citizens? Is their main purpose simply to create agreeable historic sites to visit?

We think that there is more at work than this. It can be argued that there is today a growing awareness that humankind needs to feel and to know that it has a past—a past that can be documented securely by concrete material evidence that we can all access, examine, and assess. For without our roots we are lost. Over recent generations those roots are well represented by our friends, by our families, and by our existing communities. But in a deeper sense, and in a deeper past, we are all in this together. The different religions of the world provide meaning for the lives of many people. But they do not all agree, or so it might seem, about some of the questions of human origins and early history that we have been discussing here. Some offer creation stories that are profound and illuminating. Each of these can be enriched by knowledge of the material evidence for early human development. The finds are there, in every part of the world. And more finds continue to be made.

It is abundantly clear, from the pace of archaeological discovery, that there is more to learn. That is one reason why the subject is so interesting. And it always will be. So long as the practices of conservation and mitigation are maintained we shall continue to learn more about the human past, and in that sense about what it means to be human. We hope that such will be the future of the past. And we do not doubt that it will be useful.

Building a Career in Archaeology

There are a variety of careers in archaeology—whether, for example, in the field of archaeological research (in a university or as an independent researcher), or in a more administrative capacity as a government employee, or in the business of heritage tourism. To show how an archaeological career could develop, we have invited four professionals, all earning a living by doing archaeology, to tell his or her own story.

Each is an established archaeologist but at a different stage in his or her career. Their backgrounds are also different. Yet most of them have something in common: they came to archaeology fortuitously, by chance, as it were. This is hardly surprising, since the practice of archaeology is not a major profession, such as medicine, law, or retail selling. But each of them, by some means, caught the bug. That bug, that fascination with the human past, is what drives them. The joy they express is not simply discovering and uncovering objects that have lain hidden for thousands of years. It is the pleasure of making sense of the data, making sense of the past.

Two of these archaeologists work in countries (Thailand and South Africa) outside of the transatlantic axis, between Europe and the United States, which was so significant in the early development of archaeology. It may be relevant that each did his or her postgraduate training at centers within that axis (Michigan and London respectively). Yet each now teaches graduate students in their own country—students who will themselves become the new generation of researchers, developing a world archaeology that will be fully international.

Part of that internationalism is indeed the rich experience of working in places and with people who lie outside of one's previous existence. Many of us are born and brought up in cities, so that archaeological fieldwork brings a welcome first experience of living and working with hunter-gatherers or with rural farmers in an environment very different from that of a city or university.

Each of the archaeologists is also concerned with the present and with the future, and aspires to make a difference to that future. Lisa J. Lucero hopes that her work on the demise of the Classic Maya, apparently through long-term drought, can inform our current understanding of the impact of climate change. Each sees it as part of their job both to interact with scholars in other countries, and to communicate with a wider public in his or her own homeland. The archaeologist of today, as of yesterday, is a person of wide horizons, with knowledge of the human past, and with a concern for the human future.

Lisa J. Lucero: University Professor, USA

HOW I WAS INSPIRED TO BECOME AN ARCHAEOLOGIST.   Even at high school I always wanted to know how much of a movie or book supposedly based on history was based on fact. This interest led me to obtain an anthropology degree at Colorado State University. I attended graduate school at UCLA, where the atmosphere in the archaeology program was positively electric. My interest—encouraged by my peers and professors—was to explore the foundation of political power. In the case of the Classic Maya (c. 250–900 CE) the power of rulers rested on the labor of the majority: commoners and farmers. The only way to reveal their story is to excavate commoner houses, which I have done over the years. It is amazing to peel back the layers of Maya mounds representing centuries of habitation and rebuilding by Maya families.

HOW I GOT MY FIRST JOB.   It took a few interviews before I was offered my first job at New Mexico State University, where I stayed for ten years, until I was recruited by the University of Illinois at Urbana-Champaign. I truly enjoy the academic atmosphere—I must, since I have never been out of it! I spend most of my time on various research projects as well as teaching.

Lisa J. Lucero
University of Illinois at
Urbana-Champaign
Email: ljlucero@illinois.edu

THE MOST REWARDING THING I HAVE DISCOVERED.   There is not one particular thing that I have discovered in my more than twenty years of conducting archaeology. What is rewarding are the questions I feel more and more qualified to address about human societies, including my own. What amazes me is the resilience of our species; we have overcome so much in our history. People of the past, however, have also faced challenges that they could not overcome. It is hugely valuable to identify those strategies of the past that did not work, so as to avoid history repeating itself.

Lisa J. Lucero excavating at the Maya center of Yalbac, in the jungles of central Belize.

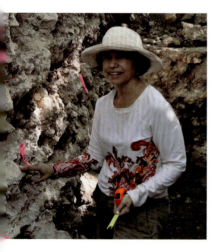

WHAT DO I RESEARCH AND HOW CAN IT MAKE A DIFFERENCE?   In the last ten years, I have been interested in how climate change—in this case, a long-term drought—played a role in the demise of the Classic Maya. In an area without permanent surface water, large and powerful centers relied on complex reservoir systems to supply water during the annual dry season, but long-term drought rapidly brought this to an end. Within several decades farmers in the southern Maya lowlands went back to living in small communities, or migrated in all directions. And this is where I can make a difference as an archaeologist—applying lessons from the past to current problems resulting from global climate change. I am involved in several organizations that bring together scholars focusing on issues of climate change and sustainability in the tropics. Our goals are twofold: avoid past missteps and highlight how ancient societies practiced sustainable ways of living.

Rasmi Shoocongdej: University Professor, Thailand

HOW I WAS INSPIRED TO BECOME AN ARCHAEOLOGIST. I initially thought about journalism as a career choice, but then became interested in archaeology. In my junior year at Silpakorn University, I wrote an article on Thai cultural heritage for a student newsletter, helped establish an archaeology club, and created a mobile exhibition on cultural heritage for schools in rural areas. These activities constituted a crucial turning point in my archaeological career: I was enjoying becoming a journalist of the past.

HOW I GOT MY FIRST JOB. In 1984, after working as a research assistant in the Archaeology Division of the Fine Arts Department at Silpakorn, I went to study at the University of Michigan; there was no graduate program in anthropological or prehistoric archaeology in Thailand. While studying at Michigan, I applied for a lectureship at Silpakorn University (one of the few teaching positions in Thailand), and returned to Thailand in 1987 to begin teaching archaeology.

WHAT DO I DO NOW? I am currently Associate Professor of Archaeology and Chair of the Department of Archaeology at Silpakorn University. I devote much of my time to students, aiming to develop their awareness of cultural heritage and a sense of responsibility to society, and to public campaigns for the conservation of Thai and other ethnic groups' heritages in Thailand. I am also engaged in a long-term project in highland Pang Mapha in northwestern Thailand, which began in 1998.

MY RESEARCH INTERESTS. My research focuses on understanding hunter-gatherer mobility organization, specifically of foragers of the late- to post-Pleistocene period (c. 32,000–10,000 BP) in the western border area of Thailand. Other interests include nationalism and archaeology, archaeology and multi-ethnic education, looting, and archaeology and the arts. My field experiences include projects in northern, western, central, and southern Thailand; Cambodia; the southwestern United States; and southeastern Turkey.

THE MOST REWARDING THING I HAVE DONE OR DISCOVERED. From the Pang Mapha project, two discoveries are highly significant (particularly as there are very few late Pleistocene sites currently known in Thailand): remains of the two oldest *Homo sapiens* found in northern Thailand (c. 13,000–12,000 BP), and the largest stone tool workshop in Thailand (c. 32,000–12,000 BP).

As I believe that the past can serve the present and the future, also rewarding is the part of the Pang Mapha project that has involved working closely with the local communities to help connect them to their

Rasmi Shoocongdej
Silpakorn University
Email: bangkokrasmi@su.ac.th

Rasmi Shoocongdej presenting the Pang Mapha project at a conference in France in 2006.

archaeological heritage, such as through art-related activities to present the history, beliefs, and meanings of the coffins that are still on site.

WHY BEING AN ARCHAEOLOGIST MATTERS TO ME AND HOW I MAKE A DIFFERENCE. I believe in searching for the truth of humankind, so I am fulfilling my dream to be a journalist of the past by doing archaeology. My search for indigenous and local archaeological knowledge and appropriate methodologies will enable me to develop an archaeology in my country that can contribute to "world archaeologies." I also hope that my work on heritage management with local communities will increase cooperation in fighting against the illegal antiquities trade and the destruction of archaeological sites.

Douglas C. Comer: CRM Archaeologist, USA

Douglas C. Comer
Cultural Site Research and Management, Baltimore
Email: dcomer@culturalsite.com
Website: www.culturalsite.com

HOW I WAS INSPIRED TO BECOME AN ARCHAEOLOGIST. I knew early on that I would be a scientist, and I was inspired to become an archaeologist not because of any strong interest in artifacts or history, but because I had a need to understand how I might be connected to other humans. In an anthropology course at Grand Valley State University, I was introduced to the work of Leslie White. He had huge ideas: culture was an extrasomatic adaptation to the environment; life was the process that counteracted the Second Law of Thermodynamics. He argued that these basic processes would be quantified as the field matured. To me, this suggested that by analyzing data, we would be able to isolate the factors that made us who we were.

HOW I GOT MY FIRST JOB. As I finished my master's degree in anthropology, the National Historic Preservation Act of 1966 was being implemented in earnest. I immediately found employment with the Colorado State Highway Department, first doing salvage archaeology. I was then loaned to the Forest Service to survey areas in the White River National Forest that were to be timbered. I had the opportunity to analyze and write up the results of some of these surveys, and on the strength of that found permanent employment with the National Park Service.

WHAT DO I DO NOW? I now run a CRM consulting firm, Cultural Site Research and Management (CSRM). I have always been convinced that the management of cultural resources should be based in scientific research and analysis, and in particular, in the collection of relevant data that can be quantified and analyzed in replicable ways. And, being a nerd, I have enthusiastically embraced geospatial analysis technologies as they have emerged. CSRM has been active in Southeast Asia, the Middle East, the United States, Africa, and Central and South America.

Douglas C. Comer in the field in Jordan, verifying the location of antiquities seen in satellite imagery.

MY RESEARCH INTERESTS. My research interests revolve around the ways in which humans utilize and structure space at all scales, including the site and the landscape. I would like to refine further the use of aerial and satellite remote-sensing technologies in archaeology and Cultural Resource Management. We cannot hope to protect archaeological resources until we know where they are.

THE MOST REWARDING THING I HAVE DONE OR DISCOVERED. Truthfully, everything that I have ever found on the ground or in aerial and satellite imagery has been interesting to me, but I'm particularly interested in the sorts of discoveries that suggest new avenues of research for archaeology.

WHY BEING AN ARCHAEOLOGIST MATTERS TO ME AND HOW I MAKE A DIFFERENCE. We live in a time in which information is far more readily available than at any time in the past. Yet while there is much more information that purports to be relevant to why people behave as they do, it has become increasingly difficult to differentiate fact from fantasy. Archaeology draws upon a reliable tradition of scholarship that includes rigorous documentation and verification procedures. As anthropologists, we know that human groups define themselves and set a course for the future by means of an imagined past. Archaeology deals with the material evidence of the past and a scientific analysis of it that can be used to bring our imaginings more in line with the realities of the world, and so make us better able to cope with those realities. It is intensely interesting and somewhat humbling to play a role in this.

Shadreck Chirikure: Archaeometallurgist, South Africa

HOW I WAS INSPIRED TO BECOME AN ARCHAEOLOGIST. If I had been asked fifteen years ago whether I wanted to become an archaeologist, I would have said "no!" My dream was to work in the finance industry. I entered into archaeology by pure chance. It all started with studying the degrees of BA General and BA Special Honours in Archaeology at the University of Zimbabwe between 1997 and 2001. We studied great civilizations, humanity's progress over time, and archaeology's potential to unlock development in host communities. In no time, I wanted to be part of this discipline that combined the thrill of discovery with learning and solving community problems.

In 2001, I was awarded a joint English Heritage and Institute for Archaeometallurgical Studies scholarship to study for an MA in Artifact Studies at University College London. I was already imagining how much I would have missed out if I had ended up in finance! At MA level, I started working in archaeometallurgy on preindustrial metal production in Africa. Generous grants enabled me to expand this research at PhD level.

Shadreck Chirikure
University of Cape Town
Email: Shadreck.Chirikure@uct.ac.za

Shadreck Chirikure in the Materials
Laboratory at the University of Cape Town.

HOW I GOT MY FIRST JOB.   On graduating with a PhD in Archaeology in 2005, I assumed a postdoctoral research position at the University of Cape Town's Department of Archaeology, becoming a lecturer in 2007. My main responsibilities include research, teaching, administration, and running the Materials Laboratory, which is Africa's only facility of its kind. The laboratory is dedicated to the study of preindustrial technologies in Africa, such as metalworking and ceramics. Our projects range from studying the technology of metal production to understanding the social context of the technology. I collaborate with leading researchers based overseas, and I have won awards for research papers and participated in award-winning documentaries.

THE MOST REWARDING THING I HAVE DONE OR DISCOVERED.   The success of my work in the Materials Laboratory led to my appointment as the head of a team of international experts working on the conservation and protection of the world-famous Oranjemund shipwreck discovered in Namibia in 2008. This sixteenth-century shipwreck contained large amounts of treasure: 28 kg (60 lb) of Spanish and Portuguese gold coins, 4 kg (9 lb) of Spanish and Portuguese silver coins, 20 tons of copper ingots, 6 tons of unworked elephant ivory, and many more artifacts together with the superstructure of the ship itself.

WHY BEING AN ARCHAEOLOGIST MATTERS TO ME.   From time to time, I write newspaper articles on archaeology and also feature on radio programs and in magazines discussing topical issues and careers in archaeology. Being an academic archaeologist allows me to contribute to national discourse through heritage protection programs, research programs, community learning, and heritage entrepreneurship projects.

Study Questions

1   What are some of the ways that humans damage or destroy archaeological sites?
2   In the United States, what are the key pieces of legislation that relate to archaeological protection, conservation, and mitigation?
3   What is Cultural Resource Management (CRM)? What percentage of archaeological work in the USA can be considered CRM?
4   Why is the publication of archaeological information so important?
5   How is archaeology relevant to today's world?

Summary

MANY NATIONS BELIEVE that it is the duty of the government to have policies with regard to conservation, and these conservation laws often apply to archaeology. Construction, agricultural intensification, tourism, and looting are all human activities that damage or destroy sites.

BUILT ON A STRONG LEGAL foundation, CRM or "applied archaeology" plays a major role in American archaeology. When a project is located on federal land, uses federal money, or needs a federal permit, the law requires that cultural resources are identified, evaluated, and if they cannot be avoided, addressed accordingly in an approved mitigation plan. A large number of private contract archaeology firms employ the majority of archaeologists in the US. These firms are responsible for meeting mitigation requirements, overseen by a lead agency and an SHPO. Publication of final reports is required, but the variable quality and usually limited dissemination of these reports remain a problem.

ARCHAEOLOGISTS HAVE A DUTY to report what they find. Since excavation is, to a certain extent, destructive, published material is often the only record of what was found at a site. Perhaps up to 60 percent of modern excavations remain unpublished after ten years. Governments and professional organizations are taking a harsher stance against archaeologists who do not publish and often will not grant digging permits to those who have unpublished work. The Internet and the popular media can help to fulfil one of the fundamental purposes of archaeology: to provide the public with a better understanding of the past.

Further Reading

The following works are useful introductions to heritage management:

Carman, J. 2002. *Archaeology and Heritage: An Introduction*. Continuum: London.

King, T. F. 2005. *Doing Archaeology: A Cultural Resource Management Perspective*. Left Coast Press: Walnut Creek, CA.

King, T. F. 2008. *Cultural Resource Laws and Practice: An Introductory Guide* (3rd ed.). Altamira Press: Walnut Creek, CA.

Sabloff, J. A. 2008. *Archaeology Matters: Action Archaeology in the Modern World*. Left Coast Press: Walnut Creek, CA.

Smith, L. & Waterton, E. 2009. *Heritage, Communities and Archaeology*. Duckworth: London.

Sørensen, M. L. S. & Carman, J. 2009. *Heritage Studies: Methods and Approaches*. Routledge: London.

Tyler, N., Ligibel, T. J., & Tyler, I. 2009. *Historic Preservation: An Introduction to Its History, Principles and Practice* (2nd ed.). W. W. Norton & Company: New York.

[See p. 345 for a list of useful websites]

Glossary

(Terms in *italics* are defined elsewhere in the glossary)

absolute dating The determination of age with reference to a specific timescale, such as a fixed calendrical system; also referred to as chronometric dating (*cf. relative dating*).

aerial survey An important technique, primarily employing aerial and satellite imagery, used in the discovery and recording of archaeological *sites* (see also *LIDAR* and *reconnaissance*).

alloying A technique that involves the mixing of two or more metals to create a new material, e.g. the fusion of copper and tin to make bronze.

ALS (Airborne Laser Scanning) See *LIDAR*.

annealing In copper and bronze metalworking, this refers to the repeated process of heating and hammering the material to produce the desired shape.

anthropology The study of humanity—our physical characteristics as animals, and the unique non-biological characteristics we call *culture*. The subject is generally broken down into three subdisciplines: *biological* (or physical) *anthropology*, *cultural* (or social) *anthropology*, and *archaeology*.

archaeobotany See *paleoethnobotany*.

archaeological culture A constantly recurring *assemblage* of *artifacts* assumed to be representative of a particular set of behavioral activities carried out at a particular time and place (*cf. culture*).

archaeology A subdiscipline of *anthropology* involving the study of the human past through its material remains.

archaeology of cult The study of the material indications of behavior undertaken in response to religious beliefs.

archaeomagnetic dating Sometimes referred to as paleomagnetic dating, this technique is based on the fact that changes in the earth's magnetic field over time can be recorded in such materials as baked clay structures (ovens, kilns, and hearths).

archaeozoology Sometimes referred to as zooarchaeology, this involves the identification and analysis of faunal species from archaeological *sites*, as an aid to the reconstruction of human diets and to an understanding of the contemporary environment at the time of deposition.

artifact Any portable object used, modified, or made by humans, e.g. stone tools, pottery, and metal weapons.

assemblage A group of *artifacts* recurring together at a particular time and place, and representing the sum of human activities.

association The co-occurrence of an *artifact* with other archaeological remains, usually in the same *matrix*.

attribute A minimal characteristic of an *artifact* such that it cannot be further subdivided; attributes commonly studied include aspects of form, *style*, decoration, color, and raw material.

Australopithecus A collective name for the earliest known *hominins* emerging about 5 million years ago in East Africa.

band A term used to describe small-scale societies of *hunter-gatherers*, generally fewer than 100 people, who move seasonally to exploit wild (undomesticated) food resources. Kinship ties play an important part in social organization.

bioarchaeology The study of human remains (but in Europe this term is sometimes applied to other kinds of organic remains, such as animal bones).

biological anthropology A subdiscipline of *anthropology* dealing with the study of human biological or physical characteristics and their *evolution*. It is also known as physical anthropology.

characterization The application of techniques of examination by which characteristic properties of the constituent material of traded goods can be identified, and thus their source of origin, e.g. *thin-section analysis*.

chiefdom A term used to describe a society that operates on the principle of ranking, i.e. differential social status. Different *lineages* are graded on a scale of prestige, calculated by how closely related one is to the chief. The chiefdom generally has a permanent ritual and ceremonial center, as well as being characterized by local specialization in crafts.

classification The ordering of phenomena into groups or other classificatory schemes on the basis of shared *attributes* (see also *type* and *typology*).

cognitive archaeology The study of past ways of thought and symbolic structures from material remains.

cognitive map An interpretive framework of the world that, it is argued, exists in the human mind and affects actions and decisions as well as knowledge structures.

cognitive-processual approach An alternative to the materialist orientation of the functional-processual approach, it is concerned with (1) the integration of the cognitive and symbolic with other aspects of early societies; and (2) the role of ideology as an active organizational force.

Computed Tomography (CT) scanning The method by which scanners allow detailed internal views of bodies, such as mummies. The body is passed into the machine and images of cross-sectional "slices" through the body are produced.

conjoining See *refitting*.

context An *artifact's* context usually consists of its immediate *matrix* (the material around it, e.g. gravel, clay, or sand), its *provenience* (horizontal and vertical position in the *matrix*), and its *association* with other *artifacts* (with other archaeological remains, usually in the same *matrix*).

contract archaeology Archaeological research conducted under the terms of federal or state legislation, often in advance of highway construction or urban development, where the archaeologist is contracted to undertake the necessary research.

coprolites Fossilized feces; these contain food residues that can be used to reconstruct diet and subsistence activities.

core A lithic *artifact* used as a blank from which other tools or flakes are made.

Critical Theory A theoretical approach developed by the so-called "Frankfurt School" of German social thinkers, which stresses that all knowledge is historical, and in a sense biased communication; thus, all claims to "objective" knowledge are illusory.

cultural anthropology A subdiscipline of *anthropology* concerned with the non-biological, behavioral aspects of society, i.e. the social, linguistic, and technological components underlying human behavior. Two important branches of cultural anthropology are *ethnography* (the study of living *cultures*) and ethnology (which attempts to compare *cultures* using ethnographic evidence). In Europe, it is referred to as social anthropology.

cultural ecology A term devised by Julian Steward to account for the dynamic relationship between human society and its environment, in which *culture* is viewed as the primary adaptive mechanism.

Cultural Resource Management (CRM) The safeguarding of the archaeological heritage through the protection of *sites* and through *salvage archaeology*, generally within the framework of legislation.

culture A term used by anthropologists when referring to the non-biological

characteristics unique to a particular society (*cf. archaeological culture*).

culture-historical approach An approach to archaeological interpretation that uses the procedure of the traditional historian (including emphasis on specific circumstances elaborated with rich detail, and processes of *induction*).

deduction A process of reasoning by which more specific consequences are inferred by rigorous argument from more general propositions (*cf. induction*).

deep-sea cores Cores drilled from the sea bed that provide the most coherent record of climatic changes on a global scale. The cores contain shells of microscopic marine organisms (foraminifera) laid down on the ocean floor through the continuous process of sedimentation. Variations in the ratio of two oxygen isotopes in the calcium carbonate of these shells give a sensitive indicator of sea temperature at the time the organisms were alive.

dendrochronology The study of tree-ring patterns; annual variations in climatic conditions that produce differential growth can be used both as a measure of environmental change, and as the basis for a chronology.

diatom analysis A method of environmental reconstruction based on plant microfossils. Diatoms are unicellular algae, whose silica cell walls survive after the algae die, and they accumulate in large numbers at the bottom of rivers and lakes. *Assemblages* directly reflect the composition of the water's extinct floral communities, as well as the water's salinity, alkalinity, and nutrient status.

diffusionist explanation The theory (popularized by V.G. Childe) that all aspects of civilization, from architecture to metalworking, diffused from the Near East to Europe.

DNA (deoxyribonucleic acid) The material that carries the hereditary instructions (the "blueprint") that determine the formation of all living organisms.

earth resistance survey A method of *subsurface detection* that measures changes in conductivity by passing an electrical current through ground soils using a resistivity meter. These changes are generally caused by moisture content, and in this way, buried *features* can be detected by differential retention of groundwater.

ecofacts Non-artifactual organic and environmental remains that have cultural relevance, e.g. faunal and floral material, as well as soils and sediments.

electrolysis A standard cleaning process in archaeological conservation. *Artifacts* are placed in a chemical solution, and by passing a weak current between them and a surrounding metal grill, the corrosive salts move from the cathode (object) to the anode (grill), removing any accumulated deposit and leaving the *artifact* clean.

electron spin resonance (ESR) This technique enables trapped electrons within bone and shell fragments to be measured without the heating that *thermoluminescence (TL) dating* requires. As with *TL* dating, the number of trapped electrons indicates the age of the specimen.

environmental circumscription An explanation for the origins of the *state* propounded by Robert Carneiro that emphasizes the fundamental role exerted by environmental constraints and territorial limitations.

ethnicity The existence of ethnic groups, including tribal groups. Though these are difficult to recognize from the archaeological record, the study of language and linguistic boundaries shows that ethnic groups often correlate with language areas.

ethnoarchaeology The study of contemporary *cultures* with a view to understanding the behavioral relationships that underlie the production of *material culture*.

ethnography A subset of *cultural anthropology* concerned with the study of contemporary *cultures* through first-hand observation.

evolution The process of growth and development generally accompanied by increasing complexity. In biology, this change is tied to Darwin's concept of natural selection as the basis of species survival. Darwin's work laid the foundations for the study of *artifact typology*, pioneered by such scholars as Pitt-Rivers.

evolutionary archaeology The idea that the processes responsible for biological *evolution* also drive *culture* change, i.e. the application of Darwinian evolutionary theory to the archaeological record.

excavation The principal method of data acquisition in *archaeology*, involving the systematic uncovering of archaeological remains through the removal of soil deposits, and other material covering and accompanying them.

experimental archaeology The study of past behavioral processes through experimental reconstruction under carefully controlled scientific conditions.

fall-off analysis The study of the way in which quantities of traded items found in the archaeological record decline as the distance from the source increases. This may be plotted as a fall-off curve, with quantities of material (y-axis) plotted against distance from source (x-axis).

feature A non-portable *artifact*, e.g. hearths, architectural elements, or soil stains.

fission-track dating A dating method based on the operation of a radioactive clock, the spontaneous fission of an isotope of uranium present in a wide range of rocks and minerals. As with *potassium-argon dating*, with which its time range overlaps, the method gives useful dates from rocks adjacent to archaeological material.

flotation A method of screening (sieving) an excavated *matrix* in water so as to separate and recover small *ecofacts* and *artifacts*.

fluxgate magnetometer A type of magnetometer used in *subsurface detection*, producing a continuous reading.

formation processes The processes affecting the way in which archaeological materials come to be buried, and their subsequent history afterward. Cultural formation processes include the deliberate or accidental activities of humans; natural formation processes refer to the natural or environmental events that govern burial and survival.

frequency seriation A *relative dating* method that relies principally on measuring changes in the proportional abundance, or frequency, observed among finds (e.g. counts of tool *types*, or of ceramic fabrics).

functional-processual archaeology See *processual archaeology*.

Geographic Information Systems (GIS) GIS are software-based systems designed for the collection, organization, storage, retrieval, analysis, and display of spatial and digital geographical data held in different "layers." A GIS can also include other digital data.

geomagnetic reversals An aspect of archaeomagnetism relevant to the dating of the Lower Paleolithic, involving complete reversals in the Earth's magnetic field.

ground survey The collective name for a wide variety of methods for identifying individual archaeological *sites*, including consultation of documentary sources, place-name evidence, local folklore, and legend, but primarily actual fieldwork.

half-life The time taken for half the quantity of a radioactive isotope in a sample to decay (see also *radioactive decay*).

hand-axe A *Paleolithic* stone tool usually made by modifying (chipping or flaking) a natural pebble.

hoards Deliberately buried groups of valuables or prized possessions, often in times of conflict or war, and that,for one reason or another, have not been reclaimed. Metal hoards are a primary source of evidence for the Bronze Age in Europe.

hominins The subfamily to which humans belong, as opposed to the "hominids," which include not only humans but also gorillas and chimps, and "hominoids," which group these along with gibbons and orangutans.

hunter-gatherers A collective term for the members of small-scale mobile or semi-sedentary societies, whose subsistence is mainly focused on hunting game, and gathering wild plants and fruits; organizational structure is based on *bands* with strong kinship ties.

ice cores Borings taken from the Arctic and Antarctic polar ice caps, containing layers of compacted ice useful for reconstructing paleoenvironments and as a method of *absolute dating*.

iconography An important component of *cognitive archaeology* involving the study of artistic representations that usually have an overt religious or ceremonial significance, e.g. individual deities may be distinguished with a special characteristic, the sun with a sun goddess.

induction A method of reasoning in which one proceeds by generalization from a series of specific observations so as to derive general conclusions (*cf. deduction*).

interaction sphere A regional or inter-regional exchange system.

isotopic analysis An important source of information for the reconstruction of prehistoric diets, this technique analyzes the ratios of the principal isotopes preserved in human bone; the method "reads" the chemical signatures left in the body by different foods. Isotopic analysis is also used in *characterization* studies.

landscape archaeology The study of individual *features*, including settlements, seen as single components within the broader perspective of the patterning of human activity over a wide area.

LIDAR (Light Detection and Ranging) A *remote-sensing* technique using the same principle as radar. Light is transmitted to a target, some of which is reflected back to the instrument. The time that the light takes to travel to the target and back is used to determine the range to the target.

lineage A group claiming descent from a common ancestor.

Marxist archaeology Based principally on the writings of Karl Marx, this posits a materialist model of societal change. Change within a society is seen as the result of contradictions arising between the forces of production (technology) and the relations of production (social organization). Such contradictions are seen to emerge as a struggle between distinct social classes.

material culture The buildings, tools, and other *artifacts* that constitute the material remains of former societies.

matrix The physical material within which *artifacts* are embedded or supported, e.g. gravel, clay, or sand.

Mesolithic An Old World chronological period beginning around 10,000 years ago, between the *Paleolithic* and the *Neolithic*.

metallographic examination A technique used in the study of early metallurgy involving the microscopic examination of a polished section cut from an *artifact*, which has been etched so as to reveal the metal structure.

microwear analysis The study of the patterns of wear or damage on the edge of stone tools, which provides valuable information on the way in which the tool was used.

Midwestern Taxonomic System A framework devised by W.C. McKern to systematize sequences in the Great Plains area of the United States, using the general principle of similarities between *artifact assemblages*.

monocausal explanation Explanations of *culture* change (e.g. for *state* origins) that lay stress on a single dominant explanatory factor or "prime mover."

multivariate explanation Explanations of *culture* change (e.g. the origin of the *state*) that, in contrast to *monocausal explanations*, stress the interaction of several factors operating simultaneously.

Neolithic An Old World chronological period characterized by the development of agriculture and, hence, an increasing emphasis on sedentism.

Neolithic Revolution A term coined by V.G. Childe to describe the origin and consequences of farming, allowing the widespread development of settled village life.

New Archaeology A new approach advocated in the 1960s that argued for an explicitly scientific framework of archaeological method and theory, with hypotheses rigorously tested, as the proper basis for explanation, rather than simply description (see also *processual archaeology*).

non-site evidence See *off-site evidence*.

obsidian A volcanic glass, the ease of working and characteristic hard flint-like edges of which allowed it to be used for the making of tools.

off-site evidence Data from a range of information, including scatters of such *artifacts* and *features* as plowmarks and field boundaries, that provide important evidence about human exploitation of the environment.

Oldowan industry The earliest toolkits, comprising flake and pebble tools, used by *hominins* in the Olduvai Gorge, Tanzania.

open-area excavation The opening up of large horizontal areas for *excavation*, used especially where single-period deposits lie close to the surface as, for example, with the remains of Native American or European *Neolithic* long houses.

paleoentomology The study of insects from archaeological *contexts*. The survival of insect exoskeletons, which are quite resistant to decomposition, is important in the reconstruction of paleoenvironments.

paleoethnobotany Also referred to as archaeobotany, the recovery and identification of plant remains from archaeological *contexts*, used in reconstructing past environments and economies.

Paleolithic The archaeological period before c. 10,000 BCE, characterized by the earliest known stone tool manufacture.

paleomagnetic dating See *archaeomagnetic dating*.

palynology The study and analysis of fossil pollen as an aid to the reconstruction of past vegetation and climates.

physical anthropology See *biological anthropology*.

pollen analysis See *palynology*.

postprocessual archaeology A range of approaches formulated in reaction to the perceived limitations of *functional-processual archaeology*. It eschews generalization in favor of an "individualizing" approach that is influenced by *structuralist archaeology*, *Critical Theory*, and neo-Marxist thought.

potassium-argon dating A method used to date rocks up to thousands of millions of years old, though it is restricted to volcanic material no more recent than c. 100,000 years old. One of the most widely used methods in the dating of early hominid *sites* in Africa.

prehistory The period of human history before the advent of writing.

prestige goods A term used to designate a limited range of exchange goods to which a society ascribes high status or value.

processual archaeology An approach that stresses the dynamic relationship between social and economic aspects of *culture* and the environment as the basis for understanding the processes of *culture* change. It uses the scientific methodology of problem statement, hypothesis formulation, and subsequent testing. The earlier functional-processual approach has been contrasted with the *cognitive-processual approach*, where emphasis is placed on integrating ideological and symbolic aspects.

provenience The place of origin or (earliest) known history of something; also the horizontal and vertical position of an *artifact, ecofact* or *feature* within a *matrix*.

pseudoarchaeology The use of selective archaeological evidence to put forward nonscientific, fictional accounts of the past.

pyrotechnology The intentional use and control of fire by humans.

radioactive decay The regular process by which radioactive isotopes break down into their decay products with a *half-life* that is specific to the isotope in question (see also *radiocarbon dating*).

radiocarbon dating An *absolute dating* method that measures the decay of the radioactive isotope of carbon (^{14}C) in organic material (see also *half-life*).

reciprocity A mode of exchange in which transactions take place between individuals who are symmetrically placed, i.e. they are exchanging as equals, with neither being in a dominant position.

reconnaissance A broad range of techniques involved in the location of archaeological *sites*, e.g. the recording of surface *artifacts* and *features*, and the sampling of natural and mineral resources.

redistribution A mode of exchange that implies the operation of some central organizing authority. Goods are received or appropriated by the central authority, and subsequently some of them are sent by that authority to other locations.

refitting Sometimes referred to as conjoining, this entails attempting to put stone tools and flakes back together again, and provides important information on the processes involved in the knapper's craft.

relative dating The determination of chronological sequence without recourse to a fixed time scale, e.g. the arrangement of *artifacts* in a typological sequence, or *seriation* (cf. *absolute dating*).

religion A framework of beliefs relating to supernatural or superhuman beings,

or forces that transcend the everyday material world.

remote sensing The imaging of phenomena from a distance, primarily through airborne and satellite imaging. "Ground-based remote sensing" links geophysical methods, such as radar, with remote sensing methods applied at ground level.

rescue archaeology See *salvage archaeology*.

research design The systematic planning of archaeological research, usually including (1) the formulation of a strategy to resolve a particular question; (2) the collection and recording of evidence; (3) the processing and analysis of these data and their interpretation; and (4) the publication of results.

resistivity meter See *earth resistance survey*.

salvage archaeology Also referred to as rescue archaeology, the location and recording (usually through *excavation*) of archaeological *sites* in advance of highway construction, drainage projects, or urban development.

segmentary societies Relatively small and autonomous groups, usually of agriculturalists, who regulate their own affairs; in some cases, they may join together with other comparable segmentary societies to form a larger ethnic unit.

seriation A *relative dating* technique based on the chronological ordering of a group of *artifacts* or *assemblages*, where the most similar are placed adjacent to each other in the series (see also *frequency seriation*).

side-scan sonar A survey method used in *underwater survey* that provides the broadest view of the sea-floor. An acoustic emitter is towed behind a vessel and sends out sound waves in a fan-shaped beam. These pulses of sonic energy are reflected back to a transducer—the return time depending on the distance traveled—and recorded on a rotating drum.

simple random sampling A type of sampling where the areas to be sampled are chosen using a table of random numbers. Drawbacks include (1) defining the site's boundaries initially; and (2) the nature of random number tables results in some areas being allotted clusters of sample squares, while others remain untouched.

site A distinct spatial clustering of *artifacts, features*, structures, and organic and environmental remains—the residue of human activity.

social anthropology See *cultural anthropology*.

soil resistivity See *earth resistance survey*.

state A social formation defined by distinct territorial boundedness, and characterized by strong central government in which the operation of political power is sanctioned by legitimate force. In cultural evolutionist models, it ranks second only to the empire as the most complex societal development stage.

stela A free-standing carved stone monument.

step-trenching An *excavation* method used on very deep *sites*, such as at Near Eastern *tells*, in which the *excavation* proceeds downward in a series of gradually narrowing steps.

stratification The laying down or deposition of strata or layers (also called deposits) one above the other. A succession of layers should provide a relative chronological sequence, with the earliest at the bottom and the latest at the top.

stratified random sampling A form of sampling in which the region or *site* is divided into natural zones or strata, such as cultivated land and forest; units are then chosen by a random number procedure so as to give each zone a number of squares proportional to its area, thus overcoming the inherent bias in simple random sampling.

stratified systematic sampling A form of sampling that combines elements of (1) *simple random sampling*, (2) *stratified random sampling*, and (3) *systematic sampling*, in an effort to reduce bias.

stratigraphy The study and validation of *stratification*: the analysis in the vertical, time dimension, of a series of layers in the horizontal, space dimension. It is often used as a *relative dating* technique to assess the temporal sequence of *artifact* deposition.

structuralist archaeology An interpretation that stresses that human actions are guided by beliefs and symbolic concepts, and that underlying these are structures of thought that find expression in various forms. The proper object of study is therefore to uncover structures of thought and to study their influence in shaping ideas in the minds of the human actors who created the archaeological record.

style According to the art historian E.H. Gombrich, style is "any distinctive and therefore recognizable way in which an act is performed and made." Archaeologists and anthropologists have defined "stylistic areas" as units representing shared ways of producing and decorating *artifacts*.

subsurface detection The collective name for a variety of *remote-sensing* techniques operating at ground level, and including both invasive and non-invasive techniques.

surface survey There are two basic kinds that can be identified: unsystematic and systematic. The former involves field-walking, i.e. scanning the ground along one's path and recording the location of *artifacts* and surface *features*. Systematic survey by comparison is less subjective and involves a grid system, such that the survey area is divided into sectors and these are walked systematically, thus making the recording of finds ore accurate.

symbol The representation (by word or visual image) of an idea or concept. The capacity to use symbols is a defining aspect of human cognition.

systematic survey See *surface survey*.

systematic sampling A form of sampling employing a grid of equally spaced locations; e.g. selecting every other square. This method of regular spacing runs the risk of missing (or hitting) every single example if the distribution itself is regularly spaced.

taphonomy The study of processes that have affected organic materials, such as bone after death; it also involves the microscopic analysis of tooth marks or cutmarks to assess the effects of butchery or scavenging activities.

tell A Near Eastern term that refers to a mound *site* formed through successive human occupation over a long timespan.

temper Inclusions in pottery clay that act as a filler to give the clay added strength and workability, and to counteract any cracking or shrinkage during firing.

thermoluminescence (TL) dating A technique that relies indirectly on *radioactive decay*, overlapping with *radiocarbon dating* in the time period for which it is useful, but also has the potential for dating earlier periods. It has much in common with *electron spin resonance (ESR)*.

thin-section analysis A technique whereby microscopic thin sections are cut from a stone object or potsherd and examined with a petrological microscope to determine the source of the material.

Three Age System A *classification* system devised by C.J. Thomsen for the sequence of technological periods (the Stone Age, the Bronze Age, and the Iron Age) in Old World *prehistory*. It established the principle that by classifying *artifacts*, one could produce a chronological ordering.

total station An optical, electronic instrument used in surveying and to record *excavations*.

trace-element analysis The use of chemical techniques for determining the incidence of trace elements in rocks. These methods are widely used in the identification of raw material sources for the production of stone tools.

tree-ring dating See *dendrochronology*.

tribes A term used to describe a social grouping generally larger than a *band*, but rarely numbering more than a few thousand; unlike *bands*, tribes are usually settled farmers, though they also include nomadic pastoral groups whose economy is based on the exploitation of livestock. Individual communities tend to be integrated into the larger society through kinship ties.

type A class of *artifacts* defined by the consistent clustering of *attributes*.

typology The systematic organization of *artifacts* into *types* on the basis of shared *attributes*.

underwater survey Geophysical methods of underwater survey include (1) a proton magnetometer towed behind a survey vessel, to detect iron and steel objects that distort the Earth's magnetic field; (2) *side-scan sonar* that transmits sound waves in a fan-shaped beam to produce a graphic image of surface *features* on the seabed; and (3) a sub-bottom profiler that emits sound pulses that bounce back from buried *features* and objects.

uniformitarianism The principle that the *stratification* of rocks is due to processes still going on in seas, rivers, and lakes, i.e. that geologically ancient conditions were in essence similar to, or "uniform with," those of our own time.

uranium-series dating A dating method based on the *radioactive decay* of isotopes of uranium. It has proved particularly useful for the period before 50,000 years ago, which lies outside the time range of *radiocarbon dating*.

varves Fine layers of alluvium sediment deposited in glacial lakes. Their annual deposition makes them a useful source of dating.

Wheeler box-grid An *excavation* technique developed by Sir Mortimer Wheeler that involves retaining intact baulks of earth between *excavation* grid squares, so that different layers can be correlated across the *site* in vertical profiles.

zooarchaeology See *archaeozoology*.

Illustration Credits

Abbreviations: a=above, b=below, l=left, c=center, r=right

(Unless otherwise indicated, coloring of illustrations for this edition was undertaken by Drazen Tomic and Ben Plumridge.)

10 St. Louis Art Museum, Eliza McMillan Fund; 12a Museum of London Archaeology Service; 12bl Çatalhöyük Research Project, Cambridge; 12br David Anderson; 13a Franck Goddio/Hilti Foundation, photo Christophe Gerigk; 13bl Johan Reinhard; 13cr Kenneth Garrett; 13br Sergio Azenha/Alamy; 17 O. Louis Mazzatenta/National Geographic/Getty Images; 19a Wiltshire Heritage Museum, Devizes; 19b Private Collection/Archives Charmet/Bridgeman Art Library; 21 F. Catherwood, *Views of Ancient Monuments in Central America, Chiapas and Yucatán*, London 1844; 22a A. Pitt-Rivers, *Excavations in Cranborne Chase*, 1893–1898; 23a Petrie Museum of Egyptian Archaeology, University of London; 23br Archaeological Survey of India; 24ac Jericho Exploration Fund; 24cl Museo Nacional de Antropologia, Arqueologia e Historia, Lima, Peru; 24bl Courtesy the Peabody Museum of Archaeology and Ethnology, Harvard University; 25 The Royal Commission on Ancient and Historical Monuments of Scotland; 28 Ray Smith; 34bl Courtesy Mrs Mary Allsebrook, Oxford; 34bc The Council for British Archaeology; 34ar The Principal and Fellows of Newnham College, Cambridge; 35al University of Colorado Museum of Natural History, Boulder; 35ac Courtesy the Peabody Museum of Archaeology and Ethnology, Harvard University; 35ar John Reader/Science Photo Library; 38 Drimi/Shutterstock.com; 40–41 ML Design (after A. Sherratt (ed.) *Cambridge Encyclopedia of Archaeology*, 1980, fig. 20.5); 44 John Sibbick; 45 Sue Cawood; 46 Annick Boothe (adapted from W. Rathje & M. Schiffer, *Archaeology* 1982, fig. 4.11); 49 Fototeka Hrvatskoga restauratorskog zavoda and Robert Sténuit; 52ar Sandro Vannini/Corbis; 52cl Egyptian Museum, Cairo; 52b Drazen Tomic (after Ian Bott); 53 After Rudenko; 54a South Tyrol Museum of Archaeology, Bolzano/Wolfgang Neeb/Bridgeman Art Library; 54b Vienna Report Agency/Sygma/Corbis; 55 Drazen Tomic (after Tracy Wellman); 56 Johan Reinhard; 57 Jada Images/Alamy; 58 Ruth Kirk; 59 National Museum of Ireland, Dublin; 62 Nick Card; 64 best-photo/istockphoto.com; 65 Wolfgang Kaehler/Corbis; 69 Annick Boothe (after Flannery (ed.) 1976); 70 Photos Shannon P. McPherron; 71a Annick Boothe (after Connah & Jones, in Connah 1983, p. 77); 71b Timothy E. Black; 73a Annick Boothe (after Oxford Archaeological Unit); 73b Rog Palmer; 75 Crown Copyright, Forestry Commission; 76a © Marty Sedluk; 76b Courtesy John Weishampel, Caracol Archaeological Project; 77l USGS; 78 Courtesy USGS and Jason Ur; 79 NASA; 80 Drazen Tomic (after Tracy Wellman); 81a © 2016 Ancient Egypt Research Associates. Photo Mark Lehner; 81b © 2016 Ancient Egypt Research Associates. Illustration Rebekah Miracle; 83a René Millon; 83b OGphoto/istockphoto.com; 85 Mandy Mottram; 88 Courtesy Dean Goodman, Geophysical Archaeometry Laboratory, University of Miami, Japan Division; 90a Abingdon Archaeological Geophysics; 90b GSB, Bradford; 92 Drazen Tomic (after M. Carver, *Underneath English Towns* 1987, fig. 2); 94–95 Photos Jamestown Rediscovery, courtesy William M. Kelso; 97l Robin Coningham; 97r Center for American Archaeology, Kampsville Archaeological Center; 98 Museum of London Archaeology Service; 99 Images courtesy Jeroen de Reu, Department of Archaeology, Ghent University; 100 Chris Ratcliffe/Getty Images; 101a Annick Boothe (after *The Courier*, Unesco Nov. 1987, p. 16, drawing by M. Redknap); 101b Annick Boothe (after *National Geographic*, supplement Jan. 1990); 102 Courtesy Robert Grenier; 104 Annick Boothe (after J. Deetz, *Invitation to Archaeology*, Natural

History Press/Doubleday & Co., New York 1967); 107 captureandcompose/Shutterstock.com; 111 Wheeler, *Ancient India*, 3 Jan. 1947; 112 Annick Boothe; 113 Annick Boothe (after Rathje & Schiffer, *Archaeology* 1982, fig. 4.17); 114l ML Design; 114r Kevin Fleming/Corbis; 115 E.R. Degginger/Science Photo Library; 118 Corpus of Maya Hieroglyphic Inscriptions and Gordon R. Willey Laboratory for Mesoamerican Studies, Peabody Museum of Archaeology and Ethnology, Harvard University; 120 Michael Worthington, Oxford Tree-Ring Laboratory; 121 Simon S.S. Driver (information from Bannister & Smiley in *Geochronology*, Tucson 1955); 123 Annick Boothe (123bl after Hedges & Gowlett in *Scientific American* 254 (1), Jan. 1986, p. 84); 124 Annick Boothe; 126–27 Courtesy Tom Higham; 128 David Hurst Thomas & the American Museum of Natural History; 129 P. Deliss/Godong/Corbis; 130 Dr Andrew Carter; 131 Javier Trueba/Madrid Scientific Films; 134 Drazen Tomic (adapted from Stringer & Andrews 2011, pp. 12–13); 135a Brett Eloff courtesy Lee R. Berger and the University of the Witwatersrand; 135b John Sibbick; 136–37 Simon S.S. Driver (with amendments by Drazen Tomic); 139al Michael S. Yamashita/Corbis; 137ar Irmgard Groth Kimball; 139cl Photo Heidi Grassley © Thames & Hudson Ltd., London; 139cr Interfoto/Alamy; 139bl Walter Wust; 142 Cameris/Shutterstock.com; 149 Annick Boothe (after Johnson 1972); 151 Tracy Wellman (after Isaac); 152 Robert Foley; 153 From B. Fagan, *In the Beginning* (6th ed.) 1988, fig. 16.4 (after Winter in Flannery (ed.) 1976, fig. 2.17); 154a Courtesy Scott W. Hammerstedt; 154b Courtesy James A. Brown; 155al Sam Noble, Oklahoma Museum of Natural History, University of Oklahoma; 155ar, 155b Werner Forman/Universal Images Group/Getty Images; 158 Charles Higham; 159 Dmitry Rukhlenko/istockphoto.com; 160a Simon S.S. Driver (after Renfrew); 160b Jeremy Walker/Alamy; 161b Bryan Busovicki/istockphoto.com; 162 Paolo Mattiae/Alamy; 163 Gary Urton; 164a British Museum, London; 164bl Musée du Louvre, Paris; 165 Nigel Pavitt/JAI/Corbis; 166l Lewis Binford; 166br Peter Johnson/Corbis; 168 John Milner Associates; 169 Chester Higgins; 170 Courtesy Landesdenkmalamt Baden-Württemberg-Archäologische Denkmalpflege; 171l From Gimbutas 1974, p. 163, drawing by Linda Mount-Williams; 171r Caroline Malone and Simon Stoddart (courtesy National Museum of Archaeology, Malta); 173l Musée du Pays Châtillonnais—Trésor de Vix, Châtillon sur Seine, Côte d'Or, France; 173r The Art Archive/Alamy; 175 Jurate Buiviene/Shutterstock.com; 178a Lucy Maw; 182l David Scharf/Science Photo Library; 182r Annick Boothe (after Scarre (ed.) 1988, p.107); 183 Philip Winton (after Piperno and Ciochon, *New Scientist* 10/11/90); 184 Philip Winton; 186 Janette Deacon; 188 After A. Marshack, *The Roots of Civilization* 1972, fig. 78b; 190 Institute of Archaeology, Chinese Academy of Social Sciences, Beijing; 193 Annick Boothe (after J. Greig, Plant Foods in the Past, *J. of Plant Foods* 5 1983, 179–214); 195 After Mangelsdorf; 196 akg-images; 198a Pat Shipman and Richard Potts; 198b Photo Curtis Marean © Dikika Research Project; 200–1 Thomas F. Kehoe; 203 British Museum, London; 206 After Vinther et al., *Quaternary Science Reviews* 29(3), 522–38; 208 County Museum, Gotland; 210 Peter Bellwood; 211 Annick Boothe; 212a Drazen Tomic (after Bruce Bradley); 212b Béatrice Schmider; 214a Ingenui/Shutterstock.com; 216 Erich Lessing/akg-images; 218 Kenneth Garrett; 219al Kunsthistorisches Museum, Vienna; 219ar Palace Museum, Beijing; 219cl British Museum, London; 219cr Zaraysk Kremlin Museum, Moscow; 219bl Ohio Historical Society, Columbus; 219bc Werner Forman Archive; 219br National Archaeological Museum, Athens; 223l ML Design (after Peacock 1982, fig. 80); 225 ML Design (after Renfrew); 227 Annick Boothe (after Pires-Ferreira in Flannery (ed.) 1976, fig. 10.16); 228a George Bass/Cemal Pulak, Institute of Nautical Archaeology, Texas; 228b ML

Design (after Bass); 229 George Bass/Cemal Pulak, Institute of Nautical Archaeology, Texas; 232 Tim Graham/Alamy; 233 Jonathan Blair/Corbis; 234 Annick Boothe; 235al Archäologisches Landesmuseum, Schloss Gottorf, Schleswig; 235ar Çatalhöyük Research Project, Cambridge; 235bl The Sutton Hoo Society; 236, 237 Forhistorisk Museum, Moesgård; 238a Annick Boothe (after Brothwell 1981, fig. 3.4); 238b Tracy Wellman (after Houghton 1980); 240cl British Museum, London; 240bl Antti Korpisaari; 240bc Elizabeth Daynès/National Geographic Image Collection; 240br Griffith Institute, Ashmolean Museum, Oxford; 241 British Museum, London; 242 Jacopin/Science Photo Library; 245 Oriental Institute, University of Chicago; 246a Illustration Aman Phull © Thames & Hudson Ltd., London; 246b Gavin Fogg/AFP/Getty Images; 247l 3LH/SuperStock; 247r Justin Tallis/AFP/Getty Images; 248 Photo Services des Antiquités de l'Egypte; 250 Javier Trueba/MSF/Science Photo Library; 252, 256 Kenneth Garrett; 257a Wim Lustenhouwer, VU University Amsterdam; 257b Reproduced by permission of Chris Henshilwood, African Heritage Research Institute, Cape Town, South Africa; 258bl Ministère de la culture et de la communication, Direction régionale des affaires culturelles de Rhone-Alpes, Service régionale de l'archéologie; 258br Anonymous/AP/PA Photos; 259ac Musée d'Archéologie Nationale, Saint-Germain-en-Laye; 259al, 259c Pablo Aries and Sergey Lev; 259ar Natural History Museum, London; 259br G. Dagli Orti/DeAgostini/Diomedia; 261l Henry Chaplin/istockphoto.com; 261r Philip Winton; 263l Annick Boothe; 263r Lucy Maw (after Mellaart); 264 Annick Boothe (after O'Kelly); 266 British Museum, London; 267 Musée des Antiquités Nationales, St. Germain-en-Laye; 269l Annick Boothe; 269ar Annick Boothe (after Burger); 269b Museo de Chavin de Huantar, Ancash, Peru; 270, 271 DAI, Photo Nico Becker; 272 ML Design; 273 Photo Scala, Florence; 276 E.Q. Roy/Shutterstock.com; 280a Annick Boothe (after Kirch); 280b Annick Boothe (after Gelb); 281c Colin Hoskins/Alamy; 281b ML Design (after Garlake); 283 akg-images; 290 Craig Chiasson/istockphoto.com; 297 Sviluppo/Shutterstock.com; 299a Courtesy Serbian Stamps Shop, Belgrade; 299b Hellenic Ministry of Culture and Tourism; 300a Jean-Claude Chapon/AFP/Getty Images; 300b Saeed Khan/AFP/Getty Images; 301 Joseph Eid/AFP/Getty Images; 302 Robert Harding Picture Library/Alamy; 304 Hiroshi Kasiwara; 305a British Museum, London; 305b Peter Eastland/Alamy; 307 Paul Bahn; 308 Emmanuel Laurent/Eurelios/Science Photo Library; 312 Antalya Museum and Museum of Fine Arts, Boston; 313 By courtesy of the Trustee of the Marquess of Northampton 1987 Settlement; 314 British Museum, London; 316 Andy Myatt/Alamy; 318a National Museum, Baghdad; 318b Marc Deville/Gamma-Rapho/Getty Images; 319 STR/AFP/Getty Images; 322cl National Geographic Image Collection/Alamy; 322ar, 322br Courtesy Great Temple Project, Mexico City; 323 Eduardo Verdugo/AP/PA Photos; 326, 327 Courtesy Archaeological Consulting Services, Ltd., Tempe, Arizona; 328al David Adamec; 328ar Kirill Trifonov/istockphoto.com; 328cl Jon Arnold Images/Alamy; 328cr Nickolay Stanev/istockphoto.com; 328bl Dmitry Rukhlenko/istockphoto.com; 328br Robert Harding Picture Library/Alamy; 332 Courtesy Lisa J. Lucero; 333 Courtesy Rasmi Shoocongdej; 334 Courtesy Douglas C. Comer; 336 Courtesy Shadreck Chirikure.

All locator maps: Ben Plumridge © Thames & Hudson Ltd, London.

Text credits
The following serves as an extension of the information on page 4. The textual contributions below are copyright © Thames & Hudson Ltd, London: pp. 94–95 and 331–36.

Useful Websites

Wikipedia archaeology portal
    http://en.wikipedia.org/wiki/Portal:Archaeology
Archaeology newsletter: Explorator
    https://groups.yahoo.com/group/Explorator/

Organizations and Societies:

Archaeological Institute of America
    http://www.archaeological.org/
Canadian Archaeological Association
    http://www.canadianarchaeology.com/
Society for American Archaeology
    http://www.saa.org/
American Anthropological Association
    http://www.aaanet.org/
Society for Historical Archaeology
    http://www.sha.org/
Biblical Archaeology Society
    https://www.biblicalarchaeology.org/
Association for Environmental Archaeology
    http://www.envarch.net/
World Archaeological Congress
    http://www.worldarchaeologicalcongress.org/
Society for Archaeological Sciences
    http://www.socarchsci.org/
American Schools of Oriental Research
    http://www.asor.org/

Magazines:
Archaeology
    http://www.archaeology.org/
Online journal finder
    http://journalseek.net/

Other:

The Archaeology Channel
    http://www.archaeologychannel.org/
Human evolution
    http://humanorigins.si.edu/
    http://www.talkorigins.org/
Egyptology
    http://www.ucl.ac.uk/museums-static/digitalegypt//
Aboriginal Studies
    http://www.ciolek.com/WWWVL-Aboriginal.html
Mesoamerican Archaeology
    http://www.famsi.org
Center for Archaeoastronomy
    http://www.wam.umd.edu/~tlaloc/archastro/
European Megalithic Monuments
    http://www.stonepages.com/

Index

Page numbers in *italics* refer to information contained in captions and illustrations.